RAF
ON THE
OFFENSIVE

R A F
ON THE
OFFENSIVE

THE REBIRTH OF TACTICAL AIR
POWER 1940–1941

GREG BAUGHEN

AIR WORLD

AIR WORLD

RAF ON THE OFFENSIVE
The Rebirth of Tactical Air Power 1940–1941

First published in Great Britain in 2018 by

Frontline Books
An imprint of
Pen & Sword Books Ltd
Yorkshire - Philadelphia

ISBN 978 1 52673 515 7

A CIP catalogue record for this book is
available from the British Library

Typeset in 10.5/13 pt Palatino
by Aura Technology and Software Services, India

Printed and bound by TJ International Ltd, Padstow, Cornwall

Pen & Sword Books Ltd incorporates the Imprints of Aviation, Atlas,
Family History, Fiction, Maritime, Military, Discovery, Politics, History,
Archaeology, Select, Wharncliffe Local History, Wharncliffe True Crime,
Military Classics, Wharncliffe Transport, Leo Cooper, The Praetorian Press,
Remember When, Seaforth Publishing and Frontline Publishing.

For a complete list of Pen & Sword titles please contact

PEN & SWORD BOOKS LTD
47 Church Street, Barnsley, South Yorkshire, S70 2AS, England
E-mail: enquiries@pen-and-sword.co.uk
Website: www.pen-and-sword.co.uk

Or

PEN AND SWORD BOOKS
1950 Lawrence Rd, Havertown, PA 19083, USA
E-mail: Uspen-and-sword@casematepublishers.com
Website: www.penandswordbooks.com

Contents

Acknowledgements

I would like to thank the staff of the National Archives at Kew, The RAF Museum at Hendon and the Imperial War Museum in London for their help over the years. Thanks again to Tony Buttler for help with images. My thanks also to all those who have encouraged me to continue this series.

Introduction

In May 1941, the survivors of the Commonwealth forces rescued from the beaches of southern Greece prepared for one last stand on the island of Crete. On 20 May, a fleet of Ju 52 transports appeared over their heads and the sky filled with parachutes as thousands of crack German airborne troops descended onto the defenders. More followed in gliders, and once the airfields had been captured, many thousands more landed in transports. There were no RAF aircraft operating from the airfields the Commonwealth forces were trying to defend. They had no air support to help beat off the invaders and no fighter protection as the Ju 87 dive-bombers once more tormented Allied troops. It had been a similar story weeks before in Greece. For those who escaped to Egypt, it was the same old question: where was the RAF? Why was history repeating itself? Why did the British Army not have something like the Stuka dive-bomber? Once again the Royal Navy had had to pluck the survivors from the beaches. Just as had been the case twelve months before, after the fall of France, it was no longer safe for RAF personnel to venture out in their air force blue uniforms. The Royal Air Force found itself rechristened the Royal Absent Force – in politer company at least. Many soldiers preferred an earthier alternative for the second letter.

The events in Crete were being followed very closely many thousands of miles away on another, much larger, island off mainland Europe. To the defence chiefs in London it was a dramatic and rather frightening demonstration of how island defences could be overwhelmed by airborne troops. Could the same happen in Britain? All the intelligence suggested that the Soviet Union was Germany's next target, but no-one expected the Red Army to be any more successful at stopping the fearsome panzers than any of their previous opponents. At best, Soviet resistance might mean a two-month postponement before Britain once more faced the might of the German Army alone. Come the late summer of 1941, Britain might once again be facing the threat of invasion. Was Britain any better prepared than twelve months before? Could airborne troops gain a foothold in Britain? Was the RAF any more ready to help the Army defend Britain?

Britain had been fortunate in 1940. Instead of launching air and ground operations simultaneously, a formula that had brought success in all previous campaigns, Hitler had chosen to try to destroy the RAF before risking an invasion. The RAF had been preparing for an air assault on the country for twenty years; it was the only battle the RAF was capable of winning, and the Luftwaffe duly suffered its first major setback. The Wehrmacht never got as far as finding out how enfeebled the British Army was and how ill-prepared the RAF was to support it. An attempt to bomb Britain into defeat by night proved equally fruitless. On its own, air power had failed to achieve much. However, in 1941, the Luftwaffe was back in harness with the German Army and the combination was once again proving irresistible as the Germans notched up rapid victories in the Western Desert and Balkans. Perhaps the next attempt to overwhelm Britain would not be preceded by an air-only campaign. The next time the Luftwaffe ventured over Britain in strength by day, it might be flying over an invasion fleet.

Chapter 1

Fighters for the Future

Throughout the Twenties and Thirties, the Air Staff had nailed their colours to the strategic bomber mast. The year 1940 had been one of fluctuating fortunes for this policy. It had started with the Air Staff certain in their belief that the stalemate on the Western Front would continue indefinitely, just as it had in the First World War, and it would be left to the opposing bomber fleets to decide the war. As soon as the Anglo-French alliance had more bombers than Germany, they thought, then the war would move inexorably towards an Allied victory. With bomber superiority, victory on the ground would be a mere formality.

Then the German blitzkrieg seemed to change everything. Poland and Norway had been defeated rapidly, but nobody imagined the panzers, supported by the Luftwaffe, would trouble the mighty French Army. Nobody expected what followed. In a mere six weeks, France was defeated; instead of the air assault Britain had prepared for, the danger was an invasion the country had not prepared for. For a brief period, the talk was of how the RAF might support the Army in defence of British shores. Hardened bomber advocates like Air Commodore John Slessor, a future Chief of Air Staff, conceded that perhaps after all there was a place in the RAF for something like the Stuka.[1] Air Marshal Charles Portal, in charge of Bomber Command, was coming up with fantastic schemes for turning ancient Vickers Virginia bombers into low-flying, anti-tank gunships.[2]

But the invasion never came and instead the country found itself engaged in the 'air-only' Battle of Britain. The war was very quickly returning to how the Air Staff had always believed wars of the future would be fought – with armies and navies playing secondary roles. Victory in the Battle of Britain restored RAF pride and confidence in its importance. The German strategy in the Battle of Britain, and the Blitz

1

that followed, seemed to be a vindication of the Air Ministry's belief that air power was the decisive factor in war. Were not the Germans turning to the very strategy the Air Staff had always advocated? All Britain had to do to guard against invasion was maintain powerful bomber and fighter forces in Britain. Germany would never dare launch an invasion fleet without air superiority, and if they did, then Bomber Command would crush it. An army was scarcely needed. It was what Hugh Trenchard – the first Chief of the Air Staff, often labelled the 'father of the Royal Air Force' – had always claimed. Domination of the air made conventional land battles impossible. Churchill agreed; he had been mesmerized for years by the seemingly unlimited power of the bomber. As far as the Prime Minister was concerned, the sole purpose of the British Army was to force the enemy to concentrate its invasion force at a particular point so that the RAF and Royal Navy could destroy it. Churchill had good reason to believe the Navy could cause havoc amongst an invasion armada. There was less justification for thinking the RAF would be as effective. In the first year of war, Bomber Command had not sunk a single enemy ship of any description.

In the summer of 1940, however, Churchill still credited the bomber with extraordinary powers of destruction. The pre-war prophets of doom had predicted bombers might end civilization; by comparison, destroying an invasion fleet seemed a relatively simple matter. Bombers also provided a route to victory. Once Britain had more bombers than Germany, victory would surely follow. Churchill's faith in the bomber gave the RAF the war-winning central role Trenchard and his apostles had fought so hard for in the Twenties. Churchill proclaimed:

> 'The Navy can lose us the war, but only the Air Force can win it. Therefore our supreme effort must be to gain overwhelming mastery in the air. The Fighters are our salvation but the Bombers alone provide the means of victory.'[3]

The Army was not mentioned. It did not have a major role either in preventing defeat or winning the war.

It was not the sort of thinking that was going to help Lieutenant General Alan Brooke, the commander of British forces in the UK, prepare for a 1941 invasion or build the sort of army that might try to win back the ground lost in1940. Much to Brooke's dismay, Churchill's insistence that the Air Force should be expanded at the expense of the Army did not provoke much disappointment in the War Office. The fate that had befallen the mighty French Army and the speed with which British expeditionary forces had been evicted from Norway and France did not encourage any enthusiasm for an early rematch with the Wehrmacht. The Army would prepare as best it could to defeat an invasion, but if the Air Ministry wanted to take responsibility for winning the war, that was fine by the War Office.

`This all led to a rather peculiar overall war strategy. By 1942 it was hoped the British Army would possess at least fifty divisions worldwide, but these would not be used to invade Europe. The British Army's offensive operations would be confined to overseas theatres, and to maximize these forces, the War Office was quite happy to maintain the smallest possible army in the United Kingdom. With support from the Home Guard and, in an emergency, training units, the War Office believed that just fourteen divisions were sufficient to defend the United Kingdom in 1941. Some thought this could drop to as low as four by 1942, when it was expected the RAF would have complete air superiority in Europe. The War Office thought seven was a more realistic minimum force, but even this was a remarkably low number to defend the entire country.[4] However, it freed the rest of the British Army for offensive action overseas. The role of the Army would be to defeat Axis forces in the Middle East and possibly later, if the conflict spread, the Far East.

This mirrored inter-war defence policy, with the bomber being the principal weapon in a major European war and the Army being required for colonial policing: in the Second World War, with Italy the enemy in North Africa, the latter would just be on a somewhat grander scale. War in the European theatre would be waged one way, but in the rest of the world it would be waged another, and nobody seemed to question this strange dichotomy. It left Brooke with the task of defeating any invading German Army with a wafer-thin force.

Even the 'air superiority' he was supposed to be relying on was not what Brooke really wanted. In the First World War, 'air superiority' had been achieved by having a superior fighter force. However, in the Trenchard doctrine, air superiority meant having more bombers. Air forces won control of the skies by bombing aircraft factories, oil refineries, airfields and communications, and making it impossible for the enemy air force to operate. Trying to defend against bomber attack was a mistake, so building fighters instead of bombers was thus also a mistake. Building more fighters just meant you were losing the bomber war. In this Air Staff model of future wars, the number of fighters you had was a measure of how close to defeat you were.[5] In the inter-war years, the Air Staff had fought fiercely to keep fighter production to

3

a minimum. When Lord Beaverbrook took over responsibility for aircraft production, there was bitter opposition to the priority he gave fighter production, even when the Battle of Britain was raging in the skies over southern England. For the Air Staff, air superiority in the European theatre meant the ability of bombers to operate at will anywhere they pleased, and it was the bomber that would achieve this, not fighters.

While the Air Ministry tried to build the massive bomber fleet that winning the war would require, Air Chief Marshal Hugh Dowding, head of Fighter Command, was trying to halt the continuing German air offensive. He had always seen his battle with the Luftwaffe as an ongoing offensive against the country rather than a battle for air superiority as a prelude to an invasion. He was so caught up in the struggle that he was scarcely aware that with the dispersal of the German invasion fleet in September 1940, his Fighter Command had won the battle. For Dowding, this dispersion was merely a clarification of the situation – there could now be no doubt that the German aim was victory by air action alone. This was seen as a far greater threat than any invading army and, as far as Dowding was concerned, the continuing struggle in the air was as critical as it had ever been.

For as long as the weather permitted, the Luftwaffe kept Fighter Command at full stretch with fighter sweeps, heavily escorted bombing raids and fighter-bomber attacks, with the British aircraft industry the primary target. Even before the planned invasion was postponed, the Luftwaffe had achieved some notable successes. On 15 August 1940, a raid on the Shorts plant at Rochester in Kent badly damaged the factory. On 4 September, the Weybridge Wellington factory in Surrey had been hit, inflicting 700 casualties. On 25 September, He 111 bombers and Bf 110 fighter-bombers halted production at the Bristol factory at Filton in Gloucestershire;[6] up to three weeks' output of Beauforts and Beaufighters was lost.[7] The next day, the Supermarine works in Southampton were the target; the two factories producing Spitfires were gutted and both had to be abandoned.

When Beaverbrook described these events to his Cabinet colleagues as 'disasters', he did not seem to be exaggerating. The Shorts attack, he estimated, had meant the loss of three months' worth of Stirling bomber output. The Weybridge raid had cost another 175 Wellingtons.[8] Fears that the German bomber force was capable of wiping out the aircraft industry seemed justified. However, it was not the disaster it seemed. When the debris was cleared away, it was found that the machine tools had survived. Where factories had to be abandoned, new dispersed production facilities were quickly set up in the region to take their place. The attack on the Supermarine works caused the loss of six weeks' worth of production,[9] but once production got going again, there was no longer a single target for German bombers to aim at. By early 1941, aircraft production was back to its previous level and increasing. German bombing had merely accelerated plans that already existed to disperse the industry. It was an early indication that bombing your way to victory was not as easy as it seemed to the inter-war theorists.

The last day of September 1940 saw the final major daylight effort against London by the Luftwaffe, when two waves totalling 200 bombers in the morning and another 100 in the afternoon headed for the capital. Late in the afternoon, forty more He 111s made for the Westland factory in Yeovil. All the raids were turned back, and fifteen bombers and no less than twenty-seven of the escorting fighters were shot down. In an attempt to reduce losses, the Luftwaffe turned to small formations of high-flying fighter-bombers. Bf 110s or Bf 109s, armed with bombs, would head for their targets at 25,000ft, with escorts operating above at 30,000ft. At these heights the Bf 109 was able to make full use of its superior altitude performance. Even the Spitfires struggled to intercept them. Attacks were less frequent than during the summer months, but the strain these high-attitude interceptions involved meant that Dowding's force was still under pressure. They also encouraged Fighter Command and the Air Ministry to focus on the high-level bomber threat, rather than other issues which in the long term would prove to be more serious. One of these neglected issues was the importance of fighter-versus-fighter combat.

The way the struggle between the opposing fighter forces had dominated the aerial battles of 1940 had not been anticipated. This was partly because Britain had prepared for a bomber assault on the entire country, rather than a battle for air superiority over a tiny corner of England. With bases in northern France, German fighters could operate over the south-east of England. Indeed, with fighters now cruising at far higher speeds, fighters could fly much further with the same endurance. For the Air Staff, however, there was a more fundamental issue. They had never believed that fighter escorts, especially single-seater escorts, could ever work. It was not just the handicap of having to carry extra fuel. Single-seaters would always be vulnerable to attacks from the rear when the time came to withdraw. As there would be no escorts, there would be no fighter-versus-fighter combat, so the Air Staff had only required heavily armed specialist bomber interceptors. The Bf 109 escorts that accompanied German bombers during the Battle

5

of Britain had demonstrated how wrong these ideas were. Britain was indeed fortunate to have fighters as manoeuvrable as the Spitfire and Hurricane, and even more fortunate that the less manoeuvrable Whirlwind, Beaufighter and Defiant that were supposed to replace them were all behind schedule. These turreted and cannon-armed fighters might be ideal for dealing with unescorted bombers, but they could not deal with fighter escorts.

By the end of the summer of 1940, there seemed no question of heavy twin-engined or two-seater fighters forming any part of Fighter Command's future daytime fighter force, at least not where enemy single-seaters were likely to be encountered. The Defiant had been a disaster, and there would be no more talk of Beaufighters replacing Spitfires on the Supermarine production line. Even the much smaller Whirlwind was not manoeuvrable enough. With Hawker and Supermarine insisting they could now fit cannon in the wings of their single-engined fighters, there was no longer any need for twin-engined fighters. The Battle of Britain had shown the importance of agility and the ability to climb fast, and on both counts the single-engined fighter had the edge. The single-engined, single-seater seemed set to remain the standard fighter configuration.

Britain was lucky to have the Spitfire and Hurricane, but both were intended only for short-range interception. Neither had been designed for fighter-versus-fighter combat, and as a result both had their drawbacks. Trials with an American Curtiss H75 Mohawk borrowed off the French had demonstrated how inferior the British fighters were in terms of agility and control. The low weight and wing area of the Bf 109 was also food for thought. The Bf 109 had much better acceleration, and the relatively high wing area of the Spitfire and Hurricane slowed the rate of roll, making it more difficult to change direction quickly. These failings were no fault of the designers; they were simply not qualities needed by fighters required to shoot down unescorted bombers flying straight and level. Now that fighters were expected to engage in dogfights, there seemed to be a case for going back to the drawing board and considering what the ideal air superiority fighter might look like.

In fact the need for a review was even greater than the Battle of Britain had suggested. Over Britain, air combat took place at ever higher altitudes, because that is how fighters gain the upper hand, and with no fighting on the ground there was no reason to fly low. When armies are engaged, and low-level observation, reconnaissance and ground-attack planes are in action, fighters have to fly much lower if they are to influence events. 'Air only' campaigns tend to take place at high altitudes; over a battlefield, the air action is more often at much lower altitudes. In an invasion scenario or with British armies in action overseas, agile low-level tactical fighters would be needed as well as high-altitude air superiority fighters. There were plenty of reasons for reviewing whether the thinking behind the next fighter on the 'cab rank', the Hawker Typhoon/Tornado family, was right for the kind of war the RAF now found itself in.

Tactics needed to change too. The large unwieldy 'vic' formations pilots were trained to fly were designed for mass attacks on bomber formations. Some squadrons had rethought their tactics and started to operate in the more flexible pairs that German pilots used, but most finished the Battle of Britain flying the same pre-war tight formations. Fighter Command had not changed that much and Dowding saw no need for it to do so. When Air Marshal Sholto Douglas took over from Dowding, he too did not see the tactics his pilots were using as a problem.

With German attacks coming in at ever-higher altitudes, what was worrying Douglas and the Air Ministry was not how to dogfight with escorts but how to reach the bombers. The fear was that when the German day offensive resumed the following spring, it would be at extreme altitudes, where any sort of manoeuvring might be extremely difficult and fighter escorts might not be necessary or possible. The nightmare scenario was German bombers cruising at 45,000ft, in clear skies, flying higher than anti-aircraft guns or interceptors could reach and having as much time as they needed to pick off aircraft factories at their leisure.[10] The problems of getting bombs anywhere near their target from 9 miles up were not really considered. The Air Ministry was very aware of the advantages of high-altitude bombing and had its own ambitions in this direction. Since the late Thirties, the Air Ministry had been looking into the option of bombing targets from altitudes as high as 40,000ft. The Air Ministry's interest in high-altitude bombing ensured that intelligence reports that the Germans were working along similar lines were taken very seriously.

Dealing with the high-altitude bomber threat was the Air Ministry's major concern, not developing the qualities required by an air superiority fighter. In 1940, there was no Air Ministry interest in releasing a fighter specification requiring designers to take more account of what was needed for fighter-versus-fighter combat, but there were no less than three new specifications for specialist bomber interceptors: F.4/40, F.9/40 and F.16/40. F.4/40, released in the spring of 1940, required a four-cannon, twin-engined interceptor with a pressurized cockpit, capable of flying to 45,000ft. Westland set about designing the Welkin to meet this requirement. Concern about high-level bombing was also driving the development of the jet-powered fighter. Since the mid-Twenties, Alan Griffith had been working at the Royal Aircraft Establishment (RAE) on his axial flow design, which compressed air by parallel rotating blades and converted the power into thrust with a conventional propeller. At the same time an RAF pilot, Frank Whittle, was investigating the centrifugal turbojet, which compressed air by centrifugal force and generated thrust directly. He presented his idea to the Air Ministry in 1930, where, ironically, it was Griffith who declared it impracticable. Undeterred, Whittle set up his own company, Power Jets, and in the late Thirties managed to attract some limited funding from the Air Ministry, and, more importantly, aroused the interest of Henry Tizard, the Air Ministry's top scientific adviser.[11]

Griffith's axial flow engine was the more compact and potentially the more efficient, but Whittle's approach was technically less complicated and the first to produce results. A demonstration by Whittle in the summer of 1939 persuaded the Air Ministry his idea was practicable. The observer from the Research and Development department seemed rather disappointed that the low output of the engine ruled out its use for long-range bombing – a reflection of Air Ministry priorities – but a short-range interceptor seemed perfectly practicable. The Air Ministry thought a maximum speed of 350mph at sea level, rising to 410mph at 40,000ft, was possible, which was impressive enough, but Whittle was convinced he could do even better.[12] He outlined the form an experimental unarmed test plane might take. Whittle was instructed to team up with Gloster, and specification E.8/39 was written around the 'Gloster Whittle 1'. The 'E' classification underlined the experimental nature of the project, but the Air Ministry was so impressed with the idea that the design team was told to bear in mind the needs of an operational fighter and the Air Ministry even suggested the plane should be armed with four machine guns.

Gloster saw no reason why development of a parallel fighter version should not begin straight away, and were soon enthusiastically predicting 400mph at sea level with just 1,200lb thrust. By May 1940 they were proposing a much more ambitions Gloster Whittle II project, a twin-engined plane armed with four cannon which, assuming Whittle could increase engine output to 1,800lb thrust, could be expected to achieve 470mph at 30,000ft. If thrust could be pushed up to 2,000lb, a staggering 515mph might be possible.[13] These predicted speeds were striking enough, but what particularly impressed the Air Ministry was that, up to 40,000ft, the higher the plane flew the more efficient the engines became. Here was the ideal antidote to the high-altitude bomber. Work immediately began on a fully fledged fighter specification, F.9/40, which was supposed to produce a fighter that was as light as possible, to ensure a high rate of climb, but also had to carry no less than six 20mm cannon. The Air Ministry was so excited by the prospect that Gloster were told to abandon work on their extremely promising twin-engined Reaper replacement for the Beaufighter (the 'less satisfactory' Mosquito was ordered instead) and focus all effort on their jet fighter.

The six cannon the Air Staff wanted had become standard for all future fighter designs. It was excessive by any standards. The Air Staff had always been worried by the cannon's low rate of fire. They believed that to score hits, a fighter pilot had to be able to put a high number of shells in the vicinity of the target, and the only way of doing this with cannon was to have a lot of them. This, however, resulted in a phenomenal weight of fire – six 20mm cannon was the equivalent of around fifty rifle-calibre machine guns. This was simply not required to destroy any bomber that RAF fighters were likely to encounter. Against the twin-engined medium bombers that equipped the Luftwaffe, even four cannon was excessive.

The RAF's Hispano-Suiza HS.404 was the most powerful 20mm cannon in the world, but it was also the heaviest. Replacing the eight machine guns of the Spitfire and Hurricane with six cannon involved a 500lb weight increase, and the much greater recoil meant more weight strengthening the wings. There were concerns that the extra weight might reduce climb performance, but nobody was thinking about how it might affect acceleration and manoeuvrability.[14] Fighter-versus-fighter combat was not a consideration. Nobody was worrying about how such a fighter might cope with escorts. It was a rerun of what happened in the Thirties. Fear of the bomber was taking British fighter design down a very familiar path.

Six cannon was a huge challenge for the fighter designer. Even the single cannon mounted in the wing of a handful of Spitfires and Hurricanes in the summer of 1940 had caused problems. The new belt-fed version of the cannon made it a little easier for designers to fit the weapon in a fighter wing, and No. 151 Squadron began trialling a four-cannon Hurricane II in August 1940, but it was much more difficult to fit four cannon into the thinner wings of the Spitfire. Supermarine were confident they would eventually manage it, but for the time being

9

the Spitfire II had just one in each wing with a couple of machine guns.[15] Undeterred by the problems, the Air Ministry was determined to go for more and Hawker was asked if it was not too late to fit six cannon in the Typhoon/Tornado.[16] Nor was it going to stop at six 20mm cannon. Even before the outbreak of war, the Air Ministry had been considering 40mm cannon and even air-to-air rockets, Dowding being particularly keen on the latter as a way of breaking up formations of bombers. In June 1940, Vickers had been asked to update their 1939 twin-engined F.22/39 proposal, the Vickers 414, by mounting two 40mm cannon in the nose or an astonishing eight 20mm cannon.[17] The new F.16/40 would be the ultimate specialist bomber destroyer.

There was no question of losing faith in the single-engined, single-seater fighter, but the only new fighters required in 1940 (F.4/40 Welkin, F.9/40 – the future Meteor – and the Vickers F.16/40) were all twin-engined interceptors. Even existing single-seaters were being made less suitable for fighter-versus-fighter combat by unnecessarily heavy armament. Nor were there any plans to take a fresh look at the qualities required by the dogfighting, air superiority fighter that would be needed for escort and winning control of the skies in an invasion scenario or fighting the tactical air battles the RAF would soon find itself engaged in overseas.

The need for such a plane became even greater when Douglas took over from Dowding at Fighter Command and immediately announced his intention to go on to the offensive. Fighters would extend the air superiority gained during the summer of 1940 over southern England to the French side of the Channel. It seemed the next logical step. The Battle of Britain had been won; the frontline in the air war would now, rather ponderously, move to the continent as the Luftwaffe was slowly pushed back. It was a model for air warfare that seemed to be inspired by the laborious advances on the Western Front of the First World War.

At least the strategy put the fighter, rather than the bomber, at the heart of the struggle for air superiority. However, it was difficult to see where this 'leaning into France' policy was going to lead. There were no plans to take advantage of any superiority gained by launching an invasion or any sort of ground operation. The offensive patrols were initially not even accompanying bombers. It was air superiority in its original sense of fighter domination, but there was no clear associated aim, apart from pushing the imaginary 'aerial frontline' ever further east. However, without any plans for a long-range fighter, it was difficult to see how much further east this frontline could be pushed. It seemed like an offensive for the sake of it, rather like Trenchard's fighter tactics in the First World War, and the danger was the end result would be the same – heavy losses for no gain.[18]

This was a very different kind of air superiority to the accepted bomber-orientated Air Staff version. It was also a complete reversal of Dowding's mantra of focusing on the German bombers and avoiding wherever possible the fighters. Dowding had not been keen about his fighter pilots crossing the English coastline, never mind patrolling over occupied France. He had been no keener about such long-range fighter missions in the First World War. The distance from Kent to the Calais region was about the same distance Trenchard had ordered fighter patrols behind the Somme front in 1916. At the time Dowding had provoked Trenchard's ire by objecting to this use of fighters and got himself sent home in disgrace.[19] Now his successor was organizing similar missions. It was a very different role for Fighter Command, requiring long-range patrolling rather than short-range interception. The German fighter force would now be the target, and fighter-versus-fighter combat would be deliberately sought. In the autumn of 1940, however, Fighter Command did not have the equipment or tactics, and there were no plans to develop either.

The only new single-seater fighter in the pipeline was a Hawker design that came in two versions: the Tornado, powered by the Rolls-Royce Vulture engine; and the Typhoon, by the Napier Sabre engine. In 1939, Hawker had been told to prepare for the production of both, even though the prototypes had not even flown yet, with the plane scheduled to enter service in July 1940. There were no alternatives if they were not a success. Nor were there any plans for a single-engined, single-seater successor. The next generation of fighters, outlined in the 1939 development programme, would all be twin-engined. The Typhoon/Tornado was to be the last single-engined, single-seater fighter.

The Tornado first flew in October 1939, followed by the Typhoon four months later. Neither was as fast as Sydney Camm – Hawker's chief designer – had originally promised, but with speeds of around 400mph, both versions met Air Ministry requirements. The Vulture and Sabre were both relatively large engines and the two fighters were correspondingly large and heavy, factors which were bound to affect manoeuvrability, but as their task was supposed to be shooting down unescorted bombers, this was not seen as a problem. Of the two, the Tornado was the lighter and had a faster rate of climb, while the Typhoon was marginally faster in level flight.

Neither was an easy plane to fly. When diving at over 400mph, the buffeting was so severe that on occasion it was enough to damage the airframe. The thick wing section selected by Camm was part of the fighter's problem. Air flows over a wing much faster than a plane flies, and the thicker the wing the greater the speed of the airflow. Like many other designs at the time, Camm was beginning to encounter the first effects of compressibility as the air moving around the wing started to approach the speed of sound. At these speeds, air starts behaving like a liquid rather than a gas, drag increases dramatically and control becomes difficult. The wing was such a fundamental part of the design that it was difficult to see what could be done without a complete redesign. Minor adjustments, like moving the radiator to the chin position, seemed to help a little, but handling at high speed remained poor.

The fighter also had some unpleasant habits at lower speeds, and if these were not problems enough, there was also trouble with the fighter's engines. The Vulture was essentially two Peregrine engines bolted together driving a single airscrew. Whirlwind pilots were discovering how unreliable this fighter's Peregrine engines were, so it was hardly surprising that the Vulture was also proving troublesome. Napier's Sabre, with sleeve valves replacing traditional poppet valves, seemed to be the engine of the future, but the new valves were soon causing endless problems. It would be the summer of 1940 before either engine was considered ready for production, and even then the decision would prove to be premature. The more the Typhoon and Tornado were modified, the more the two designs diverged, and the Hawker design office soon found itself effectively developing two entirely different planes, stretching Hawker resources to the limit.[20] Given the problems both versions were experiencing, there was even more reason for grasping the opportunity to take a fresh look at where the single-engined, single-seater fighter should go next, but nobody seemed interested. The war, it seemed, would last long enough for there to be time to develop high-altitude bomber destroyers, but no-one thought it necessary to set in motion the design of a specialist air superiority fighter.

In the meantime, Beaverbrook's short-term aim of maximizing production of the five key types (the Spitfire, Hurricane, Blenheim, Whitley and Wellington) was giving way to a better thought out, longer-term production programme. Beaverbrook wanted to increase monthly single-seater fighter production from 450 in September 1940 to around 850 by June 1941. He dare not rely on the problematic Typhoon and Tornado – at best these might contribute around 100 a month. With the new Castle Bromwich factory in the Midlands (producing the slightly improved Spitfire II) working up to maximum capacity, Spitfire production was expected to rise from 179 in September to 355 a month in June 1941. However, this still left a huge gap to fill. The only other single-engined single–seater fighter in production was the Hurricane. This was supposed to be phased out in the summer of 1941, but with the Hawker factories earmarked for the full-scale production of the Typhoon/Tornado already building Hurricanes, it seemed to make sense for them to continue producing them until the Typhoon and Tornado were ready for mass production. The Hurricane would have to make up the balance in Beaverbrook's plans. Far from phasing out the Hurricane by the summer of 1941, 1,320 more Hurricanes were ordered in September 1940 and production would increase to 330 a month.[21] The Hurricane would continue to be numerically the most important RAF fighter well into 1941.

Given the known deficiencies of the Hurricane, this was a rather remarkable turn of events. As early as the spring of 1938, it was recognized that the design was 'fast becoming obsolescent'.[22] In the early summer of 1940, Britain's desperate situation meant there was little option but to maximize the output of anything that was in production, including the Hurricane. The Hurricane I had, however, struggled against the Bf 109E. The Hurricane squadrons were helped to a certain extent during the battle by German fighters having to operate at lower altitudes to provide closer escort for their bombers, which tended to negate the superiority of the Bf 109E at high altitude and enabled Hurricane pilots to make best use of their fighter's qualities. However, the Air Ministry was very aware that Hurricane squadrons had taken a battering, and with combat taking place at ever higher altitudes, not even the most diehard supporter of the Hurricane now believed the fighter could hold its own. If the Hurricane had to stay in production, performance had to be improved, and the only quick fix was more power.

The decision had already been taken to upgrade the Hurricane and Spitfire with the Merlin XX, the first examples of which became available in the spring of 1940. The engine had a far more efficient supercharger, pushing power up to 1,460hp, a huge improvement over the Merlin III, and it also optimized engine output at two different altitudes, greatly improving power at altitude. The minimum changes to accommodate the new engine were made to a standard Hurricane I, and the prototype Mark II flew in June. With the new engine, rate of climb and service ceiling were both spectacularly improved, but it was still slower than the Merlin III-powered Spitfire I in level flight, and indeed climbed slower than the Merlin XII-powered Spitfire II. It was still inferior to the

Bf 109E in almost every respect. The power of the new Merlin XX was simply wasted on the Hurricane airframe.

For the Merlin XX-powered Spitfire III, the Supermarine design team took the opportunity to introduce various improvements. The wing area was reduced, which improved speed at the expense of some of the improved climb and ceiling. This was not actually the way the Air Ministry wanted to go, but the result was an impressive 401mph at 25,000ft, compared to the 370mph at 20,000ft of the Spitfire II.[23] This was considerably better than the Hurricane II, and, more significantly, more or less the same speed as the Typhoon and Tornado prototypes were managing. The Spitfire III also achieved this speed at a much higher altitude and climbed faster and higher than the Hawker fighters. The Spitfire III had the edge in terms of performance, had a reliable engine and the plane's extremely thin wings meant there were no compressibility problems in high-speed dives. The fighter had also already won the confidence of pilots. It was a far better proposition than the Typhoon and Tornado that were supposed to replace the Spitfire. There was already talk of getting the Americans to build the fighter.[24]

There was, however a problem: Rolls-Royce could not deliver enough Merlin XX engines to satisfy both Spitfire and Hurricane production. A choice had to be made over which should get the engine first. Unfortunately for the Spitfire III, the struggling Hurricane was in far greater need of the extra power. The Hurricane II also required far fewer changes to the production line and could be introduced with less disruption to output. The more extensive modifications planned for the Spitfire III would temporarily reduce output. It was therefore decided that the Hurricane should get the Merlin XX first.[25] As the summer wore on, the problems the Hurricane I was having in combat only seemed to prove how correct the decision had been. The improved performance of the Hurricane II helped justify the large numbers Beaverbrook was planning to build. The Spitfire would have to wait for the Merlin XX.

However, it was not just the Hurricane that was struggling. Both the Defiant and Beaufighter also needed the extra power to stay competitive. The Beaufighter was urgently needed as a night fighter, but the Hercules-powered version was a major disappointment. Archibald Sinclair, the Air Minister, made it clear late in August 1940, even before the Blitz got going, that there was no question of forgoing the Merlin XX-powered Beaufighter for the Spitfire III. The Defiant, which had gained a new lease of life as a night fighter, also needed more power to haul its bulky turret through the air. It was decided in August that the Hurricane, Defiant and Beaufighter should all have priority over the Spitfire in getting the Merlin XX.[26] In Germany, the more powerful and aerodynamically refined Bf 109F was being tested, but the British equivalent, the Spitfire III, was on hold.

The Air Ministry had made a choice between the Hurricane II and Spitfire III, but arguably the decision should have been between the Spitfire III and the Typhoon/Tornado. The Spitfire III was the quickest way of getting a 400mph fighter into service. Dropping the Tornado and its Vulture engine would have enabled Rolls-Royce to switch more capacity to the Merlin XX, and there would be no need to prolong the career of the Hurricane. Having Hawker factories build Spitfires would not have pleased Sydney Camm and the changeover would have reduced output. However, the fighter had to come out of production at some stage, and with poor weather restricting air operations, the winter of 1940/41 was as good a time as any.

However, despite the problems with the Hawker Typhoon and Tornado, there was still enormous belief in the basic design and an almost blind faith in Camm's ability to come up with first-rate fighters. The disappointing performance of the Hurricane does not appear to have tarnished his image. The teething problems with the Tornado and Typhoon were just that – glitches that would soon be overcome, it was hoped. The Air Ministry was also convinced that the power plants the Hawker fighters used were the way forward. Rolls-Royce could surely be relied on to sort out the problems with the Vulture. The Air Ministry had little choice but to believe this – planes like the Manchester bomber were relying on the engine. The case for persevering with Napier's Sabre was even stronger. Too much had already been invested in Napier's production capacity in anticipation of the huge numbers that would be required. It also used sleeve valves. Rolls-Royce had shied away from this innovation, but the experts at the Royal Aircraft Establishment were convinced that the 1,450hp of the Merlin XX was about as powerful as an engine using poppet valves could possibly get. Beyond that, sleeve valves would have to be used. The 1,800-2,000hp Sabre was the engine of the future.

Supermarine and Rolls-Royce were doing wonders squeezing the last ounce of performance out of their designs, and the Spitfire IV (a fighter variant at this stage), with the much larger 37-litre Rolls Royce Griffon, might give the Spitfire a new lease of life, but the Air Ministry felt that the Spitfire/Merlin combination was at the end of its development life. The Tornado/Vulture and especially the Typhoon/Sabre, on the other hand, were just at the beginning of theirs. In the autumn of 1940, confidence in the basic design was still so high that it was suggested the

Americans might be persuaded to build it, perhaps with an American engine. At the very least the prototype should be taken to the United States to show the Americans what a really modern fighter should be capable of.[27]

The truly outstanding fighter Britain possessed was actually the Spitfire III. In an effort to justify the decision to delay the Spitfire III, Beaverbrook's Ministry of Aircraft Production (MAP) went out of its way to play up the advantages of the Spitfire I and play down the performance of the Spitfire III. It was argued that the 365mph the Spitfire I was capable of would make it a useful fighter for many months to come. The Spitfire III, it was claimed, was only 22mph faster at 21,000ft, a rather selective statistic as it was far faster at higher altitudes. The MAP also managed to credit it with a lower ceiling, despite its higher rate of climb. It was still planned to build the Spitfire III when sufficient Merlin XX engines were available, and, as proof of intent, 1,000 were ordered in September 1940. Production plans in October even included a small number of Spitfire IIIs from January 1941, although it was not long before first deliveries were put back to the middle of 1941.[28]

Meanwhile, the first examples of the Hurricane II had rolled off the production lines in September 1940. Hurricane production was to be increased to 450 a month by June 1941 and was to be held at that level. Production would gradually switch to the Mark II version, initially with twelve machine guns but eventually with four 20mm cannon. However, the last Mark I would not leave the production lines until October 1941. Production schedules for the summer of 1941 envisaged more Hurricanes coming off the production lines than Spitfires, Typhoons and Tornados combined – and many of the Hurricanes would be the obsolete Mark I.[29]

At this point the introduction of the Spitfire III was just being delayed, but the number of planes queuing up for the Merlin XX was increasing. It was also now proposed that the four-engined Halifax bomber and the twin-engined Beaufort might benefit from it, not to mention future high-performance twin-engined planes like the Gloster Reaper and de Havilland Mosquito. Avro had been suggesting for some time that the problems with their troublesome twin-engined Manchester bomber could be resolved if the two unreliable Vulture engines could be replaced by four engines. They now resubmitted the idea, suggesting the Merlin XX would be ideal. This time Avro were given the go ahead. Whether it was confidence in the four-engined configuration, or just sheer desperation, even before the prototype flew, Merlin-powered Lancasters were included in the production programme alongside the

Vulture-powered Manchester. When the four-engined version flew in January 1941, such was the transformation, not just in performance but also the flying characteristics of the plane, that it was immediately decided to abandon the Manchester and concentrate on the Lancaster. Each Lancaster would absorb another four Merlin XX engines, and any plane contributing to the strategic bomber offensive was going to get priority over a fighter.

It was against this background that Rolls-Royce put forward a new engine, the R.M.5.S., later renamed the Merlin 45. This was basically a Merlin III engine with the Merlin XX supercharger but not the two-speed capability. Its output was lower, except between 14,000–19,000ft, where its single-speed supercharger clicked in. The Merlin 45 was a straightforward modification of the Merlin III, so current production lines would be able to continue turning out engines. Indeed, existing Merlin III engines could reasonably easily be retrofitted with the new supercharger. It had exactly the same dimensions as the Merlin III, so it could be fitted to the Hurricane or Spitfire airframe without any modifications. Here was a way of freeing more Merlin XXs for the bomber offensive. Comparative trials with the Merlin XX and Merlin 45 were ordered for both the Hurricane and Spitfire.[30]

The Merlin 45-powered Hurricane was slower, although only slightly, and climbed slower at all altitudes than the Hurricane II, and ceiling was reduced by 1,500ft. The Merlin 45 was also fitted in a standard Spitfire I airframe, the conversion being initially known as the Spitfire Ia but later becoming the Spitfire V. However, before a prototype could be thoroughly tested, the predicted performance of the Spitfire/Merlin 45 combination was compared with the known performance of the Spitfire III. This was not an entirely fair comparison, but to load the dice even more heavily against the Spitfire III, it was credited with a top speed of 383mph at 21,000ft, rather than the 401mph at 25,000ft the prototype had achieved. The predicted performance with the Merlin 45 was not quite as good as this, but it was close. At 21,000ft, the Merlin 45-powered Spitfire could match the top speed of the Spitfire III. It would be a little faster between 17,000–21,000ft, but up to 10mph slower at other altitudes. It was, however, still a considerable improvement on the Spitfire II. Most significantly of all, it appeared, on 'calculated figures', that the Merlin 45-powered Spitfire would be capable of climbing to 38,000ft, a 2,000ft higher ceiling than the Spitfire III.[31] The high-flying bomber was the threat, and the ability of the Merlin 45-powered Spitfire to climb higher made the case for the Spitfire V seem overwhelming. Early in February 1941, before the full results of trials were available, Portal (now Chief of

Air Staff) agreed that the Spitfire III should be dropped and production of the Spitfire V should begin.[32] So promising did the Spitfire V seem, that the Griffon-powered Spitfire IV was also dropped.[33]

A more basic engine seemed to be giving broadly equivalent speeds and superior altitude performance. It seemed too good to be true, and so it would prove. When the first production model flew, it managed just 369mph at 20,000ft, not the 383mph at 21,000ft anticipated.[34] This was edged up beyond 370mph in later trials, but was still lower than expected, and when the plane was delivered to squadrons, pilots did not feel it was much of an improvement on the Spitfire II. It seemed that the Air Ministry had been determined to justify a decision it felt had to be made and the available data had been interpreted accordingly. The 38,000ft ceiling figure used was an absolute ceiling; the estimated performance figures had only claimed a normal service ceiling of 36,000ft.[35] Whether by design or mistake, or a mixture of both, the Spitfire V was credited with a performance at altitude that it simply did not possess. Suddenly there were fears that it would not be long before the Spitfire V would be obsolete and the Griffon-powered Spitfire IV was hastily revived.[36] The Merlin XX-powered Spitifre III, however, did not get reconsidered.

Instead of powering Spitfires, the Merlin XX powered Hurricanes. Interestingly, although it was slower, Douglas considered the Hurricane II to be an improvement on the Spitfire I. The latter was a far better fighter at medium altitudes, but the Hurricane II could carry four 20mm cannon, while Supermarine were still struggling to get more than one into each wing of the Spitfire. Even weighed down by four cannon, the Hurricane II could climb faster and higher, and this, as far as the Air Ministry was concerned, was what mattered. Medium and low-level performance were not so useful; it was how high interceptors could fly that counted. The high-altitude bomber was the danger.

Even the Hurricane II would struggle to fly higher than 36,000ft. Enemy bombers might soon be flying higher than this, and with the Westland Welkin and jets unlikely to be available until mid-1942 at the earliest, an interim solution was needed. The Air Ministry hoped that specialized, high-altitude versions of the Spitfire might fill the gap. Rolls-Royce tweaked the Merlin 45 to produce more thrust at altitude at the expense of output at lower altitudes (the Merlin 46 and 47). This ought to enable the Spitfire to reach 38,000–40,000ft, an altitude which would require a semi-pressurized cabin. Rolls-Royce also suggested fitting the Merlin 60 to the Spitfire. This had two superchargers in series pumping even more oxygen into the engine and was intended for the high-altitude bombers the Air Staff wanted, but there was no reason why it could not power a fighter to intercept high-altitude bombers. The fighter version of the engine was the Merlin 61, which would power the Spitfire VII.[37] At this stage it was assumed that this version would pay for its excellent performance at altitude with lower performance at medium and low altitudes. Everything was being geared to deal with high-altitude bombers, with no thought given to the qualities fighters would need at low and medium altitudes over the battlefield.

Despite the priority, as the new year dawned, Douglas was far from optimistic about his Fighter Command's chances of repeating the heroics of 1940 when the weather improved and the Battle of Britain resumed. Douglas assumed the Germans would use the same tactics, with an air-only battle aimed at establishing air superiority over Britain. This would not necessarily be paving the way for an invasion. Using the same thinking behind Britain's plans to defeat Germany, there would not necessarily be any need to send in the Wehrmacht. With air superiority, the German bomber force might choose to bomb targets until Britain decided it could take no more. Britain would be defeated by the bomber, in just the same way Churchill was hoping to beat Germany.

In January 1941, Douglas was far from happy with what his command might have by the spring to deal with this threat. There was very little chance of getting any Tornados, Typhoons or the specialized high-altitude versions of the Spitfire. The best he could hope for was as many Hurricane II, Spitfire II and Spitfire Vs as possible, and many of these would only have machine-gun armament. At best, Douglas could expect just 100 Spitfire Vs by April, and only forty of these would have cannon armament. The Spitfire I and IIs were supposed to be delivered with two cannon, but continued to be built with machine gun-only armament, and many of the Hurricane IIs were the early version with twelve machine guns. So desperate was he for more cannon-armed fighters that he rather hoped more Westland Whirlwinds might be ordered.[38] The first Whirlwind squadron, No. 263, finally became operational in December 1940, but a plane whose performance above 20,000ft was rated as poor scarcely provided the high-altitude cover Douglas or the Air Staff wanted. The fighter was already being phased out as Westland prepared to build Spitfires instead, and Air Ministry assurances that Fighter Command could get two Spitfires for every Whirlwind was enough to end Douglas's interest.[39]

Unlike Dowding, Douglas chose to concentrate his best fighters in the south-east of the country. Dowding had always seen the role of Fighter Command as defending the United Kingdom from the knockout blow, so the Spitfire squadrons had been spread equally round the country. Douglas recognized his best fighters were needed in the south-east, where Bf 109s could operate, and put all his Spitfire V squadrons in No. 11 Group and three adjacent sectors – Middle Wallop in No. 10 Group and Duxford and Coltishall in No. 12 Group. There were twenty-six squadrons in these crucial sectors in January 1941, but twelve still had the Hurricane I and six the Spitfire I, which Douglas also had little faith in.[40] Douglas believed he had good reason to be worried.

Offensive operations over northern France did nothing to calm his fears. After some ineffectual fighter sweeps, the first 'circus' mission, with fighters accompanying bombers, was flown on 10 January 1941. Three Hurricane and three Spitfire squadrons escorted six Blenheims on a raid on an airfield in the Calais region. One Hurricane was lost, but three Bf 109s were claimed. It looked like a promising start, but the exaggerated claims for enemy planes shot down were to become a feature of the offensive. On 5 February, the second 'circus' operation went badly wrong. Six fighter squadrons escorted twelve Blenheims attacking the airfield at St Omer, with another five squadrons sweeping the area as the main formation returned. Only two enemy fighters were claimed, but eight pilots were lost on the operation. In fact the Luftwaffe had not suffered any losses.[41]

Immediately there were questions about whether it was a good idea to continue with the offensive. The post-mortem on the 5 February operation blamed the heavy losses on the bombers spending too long in the target area and the target being too far inland. Douglas insisted the operations continue, but subsequent missions were little more successful. A frustrated Douglas complained that German fighter pilots always seemed to have the initiative, using their superior altitude to surprise the British fighters below them. He ordered his squadrons to turn the tables on their German opponents by operating a proportion of the escorting fighters at a higher altitude, but the higher they took on the enemy, the more apparent the performance advantage of the German fighters became.[42] The Spitfire I was outclassed by the Bf 109E. The altitude performance of the superb Merlin XX helped keep the Hurricane competitive at very high altitudes, but it was an advantage that would disappear as the Germans began to introduce the Bf 109F early in 1941. This latest version of the German Messerschmitt outclassed all RAF fighters, including the Spitfire V.

Between February and May 1941, Fighter Command flew between 600 and 850 offensive sorties a month, losing fifty-five fighters. RAF pilots could only claim forty confirmed victories in reply, a claim/loss ratio that should have made it clear this was not a battle that was going Fighter Command's way.[43] Air Vice-Marshal Trafford Leigh-Mallory, the commander of No.11 Group, rather desperately suggested that if some of the 'probables' were added to the 'confirmed' victories, the Luftwaffe was losing more than Fighter Command, but few really believed the number of 'confirmed' victories, never mind the 'probables'.[44] The policy was reviewed several times, but Douglas insisted the offensive patrols continue. On 21 May, five Hurricane IIs and a Spitfire II were shot down over France, and to cap a particularly bad day, two returning Spitfires collided over their home base.[45] Following these losses, several weeks of poor weather brought the squadrons some respite.

For Fighter Command it was a hopeless struggle; too many advantages now lay with the German fighter force. The number of bombers involved was so small that they were never going to inflict substantial damage, and there were no targets in northern France that Germany needed to defend. Like Dowding had done in the Battle of Britain with Luftwaffe fighter sweeps, the Germans could choose to avoid combat whenever it suited them. Now it was German pilots who, if shot down, could be back with their squadrons the same day, whereas downed RAF pilots would spend the rest of the war in prisoner of war camps. This should have been enough to convince Douglas that flying inferior equipment over France was not the way to defeat the Luftwaffe.

Better fighters would help, and an alarmed Douglas was soon criticizing Beaverbrook for drifting into a policy of quantity rather than quality. In February 1941, he described the performance difference between German fighters and the latest Hurricane as 'disquieting'.[46] The Hurricane II was 40–50mph slower than the Bf 109F up to 22,000ft, and the situation was not much better above that height. He feared it might not even be fast enough to catch the latest version of the Ju 88 bomber. It was damning criticism for a version of the fighter that had only been in service for a few months. As for the Hurricane I, Douglas did not feel he could ask his pilots to take on the enemy in such a plane, although it 'will no doubt be useful overseas', he added, a comment which would have caused little surprise amongst commanders in the Middle East. They had got used to making do with whatever aircraft the home commands no longer wanted. For home defence, Douglas wanted the Hurricane I still coming off the production lines replaced 'at the earliest possible date' and the Hurricane II 'as quickly as possible' by the Tornado and Typhoon.[47] Portal backed up his commander, insisting that Beaverbrook give a firm date for the end of Hurricane production.[48] In April 1941, it was still planned to have fifteen squadrons equipped with Hurricane

IIs going into 1942. By this time they would only be any good for night fighting, convoy protection or 'strafing in case of invasion'.[49]

These exhortations were not going to solve the problems with the Tornado and Typhoon. Deliveries of the Typhoon were now supposed to begin in March 1941, and the Tornado in July. The first Typhoon airframes came off the production line in May. However, the only way any sort of reliability could be achieved with its Sabre engine was by building them individually, and airframe production was soon outstripping that of the engine. As for the Tornado's Vulture power plant, the decision to switch as quickly as possible from the Vulture-powered Manchester to the Merlin-powered Lancaster scarcely suggested much faith in the engine. Indeed, although plans for Tornado production were still going ahead, Rolls-Royce had already given up on ever making the engine any more reliable.

The Air Ministry knew all about the technical problems with the Tornado and Typhoon, but it was only in the late spring of 1941 that Portal seems to have become aware of their performance limitations. Portal only had in mind their limitations as the bomber interceptor they were designed to be. No-one was even thinking about whether they had the manoeuvrability to cope with enemy fighters. Speed was not a problem, but for bomber interception the fighters' poor climb rate and service ceiling were major worries. The latter, Portal now discovered, was many thousands of feet lower than the Spitfire V and Hurricane II.[50] This was scarcely the type of fighter that could deal with the much-feared next generation of German high-altitude bombers. Camm could of course claim his plane had met the requirements laid down by the Air Ministry. No-one had asked him to design a fighter capable of taking on bombers at 35,000ft. He had been tasked to design a high-speed medium-altitude interceptor, and this he had done. The Air Ministry was now paying the price for its emphasis on developing bomber interceptors. The RAF had been lucky with the Spitfire; it had turned out to be much more than the interceptor it was designed to be. They were not going to be so lucky with the Typhoon.

Tizard, now the Assistant Chief Executive Officer at the MAP, insisted Portal was being far too pessimistic, and assured him that with improved versions of the Sabre, the Typhoon's ceiling would be 35,000ft. This was scarcely much consolation to Portal; even the Hurricane II could manage that. Service evaluation of the first machines to come off the production line confirmed that the Sabre engine was still extremely unreliable and the handling characteristics of the Hawker fighter were still poor. In its existing state, the plane could not be used operationally in any capacity. Attempts to get the Spitfire V to achieve the performance it was supposed to be capable of met with only limited success. Fighter Command was forced to concede it had nothing that could match the Bf 109F; the German fighter had no difficulty outclimbing the latest version of the Spitfire and was faster at altitude.[51] If the Luftwaffe returned to British skies by day in 1941, it was going to be a very difficult summer for Fighter Command.

While the Air Staff agonized over existing and future fighter equipment, deliveries of fighters and bombers from America were continuing apace. Most, however, stayed in their packing cases, and those that were assembled never got further than storage units. When they had started arriving in June 1940, the idea had been for deliveries to continue to the UK until the danger of invasion had passed, but then to have all American planes shipped direct to the Middle East, where they would replace the mixed bag of biplanes most units still relied on. Despite the desperate straits Britain found itself in during the summer of 1940, very little was done to prepare the American planes for action.

They were all excellent planes, but they did not have the qualities the Air Staff wanted. The bombers were all designed as low-level attack bombers and did not have the range or bomb load to contribute to the strategic air offensive. They also lacked the array of power-operated turrets the Air Staff considered so essential if bombers were to fight their way through to their targets unescorted. The American fighters were fast and manoeuvrable at low and medium altitudes, but did not have the performance at altitude that was proving so important in the Battle of Britain. The American planes were ideal for low/medium-altitude fighter cover for ground forces and were precisely what would be required if there was an invasion, but this was not a scenario the Air Ministry was making any preparations for.

By the autumn of 1940, the failure to do more with the planes the United States was going to so much trouble to send was becoming a major embarrassment, if not a minor scandal. By the end of October, 900 aircraft had arrived in the United Kingdom, yet, in RAF service, only the Coastal Command Hudson had fired a gun in anger. Archibald Sinclair, the Air Minister, complained that the first thirty-two Mohawks had arrived in Britain at the beginning of July and the number had now grown to 200, but only four were ready for operations. Of eighty-seven Marylands and 144 Bostons, only eight of the former and three of the latter were ready for combat. Sinclair reminded Beaverbrook that all these were urgently required – the Mohawks and Marylands for the Middle East and the Boston for night fighting – and he demanded an explanation.[52] For someone famed for his dynamism, the Minister of Aircraft Production seemed remarkably relaxed about the issue. He insisted there was no problem, that the work could not go any faster and blamed the Air Ministry for changing its mind about the role it wanted planes like the Boston to perform: 'So you will see there has been no delay in any direction. The work cannot be progressed more swiftly, much as we desire to supply the Middle East with these magnificent machines.'[53] The Air Minister was not impressed.

At the end of 1940 there were 100 Mohawks languishing in repair and maintenance depots, but none of them were in any fit state to be issued to squadrons. These were aircraft that the British government was using the country's dwindling gold reserves to buy. The Fleet Air Arm had done much better. The first Grumman F4F Martlet (Wildcat in US service) fighter arrived in the country in August, and on 8 September the first was delivered to No. 804 Squadron, operating in defence of Scapa Flow as part of Fighter Command, with re-equipment completed in October. It was a Martlet of No. 804 Squadron that scored the first victory by an American fighter in British service when it shot down a Ju 88 on Christmas Day. It might be argued that the need to replace the squadron's Sea Gladiators was greater than any Fighter Command requirement, but the Middle East also needed something more modern than the Gladiator.

By this time the Americans were hurrying the Mohawk's successor, the Allison-powered H81 Tomahawk, across the Atlantic. The manufacturers claimed the Curtiss fighter had a top speed of 360mph, making it as fast as the Spitfire I, although performance at altitude was not quite so impressive. Whether these figures were accurate or not, nobody really knew. The first example had arrived in August 1940 for trials. The machine was assembled and delivered to the RAF in September, but when full-scale deliveries of 140 ex-French contract Tomahawks began in October, the machine had still not been properly tested. From the new year, the Tomahawks joined Mohawks in repair and maintenance depots. Sixty-nine had been assembled by the end of February, but none of them were serviceable. Most of the Tomahawks that arrived were simply left in their crates.

Portal seemed to want to do something about it. He was impressed by the manufacturer's claims, and given the known inferiority of the Hurricane I, he thought those already in this country could be used to re-equip Hurricane squadrons. This was not a bad idea, not just because the Tomahawk was a better fighter than the Hurricane I, but for purely diplomatic reasons. The American public was being told that their aircraft were playing an important part in halting the Nazi advance, but there was precious little evidence of this in the battle reports coming from Europe. President Roosevelt had promised that Britain could buy 50 per cent of anything American factories could produce, which meant many American squadrons were having to wait longer for much-needed modern equipment. Unless the Americans saw more evidence that their planes were being used in combat, they might decide better use could be made of them by their own Army and Navy air forces. This was reason enough to get some into service as quickly as possible. It was decided that the Tomahawk should equip No. 403 Squadron Canadian Air Force, which was due to form in the UK on 1 March 1941.[54] The fighter was not exactly being rushed into service.

By the end of 1940, neither the Mohawk nor the Tomahawk had even been properly tested. The plan was still to send Mohawks and all Tomahawks not required by No. 403 Squadron to the Middle East, with future American deliveries of the Tomahawk going direct to the Middle East. In December, the first batch of 100 Tomahawks were about to set sail from the United States for Africa and the first Mohawks were on their way from Britain. At this point, Air Chief Marshal Wilfrid Freeman, Portal's deputy, decided that it might be a good idea to discover any problems with the Mohawk and Tomahawk before they arrived in the Middle East.[55] It seemed rather late in the day for this.

Three months later, and seven months after the first example had arrived in the country, the first full report on the capabilities of the Tomahawk appeared. The fighter was not quite as capable as its American designers were claiming. It was not as fast as the Spitfire I, but its level, diving and even its climbing speed were superior to the Hurricane. It did not quite have the remarkable handling characteristics of its H75 Mohawk predecessor, but its controls were still rated as lighter and more responsive than the Hurricane, and it could also outturn the British fighter. Pilots reported it could climb higher than its 30,000ft theoretical ceiling and, unlike the Hurricane, the plane did not 'wallow' at higher altitudes.[56] The American fighter was thus far superior to the Hurricane I. The Hurricane II was a closer match. The huge power the Merlin XX churned out at altitude was much greater than the American Allison engine could manage, and the Hurricane II could climb far higher. It was also armed with cannon. In all other respects, however, the Tomahawk was the better fighter, especially at low and medium altitudes.

This, however, was not what Douglas wanted. He needed cannon-armed fighters that could reach and shoot down bombers at medium and high altitudes. Given that Douglas thought the Spitfire I was no longer any use, it is hardly surprising he felt he could do without the Curtiss Tomahawk. Equipping the Canadian fighter squadron with the American fighter was no more than a gesture. As for bombers, the Bostons and Marylands were no more welcome. Although far superior to the Blenheims of No. 2 Group, Portal was far more interested in converting the group's squadrons to Wellington long-range heavy bombers. Only when it was decided that the Boston was needed as a night fighter was there any urgency about getting it into service. The overall theme was the same as it had been during the summer of 1940 – strategic had priority over tactical applications of air power. If this had been the priority when an invasion was imminent, it was unlikely to change when an invasion had become a more distant prospect. Yet an invasion in 1941 was still a real possibility, and the failure to develop an effective tactical air force might still prove disastrous for the country. Looking further ahead, such a force would certainly be needed when the British Army in the UK went on to the offensive.

The low opinion of American designs was particularly embarrassing as Roosevelt was in the process of persuading the US Congress to agree to his Lend-Lease proposals, a remarkably generous scheme whereby Britain would pay nothing for American equipment. The Americans would lend it to Britain for the duration of the war, and then Britain would return whatever remained. With Britain running out of gold reserves and on its last economic legs, Lend-Lease was crucial. There was understandably opposition in the United States to the country just giving away its military equipment, despite the president's quaint analogy of it being like one neighbour lending a hose to another to put out a fire in order to save both houses. This particular neighbour planned on borrowing a lot of very expensive hoses, and there was not much chance of getting many of them back. Opposition to Lend-Lease would be even greater if it appeared their neighbour seemed not to want to use any of the hoses.

It did not help that it seemed to be common knowledge that the British thought American planes were too slow and poorly armed to be of any use, rumours which were hardly surprising since this was precisely what the Air Ministry thought. To try to correct this impression, the MAP invited journalists to visit the sites where the American planes were being assembled and watch them in action so they could appreciate the capabilities of planes like the Douglas Boston, rather generously credited with a speed of 350mph. They witnessed mock dogfights between Hurricanes and Tomahawks, where neither seemed to be able to gain the advantage over the other, in British accounts at least. Patriotic American accounts, quite naturally, but also more accurately, described how the American fighter 'outmanoeuvred and out sped the Hurricane'.[57] For the time being, American readers would have to be content with how their fighters coped with friendly Hurricanes rather than enemy Messerschmitts. American reports described with pride the large numbers of American fighters wanted by the British, but the American audience might have been puzzled by the lack of any information about the exploits of these planes in combat. There were rumours in the United States that Britain was refusing to use the planes until the results of their own exhaustive trials were known. 'I don't know who had given them this idea,' an MAP report lamented.[58] The hundreds of American aircraft piling up in storage units scarcely justified such indignation.

To Churchill's enormous relief, Roosevelt got his way and in March 1941, the Lend-Lease Bill was passed. Britain would get half the planes the United States could build and would not have to pay for any of them. If anything, however, this made it even more imperative to make some use of the equipment. It was one thing to waste British gold reserves, but quite another to waste American tax-payer's money. In April 1941, General H.H. Arnold, the head of the USAAC, visited Britain. Even on his carefully guided tour he saw recently arrived and seemingly neglected Consolidated four-engined B-24 bombers lying around on airfields apparently doing nothing, and was none too impressed.[59] Ironically, these bombers were one plane Britain was making some use of. Their long range made them ideal for patrolling the Atlantic, and they were rushed to Coastal Command within weeks of arriving. It was the failure to use the single-engined fighters and twin-engined light bombers that had been in the country for close on a year that would have more justifiably aroused Arnold's displeasure.

At the end of April 1941, 100 Tomahawks were in maintenance and reserve depots, but still none of them were operational. Nearly a year after the first American planes had arrived in Britain, not a single American fighter had flown a sortie for the RAF and not a single American bomber had dropped a bomb for Bomber Command. As far as the Air Ministry was concerned, the American planes would be fine for the Middle East – just like all the other inadequate equipment the RAF passed on to overseas commands – but they had no part to play in a modern European war. If the Air Ministry had not been so preoccupied with multi-cannon armament and so concerned about high-altitude bombers, it might have realized that in the Tomahawk it had a fighter as good, indeed in many respects better, than the Hurricane II.

The Air Ministry's disdain for the Tomahawk would have been more justified if Fighter Command had still not been so reliant on Hurricanes. Five years after the Spitfire had been ordered into production, little more than half the single-seater squadrons in the UK had the plane. No overseas squadrons were equipped with the fighter. The Bf 109 had been ordered at the same time as the Spitfire, but the German fighter force had completed conversion to the Jumo-powered version by the end of 1938, had replaced this with the second generation Bf 109E by the end of 1939 and was in the process of converting to the third-generation Bf 109F. By June 1941, 80 per cent of the German single-seater fighter force had the Bf 109F, whereas only 10 per cent of Fighter Command had the Spitfire V.

Fighter Command was numerically slightly stronger than the year before (sixty-five day fighter squadrons on 15 April 1941 compared to fifty-three, including two Fleet Air Arm squadrons, on 1 August 1940), and Douglas was concentrating his best squadrons in the south-east. However, many of his more experienced pilots had been lost over France or posted to training schools. Others had been sent overseas, and Douglas was about to lose another six squadrons to the Middle East. Ominously, the Bf 109F came with a drop tank as standard, which increased its range by 30 per cent and removed one of the most serious drawbacks of the fighter in the summer 1940 struggle. 'We must expect to have less advantage in the quality of our equipment during the next few months than we enjoyed in August last,' Fighter Command grimly recorded.[60]

Portal was not concerned by these warnings. His priorities lay elsewhere. In March 1941, he made it very clear to Air Minister Sinclair that there was no justification for switching more of Britain's resources into Fighter Command at the expense of Bomber Command.[61] Bomber production had priority. The bomber would win the war and nothing should stand in the way of the drive for victory.

Chapter 2

The Bomber Route to Victory

General Alan Brooke, commander of UK-based British forces, may have viewed the dispersion of the invasion fleet in the autumn of 1940 as providing a breathing space to prepare the Army to meet an invasion in 1941, but for Portal and Bomber Command it was an opportunity, finally, to get down to the serious business of bombing Germany into submission and winning the war. Air Commodore John Slessor of the Air Ministry Plans department thought that it might be going a bit far to suggest the RAF could win the war on its own, but continued,

> 'there is not the slightest doubt that we are not going to win it in the same way that the Germans have conquered Europe. We shall win it by the action of our bomber force, backed by the security provided by our fighters and not a "military offensive" covered by swarms of dive-bombers.'[1]

Churchill agreed entirely. He was relying on the RAF for victory. He did not believe the Army would ever be strong enough to cross the Channel and defeat the German Army, and all the Chiefs of Staff, including General Sir John Dill, Chief of the Imperial General Staff (CIGS), agreed. The Royal Navy had a crucial defensive role to play by keeping the vital sea lanes to the United Kingdom open, and both the Navy and Army might be required to defeat an invasion, but only the RAF, and in particular Bomber Command, could actually win the war. By the precision bombing of targets vital to the German war machine, Bomber Command would bring the Nazi regime to its knees.

Despite the distractions of the summer, Bomber Command believed it was already well on the way to achieving this. In September 1940, it was

29

estimated that 60 per cent of Germany's Fischer-Tropsch synthetic fuel plants had already been heavily damaged and oil production had been reduced by 15 per cent. It was also believed that attacks on aluminium plants were already affecting aircraft production, and indeed 25 per cent of German productive capacity had been affected in some way. Production in the Ruhr-Rhine and Frankfurt-Main districts had been reduced by 30 per cent just by the loss of sleep night raids inflicted on the workforce.[2]

It must have been encouraging that so much had been achieved, not only when the campaign in France and the threat of invasion had caused a dispersion of effort, but with such a small bomber force equipped with planes of limited lifting capability. In the autumn of 1940, the first examples of the next generation of heavy bombers the Manchester, Halifax and Stirling were beginning to roll off the production lines. If the arrival of these new bombers could be combined with even a moderate expansion of frontline strength, Bomber Command would surely become a truly formidable force. It is small wonder that Portal genuinely believed that if his command could focus all its efforts on the German economy, his bombers could indeed win the war single-handed.[3]

There were, however, some dark clouds on the horizon. Operating by night had slashed combat losses, but even so, at 2–3 per cent per month, they were a concern. They were higher than the Luftwaffe was suffering in its blitz on British cities. In a ground offensive, high loss rates might be acceptable over the short period of time an offensive is underway. However, in a long-term war of attrition stretching over months or even years, the cumulative effect of even relatively low loss rates can be crippling. In the first six months of the night offensive, over 300 aircraft had been lost, the equivalent of the entire frontline strength at the beginning of the campaign.

The plan at this time was to build up to a frontline strength of seventy-five heavy and twenty medium squadrons by the end of 1941, increasing to 100 heavy and twenty medium by mid-1942. This would take frontline strength up to around 2,000 bombers.[4] Early in November 1940, Bomber Command had just thirty-five heavy and nine medium squadrons. Many of the heavy squadrons were just half squadrons, and frontline strength had grown to a mere 500 machines. Members of the Air Staff blamed Beaverbrook and the priority he was giving fighter production for the slow expansion of the bomber fleet. In terms of numbers, they seemed to have a case. By December 1941, Beaverbrook hoped to be building 1,150 fighters a month, compared to 800 bombers, but even with these targets, bomber production was still getting the lion's share of production capacity. Five Spitfires could be built for one four-engined bomber, so it would require a large cut in fighter production to produce a small increase in bomber output. The Air Staff would not find many Allied army commanders agreeing that Britain was building too many fighters. The problem was that Britain simply did not have the industrial capacity to build the bombers the Air Staff wanted without taking risks with other defence requirements.

Of the bombers coming off the production line at the end of 1941, only about 200 would be the new Manchester, Stirling or Halifax 'heavies'. The Wellington would still be the single most important type, with 250 being produced a month. There was also the steel tube and plywood Albemarle (120 a month). This was a desperate attempt to produce a cheap alternative to more conventional bombers. Other significant contributions would come from the Blenheim (nearly 200 a month), but these could contribute little to the strategic offensive. Increasing bomber strength to 2,000, with a high proportion of heavy bombers, was an enormous undertaking. The very existence of the Albemarle demonstrated how aware the Air Staff was that its plans would stretch the country's resources to the limit.

This was the situation in October 1940, when Portal took over as Chief of Air Staff. The replacement of Air Chief Marshal Cyril Newall by Portal had been on the cards for some time. Although a bomber man at heart, Newall saw clearly, far too clearly for some, the needs of the other services. His flexibility was interpreted as weakness, his more open mind as a lack of conviction. Portal was the rising star, another Trenchard protégé, and had already won over the prime minister with his single-minded dedication to the bomber cause. Portal could be trusted to give the RAF's bomber offensive more focus.

Portal was not satisfied with a frontline strength of 2,000 bombers; he wanted to double it to 4,000, but Britain on its own would never be able to build such a force. The United States was one obvious way of overcoming the problem, and American planes were arriving in ever-increasing numbers. So far, however, they were mostly fighters or light and medium bombers, the types the French had ordered and the US Army preferred.

It was doubly frustrating for the Air Staff as the Lend-Lease arrangement was on the way, making a 4,000-strong bomber force very affordable. Slessor was dispatched to the United States to try to persuade the Americans to switch production to heavy bombers.[5] The Americans promised Slessor that Britain could have the majority of the heavy bombers the country was building, but unless a lot more were built this was not going to be enough. Churchill appealed to Roosevelt directly, suggesting the United States build an additional 2,000 planes a month, of which the majority should be heavy bombers.[6] There was plenty of support from the United States Army Air Corps, which was very keen to develop its own independent strategic bomber force. The USAAC, however, was still part of the Army, and the Army General Staff did not share their enthusiasm for independent bombing campaigns.

Meanwhile, Bomber Command was persevering with what it had. Portal's place at Bomber Command was taken by Air Marshal Richard Peirse. Peirse also had no doubts about the enormous destructive power of the bomber and its ability to achieve decisive results, although he was not as convinced as some about the dramatic results his new command was already claiming. Doubts were also creeping into Air Staff thinking. Peirse was told to concentrate on two targets: oil and German morale, the latter representing a significant shift in Air Staff policy. In the Twenties, Trenchard had seen morale as the primary target, but since his departure, the RAF had distanced itself from such an unworthy objective. However, the terror of the German Blitz was encouraging a harder line and it was also becoming clear that when conditions were not ideal, Bomber Command could not be as accurate as it wanted. Sometimes it might not be possible to hit anything smaller than a city centre.

German morale would be tested by attacks on twenty or thirty selected cities, 'with the primary aim of causing very heavy material destruction which will demonstrate to the enemy the power and severity of air bombardment and the hardship and dislocation which will result from it'. 'When favourable conditions obtain', the oil offensive, involving the destruction of seventeen key oil plants, would result in a heavy and possibly fatal blow to Germany.[7] A smaller effort would also be required against such targets as submarine yards, marshalling yards and bases being used by Luftwaffe night bombers. Effectively, precision bombing would only be attempted in good moonlight, which reduced the number of suitable nights to between eight and ten each month. The need for good weather cut the number even further.

Sinclair was still assuring Churchill that 'our small bomber force could, by accurate bombing, do very great damage to the enemy's war effort'. He warned that it 'could not gain a decision against Germany by bombing the civilian population',[8] but increasingly most of the bombing would be the area bombing of city centres. It was a change of emphasis that did not concern Churchill in the slightest.

Indeed, the prime minister had been actively encouraging a more indiscriminate approach. In September 1940, he tried to persuade Portal to launch widespread, sporadic attacks on German cities. Portal claimed that it was precisely because Bomber Command concentrated on specific targets that the RAF was doing so much better than the Luftwaffe. In November, Churchill proposed second-line crews, those in operational training units and perhaps army co-operation planes might shower bombs from a safe height randomly on nearby German cites 'with military targets in abundance', to supplement the efforts of the precision attacks of the regular squadrons, but Peirse insisted this would just disrupt training.[9]

Churchill was still mesmerized by the bomber's apparent enormous ability to wreak havoc. Unbeknown to Churchill, the sporadic bombing of random targets he expected second-line crews to achieve was all that his frontline experienced aircrews were managing. Peirse was more realistic than most about what his force was achieving. Against short-range targets, he estimated only one in three crews were successfully bombing the nominated target, dropping to one in five for more distant targets.[10] The Telecommunications Research Establishment (TRE), the body responsible for radar and radio research, was working on ways of improving this. Since June 1940, they had been developing GEE, a system which enabled bomber crews to identify their position from the time interval between radio signals sent from different transmitters. Trials were due to begin early in 1941.[11]

Less encouraging were efforts to use downward-looking radar to view the terrain below. This had been suggested way back in 1937.[12] When Coastal Command got the first rather primitive downward-looking radar for locating ships, crews found it more useful for detecting coastlines and helping them to navigate their way home. However, with the early low-frequency radars, there was no image as such: crews had to interpret kinks on a cathode ray tube signal to give them some idea of where they were. Attempts to use the technique to distinguish between countryside and built-up areas did not meet with much success.[13]

As well as the navigational problems, Peirse and his group commanders were also concerned by increasing losses. It was assumed that the Luftwaffe, like Fighter Command, was using radar to guide its night fighters. Fighter Command seemed to be making good progress with radar directed interceptions, and with the much deeper penetrations required to reach targets in Germany, if the German night fighter force became just as proficient, Bomber Command would be much more vulnerable than its German counterparts.[14] Indeed, geography might determine that it was a battle Bomber Command would inevitably lose. If radar ultimately made aircraft as visible by night as they were by day, then Bomber Command might find night operations just as expensive as the early day operations had been and its strategic air offensive would be back to square one.

While the loss rates were not yet considered unacceptable, they were increasing and Churchill was getting worried. On the night of 14/15 November 1940, ten out of eighty-two dispatched aircraft failed to return, the heaviest loss so far.[15] In the month as a whole, the loss rate hit 4 per cent for the first time. It seemed modest enough, but even this meant that only three out of ten aircrews could expect to survive a tour of operations. A 5 per cent loss came to be accepted as the point at which losses were becoming prohibitive. Seven per cent would be unsustainable. At this point, the future leaders and instructors would not exist in sufficient numbers to maintain the force and efficiency would inevitably decline.[16] Bomber Command was not at this point yet, but it was heading in this direction. Even the current loss rate would slow down the expansion of the force. Churchill suggested less well-defended targets should be attacked or bombers operate from safer altitudes. It might mean bombing less important targets and greater inaccuracy, but the force had to be conserved.[17] It was another good argument for just aiming at city centres.

Already, reducing losses was becoming a priority. In November 1940, Bomber Command outlined the sort of equipment that would be needed to deal with radar-directed air defences. Ideally it wanted a way of making its bombers invisible to radar, but if this was not possible, then at least a device which would tell the crew when their plane was being tracked. Radar could perhaps also be used to provide warning of an approaching fighter, and might even be used to aim defensive fire before the enemy fighter came within visual range.[18] Ground-based anti-aircraft guns were already using radar to direct fire, and the development of centimetric radar certainly provided the power and precision necessary for this to be a realistic way of defending a bomber. Bomber Command was assured these issues would get urgent attention from the Interception Committee, the body set up to examine such matters. However, even at this stage it was realized that even if such equipment could be developed, it might create more problems than it solved. Any transmissions from a bomber could be picked up and used by the enemy to locate where the signal was coming from.[19] There was a risk using onboard radar would just make it easier for the night fighter to find the bomber. It was already beginning to look like the retreat to nocturnal missions was only going to provide a temporary hiding place.

Meanwhile, it was hoped that the arrival of the four-engined 'heavies' would not only increase the bomb tonnage Bomber Command could drop, but the improved defensive armament and performance ought also to reduce losses. Indeed, a return to daylight bombing was not ruled out. The first Stirlings reached No. 7 Squadron in August 1940. With its huge 14,000lb bombload, much was expected of the plane. It was considered to be far superior to the American Boeing B-17 Fortress. Among American designs, only the Consolidated B-24 Liberator was considered anywhere near as good, but even this carried fewer bombs and had poorer defensive armament. American claims that their bomber was faster were dismissed as unlikely. Indeed, so good was the Stirling believed to be, it was suggested that the bomber should be sent to the United States, along with the Typhoon fighter, in the hope that the Americans would be so impressed they would start building the plane themselves.[20]

Such were the views in September 1940. A month later, opinions of the Stirling were not quite so enthusiastic. With the Hercules II engines, the bomber had difficulty getting into the air fully loaded, struggled to reach 12,000ft and could fly little faster than 250mph.[21] Even with more powerful Hercules engines, the plane still scarcely managed 17,000ft. The reputation of the plane was not helped by the crash of one of the first aircraft to come off the production line, and the bomber was soon dropping below the Halifax in the Air Ministry pecking order. The Halifax could not carry quite as many bombs, but it could fly higher and faster.[22] This started to reach the squadrons in November 1940. Deliveries of the twin-engined Manchester, with a performance between the Stirling and Halifax, but hopelessly handicapped by its unreliable Vulture engines, began around the same time.

None of these flew any operational sorties before the end of the year, but none of them looked like they were going to transform the prospects for Bomber Command. The previous January, Peirse had assured the Cabinet that the Stirling, Halifax and Manchester would fly so high, and so fast and be so well armed, no existing or future German fighter would be able to intercept them.[23] It now looked a particularly hollow claim. The idea of using them unescorted by day was not abandoned, but given that they could not reach 20,000ft, flew slower than 300mph and their defensive armament was not much better than the Wellington's, such aspirations seemed somewhat optimistic.

The high-altitude approach seemed to offer more chance of returning to daylight operations. Vickers was working on a version of the Wellington with the entire crew housed in a pressurized cabin. In August 1940, the prototype Wellington V, powered by turbo-supercharged Hercules VIII engines, made its maiden flight. Vickers was also developing the Wellington VI, powered by the Merlin 60 engine, the specialized high-altitude version of the Merlin XX with two superchargers in series. Vickers was also told to incorporate a pressurized cabin into its next design, the Warwick. Vickers went further, proposing a four-engined version with a new elliptical wing, capable of flying as high as 43,000ft, and this would become the Windsor.[24] While design teams set to work on these, the Americans would provide a more immediate way of testing the potential of high-altitude daylight bombing.

One of the many aircraft ordered from the United States in 1940 had been the Boeing B-17 Flying Fortress. The first American Fortress, a B-17C, flew into Britain in April 1941, along with American observers keen to see how the plane performed. The Air Ministry had never been very impressed by the Flying Fortress: it had first flown in 1935, so it was a rather old design. The Americans warned the British that the only versions of the Flying Fortress bombers they could send had no armour, self-sealing tanks or turrets and RAF officers in the United States had declared the plane obsolete.[25] However, there was one aspect of the bomber's performance that was impressive. With its turbo-supercharged engines, the Fortress managed a top speed of 325mph at 30,000ft.[26] This was twice as high as the Stirling could manage, and the Boeing bomber could fly at this altitude with an almost embarrassingly higher speed than the Stirling could manage at any altitude. This ought to put it beyond the reach of German fighters, and with its advanced Sperry bombsight, credited by its manufacturer with almost miraculous accuracy, it ought to be possible to hit even relatively small targets. The Air Ministry could scarcely believe its good fortune. Here, at last, was an American plane that really could make a useful contribution to the British war effort.

The Americans had never intended to use the plane's altitude performance to evade defences. As its name suggested, the idea was that it would fight its way through to the target, just as British bombers had been designed to do. Its altitude performance was only remarkable by comparison with the poor ceiling of recent British designs. The Americans planned to operate the plane at a more modest, although still impressive, 25,000ft, relying on tight formation flying to maximize the defensive firepower. The RAF, however, managed to get the plane to fly as high as 38,000ft. This was breaking new ground. The B-17 did not have pressurized crew compartments, and flying at such altitudes was at the edge of human endurance. A practical ceiling of 35,000ft was agreed on, but most missions were flown at 30,000–33,000ft.[27]

Even at these altitudes, the conditions aircrews had to endure were appalling. The plane had open gun positions and temperatures inside the plane could drop as low as minus 50 degrees Centigrade. No. 90 Squadron was formed within No. 2 Group to fly the American bomber. Only the fittest crews were accepted into the squadron, and a crash course in high-altitude flying and bomb dropping was initiated. Crews had to wear specially designed electrically heated suits, and even with oxygen just the slightest exertion could result in crews fainting. Despite all the problems, Flying Fortresses were dropping their first bombs on a German target (the naval base at Wilhelmshaven) little more than two months after the first machine had arrived in the country. The four-engined bomber became the first American plane to fly operations for Bomber Command. It rather highlighted Air Staff priorities. When its heart was in it, the Air Ministry had little difficulty in getting American equipment into service extremely quickly, whatever the difficulties.

While these experiments in daylight bombing were taking place, Peirse was persevering with the night offensive. Despite his doubts, he had not lost faith in precision night bombing. He may have been concerned by the high proportion of crews failing to find their targets, but he was convinced those who found them were hitting them. Peirse's main concern was the low number of bombers available, but even this cloud had a silver lining. It was very encouraging that so much had already been achieved with so few bombers. It was estimated that it had taken just 539 tons of bombs to knock out 15 per cent of the German oil industry. This was just 6.7 per cent of the total bombs so far dropped by Bomber Command, which suggested the crippling of the entire industry was well within the capabilites of the existing force, if Bomber Command could concentrate on this one target.[28] It was just a question of time before Bomber Command became the decisive force the Air Staff had always believed it would become.

The problem was focusing effort. It was a source of immense frustration to the Air Staff that, throughout the war, Bomber Command was constantly required to divert its attention from the strategic targets it had been created to destroy. There always seemed to be another branch of the armed services in urgent need of Bomber Command's support. This was hardly surprising given that Britain was fighting a war. Bomber Command frustration was an inevitable consequence of the compartmentalized structure of the British armed forces. The Air

Ministry viewed requests from the other services as distractions rather than an opportunity for different services to pool their resources and work together with a common aim.

The war in the Mediterranean was one of these diversions. As soon as the threat of invasion was lifted, Churchill saw the centre of gravity of the war moving to the Middle East, even more so after the Italian invasion of Greece, and was insisting that RAF units there be reinforced. These reinforcements included Bomber Command's most prized Vickers Wellingtons. The bomber/transport squadrons in the Middle East were re-equipped with the Vickers bomber, and in November two No. 3 Group Wellington squadrons joined them.

Then a new danger, even greater than invasion, emerged. Churchill had always feared the Royal Navy could lose the war, and in the Atlantic it seemed to be losing. German FW 200 Condor bombers and U-boats were inflicting heavy losses on the convoys that were so vital to keeping Britain in the war. Inevitably, Bomber Command was called upon to fly operations in support of the Navy. Attacks on the factories and shipyards where the Focke-Wolf bombers and U-boats were being built had to be accommodated within the general strategic offensive. Attacking ports from which the U-boats operated was even further removed from Air Staff war aims. On top of these naval demands, there was always the War Office pestering the Air Ministry about exactly how the RAF, including Bomber Command, was going to help the Army resist the invasion expected in the spring of 1941.

The good news for the Air Staff was that some progress was being made convincing the Americans to change their production priorities. In the spring of 1941, USAAC plans were still dominated by fighters, light, medium and dive-bombers, with around 16,000 of these due to be delivered to Britain. Heavy bombers had a far lower priority; only 600 were due to arrive between January 1941 and June 1942, and American heavy bomber production was going to level off at just 226 machines a month by April 1943. The visit to Britain by General Arnold, the commander of the USAAC, in April 1941 was the perfect opportunity for the Air Ministry to have its say. Portal, Freeman and Peirse all emphasized the enormous importance of long-range bombers. Peirse assured Arnold that if the American Army insisted on having bomber support, heavy bombers were just as capable of delivering it, a particularly useful argument for Arnold to use with his Army masters. Freeman had maps drawn up showing how far into Germany American light bombers would be able to penetrate. Portal told Arnold about his ambitious plans to create a force of 4,000 heavy bombers, and did his best to persuade him that Britain could find the aircrews and build and maintain the facilities such a force would require. Building the bombers was another matter. It would require 1,000 heavy bombers a month to maintain, and the British aircraft industry could only manage 500. The United States was the only alternative source for the remaining 500.[29]

Arnold scarcely needed converting; he too believed in the all-conquering might of the long-range bomber and wanted the USAAC to give it the same priority it was getting in Britain. The trip provided all the evidence he needed. He was able to return to the United States armed with facts provided by a nation with war experience. The USAAC drew up an extraordinary plan for a bomber force with 936 light bombers (Douglas A 20s), 1,248 dive-bombers, 1,060 medium (North American B-25 Mitchells, Martin B-26 Marauders), 3,995 heavy (Boeing B-17 Flying Fortresses, Consolidated B-24 Liberators), 2,040 very heavy (Boeing B-29 Superfortresses, Consolidated B-32s) and 3,740 intercontinental bombers (the enormous six-engined Consolidated B-36s).[30] The proposal was breathtaking in its scope, completely dwarfing British plans and ambitions. American heavy bomber production would start aiming for 500 a month, but Portal would need all of these if he was to achieve his 4,000 target strength. With Britain's own bomber production struggling to reach forty a month and with total frontline strength less than 500 bombers, Portal's target looked a very distant prospect.

Chapter 3

The Air Ministry Digs In

While the Air Ministry in London wanted the RAF to fight the war without any interference or distractions from the other services, this was not an option for Air Chief Marshal Arthur Longmore, the commander of the RAF units in the Middle East. General Archibald Wavell, the commander of the British ground forces in Egypt – the Western Desert Force – and East Africa, did not have the luxury of an English Channel to shield him; his makeshift forces would have to fight, and they would be relying on all the air support they could get. As happened during the brief French campaign in May–June 1940, being involved in actual ground operations inevitably affected the way the RAF was used. In France, the realities of war forced the RAF units based there to adapt, but the spring shoots of a tactical air force had soon withered once the RAF squadrons retreated to the United Kingdom and its segregated Bomber and Fighter Commands. In the desert there would be more time to develop ground/air co-operation.

Arthur Longmore was a blunt Australian who was never afraid to speak his mind. He had served with the Royal Naval Air Service (RNAS), and before the First World War had carried out the first trials with airborne torpedoes. He was an outspoken critic of the insularism Trenchard had sought to encourage in the inter-war years. He criticized the barriers that existed between services, with their 'parochial *espirit de corps*', which led to one service being incapable of using the resources of another 'without a desire to possess it and dress it in their own uniform'.[1] Such views no doubt helped him get appointed as the commandant of the joint services Imperial Defence College from 1936–1938, where he was in a position to try to break down these barriers. This was perhaps expecting too much, but, appointed to the Middle East Command just weeks before Italy's declaration of war, he would have the opportunity to apply his philosophy on the battlefield.

His Middle East command entered the war with twenty-nine squadrons, with a strength of around 300 aircraft. He found himself facing an Italian Air Force with some 1,800 aircraft. The aircraft available to Longmore were an interesting and varied collection. To a large extent, squadrons had to rely on aircraft that were being replaced in the UK, so they were often the worse for wear when they arrived. Obsolescent planes soon became obsolete as performance deteriorated in the harsh desert conditions. However, the RAF in the Middle East was lucky in that the type of planes it would need were the very types the Air Ministry did not want. Bomber Command was very quick to pack the Blenheim I off to the Middle East once the longer-range Blenheim IV arrived, but arguably the faster more manoeuvrable Blenheim I was more useful for tactical air support than the heavier Blenheim IV. The Blenheim IV was Britain's best medium daytime bomber, but Bomber Command did not particularly want this either, and the Middle East was beginning to get these too. Lomgmore was short of modern fighters, but the five Blenheim squadrons provided a modern bomber force.

The area Longmore's command covered was huge, stretching from Egypt in the west to Iraq in the east and Kenya in the south. The numerical weakness of his resources did not seem such a huge problem while France was still in the war. The combined British and French forces were sufficient to deal with the Italian threat. It was Libya that was under threat, precariously squeezed between two mighty empires. With France defeated, however, the tables were turned and it was the Italians who dominated the region and the British who felt beleaguered.

Initially, the role of the British Army in Egypt was purely defensive. Its main aim was to protect the Suez Canal and the oil fields further east. The role of the RAF was supposed to mirror that of UK-based squadrons: fighters existed primarily to defend strategic targets in the rear (cities, naval bases and lines of communication), while bombers were supposed to strike at targets deep in the enemy rear. These included targets of economic significance, and in this respect these operations were supposed to supplement those of the home-based Bomber Command. Support for the Western Desert Force would be provided by a handful of multi-purpose army co-operation squadrons.

However, in the Middle East there was no Bomber Command or Fighter Command, and therefore no compartmentalizing of air units. The RAF operated as a single force. Nor was the Air Ministry's influence so all-encompassing. In outlook, Longmore was in many ways a product of the Trenchard era. He was always anxious to extend the reach of his force, to take the fight as far behind the enemy lines as he could. From Egypt, however, it was not possible to contemplate defeating the enemy single-handedly by destroying their sources of munitions – Italy's industrial regions were well out of reach. RAF operations had to be co-ordinated with the Army to have any point. Despite the constant inter-war wrangling between the War Office and Air Ministry in London, on the ground in the colonies, counter-insurgency and air policing operations had already established a degree of inter-service co-operation. The environment was much more conducive to the development of tactical air support than was the case in the United Kingdom.

In his first instruction immediately after Italy entered the war, Longmore made it clear it was his intention 'to provide full support of the British Army in whatever operations were in progress',[2] and RAF headquarters were established alongside their Army counterparts. The Army was not seen as an unfortunate drain on RAF resources; it was why RAF units were in the region. This did not mean there were no differences of outlook. Wavell and Longmore did not always see eye to eye on how the RAF should provide 'full support', but the Air Force was prepared to co-operate with ground forces in a way that was quite inconceivable in the United Kingdom.

The Italian entry into the war was more a political act than military event, so the weak British forces in Egypt were spared an immediate assault. With one side unwilling to go on to the offensive and the other unable, another 'phoney war' seemed to be beckoning. However, unlike the stalemate that had existed on the Western Front in the winter of 1939/40, there was no political pressure on the Army or RAF to remain passive. Quite the contrary, Churchill was encouraging aggression. Army units were soon conducting raids across the Libyan frontier and the RAF was also on the offensive, attacking Italian ports and airfields. It might seem reckless to so provoke an enemy who was stronger in almost every respect, but it gave the British pilots the opportunity to test their mettle early on and gain a sense of ascendancy that was not justified by the actual forces available. Most crucially of all, the aircrews had an opportunity to learn how to get the best out of their equipment in combat situations before they were engaged in crucial battles. When the ground fighting started in earnest, crews would not be flying their planes into combat for the first time, as was so often the case with many British and French pilots and aircrews in the spring of 1940. It was offensive action in the best Trenchard spirit. It was aggressive without being reckless, and it did not incur heavy unnecessary losses. These operations helped strengthen morale and lessons were quickly learned. The day after the Italian declaration of war, around twenty-seven unescorted Blenheims attacked Italian airfields, and Fiat CR.42s and anti-aircraft fire shot down three. The intervention of Italian fighters was enough for Gladiators on air defence duties in the rear to be moved forward to escort future missions.[3] As had happened during the brief campaign in France, the RAF was learning quickly.

The RAF and Western Desert Force units maintained their aggressive stance throughout June and July, but in August it was decided to pull back to more easily defendable positions inside Egypt. On 10 August, the Army requested an air strike on Italian forces threatening some withdrawing columns. Ten escorted Blenheims were dispatched to break up the Italian force. The first request for air support from ground forces in the desert had been made and fulfilled.[4] It all seemed remarkably straightforward and uncontroversial. Nevertheless, such air support had to be rare because there was such a desperate shortage of planes. The initial allocation from the United Kingdom was just twelve Hurricanes, twelve Blenheims and six Lysanders a month, and with the Battle of Britain at its height, the delivery of Hurricanes was soon temporarily halted altogether. With the American aircraft being held in the UK until the immediate threat of invasion had passed, Longmore felt he had little choice but to conserve his strength.[5] Further strikes in support of the Western Desert Force would only be carried out if an enemy offensive was underway or imminent. It was a sensible restriction in the circumstances.[6]

Convinced that Britain was on the brink of defeat, Mussolini was anxious to engage the British in some real fighting before Britain surrendered, simply to make sure he had a seat in the surrender negotiations. To fulfil this political requirement, on 13 September, Italian forces in Libya, supported by 250 aircraft, pushed forward tentatively. British forward troops withdrew, the main British defensive line was not even threatened and no major engagement occurred. In British Somaliland, Commonwealth troops were also pulling back. Their position was totally untenable, and an Italian advance, supported by eighty-five planes, left the garrison with little option but to withdraw across the Gulf of Aden. With the slender forces available to General Wavell and Longmore, survival seemed the only sensible objective.

However, reinforcements were soon on the way, and on a surprising scale given Britain's precarious position. Churchill was very much an Empire man, and an invasion of Egypt and the possible loss of the

Suez Canal was seen as just as serious a threat as an invasion of the United Kingdom. On 15 August, with the Battle of Britain at its height and an invasion expected any day, Churchill informed Wavell that his command would be reinforced by three tank battalions, with fifty light, fifty infantry and fifty cruiser tanks. It was a substantial proportion of the total number available on the home front. Air reinforcement, however, was far more modest, but Wellingtons (six a month) would begin to join an increased monthly allocation of eighteen Hurricanes, thirty-six Blenheims, and six Lysanders.[7] It was the beginning of this strange dichotomy in defence thinking, which saw overseas theatres get priority with ground forces while the United Kingdom had priority in air resources. It all seemed very logical to Churchill. Substantial air forces in Britain would make an invasion impossible, so he therefore believed it was safe to send substantial ground reinforcements to the Middle East.

The good fortune for the Middle East was that Churchill's, and the Air Staff's, idea of a substantial air force was a bomber force that could deliver a large bomb tonnage over considerable distances and interceptors with good high-altitude performance to defend British cities and industry. Shorter-range light bombers and fighters with good low-level performance, like the planes the United States was providing, were not wanted on the home front. Longmore was told early in September that as soon as the threat of a 1940 invasion had passed, he would start getting Marylands, Mohawks and Tomahawks. The Martin Maryland was one of the best light bombers in the world, and the Curtiss Mohawk and Tomahawk, while not in the same league as the Spitfire, had many of the qualities required from fighters expected to operate at low and medium altitudes over the battlefield. By February 1941, Longmore would have all 227 Curtiss Mohawks to re-equip RAF and South African Air Force (SAAF) squadrons. Sixty-five Marylands were also supposed to arrive, and Curtiss Tomahawks would soon follow.[8] These modern planes were much needed. Many of the squadrons based outside Egypt, including SAAF squadrons in Kenya, were equipped with aircraft as old as Hawker Furies and miscellaneous Hart variants.

In the autumn of 1940, with the danger of immediate invasion of the UK fading, pressure grew to act on these commitments. Longmore wasted no time congratulating Portal on his appointment as Chief of Air Staff – Longmore's telegram anticipated the actual takeover by a couple of weeks. Longmore implored Portal to review immediately the Middle East's air allocation.[9] Admiral Andrew Cunningham, the naval commander in the Mediterranean, Wavell and Anthony Eden, the Secretary of State for War, all chipped in with their complaints. Eden viewed the problem from a politician's perspective, highlighting the political consequences if Egypt's densely populated cities should be bombed. Air reinforcements were 'the most pressing need of the hour' and he was 'frankly disappointed' by the failure to get more air reinforcements to the region.[10] Wavell too pointed out the dangers of unrest in the rear if Egypt's 'teeming cities' were bombed, and, from the tactical viewpoint, emphasized that air reinforcements were not keeping pace with the reinforcements the ground forces were receiving.[11] Finally, tension between Greece and Italy was growing and the British ambassador in Greece, Sir Michael Palairet, was already appealing for air support for Greece should Italian forces in Albania invade. At the same time, Longmore was making it clear that with the resources available to him, he would not be able to help the Greeks.[12] The Air Ministry considered this apparently organized conspiratorial lobbying for more air support rather annoying and somewhat distasteful.[13] It was the first turn in a downward spiral in the relationship between the Air Ministry and its commander in the Middle East,

Churchill set up a ministerial committee to assess the military needs in the Middle East and this recommended increasing the flow of reinforcements to the RAF, but Churchill insisted that the 'vastly inferior numbers' of Fighter Command in the UK (seventeen squadrons short of its eighty-five squadron target), the 'inadequate' strength of Bomber Command and the 'lamentably inferior' reserves the latter possessed compared to the German bomber force be taken into account.[14] Portal was more than happy to be guided by this hint, and decided that the only measures that he could take in the short term was to re-equip existing squadrons with more modern planes as they became available and to increase the frontline strength of some units. However, the Middle East was welcome to all the American planes that were available, and Portal instructed the MAP to accelerate delivery of the 450 America bombers and fighters that had been assigned to the Middle East. By the end of March 1941 it was hoped to have four-and-a-half Mohawk and six Maryland RAF and SAAF squadrons in Egypt and East Africa.[15]

A few planes did reach the Middle East through the Mediterranean before the French defeat. Malta acquired its first modern fighters by hanging on to Hurricanes that were supposed to be going to Egypt. With France defeated, however, only long-range planes could fly direct to Egypt. The only relatively safe sea route for planes without the range was round the Cape of Good Hope, which made getting any reinforcements to the Middle East a lengthy process that bit deeply into available shipping resources. To speed up delivery and save on shipping space, a base was set up at Takoradi on the West African coast. From here, aircraft would make their way to the Middle East along a string of airfields across central Africa. The trip involved flying 3,500 miles over inhospitable terrain to Cairo, a flight that took a week to complete. The first crated Blenheims and Hurricanes arrived at Takoradi on 5 September 1940, and on the 19th the first batch of one Blenheim and six Hurricanes departed Takoradi. Seven days later they arrived in Egypt, minus one of the Hurricanes which developed technical problems. It was a method of delivery that had many disadvantages, not least of which was that the planes that did survive the journey were in need of a total overhaul on arrival.[16] The initial plan was to use the route to send fifty aircraft a month.[17] It was a crucial way of getting planes to the Middle East, but it need not have been the only regular means of reinforcement; more could still have been shipped round the Cape. However, in practice, apart from the odd emergency dash through the Mediterranean, the Takoradi route became the sole route for planes that did not have the range to fly direct.

With the Hurricane, the RAF had arguably the best fighter available to either side. The Italian Air Force was only just getting its first monoplane fighters. One of these was the very manoeuvrable Macchi C.200, which was a match for the Hurricane I. The biplane Fiat CR.42 had a slight edge over the Gladiator II, but only just had the speed to catch the Blenheim. The Hurricane had a speed advantage over the Fiat biplane that was as great as the Bf 109E had over the Hurricane, although initially the value of this advantage was not appreciated.[18] As was often the case when pilots moved to high-speed monoplanes, there was a temptation to try to outmanoeuvre biplanes, which always gave the biplane pilot a chance.

The arrival of Wellingtons did much to increase Longmore's long-range hitting power. However, the fourth type being delivered, the Lysander, did not inspire much enthusiasm; indeed, the plane was soon considered a liability.[19] It was scarcely the fault of the plane; it was not obsolete, it was just that too much was expected of it. For short-range observation it was fine and losses were few, but for deeper penetrations, each sortie required an escort, which diverted fighters from other essential duties. If fighters had to escort the Lysander, then those same fighters might as well perform the reconnaissance mission.[20] It was not long before the Hurricane was given the tactical reconnaissance role.

If commanders in the Middle East needed reminding about the importance of air superiority over the battlefield, the Italians provided it at Gallabat in East Africa. Here a Commonwealth force supported by just twenty-six aircraft, including ten Gladiators, attacked across the Sudan/Ethiopian frontier. Gallabat was captured, but the Italians reacted vigorously. Six Gladiators were shot down by Fiat CR.42s during the opening hours of the attack. The Italians then moved ground-attack units to the threatened front to take advantage of the air superiority gained. The surviving fighters were unable to protect the Commonwealth forces from fierce Italian air attacks and Gallabat had to be abandoned. The speed with which the air reinforcements arrived made a significant impression on their opponents.[21]

In the Western Desert too, the British were impressed with the flexibility with which the Italians had used their air force during the minor actions that had taken place, especially with the way the Italians used obsolete Fiat CR.32 fighters to harass British columns with machine guns and light bombs. Longmore ordered trials with similarly equipped British fighters, and ancient Gauntlets were chosen for the experiment.[22] Preventing such attacks on Commonwealth forces was seen as vital. Longmore felt nothing less than immunity from enemy air attacks was required if forces were to advance, which might have been a little ambitious, but protecting Allied troops would in future be a high priority.

All this should have strengthened the case for ground forces defending Britain from invasion having similar air support. It was striking how the RAF in the Middle East was following the same path that the British Air Forces in France (BAFF – comprising the Air Component and the Advanced Air Striking Force) had followed in their brief existence. There too, fighters were initially seen as interceptors to defend targets in the rear, but the realities of actual war soon saw them committed to action over the front, fighting a First World War-style battle for air superiority. During the brief campaign in France, fighters had also been used for tactical reconnaissance and ground-attack. However, with the defeat of France this first tactical air force was disbanded and the squadrons returned to the control of Bomber and Fighter Command, where there was no framework or desire for building on the experience gained in France.

In Britain, the Army and RAF both saw events in France as proof that they had been right. To the Air Staff it seemed obvious that an air force could not support an army directly on the battlefield. In the French campaign, RAF bombers had tried and been shot down in droves. To the Army it was obvious that it could, since that was what the Luftwaffe had done. The Air Staff explained away this apparent discrepancy by suggesting that air support on the battlefield was only possible for an army that was advancing – it did not work if an army was retreating. It was a rather convenient argument for not providing support, given that the German Army was advancing most of the time. The Army might argue that the lack of air support for the defending forces was aiding the enemy advance. There was also plenty of evidence that it did work in defensive situations. In 1918, air power had played a huge role in halting a series of German offensives, and the brief Allied counter-attacks launched during the French campaign in 1940 had been constantly harassed by Luftwaffe bombing. In the Middle East, close air support was already being used to stiffen defences.

The Air Staff also maintained that air support had only worked for Germany in Poland and France because they had air superiority. Once the RAF had air superiority, the Army would get all the support it wanted. This was very dangerous thinking. Clearly, providing an army with air support is easier with air superiority. However, an army cannot wait days, weeks, months or years until air superiority is achieved before getting support. Air forces have to do the best they can whatever the situation and with whatever is available, as the RAF in the Middle East was already doing. If the enemy has air superiority, you have to develop tactics that allow you to support the army as effectively as possible in those circumstances. Arguably, if an army is losing a battle and in retreat, and the enemy has air superiority, it is in even greater need of air support than an army that is advancing with air superiority. It was the former scenario that the British Army was most likely to find itself in if it had to deal with a German invasion.

Putting off the need for air support until the RAF had air superiority and the British Army was advancing meant, in the view of the Air Staff, that it would not be needed for some time. In truth, Portal believed the bomber offensive would be so successful, it would never be needed; he did not think there would be a major battle to support. The reoccupation of German-held territories would be a mere formality against a broken enemy. The War Office went along with this argument to an extent because it genuinely believed that the German advantage on land was so great that weakening German armed forces by air attack was the only realistic way of giving the British Army a chance. Nevertheless, the War Office did not believe bombing alone could be decisive. There would be a battle on land, it would not be a formality – no matter how successful the bombing had been – and the Army would need all the support the RAF could provide to win it.

Who was right might forever remain unknown, if, in the meantime, Germany invaded Britain. Churchill and the Air Staff were convinced an invasion was simply not possible while a powerful Fighter Command existed. Even if there was an invasion, the Air Staff was convinced that battlefield air support could not help in a defensive battle. From this unpromising position, the War Office somehow had to acquire the air support the Army would need – and it was not just about defeating an invasion. Close air support requires the same tools in defence and attack. Developing the air support the British Army would need to defend its shores would hasten the day it had the support required to invade the continent.

The obstacles were immense but there would never be a better time for the War Office to get what it wanted. Much of the criticism that followed the Battle of France centred on the lack of air support. Indisputably, German use of air power to support its army had been very successful, and the Air Ministry was under a lot of pressure to provide something similar for the British Army.

The first task for the War Office was to get the Air Ministry to agree that Army needs could not be met by the 'Jack of all trades' army co-operation plane. The RAF had to start acquiring specialist planes for the different army support roles. The Army wanted not just specialist close-support planes, but also specialist tactical reconnaissance planes. The War Office pointedly referred to these as 'Tac/R', to distinguish them from the traditional multi-role army co-operation plane. Fighters also had to be attached to the Army and eventually Air Observation Post (AOP) squadrons to direct artillery. In August 1940, the War Office passed a preliminary list to the Air Ministry of the squadrons they wanted under British Army control by May 1941. The Middle East needed six close-support squadrons and six fighter squadrons for the planned three infantry corps (nine divisions) and two armoured divisions. Each corps and armoured division would also have a Tac/R squadron.

In the United Kingdom, Bomber and Fighter Command would be available for additional support, so just seven close-support squadrons would be required to support the ten infantry corps (twenty divisions) and two armoured divisions. Again, each corps and armoured division would require a Tac/R squadron. For fighter support, the War Office was willing to rely entirely on Fighter Command. A General Reserve of two infantry corps and two armoured divisions would require another four close-support and three fighter squadrons.[23] As the War Office was painfully aware, even these modest expectations added up to forty-seven squadrons, the sort of demands that had previously provoked apoplexy in Air Ministry circles. As far as the Air Ministry was concerned, every squadron attached to the Army was one less for Bomber Command. The War Office was perhaps right in believing that it could undermine its case by asking for too much, but what it was asking for in the Middle East – a huge geographical area with active fronts in the Western Desert and East Africa – was about the same as the forces the BEF had been able to count on in France, where it was defending a 20-mile front.

The Air Ministry, no doubt relieved that the demand was so modest, assured the War Office these requirements would be met. Indeed, it claimed that they had already been met. The War Office was talking about close-support squadrons under the direct control of the Army, as the Air Component had been in France, and had clearly stated they were expecting support from Bomber Command in addition to this. This additional support would be provided by the nineteen Battle and Blenheim squadrons Nos. 1 and 2 Groups had at the time. With plans to re-equip No. 1 Group with Bostons, they were ideal for the indirect support the War Office was expecting Bomber Command to provide. However, by counting these squadrons as the specialist close-support element the War Office was asking for, the Air Ministry claimed that it had more than met Army requirements. It was the sort of wily manipulation of information and reinterpretation of the facts that the Air Ministry would prove so good at and was so infuriating for those, including frontline RAF commanders, who had to deal with the Ministry.

To make matters worse for the War Office, Portal, still in charge of Bomber Command at this time, argued that since Nos 1 and 2 Groups had more than the seven squadrons the Army wanted, he was justified in converting the surplus to Wellingtons. The whole of No. 1 Group was soon re-equipping with the heavy bomber and Portal was soon dipping into No. 2 Group for reinforcements for the Wellington-equipped No. 3 Group. As for the remaining squadrons in No. 2 Group, the Air Ministry had no difficulty persuading itself the Blenheims were what the Army wanted. As an interim close-support plane, the Air Ministry had offered the War Office a version of the Blenheim IV (the Blenheim V, or Bisley).

The War Office had never been happy with the Blenheim as a close-support plane. It was fine for isolating the battlefield, the task it was expected additional support from Bomber Command would provide, but quite correctly it was believed that large twin-engined planes would be too vulnerable and would lack the manoeuvrability for low-level work over the battlefield.[24] The Air Ministry talked up the advantages of twin-engined planes for low-level operations; two engines would provide greater security against flak and enabled more bombs and armour to be carried. However, the real advantage was that it could carry more fuel and the plane could double as a long-range bomber. The Bisley had Mercury engines that offered maximum output at low altitude, armour protection and a solid nose with fixed forward-firing guns for strafing. However, the solid nose was replaceable by a glazed bomb-aiming position and the armour was detachable so that the plane could carry extra fuel tanks instead. This was supposed to be an interim quick-fix solution. The longer-term development was an entirely new light bomber that would replace the Battle and Blenheim (specification B.11/39), but this was another twin-engined plane that could be used for longer-range bombing.

Following the obvious success of the Stuka in the Battle of France, the War Office renewed its attempts to get the smaller, more manoeuvrable single-engined plane it had always preferred. Ideally, it should be capable of low-level attack and dive-bombing. Beaverbrook at the new Ministry of Aircraft Production would prove to be far more sympathetic than the Air Ministry. This ministry, created by Churchill in May 1940, was largely made up of sections transferred from the Air Ministry, so its staff were mostly RAF officers imbued with Trenchardian ideas on independent aerial warfare. However, the civilian element and the ministers who ran it were not so imbued and tended to be far more receptive to Army requirements. Beaverbrook provided the War Office with what it wanted by ordering single-engined dive-bombers from the United States. The British had taken over French contracts for the Brewster SB2A Bermuda dive-bomber, and more of these and large numbers of the Vultee A-35 Vengeance were ordered. Nobody knew what these planes were capable of – they had not even flown yet – but they were called dive-bombers and they were single-engined, which was good enough for the War Office. Beaverbrook promised the Army they would have 200 by the end of the year, a rather optimistic claim given that neither of these planes had flown.[25] Interestingly, Beaverbrook urged Eden (the Secretary of State for War) to offer to provide volunteers from the Army to fly the planes as the Air Ministry was short of pilots. Eden did indeed suggest this, and no doubt the suggestion provoked much anxiety.[26] Army pilots flying army support planes was a giant stride towards an Army Air Force.

It is easy to understand why the War Office wanted a dive-bomber. While the panzers had won the battle in France, Stukas had been the most striking feature. The screeching air brakes, boosted by a siren, made a Stuka attack a terrifying experience. Diving vertically effectively made the plane stationary with respect to the target, which made it far more accurate than level bombing. However, if the target was fixed relative to the bomber, the dive-bomber was equally fixed relative to the defending anti-aircraft guns, making them relatively easy targets. They were also vulnerable as they pulled out of their dives. To add to the dive-bombers' problems, arriving at one altitude and diving to a lower altitude made it more difficult for the fighter escorts. One way or another, dive-bombers tended to be vulnerable.

An alternative way of hitting small targets was to fly low, although this inevitably exposed the plane to ground fire. Whether this was more or less risky than dive-bombing was debatable, but a small manoeuvrable plane minimized the risk and armour ought also to help. For some time the War Office had been suggesting that older fighters being phased of service might be used. It had even approached Gloster about the possibility of converting 200 Gladiators to the fighter-bomber role.[27] The low speed of such planes was seen as an advantage, as they would find it easier to line up the target. The War Office was just as interested in low-level attack as it was in dive-bombing.

The Air Ministry opposed the dive-bomber, not because of the method of attack or its vulnerability, but because they had to be small and could not carry much fuel. Large planes cannot dive vertically, so it is difficult to develop a dive-bomber equally capable of long-range bombing. The Air Ministry was very aware that attacking from low level was every bit as dangerous as dive-bombing – there was the experience with the Fairey Battle to prove it – but there were no technical reasons why they could not be large and therefore fly long distances. The low-level attack bomber never attracted the vehement criticism directed at the dive-bomber, because it had the long-range potential the Air Ministry wanted. Vulnerability was not the issue. Indeed, by insisting on relatively large twin-engined planes, the Air Ministry was ensuring its preferred low-level plane would be far more vulnerable to ground fire than it need have been. The War Office was well aware of what the Air Ministry was trying to achieve, and it was not impressed. After one meeting in the Air Ministry, an official described the arguments used as 'palpably false and childish': 'As long as the Army is supported by aircraft which the RAF can whip away in an emergency (irrespective of whether they can do the job the Army want 100%), that's all that worries the RAF.' The Air Ministry approach was, he suggested, a case of 'Heads we win, tails you lose'.[28]

The delays were another source of frustration. The War Office was horrified when it discovered in the spring of 1940 that far from being a hasty lash-up that would be available almost immediately, the interim Bisley would not reach the squadrons until the end of 1941.[29]

Making sure it could operate as a ground-attack plane or a medium bomber involved a complete redesign, and like the previous Beaufort and Beaufighter offspring of the Blenheim, it was turning into an entirely new plane. Hardly any of the production jigs used by the Blenheim IV could be used for the direct-support version.[30]

It soon seemed the Army would not even get this. In the crisis of May 1940, Beaverbrook had decreed all effort should be focused on existing planes and the Air Ministry officials were quick to exploit the plane's dual names. By emphasizing that it was the Bisley, rather than the Blenheim V, they claimed the plane did not meet this criterion and should therefore be abandoned. The Ministry of Aircraft production had to hurriedly reassure Bristol that as a 'Blenheim follow on', the 'Blenheim V' had the same high priority as the Blenheim IV and the company was instructed to get it into production 'as quickly as possible'.[31] At best this still only meant early 1941. Having failed to get it scrapped, the Air Ministry somewhat disingenuously used the new date as evidence that it was giving the specialist close-support bomber the highest priority.

In fact, the Air Ministry was still trying to kill the project. A review of the Bisley/Blenheim V highlighted two key weaknesses; the low range (600 miles) and the poor performance above 6,000ft.[32] As it was supposed to be a low-level, short-range Army support bomber, these were scarcely weaknesses. The Air Ministry was quick to point out that the new version was going to be so different to the existing Blenheim IV that it could not be put into production without seriously reducing output, something Beaverbrook was always very sensitive about. The Air Ministry therefore suggested it would be better to return to the original idea of an Army support plane that was much closer to the original Blenheim IV and would only involve minimal changes on the production line.[33]

It seemed a reasonable argument, but the Air Ministry was still talking about a much-modified version of the Blenheim. It was still a new plane – it was just a different new plane. The wing fuel tanks, bomb sight and bomb aimer's position and the standard Mercury engines of the Blenheim IV would all be kept, as would the higher 2,000lb bomb load. However, there would be better facilities for navigation, with a fourth crew member added as a specialist navigator. If required for close-support, then the glazed bomb aimer's position in the nose would be replaced by a solid nose with a battery of four machine guns and armour plating would be added. Instead of being primarily a plane for direct Army support, that could be used for strategic bombing, the new version would be primarily a medium-altitude bomber, which could, in an emergency, be modified for the direct support role.[34] Bristol immediately complained that far from accelerating the introduction of the more advanced Blenheim, the high-altitude bombing capability would delay the production of the plane until at least June 1941. The Air Ministry was not put off and suggested the first 400–500 might have to be delivered in the original close-support configuration the company was already working on, but the ultimate version should be the medium-altitude bomber.[35]

The same emphasis on long-range capability was also influencing the next generation of 'tactical' bombers. The B.11/39 specification for a Battle/Blenheim replacement had now been renumbered B.7/40. The plane was to be capable of dive-bombing and high-level bombing, as well as tactical and strategic reconnaissance, but the emphasis was on its long-range rather than short-range capability. Like the Bisley, it was to be a relatively large machine, with a power-operated dorsal turret and ventral gun position – scarcely the small manoeuvrable bomber the Army wanted. Nor was it likely to be available for some time. The Air Ministry had already rejected Bristol's Beaubomber adaptation of the existing Beaufighter because it offered too small an advance in performance. It seemed much better to start from scratch. The Air Ministry was in no hurry to develop the plane.

The delays in developing the plane and Air Ministry 'bias in favour of its Medium Bomber role' were not going down well in the War Office.[36] Accusations that the Air Ministry was not taking the close air-support issue seriously enough led to an early August crisis meeting. The Air Ministry was very much on the back foot. Feelings over the lack of air support in Norway and France were still running high. There was a genuine fear within the Air Ministry that if they did not show some flexibility, the much-feared 'Army Air Arm' might become a reality. The Ministry continued to reassure the War Office of its good intentions, confirming that it accepted close air-support was a legitimate Army requirement. The Air Ministry even went so far as to agree that close-support was not only required in offensive action, as it had always been willing to concede. The plane also had a role in defence to relieve pressure on retreating ground forces, a far more immediate and likely scenario for British forces in the summer of 1940.

The Air Ministry agreed to organize trials in Northern Ireland with the two Fairey Battle squadrons of No. 75 Wing, which were part of the tactical air component attached to British forces there. The commander of the wing, Group Captain A.H. Wann, was no great supporter of tactical air support but would soon find himself working with Colonel

J.D. Woodall, the Army liaison officer at Air Marshal Arthur Barratt's HQ during the French campaign and a passionate advocate of the closest possible battlefield air support. The Air Ministry argued that developing a close air-support system was essentially just a matter of developing the necessary communication systems between ground and air forces. There was no intention of using the Battle squadrons for close-support in actual operations; it was just that the plane was similar to the American dive-bombers on order. Trials started early in September and within two months an interim report had been completed, describing the procedures that could be used.

While communications systems were important, it was scarcely the most difficult element to develop. No new radio equipment had to be designed; it was just a case of organizing existing equipment. Even this required no revolutionary thinking – systems for calling in close air-support had existed in the First World War.[37] The speed with which the trials were organized, systems developed and tested and a report written were a measure of how straightforward this element of the process was. It would take a lot longer than two months to develop the aircraft and weapons that would be needed.

The Army and RAF were still at loggerheads over what sort of aircraft should be developed. The Air Staff remained adamant that it should be twin-engined, but an emboldened War Office was renewing demands for a smaller single-engined plane. The War Office wanted a 300mph two-seater. Pilot and gunner would have armour protection against rifle calibre machine-gun fire to the side and below. Two 250lb bombs would be carried internally and two more externally, and it should have four fixed guns for ground strafing. Range need be no more than 400 miles. Ideally the War Office wanted a dive-bomber, although it was willing to sacrifice a steep diving capability if this reduced performance. Crucially, it was to be a specialist ground-attack plane, not a plane that could be used for long-range bombing. The War Office did not even think a new plane had to be designed: it could not see what was wrong with the existing 280mph Hawker Henley light bomber, which the RAF had dropped as a frontline bomber and was using as target tugs at gunnery schools.[38]

With criticism raging over the lack of air support the Army had received in France, the Air Ministry felt it had little choice but to concede and began drawing up specification B.20/40, although the Ministry would do its best to ensure it was not exactly what the War Office wanted. The Air Ministry could not see why the standard 'general purpose' type would not continue to meet Army needs, and insisted that the new plane must also fill the tactical reconnaissance role as 'army co-operation planes' had always done. The War Office rather reluctantly conceded the point, but felt rather 'bounced' into the decision.[39] As no-one had a clear idea of what exactly should replace the Lysander in the Tac/R role, there was no reason why B.20/40 type plane might not be the solution.

The next barrier the B.20/40 plane had to overcome was the Ministry of Aircraft production. Beaverbrook was sympathetic to the Army cause, but many of his RAF staff were not. These included Air Vice Marshal Arthur Tedder, who was responsible for development and production. He would later be credited with advancing the cause of close air-support, but there was no sign of any such inclination in the summer of 1940. He insisted that what the War Office wanted was simply not possible with a single engine. At best, 280mph could be achieved with a 500lb bomb load, which effectively meant Tedder thought it was impossible to design a brand new plane that was any better than the three-year-old Hawker Henley. Tedder reminded the War Office that the idea was to produce the best possible plane and there was little point in insisting on a single-engined plane if it was going to be second-rate.

The War Office was not persuaded. It would rather have a lower performance, more manoeuvrable single-engined plane than a large, unwieldy twin-engined one.[40] The War Office appeared to win the day. Specification B.20/40 was released to industry, requiring a highly manoeuvrable, single-engined close-support bombing and tactical reconnaissance plane. The plane was to be simple to build, fly and maintain, with a maximum weight of 12,000lb, not much more than the Typhoon/Tornado single-seater fighter. Top speed would be 280mph.[41] This was broadly the performance of the Bermuda and Vengeance dive-bombers Beaverbrook had already ordered from the United States, and indeed the Hawker Henley that was chugging around training schools. Hawker, unsurprisingly, offered its Henley, with a more powerful Merlin.

Amidst the disagreement, there was one point upon which the War Office and Air Ministry agreed. Both saw the bomb as the main weapon. Low-level attacks would continue to use 250lb bombs using an eleven-second delay so that the plane could escape the blast of its own bomb. In the French campaign, this often resulted in the bomb bouncing past the target before exploding. The most accurate weapons and most effective against many targets were fixed machine guns and cannon. While both the Air Ministry and War Office agreed that machine guns for strafing were required, neither side mentioned cannon.

By insisting on a dual close-support bomber and tactical reconnaissance role, the Air Ministry was forcing the War Office back to the traditional army co-operation concept. The advantage from the Air Ministry point of view was that the dual role ought to reduce the number of squadrons the Army would require, which had always been the thinking behind the army co-operation plane concept. In the files of the time, the B.20/40 was often referred to as the A.20/40, reflecting the Air Ministry desire to get the plane viewed as an army-co-operation plane rather than a bomber. Air Ministry officials also wanted the America dive-bombers viewed this way. They sought and were given assurance by the British Purchasing Commission in the United States that the American dive-bombers were equally capable of tactical reconnaissance.[42] It was on the face of it just a slight adjustment. Instead of equipping Army squadrons with planes with a secondary close-support capability, they would get dive-bombers with a secondary reconnaissance role.

It had never been reasonable to expect a single type to be capable of every reconnaissance and attack duty the Army might require. It was equally unreasonable for the single army co-operation squadron attached to each corps to deliver all the reconnaissance and ground-attack support that ground forces might require. Nevertheless, the War Office found itself accepting that what the Air Ministry still liked to call 'army co-operation squadrons' should be responsible for providing close air-support. As an interim measure, until the American dive-bombers arrived, the offensive capabilites of the Lysander would be improved by arming half of them with 20mm Hispano Suiza cannon, a decision originally taken in July 1940 but not acted on. A dorsal twin-gun had now been fitted and some extra armour to improve the defensive capabilities of the plane.[43] The Lysander was at least small and manoeuvrable. It would have to do until something better arrived.

That better plane would not be the B.20/40. The specification had been released, and companies were working on proposals, but the Air Ministry and its supporters within the MAP continued to work for its cancellation. They reminded the War Office it would take two years to develop the plane and questioned whether the Army would really want a 280mph combat plane in 1942. Once again, all the problems of developing anything faster were set out in detail. A speed of 300mph would be possible with the new and still experimental Bristol Centaurus radial, but this would push weight up to 16,000lb. If the War Office wanted a dive-bomber, the plane would weigh in at 20,000lb. A twin-engined plane like the Beaufort or Beaubomber would be far lighter than the single-engined plane the War Office wanted. Any attempt to meet the requirements with a single engine could only produce a second-rate machine.[44] The steep dive-bombing had never been an essential requirement, and was becoming even less important as the year wore on and evidence from the Middle East suggested low-level or shallow dive-bombing was a more efficient mode of attack.[45] For the War Office, retaining the smaller, more manoeuvrable single-engined approach was far more important than any dive-bombing capability. However, the pressure was relentless. In November, in the face of the apparently overwhelming technical evidence, the War Office finally gave in and allowed the Air Ministry to abandon the specification.[46] Designers could now focus on the larger, twin-engined bombers (the interim Bisley and B.7/40) the Air Ministry preferred, although in truth the Air Ministry was rather hoping these would disappear too.

The problems getting what it wanted emphasized how little control the Army had over the way air power was developed. The system was loaded against it. It was not enough to have a Fighter Command to defend the country, a Bomber Command to attack Germany and a Coastal Command to support the Royal Navy. There had to be an Army Co-operation Command to support the Army. The logic of an 'Army Command' was so obvious that its creation was inevitable, especially in the wake of the French debacle. But the Air Ministry was not giving up without a fight. With no land fighting taking place, the argument went, an 'Army Co-operation Command' had no operational function, a convenient argument now that British land forces had been evicted from mainland Europe. Arguably, if army support had received the same resources as Fighter and Bomber Command, British forces would not have been evicted so easily. The Air Ministry found itself having to agree to the idea of an 'Army Co-operation Command' in principle, but would still fight hard to limit its powers.

Barratt was in line to be its first commander, with Woodall his chief of staff. The Air Ministry agreed that they would have control of the army co-operation squadrons, which, rather oddly, had been under the administrative control of Fighter Command, but there was no question of it having any squadrons transferred from Fighter or Bomber Command. The suggestion that at least No. 2 Group, the only remaining daytime bomber group, should be transferred to the command was rejected. As a compromise, Eden suggested its squadrons could at least be attached to the new command for training. From here they could be loaned out to Bomber Command for actual operations.[47] This proposal was also flatly rejected. The new command was even denied the two Fairey Battle squadrons that had been involved in the close air-support trials in Northern Ireland.[48]

While negotiations on what exactly Barratt would command continued, Longmore, commander of RAF units in the Middle East, was passing on what had been learnt so far from the fighting in his theatre of the war. Much of what Longmore had to say was no more than a reminder of the lessons already learned in France. The Lysanders, Longmore declared, 'were practically useless' and precious Hurricanes were already being diverted to tactical reconnaissance duties.[49] Longmore also reminded Barratt, if he needed any reminding, that the Blenheim was too vulnerable at low level and too inaccurate at higher altitudes to provide support on the battlefield. It cannot have been of much comfort to Barratt to be told that the two types he was still forced to rely on were both proving so unsatisfactory, and the only replacement the Air Ministry was willing to develop was another version of the Blenheim. Longmore still believed the dive-bomber was the best way of achieving the required accuracy, but he also mentioned the success of Italian Fiat CR.32 fighter-bombers in the ground-attack role in offensive and defensive situations. To counter these, he was planning to equip army co-operation squadrons with fighters for forward defence.

When Army Co-operation Command was finally created on 1 December 1940, there would be little opportunity for Barratt or Woodall to apply any of this knowledge. They had no bombers or fighters under their command. All they had were the army co-operation squadrons. Since these were already firmly under the control of the army corps they served, the formation of Army Co-operation Command brought very little change. Barratt found he had very little control over anything. He would just liaise with Air Ministry through the new Director of Military Co-operation, Group Captain Victor Goddard. This was exactly what the Air Ministry wanted. For public consumption, the new command was hailed as a major step forward in army/air co-operation, but notes attached to the press release accompanying the announcement emphasized the press must not be told that the new Command had no bomber or fighter squadrons and that Barratt 'has no strictly operational role, ie that he has the direct command of nothing operating against the enemy'.[50]

As the new Command came into being, the Air Ministry set to work on its ideal replacement for the interim Bisley. The new twin-engined plane was expected to be capable of dive-bombing and tactical reconnaissance. It was to have a top speed of 300–320mph, carry 1,000lb of bombs 800 miles and be defended by a dorsal four-gun turret, twin guns in a ventral position and have four fixed forward machine guns for ground strafing. Designers were to bear in mind the possibility of extending the range to 1,400 miles.[51] The Air Ministry clearly had much more than tactical targets in mind – this was enough to bomb Berlin. Its main advantage over the American bombers already in the country was deemed to be its comprehensive defensive armament. Despite all the evidence to the contrary, the Air Staff was still convinced that if you fitted enough guns to a bomber it could beat off fighter attacks. The requirements were bound to lead to a heavy, large and cumbersome plane. Dive-bombing, ground strafing and tactical reconnaissance might have been included among its roles, but nothing else about the proposal suggested it might be a success over the battlefield.

The Air Ministry decided that perhaps after all the Beaubomber would be a reasonable basis for a plane meeting these requirements.[52] The plane was rechristened the Beaumont, but like all offspring of Bristol's original Type 142 civil transport, it was effectively an entirely new plane.[53] Initially a first flight was not expected until the summer of 1941, which meant it would struggle to be available in any numbers in the event of a 1942 invasion. By March 1941 the first flight had been put back to early 1942, with the type becoming operational in 1943. Doubts were then raised over whether, by this time, it would have any performance advantage over the American types likely to be available. To ensure it did, the army co-operation and dive-bombing capability was dropped – the American Vengeance and Bermuda would cover these roles – and the new Centaurus radial would be used. This engine was expected to be in production by the end of 1942 and ought to give the light bomber the very creditable speed of 370mph.[54] Normal range was pushed up to 1,000 miles. By this time there was absolutely nothing left of the original Beaufighter. The new plane, the Bristol Buckingham, was not now expected to fly until the summer of 1942.

Any pretence that it had any close air-support capability was soon abandoned – it was just another medium bomber. Portal wanted it mainly because he thought it wise for Britain not to be relying totally on American imports. The bomber was seen as a replacement for the Beaufighter and Beaufort as well as the Bisley, but despite this, planned production was only twenty to twenty-five per month, just enough to keep the British aircraft industry in the medium bomber market. Even then, production of the Buckingham would only go ahead if it did not interfere with heavy bomber production.[55] As Tizard pointed out, it obviously would, and given the almost impossible number of heavy bombers Britain was hoping to build, it was difficult to see how it would ever go into production. It was certainly not going to be available for a very long time.

There was little chance of the Bisley in any form arriving in time for a 1941 invasion. Given that the original idea had been to get an interim solution into service for the summer of 1940, this was quite some delay. The Air Ministry now regretted its previous commitment to allow 400–500 of the specialist ground-support version to come off the production lines before the medium-altitude version. It wanted all work on the former suspended until the end of 1941 to accelerate the development of the bomber version. The Air Ministry went back to arguing that close air-support was not possible in defensive situations, emphasizing that this was especially true in an invasion scenario. It would only be needed once the Army went on to the offensive in Europe, a prospect that in most people's minds was so distant that it could be discounted. There was therefore no need to worry about any close-support capability. The Blenheim V would only be built as a medium-altitude bomber. As a precaution, some conversion packs might be developed to enable the plane to carry machine guns for ground strafing.[56] The close air-support role was now no more than an afterthought.

There was no chance of the American dive-bombers arriving in time for a 1941 invasion. The Air Ministry and War Office appeared to be very poorly informed about the status of the American Bermuda and Vengeance programmes. In December 1940, the British Purchasing Commission in the United States reported that both these planes were behind schedule and deliveries could not now be expected before June 1941. In fact, the situation was even worse. The prototype Vengeance did not fly until the end of March 1941, and the Bermuda did not take to the air until the following June. Air Chief Marshal Freeman assured the War Office he appreciated the importance of these aircraft and everything was being done to speed up deliveries, but in truth the Air Ministry was thinking of replacing them with twin-engined bombers.[57] Slessor, in the United States, insisted that the twin-engined Boston and Baltimore 'specifically ordered for use as Army support bombers', were a much better bet than the single-engined dive-bombers.[58] To compensate for the delays, Freeman suggested re-equipping six army co-operation squadrons with the Blenheim.[59] The Air Ministry seemed determined to fill the army-co-operation squadrons with twin-engined planes. Only the desperate shortage of Blenheims prevented this from happening.

Using fighters was considered as another interim solution for tactical reconnaissance. By the end of 1940, this should have been much more than just an interim solution. For some time, unarmed Spitfires equipped with cameras had been flying strategic and tactical photo-reconnaissance missions. There was even a short-range, armed Spitfire G for low-level photo-reconnaissance. Hurricanes in the Middle East were also being equipped with cameras. However, in the UK there was real resistance to using fighters for reconnaissance. There were occasional suggestions in the summer of 1940 that the unused American fighters could be issued to army co-operation squadrons, but nothing came of this. In the Middle East it was different. Longmore's Command was not exactly overflowing with Hurricanes, but even they had decided it was worth reassigning some to the tactical reconnaissance role. There was no reason why some of the Hurricane Is coming off the production lines in Britain could not also be fitted with cameras. The idea was suggested in September and December 1940, but again rejected.[60] At the height of the Battle of Britain this was perhaps understandable, but by December 1940 there should have been fewer objections.

It was Goddard who finally got some movement on the issue. In January 1941, with an air of desperation, he asked if there were any fighter types he could use to replace the Lysander. He was offered the Tomahawks which were about to be sent to the Middle East, and it was agreed one army co-operation squadron would be experimentally equipped with the fighter. By February this had risen to three. This, together with the planned Canadian fighter squadron due to get the Tomahawk, would absorb the first batch of 140, none of which would now go to the Middle East.[61] Ironically, having been denied the Hurricane, the army co-operation squadrons were now to get the superior Tomahawk.

Using the Tomahawk for tactical reconnaissance was still seen as a makeshift, interim arrangement by both the Air Ministry and War Office. It was still believed that larger planes like the Vengeance and Bermuda were needed to carry cameras for photo-reconnaissance, even though the Spitfire and Hurricane were demonstrating there were no insurmountable problems to fitting cameras in single-seaters. Nor could the Tomahawk perform any of the other roles expected of army-co-operation squadrons. It could not carry bombs, so it could not be used for ground attack. It was also difficult to imagine it directing artillery fire.

This was the one role the Lysander was perfectly capable of doing – it was just a rather expensive way of doing it. Flying a few hundred feet into the air did not need a sophisticated machine with a supercharged engine. For some time the artillery arm had been experimenting with light sports planes. The Air Staff thought the idea of flying in the battle zone in a plane with the performance of a First World War B.E.2 was bizarre, but the planes the Army wanted were cheap and using them would free production resources for more important aircraft. They were therefore quite happy to go along with War Office plans. The main opposition came from Barratt. He also could see no place on the battlefield for a slow, 100mph unarmed observation plane, although this did not stop him from suggesting the Army should try man-carrying kites as an alternative.

Barratt wanted all further research into the Air Observation Post concept ended, and it took the personal intervention of Brooke to keep the experimental flight in being.[62] Stinson Vigilants ordered from the United States were supposed to arrive before the end of 1940, but well into 1941 there was still no sign of them. Until these arrived, trials could not even get going, although it ought to have been possible to do something with the previously rejected Taylorcraft. As it turned out, it was this plane rather than the Vigilant that would eventually be adopted. It was yet another tactical application that with a little urgency might have been available for a 1940 invasion, should have been available by 1941, but would probably not now become available until 1942. In this particular case, both the War Office and Air Ministry were equally responsible for the delays.

Organizationally, the services had been slow to put in place any measures to enable closer ground/air co-operation. In the autumn of 1940, only after the immediate invasion threat had passed was an attempt made to centralize air support operations with a Combined Central Operations Room (CCOR), with Army and RAF officers working side by side directing operations.[63] This was a belated step in the right direction, but the chain of command was just as long as it had been for UK-based squadrons in the Battle of France. Requests for support still had to pass from corps commanders up to Army level and the Commander of Home Forces, then down to C-in-C Bomber Command and finally to the squadrons.

The Wann-Woodall report in late October 1940 laid the foundations for a more streamlined approach to close air-support. It was only supposed to be dealing with situations a future advancing British Army might find itself in, but there was no reason why some of the principles could not be applied in more defensive situations. It described how the speed of modern warfare had made it necessary for aircraft to support advances once they had passed beyond artillery range, but it also described how defending as well as attacking armoured formations would be able to make use of close-support. It was proposed that Close Support Bomber Control (CSBC) would direct the support. These would have direct radio links with the operations rooms at bomber bases and 'tentacles' located with army units at the front. Typically, a single CSBC would operate with two army corps and an armoured division, with tentacles at division and brigade levels. The CSBC would be located at the most appropriate army headquarters, which might be at commander-in-chief, corps or divisional level, depending on the scale of the operation, thus avoiding the lengthy chain of command of the recently instituted CCOR system. A response time of 90 minutes was hoped for.[64]

The report also mentioned the possibility of aircraft in the air being on call for air strikes. This was by no means a new idea; Slessor had pioneered it in colonial air operations in the Thirties in India. The report emphasized that this would only be possible with air superiority, as the waiting planes would be vulnerable to interception. It was therefore a procedure for the more distant future, but this 'cab rank' system would later become an important element of RAF tactical air support. The report recommended a Close Support Bomber Group with a reconnaissance group, a fighter group and a bomber group, the latter with eight squadrons. This implied considerably more army support squadrons than the seventeen the War Office had requested. The squadrons had to be under direct Army control. The process could not wait for decisions to be made at the different RAF levels of command, and indeed run the risk of the request being rejected.[65] The proposed arrangements were much closer to the system used in the First World War, with more control and responsibility being assumed lower in the chain of command.[66] However, the system needed specialist aircraft, capable of hitting small targets on the battlefield. It was acquiring the right aircraft that was the major obstacle to further progress.

The recommendations of the Wann-Woodall report were initially accepted without comment by both sides, although in the case of the Air Ministry this was more an indication of its perceived irrelevance than any sense of approval.[67] When pushed for a response, the Air Ministry again insisted that the close air-support proposed by Wann-Woodall was not relevant in a defensive struggle, the only sort of combat the British Army would find itself involved in if there was an invasion. Such a system would only be useful at some future hypothetical stage of the war when British forces returned to the offensive on the continent.

By December 1940 the joint Army/RAF signals units required by the Close Support Bomber Control Groups were being created. The first was to be ready by 15 January, with two more by 15 February. Each of the six home commands would eventually have its own Control Group and, almost as an afterthought, there were plans to send one to the Middle East.[68] However, the Air Ministry insisted no special aircrew training or aircraft were required:

> 'Medium bomber squadrons are regarded by the Air Staff as having close and direct support as a primary role when so required and all such squadrons are to be fully trained in these roles, close support in particular, as a matter of course.'[69]

Wann reassured the Air Ministry that compared to the skills required for strategic bombing, tactical air support was a relatively straightforward business. It did not take pilots long to distinguish between a tractor and a tank, Wann explained.[70] It was far more complicated than this. Bombing a factory from medium altitude was very different to hitting a small battlefield target. The former required a meticulous approach; for the latter, pilots had to act fast, hit the target and make their escape before the defences could react. Wann's idea of bombers roaming the battlefield attacking targets individually with one bomb at a time gives some idea of how unrealistic Air Ministry ideas on battlefield air support were.[71] With tactics like this, it was not surprising they believed it was impracticable. The operations of the Fairey Battle squadrons in France should have made it clear that operating at low level was risky and planes could not afford to loiter looking for targets. The inexperience and lack of realistic training had been one of the reasons for the high loss rates suffered by the Battle squadrons in the Battle of France.

The Army began incorporating Woodall's ideas into their thinking, but it was a tentative, cautious, almost apologetic process. The War Office seemed to be willing to accept the Air Ministry notion that all this talk of close air-support was only relevant to some distant future time when British armies were once more advancing. In fact, in the Middle East the RAF was already supporting the Army in offensive and defensive situations, and Wavell was about to launch the largest Allied offensive of the war so far. Before this, though, the RAF would find itself called in to support the latest victim of Axis aggression.

Chapter 4

Greek Discontent

The air reinforcements that arrived in the Middle East in the autumn of 1940 may not have given Longmore the frontline strength he required, but he had a reasonably balanced and equipped force. The Wellington squadrons provided an effective long-range strike force, the Blenheim was just about fast enough to operate by day and the Hurricane was superior to any Italian fighter. Substantial numbers of tanks had arrived to provide mobility on the ground and Wavell was sufficiently encouraged to start thinking about going on to the offensive. The Commander-in-Chief planned a major raid which, if all went well, might even lead to the recapture of Sidi Barrani, recently vacated by the British. The attack was due to be launched on 14 November; to ensure security was maintained, Wavell did not even take the risk of telling London. However, events on the other side of the Mediterranean were about to upset Wavell's plans. On 28 October, Italian forces invaded Greece and Britain immediately offered its support.

It was potentially a significant moment. Britain had a new ally and a foothold on mainland Europe. For Wavell and Longmore it was unfortunate timing, but for Churchill and Portal it was a marvellous opportunity. Politically, there was much enthusiasm for establishing an Allied presence in the Balkans and possibly bringing countries like Turkey and Yugoslavia into the anti-Axis camp. Churchill was particularly delighted to have the opportunity to secure the use of Suda Bay in Crete as a naval base, and was anxious to give Greece the maximum support possible. Britain could not afford to allow another ally to be defeated. The world was watching, with Turkey and Yugoslavia in the front seats. Troops were out of the question, but Churchill wanted aircraft sent and as much military equipment as Britain could afford. Churchill ridiculed an initial list of military supplies he was presented with, and demanded a far greater effort.[1] A revised list included twenty Hurricanes.

Beaverbrook was horrified by Churchill's willingness to help. In a blunt message to the prime minister, he complained that his reserves of Hurricanes and Spitfires were down to 425 and falling, and pleaded with Churchill not to let any more leave the country. Could the Greeks not make do with Defiants, he wondered.[2] Middle East commanders might wonder how such substantial reserves could provoke such anguish. The Middle East would struggle to match these reserves if it counted every derelict wreck of a biplane in the entire region. Even Portal felt compelled to point out how absurd Beaverbrook's claim was, with production of Spitfires and Hurricanes both exceeding losses.[3] Churchill and Portal seemed determined to help the Greeks, and the twenty Hurricanes were supposed to set sail for Greece in December.

Longmore had already made it clear that the Greeks could not expect any help from the Middle East. His priority was to maximize the forces available for Wavell's forthcoming attack. Although the Balkans came within Longmore's domain, he hoped that if air reinforcements did have to go to Greece, they would be organized, resourced and maintained entirely from the United Kingdom, rather than putting further strain on his limited resources. However, urgent appeals from Michael Palairet, the British ambassador in Athens, forced a rethink. Longmore, with the approval of Eden, Secretary of State for War, who happened to be in Egypt at the time, rather reluctantly dispatched one squadron, No. 30, equipped with a mixture of Blenheim IF fighters and Blenheim bombers, as token support.[4] Longmore was not anticipating a long-term commitment: the Blenheim squadron was supposed to be a mere gesture. He told Portal that he had no idea how this squadron could possibly be maintained in Greece if the country managed to resist longer than ten days.[5] Clearly he did not believe it would take Italy long to conquer Greece.

Churchill and Portal were already planning a far more substantial RAF force. The Air Ministry had previously been most reluctant to dispatch priceless heavy bombers to the Middle East as no worthwhile targets were within range from Egypt, but all that changed with the possibility of operating from mainland Europe. For Portal it was not about stopping the invading Italian forces; he was far more interested in targets in south-east Europe, especially the oil refineries in pro-German Rumania that would now be within range. It was not just the Air Ministry that saw the potential. Eden and even Wavell enthused over the possibility of bombing the Italian naval base at Taranto or the capital

Rome from bases in Greece. Taranto was an important military target, but Rome had no military or economic significance. It was not just the Air Ministry and Churchill that thought bombing cities to intimidate was a good use of air power.[6]

Churchill envisaged a force of four Wellington squadrons operating from Greece. The prime minister still had delusions about the influence such a small force could wield, the same delusions that had inspired his own colourful rhetoric in the mid-Thirties when he had so vividly described the horrors that awaited London.[7] As far as Churchill was concerned, four Wellington squadrons, capable of dropping 100 tons of high explosives on any chosen target, was a truly mighty force, one that could smite the enemy wherever he dared expose himself and dominate an entire theatre.

The Air Ministry was set the task of working out the details. There were doubts about the ability of the Greek Air Force to protect any RAF bases on the mainland. The Greek fighter force consisted of five French Bloch 151s and twenty-four Polish PZL P.24s. The Polish fighters were rated by the Air Ministry as obsolescent, although they were arguably superior to the Gladiators it was expecting RAF squadrons to use. The Bloch 151, while rated as modern, was not much better than the PZL P.24. The Air Ministry assessed the air defence capabilities of the Greek Air Force as negligible, and it was therefore decided that the bomber force would have to be based in Crete with its own defensive fighter squadrons. Four Hurricane squadrons would be needed to protect the Wellington bases.[8] In total, therefore, the idea was to have a force comprising four Hurricane and four Wellington squadrons.

As attractive as a long-range bomber force in the Balkans was to the Air Staff, Portal had no intention of creating this force at the expense of Bomber Command. He pointed out that the eight squadrons and all their ground support would have to go via the Cape, and therefore could not possibly be operational until February 1941. By this time existing Air Ministry expansion plans for the Middle East already required another four-and-a-half fighter squadrons. Furthermore, it was planned to increase frontline strength of existing bomber units by fifty-six aircraft, which was the equivalent of three-and-a-half squadrons. This was, therefore, pretty much the force Churchill was proposing. It was already planned to convert the two bomber/transport squadron to Wellingtons, and Portal suggested two Blenheim squadrons could convert to the Wellington by mid-January. The entire force could come from the existing reinforcement plans, albeit at the expense of some of Longmore's tactical day bomber force. Churchill would have the bomber force he required, with the fighters to protect them, without weakening Bomber or Fighter Command.[9]

Churchill was not impressed. The prime minister was 'distressed' that anyone could possibly have imagined he only intended to have his force in action by the following February. Furthermore, he wanted his Wellington force to be on top of any expansion the Air Ministry already had in mind. He suggested that the Wellingtons could be flown to Greece via Malta. The Hurricanes could also be flown off a carrier to Malta; if they did not have the range to reach Greece from there, they could land on another carrier to refuel. The Royal Navy would get the ground crews and support equipment there somehow, and if more was required it could be improvised from Middle East personnel and resources, which, Churchill was convinced, were far in excess of existing requirements anyway.[10] Churchill's proposal was as unworkable as the Air Ministry's was devious. In the end, as a compromise two Bomber Command Wellington squadrons were flown out, to join the two squadrons converting to the Wellington.

Churchill immediately congratulated Longmore on his prompt response in dispatching the single Blenheim squadron and informed him that a more formidable force of four Wellington and four Hurricane squadrons was to operate from Crete 'to assist in the defence' of Greece.[11] How much assistance the Greek General Staff might expect from heavy bombers that normally only ventured out under cover of darkness was another matter. It was certainly not the sort of bomber force the Greeks might have chosen to support their army on the battlefield. Portal, however, insisted that the Wellington was by far the best bomber 'for the direct support of Army operations'. Portal argued that for tactical purposes the Wellington was far superior to the Blenheim. It carried more bombs, had better defensive armament and, he claimed, was only slightly less manoeuvrable.[12]

Terminology at the time was not always consistent. 'Direct support' was often used to mean close air-support on the battlefield (as opposed to indirect support beyond the battlefield) as well as support beyond the battlefield (as opposed to strategic bombing). Portal was probably shrewd enough to use the ambiguity to his advantage. The reference to manoeuvrability conjured up an image of lone Wellingtons engaging targets on the battlefield, but the Blenheim was already considered too large and unmanoeuvrable for the close-support role. The Wellington was much slower, twice as heavy and nearly twice as big, and was more than slightly less manoeuvrable. Portal had always vehemently opposed any bomber intervention on the battlefield, and the instructions Longmore was given for using these bombers were very clear:

> 'Our experience in France proved direct support [for] land forces [was] best provided by attacking lines of communication where congestion likely to be greatest and not necessarily in the battle area.'[13]

In truth, Churchill was not thinking about how these Wellingtons might support the Greek Army. The naval base at Taranto and other targets on mainland Italy were more what he had in mind.

Portal saw no reason why the Wellington should not operate by day. He argued that Italian fighters would be quite a different proposition to German fighters, and, operating in flights of three, the bombers should be perfectly capable of looking after themselves.[14] It was another chance to prove the Air Staff had been right about self-defending bomber formations. There was no reason why the Wellington could not operate by day – the plane was no less suitable for day operations than the German He 111 – but as with the German bomber, it was only possible with a fighter escort, and this was not Air Staff policy.

The Air Ministry warned Longmore it would take time to organize the dispatch of these squadrons, and since time was of the essence, the maximum effort would initially have to be made from Middle East resources. The prime minister made it very clear to Longmore what he expected; he wanted another Gladiator and two Blenheim squadrons sent to Greece immediately to join No. 80 Squadron, followed by another Gladiator squadron as soon as possible. He promised Longmore replacements would soon be on their way. Thirty-four Hurricanes and pilots were to be rushed to Takoradi aboard the aircraft carrier HMS *Furious*, and thirty-two Wellingtons were to fly to Egypt via Malta, all arriving by 2 December.[15] In terms of actual squadrons, Longmore was only getting one Hurricane and two Wellingtons to make up for the five he was expected to deploy in Greece. It was scarcely the additional eight squadrons Churchill had in mind.

Longmore objected and Eden, fully aware of Wavell's plans to take the offensive, supported him, but Churchill, who was still in the dark about Wavell's 'raid', would truck no opposition. Eden made it as clear as he dared in a telegram that Wavell was planning 'a blow against Italians in Western Desert'.[16] However, even Wavell was playing down its significance; it was merely a large-scale raid which only might develop into something more substantial. Whether Churchill missed the significance of Eden's telegram or chose to ignore it is not clear, but as far as Churchill was concerned a bridgehead on mainland Europe, even in an unpromising location in the Balkans, was a far more interesting proposition than Wavell's proposed 'blow'. The instruction from London was clear: the suggested air reinforcements were to go to Greece. Longmore found his weak resources having to cover three fronts – East Africa, the Western Desert and now Greece – not to mention Malta and various naval commitments. Wavell felt he had little choice but to postpone his attack.

Churchill was not particularly sympathetic to Longmore's plight, partly because the prime minster did not believe Longmore was as short of aircraft as he claimed. Indeed, so suspicious was he that he ordered a stocktaking of Middle East air resources, and when he discovered there were 1,000 planes and 1,000 pilots in the Middle East, but frontline strength was only around 400, he let Portal know how unimpressed he was.[17] In fact there was nothing particularly disproportionate about these figures. One quarter of the aircraft in the theatre were undergoing major repairs requiring up to two months to complete. Training schools accounted for a further 20 per cent. Many of the 'combat planes' were genuinely obsolete Harts, Vincents and Hardys. Even relatively modern planes, like the Gladiator I, were so worn out after years of operations in harsh desert conditions that Longmore considered them useless as frontline combat planes. As for pilots, the figures included instructors, ferry pilots and any staff officers who could fly.

Although often exasperated by Longmore's constant demands for more, the Air Ministry was more aware than Churchill of the problems he faced. The ministry understood the harsh conditions the planes had to operate in and the less-than-ideal repair facilities available in the Middle East. However, the Air Ministry did not see the difficulties Longmore faced and the responsibilities his command had as any reason to increase the number of aircraft being supplied to the Middle East. Every plane that went to the Middle East was one less to defend Britain or, more significantly, join the strategic air offensive against Germany. The build-up of the offensive capability of Bomber Command was progressing at a snail's pace, much to Churchill's as well as Portal's immense frustration. The supply of aircraft to the Middle East had to be kept to an absolute minimum.

Portal was becoming as frustrated with Longmore as Longmore was with the Air Ministry. From Portal's perspective, Longmore could not see the big picture; he did not seem to understand the secondary nature of the tactical operations he was engaged in, compared to the crucial war-winning strategic air offensive. For the Air Ministry, the Middle East only became of any interest at all when it could supply bases from which targets of economic value in Europe could be bombed. Longmore's reluctance to send his squadrons to Greece, where they could reach significant targets, as well as his constant demands for more resources, were causing increasing irritation in London. When, in December, Tedder was sent out to join Longmore as his second in command, Freeman instructed him to make sure Longmore understood everyone was getting tired of his 'Moan, moan, moan' attitude.[18] When his time came to take command, Tedder would not forget this criticism.

It was not just Longmore who was moaning. The Greeks were also desperate for more aircraft and were sending a string of requests for aid via Palairet, the British ambassador. The Greek Air Force started the campaign with three bomber (one Battle, one Blenheim and one Potez 633), four fighter (one Bloch 151 and three PZL P 24) and four ground support squadrons equipped with ancient French Potez 25s, Breguet 19 biplanes and some more modern German Henschel HS 126s: in total, forty-five fighters, thirty-five bombers and fifty ground support planes.[19] It did not help that most of these planes had been supplied by Germany or countries occupied by Germany.

The Greeks were having particular problems keeping any of their French Bloch 151 fighters serviceable, and this squadron had to stay in the Athens area, but the rest were immediately thrown into the defensive battle being fought on the Albanian border. Pilots flew several sorties a day; the bombers attacked Italian airfields in the rear, while the Potez and Breguet ground support planes concentrated on Italian troop columns in the battle zone, proving particularly useful against attempts to outflank the Greek defences using obscure mountainous tracks. The PZL P.24s attempted to break up attacks on Greek positions in the frontline and communication centres in the rear.[20]

Greek Air Force losses were relatively light, but after a week of intensive operations, serviceability rates were dropping alarmingly. The Greeks were assured that RAF reinforcements were on the way and would be in place by 15 November, but the Greeks also desperately needed replacement aircraft for their own squadrons. The Greek government pleaded with Churchill for sixty 'Hurricanes or Spitfires'.[21] It probably did not occur to the Greeks that a plane like the Spitfire had yet to reach RAF squadrons outside the UK, and even Hurricanes were in desperately short supply. Palairet put as much pressure as possible on the Foreign Office to ensure the Greeks got as many aircraft and as much RAF support as possible.[22]

72

Longmore could not spare any aircraft from his own command to reinforce Greek squadrons, but he decided that the Greek Air Force 'badly needs intelligent direction of its activities'.[23] He suggested to Portal that Air Commodore John D'Albiac, the RAF commander in Palestine, should be sent to Greece to take command of the RAF squadrons there and provide the advice he felt the Greeks needed. D'Albiac was given very clear instructions about how he was to use the forces available to him. The bombers were there to bomb strategic targets and the fighters were there to defend the airfields the RAF was operating from. They were mini Bomber and Fighter Commands. He was not to allow his bombers 'to be used as artillery or participate in the actual land operations unless the military situation become so critical as to justify the temporary diversion of our bombers from strategic bombing to support the Greek land forces'.[24] It was all in line with the philosophy behind air operations in the French campaign and seemed to be straight out of the standard Air Ministry war manual. In fact, the directive was drawn up in the Middle East by Longmore's Senior Air Staff Officer, Air-Vice Marshal Peter Drummond. It seemed somewhat out of step with the way the RAF was being used in the Western Desert and rather underlined how even its commanders like Longmore, who appeared to be fully behind the tactical needs of the Army, at heart preferred a more indirect role for the RAF. With no British ground forces to support in Greece, there was a tendency even from the Middle East Command to revert to a purer form of air warfare.

D'Albiac was told he would be 'an independent Air Force' commander and would most definitely not be under the Greek General Staff, although he was to take Greek tactical intentions into account when planning his strategic operations.[25] As there were no British ground forces involved at the front, it was perhaps easier to maintain a dispassionate distance from any problems the Greek Army might be facing. Running RAF operations independently of the struggle on the ground was an approach D'Albiac was very comfortable with. Even when Commonwealth ground forces were later involved, the RAF in Greece retained a degree of detachment. The War Office would later argue that the RAF in Greece was never under the control of the Army in the way the RAF in the Middle East was, and was therefore less successful.[26] The force certainly seemed to be more under the sway of the Air Ministry in London than the RAF in the remainder of the Mediterranean.

In the meantime, the Greeks seemed to be managing quite well without British help or advice. In admittedly appalling weather, the Italian advance was first slowed and by mid-November halted completely. Greek forces were soon counter-attacking, with the main opposition coming from low-level attacks by the Italian Air Force. The air support, especially the fighter support, Britain had promised was eagerly awaited to back up the much-diminished efforts of the Greek Air Force. The fighter Blenheims of No. 30 Squadron, based near Athens, flew their first operation on 4 November. The bomber Blenheims of No. 84 Squadron followed on 10 November, with a raid on the Albanian port of Valona. However, there was no sign of the promised single-seater fighters the Greeks needed over the front. On 14 November, the Greek forces launched a major counteroffensive and within days the Italian invaders had been ignominiously flung back into Albania all along the front. Soon the Greeks were closing in on Korista, the largest city in south-east Albania. While Italian resistance on the ground appeared to be crumbling, the Italian Air Force responded by launching a furious and effective assault on the advancing Greeks, exposing the shortage of Greek fighters and highlighting the absence of RAF fighters.

Palairet found himself explaining to the Foreign Office how badly let down the Greek King George II and General Staff felt by the failure to get all the RAF support in place by 15 November as promised. Italian Air Force operations were demoralising Greek troops. As well as RAF support, he suggested that perhaps some Hurricanes could be 'lent' to the Greeks to reinforce their own squadrons.[27] The Greek king sent a personal note to King George V reinforcing this message. The first single-seater fighter squadron, No. 80, with Gladiators, arrived on 18 November. Plans to use these for airfield defence were put to one side and the squadron was immediately sent forward to operate over the frontline. It flew its first sorties in the Korista area on 19 November, shooting down four Italian fighters on its first patrol.[28] In response to the complaints reaching London, the Air Ministry instructed Longmore to dispatch the second promised fighter squadron (No. 112) to Greece along with an extra twelve Gladiators, as a reserve for British or Greek squadrons, and this too was to operate over the frontline.[29] Twelve pilots from the squadron duly flew to Greece early in December, handed over their Gladiators and flew straight back to Egypt. One flight of the squadron stayed long enough to participate briefly over the Albanian front, before it too returned to Egypt. It was just long enough for Longmore to claim that he had kept the promise to deploy a second fighter squadron. Meanwhile, the fifth squadron promised in the first wave, No. 211 with Blenheims, had flown its first mission on 27 November, bombing the Albanian port of Durazzo.

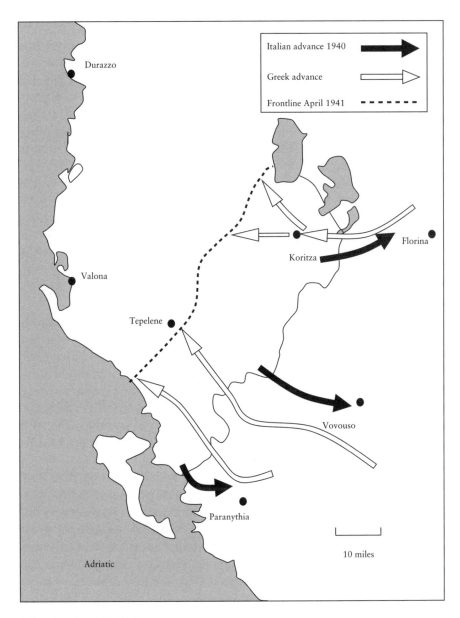

Albanian front 1940-41

Palairet's demands for more RAF air support cut little ice with Churchill. He was incensed by what he considered the ambassador's unreasonable demands and suggested he get his air attaché to explain to him the realities of transferring aircraft from one country to another.

It was an interesting change of heart from someone who had recently suggested it was just a question of getting fighters to hop from one aircraft carrier to another. The five RAF squadrons transferred to Greece, Churchill went on (he was including the brief intervention of No. 112 Squadron), and twelve Gladiators for the Greeks added up to eighty-four aircraft, which, Palairet should understand, represented a high proportion of the Middle East air strength, and left the RAF on other fronts in the region severely depleted.[30] This was all true, but merely underlined the inadequate strength of the RAF in the Middle East. The air reinforcements sent to Greece might be a large proportion of Middle East strength, but it was a tiny proportion of the total overall RAF frontline strength. There was a clear imbalance of forces when 1,000 high-quality day fighters, with substantial reserves, were stationed in Britain and largely idle with the Luftwaffe bombing by night, while on the fronts where British, Greek and Commonwealth forces were engaged, the RAF was severely outnumbered and had to make do with equipment that was second best.

This disparity was not so obvious in London. Palairet's demands were being considered by Churchill and his Cabinet as they struggled to take in the horror of the Coventry raid on the night of 14 November, in which almost 450 Luftwaffe bombers destroyed much of the city and inflicted heavy loss of life. There was no certainty the Germans would not return to day bombing and, from Churchill's perspective, the 1,000 frontline Hurricanes and Spitfires available, and the reserve of 300, did not seem in the least extravagant. From the perspective of the Middle East, such untold riches looked very extravagant.

The Greeks may not have been happy with the speed that RAF squadrons were arriving, but they were even less pleased with how they were being used. The fighters over the front were very welcome, but D'Albiac was using his bomber squadrons to attack the Adriatic ports of Valona and Durazzo, through which Italian supplies were arriving. These were perfectly legitimate targets. Many of the problems the Italians had in this campaign stemmed from the low capacity of these ports, and bombing them could only increase the difficulties. However, the Adriatic ports were not where their Greek hosts wanted the RAF to operate, especially when crucial battles on land were taking place. The Greek Army wanted the Blenheim used like their bomber and army support squadrons, attacking troop concentrations and similar targets at the front. D'Albiac patiently set about explaining to the Greeks how air power should be used. He was soon claiming success in getting the Greeks to 'reorganise their Air Force on modern lines' and had 'more or less' got agreement that he should have 'a very large measure of control' over the Greek Air Force.[31] This was not quite how the Greeks saw it.

D'Albiac's attempts to persuade the Greeks that tactical air support over the battlefield as practised by the German, Italian and Greek air forces was not a correct use of air power, had, unsurprisingly, made little impression on the Greeks. D'Albiac insisted that if the Italians had not made the mistake in the early days of their offensive of wasting their air effort on bombing 'undefended villages' in the tactical zone and had concentrated instead on preventing Greek mobilization, the Greeks might not have been able to hold the Italian advance.[32] British air strategy was based on the solid experience gained in the Battle of France, D'Albiac assured his hosts. The Greeks, however, did not take kindly to being lectured on the correct use of air power by their new ally, especially an ally using its experience in the Battle of France as an example of how to do it properly. The official Air Ministry narrative on the Greek campaign would later fully support the stance D'Albiac took, but was also forced to observe that 'there was the inconvenient certainty that … the Battle of France was manifestly not a victory'.[33]

The Greek king personally expressed his own bitter disappointment at the apparent lack of willingness of the RAF to get involved where it really counted. The king told D'Albiac that Greek pilots were flying up to six sorties a day over the front, while the RAF long-range bombing missions meant British pilots could only manage one. Air support for the Greek Army was desperately needed. The small Greek Air Force had lost nine planes in two days, and the king was fearful that it would soon be destroyed. As far as D'Albiac was concerned, these heavy losses merely confirmed the Greeks were not using their air force correctly. As a concession to Greek pressure, D'Albiac reluctantly agreed to support the Greek attack on Koritza with three of his bombers The three Blenheims, escorted by six PZL P.24s, were used to attack Italian positions near the front. One was lost and D'Albiac claimed the escort provided by the Greeks, a luxury most Greek bombing missions usually had to do without, had been ineffective and he was reluctant to repeat the experiment.[34] The Greeks would have to continue their offensive without RAF bomber support. Nevertheless, the offensive was a success and Koritza fell on 22 November. RAF fighters played their part, but the British were not winning any friends with their refusal to commit their bombers tactically.

Portal was sympathetic to the Greek request for fighters and thought the twenty Hurricanes due to go should be sent, provided D'Albiac felt the Greeks could make good use of them. D'Albiac, however, was far from convinced this was the case. He believed that Greek pilots 'operationally had a lot to learn before they would get full value out of really modern aircraft'. Such views reinforced scepticism within the Air Ministry. Air Commodore Charles Medhurst, in the Air Ministry Plans department, did not believe it was wise to sacrifice Britain's other interests to keep the Greek Air Force in being. No modern aircraft should be supplied to them; they would have to make do with any obsolete aircraft the RAF no longer needed.[35] As had been the case with the Poles and Czechs during the Battle of Britain, there was an unfortunate tendency to underestimate the capabilities of any aircrew not of Anglo-Saxon origin. Even without these prejudices, there were reasons for not giving the Greeks any Hurricanes. With some RAF fighter squadrons in the Middle East, not to mention Greece, still awaiting their first Hurricane, allowing Greek pilots to get them first would not have been a popular move.

Longmore saw the obvious logic of making sure trained Greek pilots had planes to fly but was also painfully aware of his own shortage of material, and any perceived inadequacy in the quality of Greek personnel was a convenient reason for not dipping into his limited reserves. Longmore persuaded himself that giving the Greeks bombers would be a waste of good aircraft. They would not have the necessary skills to bomb by night, nor the ability to fly in formation as required by day bombing. A fighter, perhaps one that could carry bombs, was more suitable equipment for air forces like the Greek one, he suggested, leaving the serious business of fighting a proper air war to the RAF.[36] It neatly summarized attitudes that were common both within and beyond the walls of the Air Ministry. It would seem that fighter-bombers were only suitable equipment for second-rate air forces and second-rate pilots.

Meanwhile, the Greeks had turned to the Americans for help. The plucky Greek resistance was getting a lot of coverage in the United States, where there was no shortage of sympathy for the underdog. Unfortunately, the Greeks would find the British were still blocking their path. The Greek government asked for sixty 'modern fighters'; President Roosevelt promised thirty and possibly the full sixty, but pointed out that the United States was under an obligation to give Britain priority with military exports.[37] It was therefore up to the British to sanction a diversion from their Curtiss Tomahawk contracts, and the British were asked for their consent.[38] The Greek government stepped up the pressure by appealing directly to Churchill.[39] Sinclair, the Air Minister, was not keen. He rather pedantically pointed out that there had been no formal request, and, in any case, it would cause disruption out of all proportion to the military value of Greek Tomahawk squadrons. It would take too long to deliver the fighters from Britain, and any supplied directly by the United States via Takoradi would mean one plane less for the RAF in the Middle East. In any case, deliveries from the United States could not arrive before the spring. To begrudge an ally the use of a fighter that Britain was in no great hurry to use itself seemed rather miserly.[40]

The Foreign Office agreed with the Air Ministry. It saw no reason why Britain should give up any of its American aircraft to equip the Greek Air Force. Doubts about the ability of the Greeks to make use of modern equipment were again a comforting argument. Spares and where the Greeks would get them from seemed to be another much-cited reason for not letting them have American aircraft, although the answer was, presumably, the same place Britain was getting them from – the United States. Portal left Longmore with the delicate task of explaining to the Greeks that 'aircraft without spares, tools and equipment are useless',[41] which the Greeks scarcely needed to be told as they struggled to keep their French Bloch 151 and Potez 633, Polish PZL P.24 and German Henschel HS 126 aircraft serviceable. American spares would be considerably easier to acquire than spares from Vichy France, occupied Poland and Nazi Germany.

Sinclair argued there would probably be some Mohawks available by the new year. Alternatively, if the Americans got the fighters from non-British contracts, and the Americans agreed to deliver them themselves, without taking up shipping space required by British deliveries, Britain had no objections. Portal was asked for his opinion, and he agreed that sending untested and untried Tomahawks would not be a good idea, but again insisted that Hurricanes would.[42] Churchill was doing his best to override the objections but found his efforts thwarted. The twenty Hurricanes that Churchill wanted to go to the Greeks were supposed to be added to a convoy leaving in December, but Churchill was told the convoy was already full and was assured that the Americans were 'thinking of' sending fighters out of their own supplies.[43]

Meanwhile, Palairet was furious at the British decision effectively to veto the delivery of the Tomahawks. The Foreign Office explained that the Greeks lacked the personnel and experience to handle such modern planes, so the American fighters would be wasted on them. If these aircraft went to the Greeks, RAF units, which would be able to make far better use of the American fighters, would be denied this equipment. If the Greeks had dollars to spend, they should spend it on other military equipment and leave the air war to the RAF. However, the Greeks would not be denied all assistance, Palairet was assured. The Air Ministry had instructed Longmore to pass over its Gladiators and Gauntlets to the Greeks as his squadrons re-equipped with Hurricanes and Mohawks.[44]

The British attitude was not going down at all well in Washington. It all looked rather selfish to the Americans, who started to apply a little more pressure. There was an as yet unallocated batch of 194 Tomahawks, half of which would normally go to Britain, but for political reasons, the Americans informed the British, they were thinking of allocating thirty to fifty to various South American countries, restricting the British allocation to fifty. If, however, Britain was willing pass on thirty to fifty Tomahawks already in their possession to the Greeks, the British allocation would be increased to between eighty and 100. The Greeks would get their fighters straight away and the British, in the long run, would be no worse off.[45]

The British were not impressed by this arm-twisting; they insisted that under Roosevelt's 'fifty-fifty' promise they were entitled to half of whatever the United States produced. As an alternative, the Americans patiently suggested Britain hand over an equivalent number of modern fighters from their stocks, the type being left for the British and Greeks to agree on, and these would later be replaced by an equivalent number of Tomahawks. News of this compromise reached London with the warning from British officials in Washington of how dimly the British attitude was being viewed. There was a serious danger of alienating the Roosevelt administration, and they urged that the American compromise be accepted.[46]

Rather grudgingly Sinclair agreed, although the general British attitude was that the British were doing the Americans a favour. It was argued that Roosevelt had made rash promises to the Greeks without any idea how they could be acted on, and Sinclair was rather patronizingly just agreeing to help the American president out of his difficulty. The Greeks would be offered thirty British fighters. It was hardly a major commitment: it was only ten more than the twenty Hurricanes that had failed to get on to the December convoy. The thirty fighters would not be Hurricanes, however. The Greeks were offered Gladiators or Defiants. The latter just about satisfied the American requirement that the fighters should be 'modern', but it was hoped that the Greeks would be sensible and accept Gladiators. This was a fighter the RAF was already using in Greece, so spares would be less of a problem, and indeed a few Gladiators had already been handed over to the Greeks. The Greek ambassador was told they would get a plane 'such as the Defiant', and he was apparently very grateful – he clearly did not know what a Defiant was – and reported back to his government on the offer.[47]

Meanwhile, Air Marshal Christopher Courtney, responsible for supplies, was given the task of finding these fighters. He reported that both the Defiant and the Gladiator would have to be shipped, as neither had the range to use the Takoradi route. There were not enough Gladiators left in Britain anyway, and the Middle East certainly could not afford to pass any more over yet. No one had ever considered how Defiants would be packed for dispatch overseas, so this would take time to organize. Before these problems could be tackled, the Greek authorities in Athens, where someone clearly did know what a Defiant was, declared the plane was unsuitable, and insisted on the Tomahawks the Americans had promised.[48] The British were horrified by the temerity of the Greeks and believed they would get their comeuppance if they insisted on embarrassing the American president by rejecting the British offer.[49] American patience was indeed wearing thin, but not with the Greeks.

Sinclair was by this time convincing himself that the British promise of thirty fighters could be met by counting the Gladiators that RAF squadrons in the region were already handing over as they converted to Hurricanes. However, to Sinclair's frustration, the Greeks insisted they wanted their thirty modern fighters as well. Again grudgingly, and again to help the Americans out, Sinclair decided that thirty of the Mohawks that were being sent to the Middle East would go to the Greeks, 'as soon as these are sufficient and the type is proved in service', which left plenty of opportunity to delay actually handing them over.[50]

Eden, who had just taken over at the Foreign Office, was very worried about the unfortunate impression the whole affair was having in Washington and Athens, and instructed Beaverbrook to sort it out.[51] The next day, Christmas Day, Washington and Athens were told that the Greek Air Force was to get thirty Mohawks, a tried and proven plane, they were assured, that was to become standard RAF fighter equipment in the Middle East, and the first batch was already on the way.[52] It was tried and proven in French service, but this was scarcely the case for the RAF. None had flown operationally. The RAF had tested an early version of the fighter, powered by a Pratt and Whitey Twin Wasp, that they had borrowed off the French, but most of those being delivered to Britain were the Mark IV powered by a Wright Cyclone 9 engine. None of these had been tested, let alone flown in action.

The first four Mohawks reached Takoradi on 17 December; the first one, a Mohawk IV, flew ten days later, but crashed, killing the pilot.[53]

This was just weeks after Freeman's belated suggestion that it might be a good idea to test the American fighters before the Middle East got hold of them, in case there were any problems. Takoradi had found the problem; the fighter needed an air filter to operate in tropical conditions. Portal had to inform Longmore that the Mohawk had fallen through because of engine problems and, mysteriously, 'the disinclination of the US government to co-operate'.[54] Until an air filter for the Cyclone engine was designed, the Mohawks were no use to anyone, Longmore or the Greeks. All this meant that by the end of 1940 the only reinforcements the Greek Air Force had received were seventeen worn-out Gladiators handed over by the RAF, and there was no prospect of anything more modern in the immediate future. As a substitute for the Mohawks, it was finally agreed that the Greek Air Force should get eighteen Tomahawks, but none of these planes had even got as far as Takoradi.[55]

By this time the Americans had given up on Britain and decided to sort out the problem themselves. In January, Roosevelt offered the Greeks sixty US Navy Grumman Wildcats, although not before checking with John Slessor – now an air vice marshal – who was in the United States at the time, whether he thought the Greeks would be able to make efficient use of the plane. It was not just the British who had their doubts about the non-English speaking world. Fortunately for the British, the Americans were not being so inquisitive about how efficiently Britain was using its American aircraft. Slessor was no more upbeat than the Air Ministry about the capabilities of Greek pilots, emphasizing that the Greeks had no experience with modern planes and would find it difficult to keep them operational. Nevertheless, Slessor encouraged the Americans to go ahead, partly because, as he candidly informed the Air Ministry, 'in certain contingencies' Britain might come into possession of the planes and they might prove quiet useful for British aircraft carriers.[56] It seemed somewhat strange to be speculating so prematurely about how Britain might benefit from the future defeat of another ally. The Americans bypassed any further British involvement by shipping the Wildcats across the Pacific.[57]

The American frustration was beginning to show in some of the decisions the government was making. Roosevelt decided that 100 of the Tomahawks that had been allocated to the British would now go to the Chinese to help protect the Burma Road. This caused howls of protest in the Foreign Office. The British ambassador was instructed to point out that the Chinese need could not possibly be as great as that of the British, and indeed of the Greeks, the Foreign Office added quite unashamedly. The whole British approach was causing huge embarrassment in British diplomatic circles in Washington, where the British Purchasing Commission pleaded with the Foreign Office not to keep instructing the ambassador to make such a fuss about where the Americans chose to send their own fighters.[58]

It was not the most glorious episode in British inter-Allied politics, but it was typical of the attitude the Air Ministry had shown to all allied air forces. It was clearly in British interests to get fighters to pilots on active fronts with nothing to fly, whatever their nationality. It had been the same story in previous campaigns. In May 1940, Belgian fighter squadrons just needed replacement Hurricanes and Gladiators to keep flying, but appeals for help were ignored. Too many experienced Poles and Czechs had been left on the sidelines during the Battle of Britain. Now experienced Greek pilots were being denied the planes they needed. Britain needed to change its attitude towards allies.

The Americans were understandably frustrated that the British could not pluck fifty of the many hundreds of single-seater fighters the United States had sent and pass them over to the Greeks. It would never have occurred to the Americans that hardly any of the fighters they had been sending to the British these past six months were in any fit state to serve with any air force. Even without the American planes, the number of aircraft in the United Kingdom was substantial, more than enough to re-equip a handful of Greek squadrons. To obstruct the delivery of American planes and be so reluctant to supply British planes to a fighting ally was perverse, but arguably the Greeks were being treated no worse than the RAF units in the Middle East. The Greek Air Force may have been at the very bottom of Air Ministry priorities, but Longmore's command was not much higher up the scale.

Meanwhile, D'Albiac was pursuing his air offensive against the Albanian ports. Initially, both Wellingtons and Blenheims were sent out by day, but for the Wellington it would be a very brief foray into daylight operations. On 5 November, six Wellingtons of No. 70 Squadron set off unescorted at dawn for Valona. The protective cloud cover deserted the bombers over the target area, Italian fighters intercepted, two Wellingtons were shot down and two more were damaged. It was, according to D'Albiac, just bad luck, but it was the end of Portal's theory that the Wellingtons could look after themselves against Italian fighters; future missions would be flown under cover of darkness.[59] Blenheims continued by day, flying nearly 300 sorties from November to the end of January. Wellingtons flew missions against the Albanian ports and more distant targets like Brindisi in southern Italy.[60] This was one of the ports Italian supply ships to Albania were sailing from, but the further the attacks on communications were from the frontline in Albania, the less effect they had at the front. Churchill's Wellingtons were not having the impact the prime minister had been anticipating.

The desperate Greek Army requests for some air support on the battlefield may not have made any impression on the Air Ministry, but as soon as the Greeks showed any inclination to attack targets further afield, there was immediate interest. These proposals normally came from political circles within Greece, and the motivation was often more political than military. Like Churchill, Greek leaders also had rather exaggerated ideas of what bombers could achieve. Soon after the Italian invasion, the Greek king had suggested Britain could knock Italy out of the war by bombing the country from Greece.[61] RAF bombers in the UK could attack targets in Italy and fly on to Greece to continue operations from there. The Greeks also hoped that the very existence of a fleet of RAF bombers, within striking distance of the Rumanian oil fields, might be sufficient to deter German intervention from Bulgaria or Rumania. Such thinking was not so far removed from Air Ministry plans to open a strategic air offensive from Greece. If the Greeks wanted more air support, it was suggested they should build airfields heavy bombers could use.[62] Longmore was also told that establishing airfields for heavy bombers in Greece should be one of his top priorities.[63] Portal was now warming to the idea of a major air presence in the region. Early in December, plans were laid to send six fighter and four bomber squadrons from the UK, and raise another two in the Middle East, to bolster Greece and perhaps encourage Turkey to join the Allied fold.[64]

While D'Albiac continued his air offensive against Italian ports, and Portal and the Air Staff fretted about delays in the construction of bases heavy bombers would use to strike even more distant targets, Wavell and Longmore were about to give a demonstration of armoured forces and tactical air power working together that was as impressive as any provided by the German Wehrmacht.

Chapter 5

Desert Blitzkrieg

For Wavell's 'raid in strength' (Operation Compass), Longmore drew in resources from the distant corners of his command to replace the squadrons sent to Greece. The Commonwealth air force units supporting the attack were commanded by Air Commodore Raymond Collishaw, a Canadian fighter ace of the First World War. He had under his command two Hurricane squadrons, with a third just arriving from the UK and four Blenheim daytime bomber squadrons. For army co-operation, No. 208 Squadron had been joined by Nos 3 (RAAF) and 6 Squadrons from Palestine. These were equipped with a variety of planes. No. 6 Squadron was flying Lysanders, No. 208 Squadron had a mixture of Lysanders and Hurricanes and the Australian squadron had four Gauntlets for dive-bombing and eight Gladiators to provide escort and air cover for forward troops.[1] While Woodall in the UK was proposing Close Support Bomber groups with bomber, reconnaissance and fighter elements, in the Middle East the idea had evolved quite naturally.

For more indirect support there were four heavy squadrons based in the Nile Delta (three Wellington and one Bombay). These would strike at ports and other communication targets in the rear. The Blenheims would attack lines of communication approaching the battle zone and enemy airfields, but would also back up the efforts of the army co-operation squadrons over the battlefield. It was a small force, with a greater long-range than close-support capability, an imbalance that Longmore was aware of. Blenheims were far more useful to him than the Wellingtons Bomber Command was so grudgingly parting with. Longmore caused some consternation in London when he presumed that he was getting so many Wellingtons because the Air Ministry had

'Wellingtons to spare'.[2] What he really wanted, he told Portal, was high-speed day bombers like the Maryland to replace the Blenheims.

The handful of Hurricanes that had arrived had the performance to challenge the much larger Italian fighter force, but Longmore did not see the Hurricane as an air superiority fighter. Compared to Italian fighters, the Hurricane was fast but not particularly manoeuvrable, and pilots initially had problems dealing with the much slower but nimble Fiat CR.42 biplanes. The Hurricane had obvious value as a bomber interceptor, especially as the Gladiators struggled to catch the Italian Savoia-Marchetti SM.79 bombers, but Longmore felt the Gladiator was a better fighter for operations over the battlefield.[3] It was not the first time, nor would it be the last, that pilots flying the latest generation of fighter had problems when confronted with older but slower and more manoeuvrable planes. The solution would always be the same: to use the higher speed in hit-and-run attacks from altitude rather than slow down and try to outmanoeuvre the enemy. Rather than use the few Hurricanes to challenge Italian fighters, Longmore decided to use them in ground strafing attacks on rear targets, preferably ones with little anti-aircraft protection. Longmore hoped this would force the Italians to divert their fighters to deal with the threat and tie them up in vain attempts to catch the faster Hurricane.[4] It was a rather negative use of a fighter force, but it ensured Hurricane pilots became very familiar with the ground-attack role.

Wavell was still determined to keep expectations low and still considered the operation no more than an exploratory raid, but in General Richard O'Connor, Wavell had a commander who could exploit to the full any opportunities that might arise. Although the attacking Commonwealth force was outnumbered three-to-one, with the slow but heavily armoured Matilda it had a tank that no Italian anti-tank gun could pierce.

The first target was the recently vacated port of Sidi Barrani. The Commonwealth forces had to advance 60 miles into uncontested desert to take up positions to the south of the port and its ring of defensive strongpoints. Hurricanes and Gladiators covered the advance, but their protection was scarcely necessary. The weather was poor, many Italian airfields were waterlogged and those aircraft that were able to take off did not spot the advancing columns through the low cloud. On the morning of 9 December, attacks were launched on the forts surrounding the port, with bombers, including the Gauntlet dive-bombers, paving the way for the infantry assaults.[5] By later standards it was on a very small scale, but the support helped ensure the forts were rapidly overrun.

It was precisely the sort of support D'Albiac was so reluctant to provide Greek forces. The ground-strafing Hurricanes added to the confusion in the rear, but rather than just lead the Italian fighters a merry dance, the Hurricane pilots took on their pursuers and soon discovered that if they avoided dogfights, the Italian fighters were very vulnerable. The Hurricanes claimed eight Fiat CR.42s and three SM.79 bombers on the first day, and over the next few days the Hurricanes claimed a steady toll of Fiats. Longmore was soon reassessing the value of the Hurricane as a fighter and asking for as many as possible to be sent as quickly as possible, by any means available.[6]

On the ground, elements of the 7th Armoured Division headed for the coast road at Buq-Buq to cut off the Italian line of retreat westwards from Sidi Barrini. Four Bombays showered 600 24lb bombs over Sidi Barrani and Bardia to discourage any attempts to dispatch forces from these fortresses to unblock the road. More bombing sorties preceded the assault on Sidi Barrani, and by the evening of 10 December, most of the port had fallen. On the 11th the bombers focused on Italian units fleeing westwards towards Bardia. Resistance on the ground was unexpectedly weak, but in the air there was some tough fighting. In one engagement on 13 December, five Gladiators of No. 3 RAAF Squadron were shot down by Fiat CR.42s. Initially the Italian Air Force focused on airfields and other targets in the rear, but with their troops on the ground in trouble, all effort was soon focused on the advancing British armoured forces.[7]

Despite the pockets of Italians still holding out on or near the Egyptian frontier, there was no thought of consolidation. Instead,

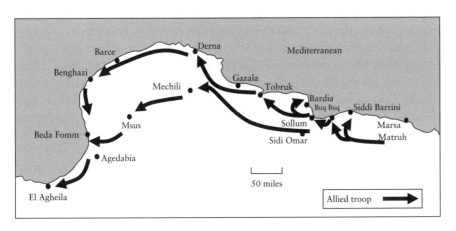

Operation Compass December 1940

the 4th Armoured Brigade boldly pushed on to cut off Bardia. On 14 December, the Italian Air Force made its biggest effort so far; over 200 sorties were flown by Fiat CR.32 and CR.42 fighters, Breda 65 fighter bombers and SM.79 medium bombers, principally against the rapidly advancing 4th Armoured Brigade. Despite the losses inflicted, by the 15th the tanks were established on the Bardia-Tobruk road. The two divisions available to O'Connor, however, were simply insufficient to deal with the large number of Italians they were surrounding. Sidi Omar fell on 17 December, but Italian forces elsewhere escaped to reinforce the Bardia defences.

It was the power and speed of the armoured thrusts that was largely responsible for unhinging the Italian defences, but the air support the Commonwealth air forces received played its part. The experiment with the Gauntlet dive-bombers was apparently a success. After four days of operations, during which twenty-three sorties were flown by the handful of available Gauntlets and no aircraft lost, a lack of spares forced the unit to be withdrawn. It was simply impossible to keep the obsolete Gauntlets in the air. However, having helped achieve the initial breakthrough, it was not felt they would be needed again as the attack entered a more mobile phase and there was no effort to find an alternative bomb-carrying fighter. The dive-bomber was apparently seen as a breakthrough weapon, not one for dispersing enemy forces in retreat or supplying mobile air support for friendly advancing forces. It was a very short-lived return for the fighter-bomber.[8]

In the first week of operations, the Italian Air Force flew around 1,000 fighter and bomber sorties, compared to just 400 flown by the RAF.[9] However, the Hurricane had stamped its authority on the air war and even the much criticized Lysander had performed better than expected.[10] As the AOP Austers would demonstrate in later campaigns, there was nothing wrong with the idea of a low-performance plane flying over the frontline and directing artillery fire. More dangerous, longer-range reconnaissance was left to Hurricanes. Only half a dozen planes had been lost in the first week of operations, but many had become unserviceable. The lack of reserves and problems supplying squadrons that had moved forward was soon forcing Longmore to scale back operations. In the second week of operations, less than 200 sorties would be flown, of which around 150 were bombers. In the third week, the number of bomber sorties fell to just fifty.[11] The retreating Italians were struggling too as airfields and equipment had to be abandoned, but reinforcements were much closer to hand and fresh Italian Air Force units were soon flying into North Africa. The Italian reinforcements included the first squadron of monoplane Fiat G.50 fighters, to help deal with the Hurricane. The stiffening resistance in the air was soon noticed, and intelligence suggested further reinforcements were on the way. Longmore warned the Air Ministry that some of his squadrons were down to just a handful of serviceable planes and there were virtually no reserves. Longmore complained that he was not even getting the aircraft he had been promised. By his estimation, so far 100 fewer than expected Blenheims had arrived via the Takoradi route.[12] The Air Ministry assured Longmore that reinforcements were on the way, but these were not going to arrive until early January.[13]

In truth, everyone was taken by surprise by the success of what had never been intended as more than a large-scale raid. Wavell and Longmore could scarcely complain too much about the lack of resources for an offensive that originally had such limited aims and about which they had been so reluctant to keep London informed. Nevertheless, he was not getting what he had been promised, and with commitments in Greece and Wavell already planning to take the offensive in East Africa, Longmore clearly did not have the resources he needed.

After a pause to allow more supplies to be moved up and the air units to gain a semblance of their former strength, the assault on Bardia was launched on 3 January 1941. On the two nights preceding the assault, RAF Wellingtons and Bombays, together with Fleet Air Arm Swordfish, dropped 50,000lb of bombs on the citadel and each stage of the ground advance was preceded by Blenheim strikes.[14] Lysanders hovered over the frontline directing artillery fire, and British warships offshore added to the barrage. Italian opposition in the air was noticeably stiffer, and although Blenheim losses were not excessive, a large number of planes were damaged and rendered unserviceable by the defences. Nevertheless, the port fell on 5 January. It was another resounding victory for Commonwealth forces. By this time the 7th Armoured was already moving swiftly to block the road running westwards from Tobruk.

These were dramatic, unexpected victories that lifted the morale of a nation suffering nightly attacks by the Luftwaffe. An excited Churchill had not been expecting anything like this. Not even Wavell had dared hope for this scale of success. It put the role the British Army might play in the war in a completely different light. Wavell's army was supposed to just defend the Suez Canal, not win campaigns. There seemed no reason why the advance should not continue until the Italians had been pushed out of the continent entirely. There was talk of capturing Sicily. An Italian surrender might follow.

Such speculative musings, however, were interrupted by disturbing evidence that Germany was showing more interest in the Mediterranean theatre. Luftwaffe units were beginning to operate over Malta, and there was an increasing German presence in Rumania and Bulgaria. British intelligence suggested an invasion of Greece from Bulgaria might well take place as early as March, possibly even sooner. This was where Churchill perceived the centre of gravity of the war was shifting. Establishing an anti-German front in the Balkans, perhaps with Yugoslavia and Turkey, seemed a very attractive proposition. It was not just intervention in Greece that was on the agenda. Wavell was told to start thinking about dealing with the Dodecanese, which provided the Axis with bases within range of the Suez Canal. Malta had to be made secure. Churchill was also insisting that Wavell maintain the offensive in East Africa. All this was in addition to the air and a probable future ground commitment in Greece.

These were extraordinarily ambitious and far-ranging objectives. The Chiefs of Staff could at least claim that in terms of ground forces, Wavell was getting just about everything Britain could afford to send. (Brooke would argue a bit more than was safe to send.) However, the air reinforcements had always been on a significantly lower scale. There was a huge imbalance between the air forces available in the Middle East/Balkan theatre, where the RAF was engaged over three fighting fronts, and in the UK, where no land operations were in progress or planned. In the entire Middle East/Balkan theatre there were thirty-three squadrons (sixteen bomber, ten fighter, two naval and five army co-operation/general purpose),[15] compared to 169 squadrons in the United Kingdom (forty-five bomber, eighty-one fighter, thirty Coastal Command and thirteen army co-operation).[16] In Churchill's mind, the imbalance was perfectly justified. Coastal Command was fighting a battle that was at least as crucial as any other the country was engaged in. Fighter Command was needed to guard against the knockout blow and deter invasion. Bomber Command was the means by which Churchill hoped to win the war.

The air situation would not have been so serious if Longmore had been getting what he was supposed to. The prime minister, quite justifiably, made much of the problems Britain had moving aircraft from one theatre to another. It took two to three months to get supplies round the Cape, with more time needed to assemble the aircraft. The Takoradi route took less time, about six weeks from UK to Egypt. Even the risky route straight through the Mediterranean took two weeks. With internal lines of communication, it was much easier for the Italians and Germans to switch resources from one front to another.

Relying on the Takoradi route was proving problematic. When it was set up, it was hoped it might delver fifty aircraft a month, which was never going to be enough to support an entire theatre. In the first four months of operation (September to December 1940), 139 planes were assembled at Takoradi and 108 were dispatched to Egypt. It was early days for the organization, but with forty-nine dispatched in December, deliveries had just about reached the first target. However, by January the target had been increased to 100, and was subsequently increased to 120 and finally, in March, 180 (fifty Hurricanes, fifty Tomahawks, sixty Blenheims and twenty Marylands).[17] Nobody really knew what might be possible; these were no more than administrative guesses, driven upwards more by the need to get more aircraft to Longmore, rather than any analysis of the route's capacity. Relying on this as the sole regular means of supplying aircraft to the Middle East was a decision based on hope rather than evidence.

In 1941, aircraft began arriving from the United States in substantial numbers. The first Maryland light bombers arrived in Takoradi in January, followed in February by the first batch of 100 Tomahawks. In February and March, no less than 400 British and American aircraft were expected to arrive at the Ghanaian port. These included another ninety-one of the now grounded Mohawks, but this still left 121 Tomahawks, sixty Hurricanes and 120 Blenheims. However, arriving in Ghana and reaching Egypt were two quite different propositions.[18] Even in December, Churchill was worrying about the disparity between aircraft arriving at Takoradi and the number being sent on to Egypt. Unassembled aircraft were piling up and it seemed the facilities could not cope.[19] In January, only twelve Blenheim IV, two Wellingtons and one Maryland would reach Longmore. The number of planes reaching Longmore rose to seventy-two in February, but this was still well short of the revised targets.

The Middle East could not rely solely on what the Takadori route could deliver. Using some of the shipping capacity to transport aircraft round the Cape would obviously mean something else had to be sacrificed, but the problem was one of balance. The Army was in desperate need of every cubic foot of shipping capacity to support its operations in East Africa and the Western Desert. However, the RAF was even less able to provide adequate air support on all these fronts. More air and fewer ground forces would make for a better-balanced overall force. With more ground than air forces, there would always be the temptation to use ground forces without the air support they needed.

Any acceleration of deliveries using the route round the Cape would come with a three-month time lag. For more aircraft to arrive in March, the process had to be set in motion in January. Ironically, on 6 January Churchill was urging more effort should be made in case there was a German invasion of Greece, although he was more interested in making sure there would be airfields for Hurricanes in Crete and Greece than actually delivering more Hurricanes. 'The call when it comes may be urgent. Everything must be set in train now,' he urged.[20] With hindsight, this rousing call should perhaps have set the Air Ministry thinking. But an alternative way of getting sufficient aircraft to the Middle East was not set in motion and so, come the spring, Longmore would be relying on whatever the Takoradi route could manage.

It was not just the numbers of planes sent to the Middle East that was a problem; quality was also an issue, and would become more so as the evidence grew that German forces were about to become involved. If supply lines and other considerations meant the Middle East RAF would always be small, it was even more important that it should be a high-quality force. An Air Ministry lack of interest in tactical planes meant the Middle East was getting the Blenheim, the best day bomber Britain possessed, and even better American light bombers were to follow. However, the fighter squadrons also needed the best, especially as evidence grew that Germany was about to intervene. Churchill seemed to accept this and was willing to take risks to make sure the Middle East got them. Early in January, Churchill took the aircraft carrier HMS *Furious* out of vital convoy protection duties to ensure Longmore's fighter squadrons got 'the best machines' before they had to face the Luftwaffe.[21]

Churchill, however, was not sending 'the best machines'; the only fighter he was sending was the Hurricane I. The Hurricane had emerged from the Battle of Britain as a national icon that had helped save the country. This was fine from the propaganda point of view, but as the Air Ministry was very aware, it had struggled; at the end of the Battle of Britain, replacing the Hurricane I was one of Fighter Command's most urgent priorities. Fortunately for Britain it was still superior to anything the Italian Air Force had, and this helped justify its continued use in the Middle East. However, as Churchill had pointed out, it was now only a matter of time before Longmore's squadrons came up against the Bf 109.

Churchill seems to have been taken in by Britain's own propaganda on the Hurricane issue. He rarely distinguished between Hurricane and Spitfire; the two seemed interchangeable in his mind. It was perhaps up to Portal to explain that the Hurricane could not deal with the latest German fighters, but he chose not to enlighten the prime minister. If the German fighter force was going to be challenged, Longmore and

D'Albiac needed Spitfires, preferably the very latest version. Not even the Hurricane II or Tomahawk would do. As it was, the Middle East was still having to make do with the Hurricane I as its 'best' fighter, and some squadrons were having to persevere with the Gladiator.

Churchill was being dragged in two directions. Longmore's success in the Western Desert and Italian reverses in Albania whetted his appetite for more military success on the ground, but his overall war aim was still to win the war by the bombing offensive. It was convenient to believe that the Middle East did not really need the air reinforcements it was demanding, indeed was already awash with aircraft and pilots that were not being used. Churchill was never slow to remind everyone about the 1,000 planes and 1,000 pilots his censuses of Middle East resources revealed.

In Greece, the growing German presence on the country's northern frontier made it even more crucial to capture the port of Valona. With their western flank secure, the Greeks could redeploy their forces to deal with a possible German invasion. With neutral Turkey and Yugoslavia looking on, not to mention an Air Staff anxious to use Greece as a base for strategic bombing, Britain had good reasons for giving the Greeks all the help they needed. The country provided a priceless bridgehead on mainland Europe. With the victories over the Italians in the Western Desert, the Commonwealth western flank seemed secure and Churchill felt sufficiently confident to offer the Greeks ground forces, an option that Churchill had previously studiously avoided. Whether the resources existed in the Mediterranean for another major commitment was another matter. Britain's prestige was at stake; the country could scarcely afford to be evicted from mainland Europe for a third time.

Churchill offered the Greeks troops, backed by artillery, tanks and five more RAF squadrons. Once suitable airfields were available – and by this Portal meant airfields capable of operating heavy bombers – an air component of fourteen squadrons was envisaged. As it turned out, the ground forces Britain offered were so limited that the Greeks decided it was not worth the risk of antagonizing Hitler by inviting Commonwealth ground troops into the country. The air reinforcements, however, were gratefully accepted, although there was no question of provoking Germany by the sort of strategic operations Portal was hoping to launch from Balkan bases.

The extra air commitment should have been covered by existing arrangements. In December, Portal had set in motion plans to increase the number of squadrons in the Middle East by twelve, because of possible new commitments in Greece or Turkey. He had even got as far as telling

Longmore. However, even before the Greeks formally turned down the British offer, Portal changed his mind. Portal probably already realized he was not going to get permission to attack strategic targets. His official explanation was that there was a decreasing chance of a Balkan front and Churchill had ordered him to accelerate the expansion of Bomber Command.[22] It cannot have helped Longmore's mood that the problem was not a lack of resources or the means to get reinforcements to the Middle East; it was just that Portal had changed his mind.

The five squadrons the Greeks had accepted would still have to be sent and they would have to come from what was available in the Middle East. Longmore objected to the loss of these units while what was now a full-scale offensive in the Western Desert was still in progress, but Churchill was in no mood to debate the issue. He sent Wavell and Longmore a very firm reply, making it very clear that Greece was the priority. The issue was not up for discussion and he expected 'prompt and active compliance'.[23]

It meant more of the limited air resources available would be used where British forces were not in action, so the imbalance between ground forces and air support would be even greater where they were in action. No. 33 Squadron (Hurricanes) and No 11 Squadron (Blenheims) made their way to Greece, the latter taking the surviving Blenheims of No. 39 Squadron to bring it up to strength, while the latter squadron withdrew to convert to the long-awaited Marylands. In the months to come, more and more squadrons would find themselves stranded in the rear waiting for aircraft to arrive.

Wavell expressed his dismay to Dill, the Army CIGS, about yet more squadrons going to Greece, despite the desperate shortage of aircraft in the theatre. Portal took exception to what he saw as Longmore actively encouraging commanders of the other services to support his protests about the low aircraft delivery rates. Air commanders colluding with other services was considered disloyal to say the least. Relations between Portal and Longmore were deteriorating fast, and were about to take another turn for the worse.

Churchill had not given up on bringing Turkey into the Allied camp by providing 'the additional air support they need to sustain their famous military qualities'.[24] Again Churchill saw no distinction between a strategic bomber force and one that could genuinely 'sustain' Turkish troops on the battlefield. Churchill promised the Turkish president ten fighter and bomber squadrons, along with 100 anti-aircraft guns and crews, and these were already on their way. These ten squadrons would be reinforced by the five promised to Greece should that country be defeated. Churchill assured the Turkish president that any build-up of German forces in Bulgaria would, if the Turks agreed, constitute sufficient justification to use these bombers against lines of communication the German were using and, more importantly from Portal's point of view, Rumanian oil fields.[25]

When Portal told Longmore these ten squadrons would also have to come from the resources available to his command, the Middle East air commander was dumbstruck. He told Portal he was 'astounded' by the suggestion, and that Portal clearly did not understand the situation he was facing.[26] Indeed he did not, but from Portal's perspective, Longmore did not understand the huge opportunity this offered to strike at Axis oil targets. There was a yawning gulf between the way frontline commanders in the Middle East and the Air Ministry in London were viewing the war. To Longmore's enormous relief, the Turkish president turned down the British offer.

The decision by the Greek government not to accept British ground forces opened up the possibility of continuing the advance in the Western Desert. Wavell would be allowed to try to take Benghazi, although efforts would then focus on creating a four-division mobile reserve in Egypt, which, Churchill assumed, would soon be required to deal with the inevitable German invasion of Greece. The Commonwealth air forces were not in a good position to provide much assistance, but the lack of air support was not so obvious while forces on the ground were making such huge progress against a demoralized, retreating Italian Army. Tobruk was the next Italian stronghold surrounded. Time was needed to bring up the resources to reduce the fortress, but it was not enough time to enable the Italians to regroup. The assault on the citadel was launched on 21 January. For three hours before dawn, a handful of Wellingtons droned over the city dropping bombs, causing confusion and, more importantly, helping to conceal the noise made by the British tanks moving into position. The Blenheims again supported the ground assault, flying eighty-eight sorties during the course of the day. Hurricanes strafed and Lysanders directed artillery fire. Royal Navy warships also joined in the bombardment. This time resistance in the air was almost non-existent. The artillery bombardment from ship and land continued through the night, a few Wellington bombers adding to the confusion. In thirty-six hours the RAF had dropped 60 tons of bombs in 100 sorties. Next morning there was very little resistance and the port was occupied.[27]

O'Connor now struck inland towards Mechili, but unexpectedly the Italians pulled out without a fight. RAF reconnaissance spotted the withdrawing forces on tracks not on British maps. Fuel shortages delayed the chase on land, but the RAF did its best to strafe and bomb the retreating columns. However, the number of sorties was dropping rapidly. Italian columns attempting to retreat towards Benghazi were also bombed and strafed, but in three days the Blenheims could only manage forty sorties.[28]

Nevertheless, the Italian forces were in disarray and O'Connor had no intention of allowing them time to regroup. Armoured forces raced round the coast road to Benghazi, and as it became clear the Italians were not even going to try and hold this port, elements of the 7th Armoured Division were dispatched across the barren terrain to Beda Fomm, on the coast south of Benghazi, to block any escape from Cyrenaica. In the air, the surviving handful of Blenheims and Hurricanes strafed the retreating columns whenever and wherever they could. Captured Italian fuel dumps helped keep the planes in the air, but with the extended lines of communication, there were huge problems keeping any planes serviceable, although the Italian forces were so disorganized, there was scarcely any need for air support. After several attempts to break out, the trapped Italian forces surrendered. An attacking force of just two divisions had advanced 500 miles, destroyed ten Italian divisions, captured 400 tanks and 850 guns, and the road to Tripoli was open.

It was by any measure an astonishing victory. O'Connor's tanks had again played the central role, demonstrating what was possible when a commander was willing to take risks, but the RAF had played its part too. Air reconnaissance had kept the land forces reasonably well informed about enemy movements, while fighters had blunted efforts of the Italian Air Force to intervene and had provided morale-boosting air support for the advancing infantry. It was, however, all on a very small scale. Against better-equipped opposition, Commonwealth air forces would need to be far more prepared. More and better planes were an obvious need, although not one Tedder put too much emphasis on. Greater mobility, Tedder noted, would be useful. Army co-operation squadrons, more used to manoeuvring with the army, were much better at keeping up with the advance and maintaining operational strength. In actual operation, Tedder noted that bombs by and large did not cause much damage; it was strafing that appeared to have inflicted more casualties.

It was a catastrophic time for Italian armed forces on all fronts. In Eritrea, Italian forces had retreated to the more easily defendable Keren region. Initially the Italian Air Force was much in evidence, but the Italians were completely cut off and without adequate reinforcements the level of Italian air operations steadily dwindled. The Commonwealth air forces, led by Air Commodore Leonard Slatter, gained superiority and then supremacy, and close army/air co-operation ensured this was fully exploited. A squadron commander was attached to army HQ to co-ordinate air operations, his experience proving invaluable in deciding what were and what were not reasonable targets for air attack. Flights equipped with Hardys, Lysanders and Gauntlets were attached to divisions for tactical reconnaissance and dive-bombing in response to requests from forward troops, while Blenheims and Wellesleys escorted by Hurricanes attacked aerodromes and communication targets further in the rear. Resources were used flexibly. If the Hurricanes and Gladiators on fighter sweeps encountered no opposition, they strafed any targets they came across. The close support involved attacking artillery, troops concentrating for counter-attacks and forward enemy positions. This close support was particularly valuable when Commonwealth forces had to storm fortified hilltop positions. The attacks were often very close to friendly forward troops, but there were no losses to friendly fire.[29]

For the final assault, Blenheims, Gauntlets, Wellesleys and Hardys bombed, dive-bombed and strafed enemy positions. A late revival by the Italian Air Force could do little to prevent what the Italian commander, General Frusci, described as the constant torment the Commonwealth air forces inflicted on his troops. It was the sort of ground/air co-operation that in Britain provoked bitter inter-service controversy, endless conferences and extensive trials. In Greece it had been officially banned. In Africa, however, it was the obvious way of using the available aircraft. After eight weeks of intensive fighting, Keren was taken on 27 March. The Italian naval base at Massawa fell on 7 April, opening the Red Sea to American shipping and a new route for reinforcing the Middle East. In his report on the campaign, Slatter recommended the development of longer-range fighters for ground attack and specialized bombers for hitting pinpoint targets. As far as Slater was concerned, this meant dive-bombers.[30]

The advance northwards into Sudan from Kenya encountered less resistance. The ground forces were supported by the South African Air Force, with bomber support provided by a squadron of Fairey Battles and one of Ju 86s. There were also two squadrons equipped with Hawker Hartebeests, a version of the Hawker Audax built in South Africa. There were also a couple of Hurricane squadrons (one of which still had some Hawker Furies). The bombers were supposed to be replaced by Martin Marylands, but in January 1941 only a couple were available and these

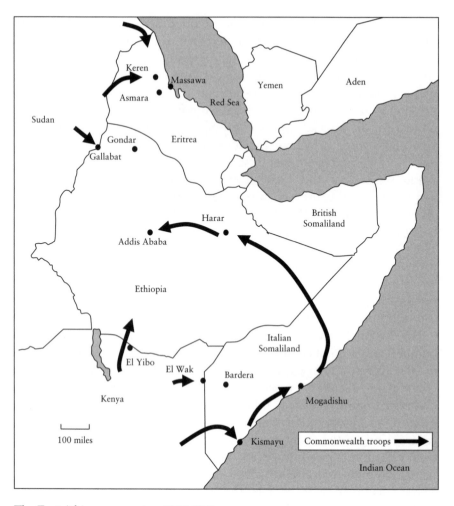

The East African campaign 1940-1941

were used for reconnaissance. The Fairey Battle, the most modern bomber available, would soldier on until August 1941, suggesting that perhaps more use could have been made of the many stored away in the UK. The Hawker Hartebeests would continue flying reconnaissance and ground-attack missions right up to the very end of the East African campaign in November 1941.

Junkers 86s, Battles and Hartebeests bombed airfields and communications in the rear, and enemy artillery and trenches at the front, although initially most attacks were in the rear as there was little resistance on the ground. Mogadishu was captured on 25 February. As the

98

Commonwealth forces struck inland towards Harar, encounters with enemy fighters became more frequent and bombers were immediately provided with fighter escorts. With decisions ruled by common sense rather than doctrine, it all seemed remarkably straightforward.[31]

Resistance on the ground was also increasing, and the need for more closely co-ordinated air support led, on 1 April 1941, to the creation of a 'close-support flight' with four Hawker Hartbeestes and four Gloster Gladiators, mirroring the similar flight created in the Western Desert. Again this was all happening without any controversy or fuss. An air force officer moving forward with the ground forces was able to call in close support whenever it was required. The scale was small, but wherever Commonwealth troops were fighting in Africa, they were getting limited but well-focused support.

On 5 April, Addis Ababa formally surrendered before troops even reached the city. The back of Italian resistance in East Africa had been broken, but it would be November before the final strongholds fell and up to the very end, RAF and SAAF squadrons continued to provide very close air support for the ground forces involved in these mopping-up operations. One addition to their strength was the Curtiss Mohawk. Twenty, with full modified engines, arrived in Mombasa from Britain in July, and in August were issued to No. 3 SAAF squadron for use as a fighter-bomber. In November 1941, sixteen months after the first Mohawk came into British hands, the plane flew its first missions.[32]

The circumstances that existed in the Middle East made it far more natural for air forces to be used for more direct support of ground forces. There were usually no obvious strategic targets to distract the RAF, and close co-ordination between air and ground forces was much easier to organize when at most a couple of divisions, sometimes only a couple of brigades, were involved, operating along narrow fronts, which simplified the task of deciding where the planes might be needed. It would be much more complex with far larger fronts to cover and more substantial forces engaged. However, RAF thinking in the UK had to start moving in the same direction if it was to become a force capable of playing a part in helping the Army either defeat a German invasion or, thinking further ahead, support an Allied invasion of the continent.

Chapter 6

Preparing for Invasion

Although Britain's priority in the winter of 1940/41 had to be to make sure its armed forces were ready to deal with an invasion, the organization, tactics, equipment and, most important of all, mindset of commanders would need to be precisely the same as those required when the time came to take the offensive and cross the Channel. Such offensive action was far from General Brooke's mind in the autumn of 1940. Even after German invasion barges began dispersing, scares continued to keep the Army on the alert and few doubted that the return of better weather in the spring of 1941 would see a fresh attempt to complete the Nazi conquest of north-west Europe. For Brooke, in charge of forces in the UK, it was a race against time; partially trained and poorly equipped troops had to be turned into divisions he could count on. He also had to convince the Air Ministry that his soldiers should get the sort of air support Commonwealth forces were getting in Africa.

There were some encouraging signs. With the greater responsibilities that came with the position of Chief of Air Staff, Portal was taking the danger of invasion very seriously, and he was from convinced the RAF was ready. 'It has been reported to me that it is not generally appreciated in Operational Commands, and even within the Air Ministry itself, how much has to be done,' he confided in Peirse, his successor at Bomber Command.[1] Progress had been slow and unnecessary delays had occurred: 'Many methods of cooperation must be revised in the light of experience gained in France.' Portal seemed to have forgotten that while at Bomber Command, he had bitterly opposed using his bombers to support Allied armies in France. Exercises were being organized by the War Office to test the defences, and Portal made it very clear to Peirse that Bomber Command must give its full support. 'Failure in this involves the risk of failure in battle if the threat of invasion materialises in the Spring [sic],' Portal warned. The exercises were to be as realistic as possible as they might be the last before invasion became an imminent possibility. It seemed the new broom was determined to make a fresh start.[2]

Bomber Command seemed to be willing to play its part. For the Victor anti-invasion exercises in January 1941, notes prepared by Bomber Command stated that heavy as well as medium bombers by day and night, but mainly by day, would be used against the ports of embarkation, transports crossing the sea and the attempted landing zone. This sounded promising, but there was little sign that the lessons of the French campaign had been taken on board. It seemed that no direct fighter escort was thought necessary for daylight operations; Fighter Command would be around in some numbers and this ought to be sufficient.[3] This was the sort of indirect protection that had proved so disastrously ineffective during the Battle of France.

As was the case in the summer of 1940, it is hard to believe that if it had been a real invasion rather than a paper exercise, the heavies really would have been so readily committed. Such was the damage Bomber Command believed it was inflicting on German industry, that the argument that it would be a mistake to release the pressure would no doubt have been as persuasive as it was during the Battle of France. The notes for the Victor exercise even suggested that any German preparations for an invasion should be viewed with suspicion as they might just be an attempt to divert Bomber Command effort from the pounding it was giving German industry.[4] Even if used against an invasion fleet, it is difficult to imagine the heavies would have been used by day. There was certainly no serious preparation for daylight operations. Formation flying was a dying art, and the casual suggestion that no close escorts would be required did not bode well. Either lessons had been forgotten or Peirse was just going through the motions to keep his War Office counterparts happy.

Direct support on the battlefield was definitely not on the agenda. Indeed Group Captain Victor Goddard, Director of Military Co-operation, made it very clear that the aim of these exercises was to rid Brooke of the notion that the Army should have close-support bombers.[5] Peirse's attitude was quite clear: 'I hope no requests will be made to bomb forward troops either to relieve pressure or cooperate in attack.' Nor could Bomber Command be expected to deal with fast-moving enemy columns. In all probability these would not be found and there would be a grave risk of bombing one's own troops, he insisted.

Peirse recalled the losses suffered over Maastricht in the 1940 French campaign, although these missions were not flown in close support of forward troops; it was a communications target in the rear, the sort of target Peirse was claiming he was quite happy for his bombers to attack. Without effective escort, Peirse was quite right to believe Blenheim losses would have been just as heavy as they had been over Maastricht.

Examples of providing close support were included in the Victor exercise mainly to demonstrate how futile they would be. Army Co-operation Command tentatively outlined a scenario where 'the situation on land has become so serious' that the medium bombers should be used for 'direct and close support' for a counter-attack, but even Army Co-operation Command was emphasizing that this was not a normal role, even for medium bombers.[6] Peirse suggested that the Army needed to be reminded that Bomber Command did not have the dive-bombers necessary for attacks on precision targets such as bridges, although the War Office scarcely needed reminding about that. Peirse was not pointing out a weakness in his equipment that needed correcting; he was merely pointing out that bombing bridges and enemy columns were not what his bombers were for. Indeed, with four-engined heavies replacing twin-engined bombers, his command was becoming progressively less suitable for tactical bombing. If Bomber Command ever got involved in supporting ground forces, it could only be as a desperate last resort, he insisted.[7] During the exercise there was a single attack by Wellingtons on an armoured column, but in the post mortem this was considered to have been an uneconomic use of the bomber force. In the case of the cumbersome Wellington this was no doubt true, but again the aim was to demonstrate this was not how Bomber Command should be used rather than to highlight problems.

This did not mean the RAF did not have suitable equipment for such attacks. Peirse was quick to point out that Training Command would, in the event of an invasion, be expected to put around 240 planes into the air as part of the Banquet scheme. This was a desperate 1940 plan to throw every available plane, including trainers, against invading German forces. Peirse claimed that the low speed and high manoeuvrability of planes like the Hawker Hart would make them extremely tricky targets for enemy fighters. Enemy anti-aircraft fire might be a problem, he conceded, but such planes should nevertheless make effective dive-bombers.[8] In the first year of war, slow-flying obsolete biplanes had proven surprisingly successful in the ground-attack role, but they were scarcely weapons of choice. The best the RAF could manage in the UK, with the pick of the available resources, was no better than an equipment-starved SAAF was having to use in East Africa. In 1940 the Banquet scheme had been a desperate measure; in 1941 it had become the preferred option.

In the post-exercise discussions, Air Ministry representatives distanced themselves from any previous commitment to provide bomber support on the battlefield. They again emphasized that their agreement to develop close air-support was purely to help the Army achieve a breakthrough in some future offensive. It was not a normal mission for defensive operations, and especially not for an invasion. In a concession to the War Office, and despite Peirse's objections, from January 1941, No. 2 Group Blenheim aircrews began their training programmes on how to deliver close air-support. Training for each squadron consisted of only a three-day course, and getting the programme started did not attract the urgency Portal was demanding.

Indeed, it would seem that Portal's concerns over invasion were soon on the wane, perhaps influenced by Churchill's rather dismissive attitude towards the threat. The prime minister cum minister of defence took the Chief of Air Staff more into his confidence than other service leaders, and the two spent much time at Chequers mulling over the course the war was taking. Churchill ridiculed the assumptions made in the simulated invasion exercises, claiming they suggested that far more troops could be landed than could possibly be the case. He mockingly suggested that if the staff officers were so confident the Germans could do this in the face of the Royal Navy, then the same staff officers should draw up similar plans for a British invasion of France, which he would unhesitatingly recommend to the War Cabinet. Such talk no doubt helped clear Portal's mind of any lingering doubts.

Churchill stuck to his belief that Germany would have to achieve air superiority before launching an invasion, so it was only necessary to ensure Fighter Command was strong to prevent one being attempted. It was a dangerous assumption. This had been the German strategy against Britain in 1940, but in Poland, Norway and France they had not sought air superiority first, air and ground operations having begun simultaneously. Churchill was also relying too heavily on the bomber. With his apocalyptic pre-war vision of mass destruction from the air, Churchill was convinced that Bomber Command could smash an invasion fleet. Churchill happily accepted the Air Staff line that bombing one target was like bombing any other target. He was not the least bit interested in the specific capabilities of the aircraft equipping the RAF or what the aircrews were trained to do. He was just happy to have a 'fleet in being', air and naval forces so powerful they would prevent an invasion even being considered. Despite assurances to the contrary, RAF bomber crews were not trained to hit naval targets or tactical targets in support of ground forces. If an invasion fleet set sail, the Royal Navy might turn it back, but the RAF would be far less effective than Churchill imagined. It was this misplaced faith in the deterrent value of Bomber and Fighter Command that gave Churchill the confidence to pour ground forces into the Middle East, without worrying about the consequences for home defence. Churchill's willingness to commit ground forces to the Middle East, along with his reluctance to commit air units, left Wavell in the Middle East complaining about the air support he was getting and Brooke on the home front fretting about the strength of his ground forces.

In Churchill's war strategy, the state of the Army in Britain was irrelevant. Brooke's complaints about the shortages of basic weapons and ammunition were beginning to annoy the prime inister. He believed Brooke was exaggerating the danger of invasion to gain preferential treatment for the Army.[9] Portal's fellow chiefs, Dill and the First Sea Lord Dudley Pound, attempted to persuade Churchill an invasion was every bit as likely as Brooke was claiming, but Portal and Churchill both needed to believe it was not. Both wanted the maximum resources to go to the strategic air offensive, and Churchill wanted to send as many ground forces to the Middle East as possible. The prime minister and his Chief of Air Staff provided each other with the reassurance they both needed.

Since the Army was not really needed, an air force to support it was not required either. Close air-support was certainly not needed. Within the Air Ministry there was a determination to make the war conform to its beliefs. The importance of German tactical air-support was questioned. There was nothing to prove the German Army would not have been just as successful without the Stuka. After all, one assessment continued, air support had only been successful in the Polish and French campaigns. Nor was the Luftwaffe always used to support the army, as the bombing of Rotterdam demonstrated, the report triumphantly declared.[10] In fact, even this was close air-support for German forces trying to break through Dutch defences. The War Office found it impossible to penetrate the barrier of wishful thinking and self-delusion. The Army already faced huge challenges trying to get to grips with the new era of mechanized warfare that the panzers had ushered in, but it was having to waste energy just to get the Air Ministry to be realistic about the Army's need for tactical air-support. After more than a year of war, the UK-based RAF was still less proficient in army support than it had been in 1918.[11]

While Portal was becoming ever more part of Churchill's inner circle, Dill was rapidly losing the confidence of the prime minister and an undermined War Office was proving feeble in its attempts to oppose the increasing dominance of the RAF. Talks between the War Office and Air Ministry held in February 1941 were supposed to clear the air about the whole army air-support issue, but it soon became clear to Dill it was about how army air-support might be whittled back even further to help boost Bomber Command. Portal was adamant: 'There is little prospect of defeating the enemy Air Force except by the development of a superior bomber force.'[12] Medium bombers were not needed; the continuation of their production rested on 'the possibility of our sending an Army to the continent before Germany is beaten' and the 'tactical feasibility of close support', the implication being both were rather unlikely. If bombers had to support the Army, heavy bombers could do it far better than specialist close-support planes like the Bisley or Beaubomber, which Portal wanted to abandon completely. Close support was not likely to be of value except in exceptional circumstances. For the War Office, it was all very alarming.

The 19 February 1941 meeting was a small affair in Portal's office and was essentially about how Army Co-operation Command could help increase the strength of Bomber Command. Dill's deputy, General Robert Haining, was there but Brooke was not present to defend his corner. Goddard was also there, supposedly to provide a neutral, balanced view, but there was little doubt which side of the divide he was on. He could not see what the War Office had to complain about; it had the seventeen close-support squadrons it had requested in 1940, if you counted the Bomber Command Blenheim squadrons as specialist close-support planes. This set the tone for the rest of the meeting.

With not even an outline plan of how the Army might win the war, Haining had to agree that the strategic bomber offensive was the only way Britain had of attacking Germany, and therefore all effort should go into increasing the long-range bomber effort at the expense of the other services. The additional army co-operation squadrons that the expanding Army required would not be created. Indeed, the strength of existing squadrons would be cut by a third. Each squadron would have just eight planes, allowing sixty aircrews to be transferred to Bomber and Fighter Command. Haining also found himself agreeing that the Army at this stage should not be so much interested in the actual equipment required for close air-support but merely the organization, signals systems and training. He accepted that the Army could not expect a specialist close air-support plane. Any plane designed for army support had to be capable of contributing to the strategic air offensive, at least until an increase in aircraft production allowed the development of more specialist planes.[13]

The War Office had hoped to get back the two strategic reconnaissance Blenheim squadrons (Nos. 53 and 59) that had been attached to the Air Component in France but had subsequently been loaned to Coastal Command. Instead they got a flight (No. 1416) of photo-reconnaissance Spitfires. In the context of the other decisions it was a victory.[14] With no enemy to engage, and no plans to go onto the offensive, it was perhaps embarrassing to have army co-operation squadrons doing nothing while Bomber Command was fully committed to the struggle. Even so, with a possible invasion of the UK only months away, the War Office response appeared rather lame.

Ironically, on the day his army co-operation force was slashed and hope of developing an effective close air-support element scuppered, Brooke was having what he believed to be a constructive discussion with Peirse at Bomber Command headquarters on the help his bombers would provide if it came to an invasion.[15] Brooke was furious when he heard what had been agreed in his absence. Haining rather defensively assured the Army commander that the Air Ministry had promised the reduction in army co-operation squadron strength was only temporary and would be made good by the end of the year, which would not have helped much if the invasion battle had been fought and lost by then. Churchill would adjudicate if Brooke wanted to take the matter further, Haining explained, but he thought it would be a waste of time to reopen the issue.[16]

As a concession, Goddard had agreed to conduct a joint Air Staff/ General Staff study of close air support in an invasion scenario, although presumably this was just to clarify that it would not be needed. A start was made with the training of No. 2 Group squadrons in direct-support missions, and it seems that Barratt ensured that this included how the force should be used during an invasion rather than just in support of a future advancing British Army. The content of the training proved to be rather academic as hardly any took place, thanks to a combination of poor weather, technical problems with radio equipment but mostly a lack of RAF interest.

By March, the War Office was beginning to show increasing frustration with the way the training was going. It also pointed out that there was little point in training crews for close-support duties if they were promptly lost on Bomber Command operations over Germany, and wanted the few crews that had been trained held back from such operations. The idea that No. 2 Group pilots be kept out of the battle on the 'off chance' that they would be required for close support struck the Air Ministry as absurd. Both sides had a point, but Air Ministry certainty that the bomber offensive was crucial to the outcome of the war and invasion was not a serious possibility made the gulf in the two outlooks even wider.

Peirse, meanwhile, was growing concerned that, having, in his own mind at least, settled the close-support issue, the situation had now 'deteriorated', with many Army officers under the impression that, in the event of an invasion, Bomber Command would intervene on the battlefield.[17] Peirse was anxious that divisional and brigade commanders should be made aware this was not going to happen. Even if at some distant future point in the war the Army did cross the Channel, close air-support would simply not be tactically feasible. Attacking communications leading to the battle zone was, in the Air Staff's and Peirse's view, the best and only way of supporting operations on the ground. The Air Ministry seemed oblivious of the much closer air-support Commonwealth ground forces in the Middle East were getting.

Bomber Command issued an Instruction on the operational uses of its aircraft in the event of an invasion in which no mention was made of close support. Sea lanes and exits from the bridgehead would be bombed, but no targets nearer the frontline. For close support, the Army was reminded about the 'dive-bombers' of Training Command. These, a Bomber Command Instruction of March 1941 stated, were to be centralized and under the direct command of GHQ Home Forces. On paper this represented a force of 250 machines that could be used for supporting the Army, and certainly appeared to go a long way to meeting Army demands. However, when the War Office enquired as to exactly how this sizeable force of planes was to be actually deployed in such a way that it could be used *en masse*, it transpired that no way existed. The only plan was the one formulated in the summer of 1940, which envisaged flights of these trainers being attached to army co-operation squadrons. The number that could be deployed over the front would be limited by the number and location of army co-operation squadrons. That meant one Banquet close-support flight of half a dozen trainers would be available to support a corps or armoured division – that is if it was lucky enough to have an army co-operation squadron.

Goddard, supposedly responsible for developing ground/air co-operation, settled any lingering doubts about the role of the close support by insisting that its sole purpose was to support offensive operations overseas, not in the UK. It had not been 'possible to visualise the circumstances in which it would prove to be an economical employment of bombers during operations against an invasion'.[18] Training in the communication systems required would continue, but Goddard agreed with the War Office that there was little point in training crews in close air support if they were likely to be lost on normal Bomber Command missions. His solution, however, was to end the No. 2 Group training programme.[19]

The RAF attitude to co-ordinating operations with the Army was summed up by procedures Bomber Command was to follow during an invasion if communications with higher commands broke down. Various methods for re-establishing contact were suggested, and if all these failed then bombers were to be sent out on reconnaissance missions in an attempt to locate suitable targets. If this failed, 'as a last resort' the local Army commander was to be contacted.[20] In the Middle East this had become the standard preferred option, not a last resort. The RAF in the United Kingdom was not prepared, and was not even preparing for an invasion. Without air support, and weakened by the reinforcements sent to the Middle East, the Army would be at an enormous disadvantage. Britain was perilously vulnerable to an invasion – far more vulnerable than Churchill imagined. The Royal Navy was a very real barrier and might well defeat an invasion fleet, but if the Wehrmacht overcame this barrier, the Germans would be pushing at an open door.

While the Air Ministry struggled to visualize the situations in which close support might be required, the Greek Army was having no such difficulty. Unfortunately, the Greek Air Force had almost ceased to exist, not through lack of pilots but a lack of planes. When the Greeks asked what had become of the promised Mohawks, the Foreign Office indignantly pointed out that Britain had never promised immediate delivery. Indeed, with the Mohawks grounded while an air filter was developed, they had become a very distant prospect. Nor was there much chance of the Greeks getting the eighteen Tomahawks that were supposed to replace them.

When the first Tomahawks arrived in Takoradi from the United States, it was found that they also lacked the necessary air filters and other equipment needed for operations in the tropics.[21] A slanging match ensued between Portal and Beaverbrook over who was responsible. Portal could not believe the MAP had allowed the delivery of planes not ready for operations; Beaverbrook retaliated by insisting it was the Air Ministry's job to sort out the fine details. Beaverbrook also emphasized it was Portal himself who had claimed the planes would not need any modifying.[22] In any case, Beaverbrook added, the MAP did not have the staff overseas to do anything about it. An unimpressed Portal thought at the very least that the MAP could find out what the planes lacked before they arrived in the theatre, even if they were powerless to solve the problem at source. The fact that the RAF had taken delivery of quite a large number and had not bothered to test the type scarcely reflected well on the Air Ministry or the MAP. Urgent orders were issued for the delivery of air filters and desert flying equipment to be dispatched to the Middle East, but in the meantime the crated Tomahawks stayed in Takoradi. Neither the Commonwealth nor Greek squadrons would be getting Tomahawks anytime soon.

In the meantime, the only reinforcements the Greeks were getting were any Gladiators and Blenheim 1s that RAF squadrons no longer needed as they re-equipped with Hurricanes and Blenheim IVs. In December 1940, fourteen Gladiators allowed the re-equipment of one of the PZL P.24 squadrons, and this became operational in January, but that was about it.[23] Middle East HQ emphasized how short of aircraft they were and could not afford to give the Greeks any Blenheims.[24] The Greek Air Force was withering away. With so few aircraft of their own, the Greeks became even more desperate for the RAF to take over the close air-support role. As vulnerable as Italian lines of communication were, a handful of sorties was never going to achieve much against distant ports, and, the Greeks argued, the RAF could fly far more sorties against less distant targets.

The Greeks were right in believing that the fewer planes you have, the greater the need to use them closer to the front. A small number of aircraft will always achieve more in conjunction with other arms than they can by trying to achieve results on their own. The Greek government and military authorities, not to mention the British military attaché in Greece, were all lobbying intensely for RAF units in Greece to switch their efforts to supporting the Greeks Army. A beleaguered D'Albiac was becoming paranoid, claiming even the Reuters news agency appeared to be part of an anti-British conspiracy with its rather unflattering accounts of the contribution the RAF was making in the Greek struggle.[25]

The pressure seemed to tell; in February 1941, D'Albiac formed a 'West Wing' with a bomber and a fighter squadron to provide direct support for the proposed Greek drive on Tepelene, the last major town before the port of Valona. It was a deployment very much against D'Albiac's better judgement, but the Greeks insisted that it was crucial that the morale of the attacking troops be sustained by air support on the same scale they themselves were suffering at the hands of the Italian Air Force.[26] As the writer of the official narrative put it:

'Allowance had to be made for Greek temperament – for the possibility that for reason of morale it might at a particular moment be more important to show the Greeks that they had air support than to use that support in the most scientific way possible.'[27]

It was a sentiment which reflected the patronizing attitude of the British towards their allies, both in 1941 and in 1945 when the narrative was written. It did not seem to occur to the writer that maintaining the morale of friendly troops and helping them to win a battle might be a very good 'scientific way' of employing the available air resources.

Between 11–18 February, around 100 Blenheim sorties were flown in support of the Greek assault on Tepelene. The targets were generally roads leading up to the front rather than battlefield targets, but they were relevant to the ongoing struggle on land and this was the best way of using a plane like the Blenheim. These operations were escorted, and when no enemy fighters were encountered, the escorts joined in the attack. Italian resistance on the ground, however, was fierce and the assault on Tepelene failed. The Blenheims returned to attacking Adriatic ports, but an Italian counter-attack on 9 March provoked renewed appeals for closer air-support and once again the RAF responded as best it could.[28]

D'Albiac rather disdainfully described these operations as successful 'from a purely local spectacular point of view', but it was a local spectacle much appreciated by the Greek troops.[29] D'Albiac later agreed that the esteem in which RAF personnel were held was never higher than at this time.[30] Even so, he still believed it was a misuse of his forces and that the Italian counter-attack merely proved that his bombers should have been trying to prevent the Italian build-up by attacking the ports reinforcements were coming through.[31] Prior to February 1941, this was what the RAF had been trying to do, and even D'Albiac had to concede that with so few planes, achieving worthwhile results was always unlikely.

The support continued until 14 March when, on instructions from London, the RAF units were switched to rear targets, mainly the two key ports of Valona and Durres and nearby airfields. The staff officers with the 'West Wing' found themselves in the awkward situation of having to turn down desperate appeals from their Greek allies for urgently needed fighter and bomber support. It would appear that not all these pleas were rejected as some Blenheim raids were flown on lines of communication immediately behind the battle zone.[32]

The approaches adopted by the Greeks and British mirrored the tactical versus strategic debate over how air power could best support land forces. Both the British and Greeks saw Valona as the key to the battle for southern Albania. The British believed that bombing the port would lead to the defeat of Italian forces. The Greeks wanted to capture the port by defeating the Italian army. The British approach was based on a grossly exaggerated idea of what a small number of bombers was capable of achieving. It was assumed that the RAF bombers were delivering the same level of destruction Bomber Command was believed to be achieving over Germany. With the enemy starved of supplies, victory on the battlefield would inevitably follow: indeed, the battle on land might be a mere formality. It was, on a much smaller scale, the British strategy for defeating Germany.

The Greeks more realistically saw attacks on supply lines as useful, but not as useful as helping achieve a decisive victory on the battlefield. It would take time for a bomber offensive against the ports to achieve useful results, and time was something the Greeks did not have. Only victory on the battlefield could produce the quick results the Greeks needed so that they could switch their forces to meet a German invasion. Concentrating all air effort on the battlefield was more likely to bring about a sudden collapse of Italian resistance than attacks on communication targets in the rear.

The Italian counter-attack spelt the end of any hopes that the Greeks might have had of moving forces from the Albanian front. The build-up of German forces in Bulgaria was continuing and an alarmed Greek government felt obliged to reconsider Churchill's offer of ground forces. Commonwealth troops were now welcome, and with apparently no Axis threat in the Western Desert or East Africa, it seemed safe to oblige. The Greeks agreed to start constructing and manning a defensive line, the Aliakmon Line. It involved conceding the north-east of the country (Macedonia and Thrace), but would be much shorter and easier to defend and would be reasonably well-placed to block a German advance across the Bulgarian or Yugoslav frontiers. The Greeks had little with which to man the line, and only one Commonwealth division was expected to be in place by the end of March.

The British Chiefs of Staff and Cabinet were initially buoyed by hopes that Yugoslavia and Turkey would join the struggle. However, it was soon clear neither would intervene, and to make matters worse the Greeks decided not to abandon the north-east of their country after all but try to hold a line much further east in Macedonia. The whole scheme was beginning to look very problematic, but commanders in the Middle East still believed the German Army could be held and the Allied deployment went ahead. Wavell, Longmore, the Greek king and government, their Army generals and the British ambassador, however, were all united in pointing out that despite the obvious Allied weakness on the ground, air support was an even bigger deficiency.

In London, the air situation was not causing the same degree of alarm. On 6 March, the Cabinet met to discuss the apparently deteriorating chances of a successful intervention in Greece, and the lack of air support was one of the issues. Portal told the Cabinet he believed the Luftwaffe had 475 aircraft in Rumania. Discounting reconnaissance and army co-operation planes, this could be reduced to 160 bombers and 160 fighters, which, in Portal's eyes, was a more accurate measure of air strength The RAF had five bomber squadrons in Greece, but three Wellington squadrons would soon be arriving to reinforce them. Three fighter squadrons and a flight were also in Greece. The proportion of the remaining seven fighter squadrons in the Middle East that could be used as reinforcement depended on the situation on other fronts, but two more fighter squadrons were due to be formed by the end of March, and this ought to make it easier to send more fighters to Greece.[33] It was perhaps a rather more upbeat assessment than Longmore would have given.

A wavering Churchill was encouraged by Portal's figures, the three Wellington squadrons probably making a particularly strong impression. He described how soon there would be 'strong air forces' in Greece, and although they would still be outnumbered, he pointed out that numerical inferiority had never prevented the RAF from inflicting heavy losses on the enemy, which to Churchill was what air warfare was all about.[34] There was no discussion as to whether the RAF would be able to do much to support the Australian and New Zealand divisions that were going to be doing the actual fighting on the ground.

Churchill and Portal were frustrated by the Greek request that the RAF take no action until Greece was actually attacked, which meant not only could German movements towards the Greek frontier not be bombed but, more significantly from Portal's point of view, neither could Rumanian oil fields. Portal felt the military argument for bombing Rumania and Bulgaria straight away was unanswerable, but he agreed it was difficult to override the wishes of the Greeks as long as RAF forces in Greece were so weak. However, the arrival of the three Wellington squadrons ought to change that.[35] Portal's mind was focusing purely on the strategic air war. Three Wellington squadrons were not going to do much to stop the German Army. There were all sorts of reasons why Churchill and his Chiefs of Staff were becoming increasingly nervous about the Allied intervention in Greece, but the air support the RAF might be able to provide for the Army was not one of them.

Even D'Albiac was more interested in the strategic possibilities than the tactical battle his squadrons might soon be engaged in. Just days before the German offensive, he was telling Longmore that he should try to persuade the Air Ministry to get the latest heavy bombers, like the Stirling and Manchester, out to Greece, so that this valuable and, with Commonwealth troops involved, far more secure foothold in Europe could be used for strikes on targets deep inside Southern Europe.[36] Ensuring these Commonwealth troops had the air support to secure the foothold would have been a more worthy priority. The Spitfire would have been a more useful plane to pester the Air Ministry about.

The decision to accept the offer of Commonwealth troops came at the worst possible time for Longmore. RAF squadrons were seriously under strength. There were not enough aircraft to replace losses in existing squadrons, never mind replace obsolete planes. Portal's schedules in London might have the dates squadrons were due to be formed, and Longmore did indeed have the pilots, but he did not have the aircraft. He had nothing like the resources he needed to cover yet another active front. The Takoradi route was still struggling to meet its commitments. The MAP was still trying to develop a satisfactory air filter for the Mohawk. The problems with the Tomahawks seemed to have been resolved, but neither these nor the Marylands were reaching the Middle East in any numbers. Churchill continued to rage at the hold-up in Takoradi. In March, there were 195 aircraft piling up at the base, twenty had arrived in the last week but only five had been dispatched. He ordered Portal to do something about it, but Portal was equally frustrated. It was not just a shortage of vital equipment, as the technicians were struggling with the more unfamiliar American planes. It seems that it was not just the Greeks who were not up to the task of dealing with unfamiliar modern equipment.[37]

The American Tomahawk was Longmore's best way of improving the quality of his fighter force, but he seemed blissfully unaware of this. He had taken some persuading that the Hurricane was a better tactical fighter than the Gladiator. He had now been won over by the Hurricane's qualities, but seemed unaware of how outclassed the Hurricane I was by the BF 109E. For Longmore, the Hurricane I was the ultimate fighter, and indeed compared to Gauntlets and worn-out Gladiators it was a huge improvement. As far as Longmore was concerned, the Tomahawk was an untried, unknown quantity and no great loss, while the Hurricane was tried and trusted.

The Air Ministry tried to convince him of the merits of the Tomahawk, claiming a 'non-operational squadron' had proven the Tomahawk could easily match the speed and climb of the Spitfire, although why they did not know the fighter's exact speed was not explained. It was, the Air Ministry insisted, also very manoeuvrable and easy to handle. With bullet-proof windscreen and self-sealing tanks, it seemed like Longmore was getting an outstanding plane, and it was suggested he give the American fighter priority at the Takoradi assembly line, even if the workforce there was struggling with the American assembly instructions.[38]

It is difficult to avoid concluding that the Air Ministry was deliberately over-selling what it believed to be an inferior American fighter. At the time Longmore received the upbeat assessment, the fighter had not even been properly tested and had certainly not been issued to a 'non-operational squadron'. This seemed to be a rather fancy name for an RAF Maintenance and Storage Unit. The Air Ministry's description seems to have been based on a combination of manufacturer's claimed performance and the improvements, like self-sealing tanks, that had been introduced, which reduced this performance. The Tomahawk was not as good as the Spitfire, but it was the best fighter available to Longmore.

Longmore was not persuaded, and would have been even less convinced if he had known how reluctant the Air Ministry had been to make any use of the Tomahawk. Longmore did not want to become reliant on an American fighter, and no doubt feared it was another Air Ministry attempt to dump second-rate material on his command.[39] He was right about Air Ministry motives, but as the Air Ministry would discover when it did finally get round to testing the Tomahawk, it was a vast improvement on the Hurricane I and in many respects better than the Hurricane II. When Dill told Portal about Longmore's doubts about the Tomahawk, Portal made no effort to change his mind. He assured Longmore he would continue to get Hurricanes, and it was up to him which type Takoradi should give priority to.[40]

The Marylands were no quicker coming through. Longmore had already withdrawn squadrons from the front to re-equip with the American bomber, and fifty were due to arrive in Takoradi in February and March. However, again there were complaints about the American aircraft being complicated to assemble. Longmore, adopting an engrained British distrust of anything foreign, was quite happy to allow

Takoradi to concentrate on the Blenheim. Of the 195 planes in Takoradi in mid-March, 135 were American, but by the end of March only two Tomahawks and nine Marylands had made their way to Egypt.[41] The RAF in the Middle East was left relying almost totally on the more familiar but more dated British types, when far more advanced American planes were available.

Even the trusted British planes were only trickling through. After the Churchill-inspired rush of Hurricane reinforcements at the beginning of the year, with forty-four arriving in January, the monthly deliveries dwindled to just thirteen in March. Blenheims were consistently below the promised sixty – only eighty-five arrived in the first three months of 1941. The only aircraft delivered around the Cape in these three months were six Lysanders. Only 209 aircraft arrived in the Middle East in the first three months of 1941 by any route. It was nothing like what was required. While Portal was confidently reassuring the Cabinet that Longmore was forming more fighter squadrons, there were four fighter squadrons waiting to be re-equipped before a start could be made on the six squadrons that were forming. Nor could army co-operation squadrons be expected to carry on with Hardys. Ideally, the Lysanders also needed replacing.[42] Longmore insisted he could not rely solely on aircraft coming through the Takoradi route, and appealed to Churchill and the Air Ministry to send aircraft round the Cape and across the Pacific to Basra.[43]

Longmore's frantic appeals were not well received in London. For some time, Churchill had been taking exception to the tone of Longmore's complaints, and instructed Portal to tick him off.[44] 'I feel bound to tell you that further emphasis on your shortage of aircraft is quite unnecessary,' Portal snapped in Churchillian style.[45] Longmore replied, taking 'grave exception' to the comment and set about using any channel of communication to get his message across.

The more he enquired about what was going on, the more incensed he became. Longmore discovered that the Tomahawks already delivered to the UK, which were supposed to come to him once the summer invasion scare had passed, were now being assigned the army co-operation role in the UK. Apparently forgetting his doubts about the fighter, he let Eden know of his displeasure at the decision. Portal was forced to explain to Churchill that this had been under consideration, but he now declared this decision had been reversed and that Longmore had been assured he would get most of them, which might have been news to the army co-operation squadrons which were still expecting to get the plane.[46]

Portal also claimed that Longmore had misunderstood the situation and he would have got replacement British fighters anyway. However, since Takoradi was still having trouble handling the 100 that had been delivered in February, Portal felt that it made sense to prepare further Tomahawks for desert combat in Britain before they were dispatched to Takoradi. It did indeed make sense. However, although the MAP had been working on this tropicalization process since January, there were still none ready for dispatch in March.

The next nasty surprise for Churchill and Portal was a report, dated 17 March, via Cunningham, the Naval commander in the Mediterranean, that Wavell was complaining that in February and so far in March only one Hurricane had been delivered. Churchill exploded at this absurd claim.[47] Portal promptly checked up on the figures and triumphantly announced that in the month and a half in question no less than twenty-seven Hurricanes had arrived in the Middle East.[48] In his moment of triumph, Portal did not seem to appreciate that four Hurricanes a week was scarcely enough to support air fighting on three fronts and re-equip units still having to make do with the Gladiator, not to mention the fighter squadrons Portal had assured the Cabinet were in the process of forming.

Wavell, however, pointed out that he had actually said only one Hurricane had arrived in Takoradi in February. He was right. An indignant Portal explained to Churchill that this was only because forty had been rushed through in January to help Longmore continue his advance in Cyrenaica. These, he claimed, were not supposed to be additional planes, but were merely an advance on future allocations, which therefore dropped to close to zero in February to compensate. Given that the Mediterranean was the only theatre in which British forces were in contact with the enemy, it was parsimonious to say the least, but as far as Portal was concerned, Longmore was just trying to get more aircraft than what he was entitled to.

The figures scarcely suggested Longmore was being greedy. He was supposed to have got a one-off increase of thirty-two Hurricanes to compensate for the dispatch of fighters to Greece, and his monthly allocation of Hurricanes had been increased from eighteen to thirty. For the months November to March, he should have got at least 172 Hurricanes. In fact, including deliveries to Malta, only 133 Hurricanes were dispatched to the Middle East. Only seventy-eight planes of all types arrived in March, well short of the previous 120 target, never mind the new 180 target.[49] Portal's claim that Longmore was asking for more than he was due was scarcely borne out by the figures.

116

Churchill, however, thought Longmore was putting about 'trick statistics', which was rather ironic given the questionable validity of the statistics Portal had conjured up in his own defence.[50] Portal had to concede that the facts Longmore seemed to be putting about were essentially correct but not 'the complete picture'.[51] Portal complained to Churchill that this was typical of what he had to put up with from Longmore, and had to admit relations between Longmore and the Air Ministry were not 'smooth'. He suspected Longmore of orchestrating the comments on aircraft shortages now coming via Cunningham and the Foreign Secretary, Eden. Longmore seemed to believe the Air Ministry was keeping the true state of his plight to itself, and suggested a message direct from the prime minister might put him straight.[52]

Churchill duly obliged with a furious communication on 29 March in which he accused Longmore of deliberately spreading false information among other commanders in the Middle East, which was even finding its way to Commonwealth leaders. Apart from the 'absurd' Cunningham Hurricane claim, Jan Smuts, the South African Prime Minister, had spoken of Beaverbrook hoarding material unnecessarily in Britain to the detriment of the war effort in the Middle East, which led Churchill to conclude that 'there must be some talk emanating from your Headquarters which is neither accurate nor helpful'.[53] Longmore's unappreciative attitude was most unwelcome. Enormous risks were being taken to get him the planes he wanted; the Royal Navy was having to do without vital carriers in the Battle of the Atlantic to transport them. The gist of the message was that Longmore should be more grateful for what he was getting. The Navy, however, was on Longmore's side. Cunningham, the source of the furore, mockingly admitted he was getting his facts wrong. It had been quite inaccurate to suggest that only one Hurricane had been delivered in the period February to mid-March. In fact, the single Hurricane that had arrived in February had been followed by two more in the three weeks up to 20 March.[54]

Churchill convinced himself he could do no more to support operations in the Mediterranean and felt he had good reason to feel aggrieved. From his perspective it seemed huge quantities of aircraft were being poured into the Middle East, but appeared to be disappearing like 'water in the desert sand'.[55] He still could not believe that with 1,000 planes in the Middle East, frontline strength, according to the latest figures, was only 300 aircraft. It was all an example of 'frightful mismanagement and futility'.[56] Middle East commanders might argue that the mismanagement and futility had more to do with the large numbers of planes held in stores in the UK. Even the planned 180 planes a month that were supposed to be going to the Middle East were scarcely adequate for such a huge theatre – the seventy-odd planes that were actually arriving each month was unquestionably inadequate. Even worse, these planes were not 'the best machines worthy of the quality of the pilots in the Middle East' that Churchill thought them to be.[57]

Churchill may have had romantic ideas about the quality of the Hurricanes that Longmore was getting, but Portal knew better. Douglas at Fighter Command had made it perfectly clear to him that the Hurricane I was no longer acceptable as frontline equipment. If Portal needed a reminder about the hopeless inferiority of the fighter, the struggle over Malta would provide it.

Chapter 7

Discord in the Ranks

German air units had begun to arrive in the Mediterranean in December 1940. Initially they were mostly dive-bombers and specialist anti-shipping units to reinforce Italian efforts against the British convoys that were supplying Malta and Egypt. The tiny island, halfway between Sicily and Libya, was now seen as crucial to British fortunes in the Mediterranean and the Chiefs of Staff had instructed Longmore, the RAF commander in the Middle East, to make the defence of the island his first priority. Longmore's problem was that he had far too many 'first priorities'.

So far Malta had been a fairly inconspicuous outpost. The defeat of France left the island hopelessly isolated from any friendly territory and there were times when the British could scarcely believe they had been allowed to retain control of what was effectively an unsinkable aircraft carrier handily situated to attack the shipping lanes between Sicily and Libya. Wellingtons on their way to Egypt had briefly paused on the island to deliver an attack on the mainland, small compensation to the Air Ministry for the loss of these valuable long-range bombers to the Middle East. However, there was a reluctance to launch too many raids from the island for fear of drawing Italian attention to its strategic value and its obvious vulnerability.

Initially, Italy showed every intention of making life difficult for the islanders. June and July 1940 saw a series of heavy air raids, initially opposed by just six Sea Gladiators, three which were immortalized as Faith, Hope and Charity, flown by an assortment of pilots who happened to be on the island. There was, however, already an early warning system – the first radar station had been established in 1939, and a second joined it in June 1940.[1] The Gladiators were soon reinforced by a handful of Hurricanes that the island held on to from

119

a batch on their way to Egypt via France. These gave the defenders a qualitative edge over any Italian fighter and the firepower to deal with the bombers. The Hurricanes seemed to make a difference, and from August onwards the number of raids steadily declined.[2] In the first six months of war with Italy, little more than 600 bombing sorties had been flown against the island, scarcely a huge effort.[3] By the end of the year, a Hurricane, a Wellington, a Sunderland and a Swordfish squadron were operating from the island, along with a reconnaissance flight of Marylands.[4] However, neither these nor the light naval forces operating from the island had yet made much impression on Italian shipping. Only 2 per cent of the supplies to Libya had been lost in 1940.

The German reinforcements that arrived in December initially comprised three bomber groups, which soon made their presence felt. One of their victims was the aircraft carrier HMS *Illustrious*, damaged as it escorted one of the rare convoys routed through the Mediterranean to Egypt. *Illustrious* was forced to seek refuge in Malta, and while repairs were underway the full fury of the German bomber force was unleashed on the naval base and RAF airfields. The carrier was able to limp back to the relative safety of Alexandria, but the Luftwaffe attacks on the island continued. For Malta and its people it was the beginning of a merciless siege. The relatively small German force flew four times as many bomber sorties in the first five months of 1941 as the Italian Air Force had managed in the preceding five months; apart from supplying some escorts, Italian participation ceased.

In February a single squadron of Bf 109Es, with just nine pilots, arrived in Sicily to support German bombers and made an immediate impact. For four months this squadron terrorized the Hurricane force. The German unit claimed over forty Hurricanes, without losing a single pilot. German bomber losses over Mata dropped from twenty-one out of 451 sorties flown in January to just six out of 755 sorties in May.[5] On 15 February, the RAF commander on Malta, Air Vice-Marshal Forster Maynard, appealed for immediate help. The incessant and increasing attacks were wearing down his small fighter force, the Bf 109E was outclassing the Hurricane – especially at altitude – and there was only so long they could continue suffering losses for no gain. He needed more fighters, but even more importantly he needed better fighters, either the Spitfire or the Hurricane II, he suggested.[6] As an alternative, Portal suggested Longmore give priority to Malta with the first Tomahawk deliveries, but this was scarcely a solution since the fighter was grounded.[7] At the beginning of March, the governor of the island, Lieutenant General William Dobbie, stepped up the pressure with an impassioned appeal for more and better fighters.[8] The pleas paid off and it was decided that the Maltese squadrons should be the first overseas units to get the Hurricane Mark II. However, it was only a question of time before the squadrons in Greece and the Western Desert would also have to take on the Bf 109E.

Palairet, the British ambassador in Greece, was keeping up the pressure on London, warning of dire consequences if adequate air support was not provided. He told Churchill that according to his sources, the Germans had 600 aircraft in Bulgaria and the Italians nearly 500 in Albania. If the Greek Army and population could not be protected from air attack, there could only be one outcome. Portal claimed he was exaggerating: he said the Italians only had about 250 aircraft and there were just 500 German aircraft in Bulgaria and Rumania, of which 100 were army co-operation and did not really count. Given that the RAF had a theoretical strength of around 160 planes, of which only about eighty were serviceable, and the Greek Air Force scarcely had any planes it could put into the air, it did not matter what was excluded or which estimate was right – the Luftwaffe had the numbers and the quality to dominate the skies.[9]

Having assured the Cabinet that Longmore had the fighter resources to reinforce Greece, Portal was rather anxious to prove he could. He had a look at Longmore's deployments and accused him of having too many fighter squadrons in East Africa. Portal noticed that there was a fighter squadron based at Aden, which seemed a luxury that Longmore could not afford, and he suggested he move it north.[10] Longmore responded that with ten worn-out Gladiator Is this squadron was scarcely a luxury. Throwing it against the Luftwaffe would just be a waste of good pilots. He would move it north as soon as he had Hurricanes for the squadron; in the meantime they could achieve far more against obsolete Italian planes than the pick of the Luftwaffe. Even Portal could see that in the overall scheme of things, one squadron, whatever it was equipped with, was not going to make much difference.

Portal was suddenly beginning to appreciate the scale of the problem facing Longmore, and realized that something had to be done about it. On 25 March, he laid down the facts before his staff. The shortage of fighters in the Middle East was now very serious; the RAF might be outnumbered three-to-one. Meeting any single threat might require every one of the ten fighter squadrons the RAF had in the theatre. The number would have to be raised to at least fifteen as quickly as possible, and sufficient planes would have to be delivered to maintain these and two or three Greek squadrons, which he now appeared to hope might be available to help out. Even more significantly, he now accepted the Hurricane I was outclassed and it would be necessary to go over to the Hurricane II as soon as possible.[11] It was late March 1941; the German invasion of Greece was just days away. The change of heart was far too late.

There were now desperate attempts to get more fighters to Longmore. Portal was told he could get 110 Hurricanes to the Middle East in ten weeks, 145 if the aircraft carrier HMS *Furious* was used, but, he observed, 'obviously even this higher number is totally inadequate'.[12] Attitudes really were changing. Takoradi had to do much better than just eleven fighters a week. He now agreed with Longmore that new routes had to be found for getting fighters to the Middle East. More use had to be made of convoys going round the Cape. One hundred might be squeezed on a convoy about to depart, and this ought to get to the Middle East by late May.[13] This, however, could only be done at the expense of the mechanized transport for the 50th Division, which was being sent to the Middle East. Portal readily conceded this was needed just as much, but, as Portal was now quick to point out, without fighter cover, these Army reinforcements would not be able to achieve much anyway.[14] This was true enough, but unlikely to impress the War Office at this late stage.

Portal now realized that disaster was looming. Courtney, in charge of supplies for the RAF, was told to give the matter his personal attention, with the grim warning that 'the consequences of failure to maintain our fighter force in this area will be very serious indeed'.[15] The response was not encouraging. Courtney was doing all he could, and the MAP was asked to increase output of tropicalized Hurricanes to 120 a month.[16] But Takoradi was still the bottleneck; the trans-African route was nowhere near the latest target of fifty a month. Clearly other routes had to be found to get all these Hurricanes to the Middle East.[17]

Courtney was trying to use other routes. Sixty might be squeezed on Churchill's emergency Tiger Convoy, which was going to risk the Mediterranean route to get tank reinforcements to the Middle East. Another twenty to thirty could perhaps be sent in unescorted cargo ships heading round the Cape. Portal pleaded with the War Office to squeeze a few more in Cape convoys, and eventually around sixty were sent by this route but they could not start arriving until July.[18]

As these measures were put in place, German forces in North Africa were on the move, which triggered a more radical reappraisal. Portal argued that Fighter Command was stronger than it had been in 1940, yet, now the Germans were committing to the Mediterranean theatre, a Luftwaffe assault on Britain could not possibly be as strong. Portal

122

therefore decided to move six complete Fighter Command squadrons equipped with the Hurricane II to the Mediterranean. Furthermore, the Takoradi and Cape supply routes would be supplemented by American planes sent to Basra or directly to Egypt through the Red Sea once Italian forces had been cleared from Eritrea.[19] These first direct shipments across the Pacific began to arrive in the Middle East in June. However, it was all much too late to avert the disaster that was about to plunge the Allied cause to its lowest point since Dunkirk.

On the same day that Longmore received Churchill's dressing down he also had to deal with complaints from the Greeks that the RAF had virtually disappeared from Albanian skies.[20] The Greeks, desperate to eke out more support from their ally, were exaggerating, but not by much. There were too few RAF squadrons to give the Greeks what they needed in Albania, never mind meet the likely challenge of the Luftwaffe over northern Greece. There was very little Longmore could do about it. His scanty forces in North Africa were already hopelessly stretched.

Five days before the Greek complaint and Churchill's reprimand arrived, General Erwin Rommel, commander of the *Deutches Afrika Korps* in North Africa, had begun moving forward. It was just a reconnaissance in strength, but El Agheila fell virtually without a fight. Initially there was still no real concern. Following the massive defeats inflicted on Italian forces in the Western Desert and East Africa, it was believed that no serious threat could possibly emerge anywhere on the African continent. British intelligence believed the newly arrived German forces – the 5th Light and 15th Panzer Divisions – could not possibly be in a position to launch a major offensive until at least May. It was scarcely a misjudgement – the German High Command had come to exactly the same conclusion. Unfortunately for the British, Rommel had not.

Rommel followed up his capture of El Agheila with an attack on the more heavily defended Mersa Brega. He had only a handful of tanks, and just seventy-five Ju 87s and Bf 110s, but the Commonwealth forces were also weak on the ground and in the air there were just two Hurricane, one Blenheim and one Lysander squadrons. In a dramatic reversal of fortune, Commonwealth resistance crumbled just as quickly as Italian forces had four months earlier and Rommel's raid rapidly turned into a full-scale offensive. Confusion reigned as RAF reconnaissance reported that enemy columns were advancing on Msus in Cyrenaica. In a move that would later cause bitter recriminations, the petrol dumps there were blown, limiting the manoeuvring power of those tanks that were available. Just as O'Connor had done, Rommel kept driving his small force forward, ensuring the Commonwealth forces had no time to recover their balance. To make matters worse, in the confusion, O'Connor himself was taken prisoner.

The appearance of the Ju 87 dive-bomber did much to tip the psychological battle in favour of the Axis forces. It was all very well claiming from the safety of the Air Ministry that the bombs did little damage, but troops continued to be unnerved by the weapon, especially those with no previous experience of it. There was plenty of proof of how vulnerable the dive-bomber was as RAF fighters tore into them, claiming no less than fourteen on 5 April. Bf 110s were also being claimed on a regular basis and both types were considered relatively easy targets by Commonwealth pilots. In the air there was nothing for them to fear – not yet anyway.[21]

The few available Blenheims did their best to slow down the advance with daily attacks on the German columns. Tedder, temporarily in command of the Commonwealth air forces, was anxious that his squadrons should do something to relieve the hard-pressed ground forces, and Hurricanes were ordered to back up the efforts of the Blenheims by strafing enemy columns.[22] However, Rommel's advance was even swifter than O'Connor's had been. Benghazi fell; reinforcements were rushed into Tobruk so that at least this citadel might be held even if bypassed. Blenheims, dropping large numbers of anti-personnel bombs, were particularly effective in stiffening the defences around the port. The retreating Commonwealth columns were at least spared air attack, partly because, with only the Bf 110 to deal with, the Hurricanes remained an effective force, but also because German air support was limited. It never quite became a rout and, contrary to Air Ministry dogma, the RAF had played a part in slowing down the German advance and when a stand was made, strafing and bombing helped stiffen resistance. Tobruk held on and took the sting out of the German advance, but the majority of Commonwealth forces were back where they started at the beginning of December.

Meanwhile, events were now moving fast in the Balkans. Yugoslavia seemed to have decided its best interests lay with an accommodation with the Germans and signed the Tripartite Pact on 25 March, but a coup two days later saw the government overthrown and the agreement overturned. Negotiations between the British and Greek military, complicated by the uncertain position of Yugoslavia, failed to hammer out an agreed strategy for the defence of Greece. The Greeks were determined to defend as much Greek soil as possible by making a stand in Macedonia on the Metaxas Line, close to the Bulgarian frontier. The British, fearing this line of defence would be outflanked by any German drive through south-eastern Yugoslavia, still believed the more southerly Aliakmon Line was the only viable option.

Most of the Greek Army was still engaged with Italian forces in Albania, and only half of the remaining six Greek divisions joined a New Zealand division, an Australian division and a British armoured brigade on the Aliakmon Line. The rest were deployed further west in Macedonia. The Greek divisions, however, were seriously under strength and the Commonwealth forces were still trying to move into position. The German forces assigned to the invasion of Greece had been reduced by the sudden need to invade the recalcitrant Yugoslavia simultaneously, but still consisted of six infantry, two motorized and two armoured divisions. Nevertheless, given the nature of the mountainous terrain, a successful defence should by no means have been beyond the capabilities of the limited ground forces available to the Allies.

It was in the air that the real disparity in strength lay. More Gladiators and a handful of Blenheim Is had been handed over to the Greeks, but the squadrons were in a pitiful state. Portal was quick to blame Longmore and the Americans for the failure to get modern fighters to the Greeks.[23] In fact the Americans could have done no more, and Wildcats were on their way across the Pacific. On 1 March, the Air Ministry promised the Greeks that they would get eighteen Hurricane Is just as soon as Nos 80 and 112 Squadrons had replaced all their Gladiators, but it was doubtful they would become available any sooner than the Wildcats. When the Germans invaded Greece in April 1941, one Greek squadron was equipped with Gladiators and the remaining three with what was left of the Bloch 151 and the PZL P.24s. In desperation, some of the Greek Navy's Do 22 floatplanes had their floats replaced by wheels and were issued to reconnaissance squadrons. Even Avro Tutor trainers were issued to squadrons for short-range observation duties. What should have been a battle-hardened force was scarcely capable of making any serious contribution.

Dwarfing both the Greek and British air contingents was the air force of Britain's new ally, Yugoslavia. It possessed around 500 frontline planes and, with nineteen fighter squadrons, had the most powerful Allied fighter force in the region. It also had the only fighter capable of challenging the German Messerschmitts – six Yugoslav squadrons being equipped with Bf 109Es supplied by Germany. However, they also had four squadrons that had to make do with the ancient Hawker Fury II. The other nine were equipped with Hurricane

Is and a handful of Yugoslavia's own mediocre Rogožarski IK-2 and more advanced IK-3 fighters. Bomber squadrons were equipped with British Blenheims, German Dornier 17s and Italian Savoia-Marchetti SM.79s, reflecting the efforts made by all the major powers to win over the country.

RAF strength in Greece had been increased to nine squadrons – four fighter squadrons (two Hurricane, one Gladiator and a night fighter Blenheim IF), four bomber squadrons (two Blenheim I, one Blenheim IV and one Wellington) and a Lysander/Hurricane army co-operation squadron, which arrived on the day of the invasion. D'Albiac seemed prepared to use these to support the Allied forces as best they could; close air support was included in the list of tasks the Blenheim squadrons might have to perform.

Longmore was far from happy with the quality of the planes available to him. He sent on D'Albiac's request for Stirlings and Manchesters to London, adding the Typhoon, Beaufighter and Blenheim V. If they could not be sent, he rather mischievously asked for advice on how he should explain to other Middle East commanders why they were not getting the latest RAF equipment. For Churchill and Portal this was the last straw – Longmore's days in command were numbered.

Longmore was right. The long line of communication might explain why there were only three day-fighter squadrons deployed in Greece, but they should at least have been equipped with the best Britain had. Relying on Gladiators and Hurricane Is, and reserving Spitfires for the defence of the UK, was rather like the Luftwaffe holding back its Bf 109E/F squadrons to defend Berlin and supporting its invasion of Greece with Arado Ar 68 biplanes and Jumo-powered Bf 109s. However, the Spitfire was mysteriously absent from Longmore's wish list. It was an odd omission – Longmore was clearly not afraid to ask for what he wanted. Longmore does not seem to have been aware of how superior the Spitfire was to every other available fighter. Even the Spitfire I would have been a huge improvement.

On 6 April, the Germans launched their assault on Greece and Yugoslavia. For the Luftwaffe it was a return to a more familiar role. Attempts to win glorious victories on its own over Dunkirk, and later over Britain by day and night, had ended in failure. It was back now doing what the Luftwaffe, and indeed any air force, did best – collaborating with other branches of the armed services. Once more the combination of ground and air forces would prove irresistible. Initially the main thrusts were aimed at Yugoslavia and the Greek forces in the north-east of the country protecting Macedonia. With over thirty

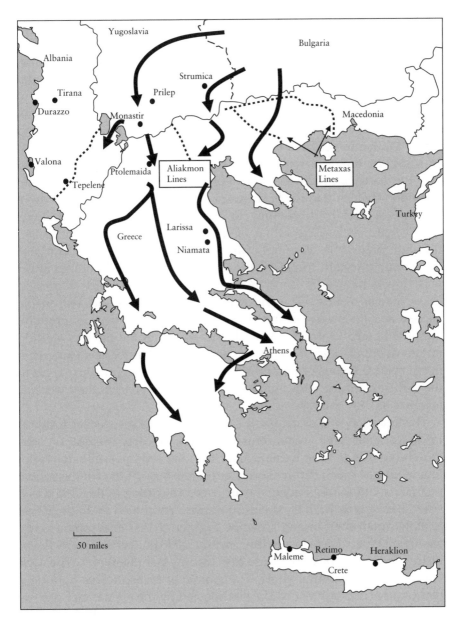

German invasion of Greece April 1941

divisions, a 500-strong air force and easy terrain to defend, on paper Yugoslavia appeared an awkward opponent. As it turned out, the Yugoslav Army was poorly equipped and the country was so ethnically splintered that in some regions the German invaders were welcomed as liberators. Where they offered resistance, Yugoslav forces were soon in retreat.

Further south, RAF Hurricanes of No. 33 Squadron were soon patrolling over Greek lines on the Bulgarian border. Squadron Leader Pat Pattle, the RAF's leading ace in Greece, shot down two Bf 109s in minutes, demonstrating how the best pilots could make a mockery of fighter performance figures.[24] On 6 and 7 April, fifteen Blenheims and seven Wellingtons, the latter venturing out by day, bombed targets in southern Bulgaria without suffering any losses. On the 8th and 9th, the focus moved west, thirty-one Blenheims attacking German columns advancing towards Strumica in south-east Yugoslavia, a drive which was already threatening to outflank the Greek Metaxas Line. By 10 April, it was clear that German forces advancing unchecked through Yugoslavia were not only outflanking the Metaxas, but also the Commonwealth forces on the Aliakmon Line, and bomber effort was directed towards German troops advancing towards Monastir. These attacks against German forces were carried out with reasonable success and no losses. For the most part the bombers were escorted by admittedly small formations of Hurricanes, with the fighters strafing targets of opportunity if there were no enemy fighters. The attacks were not powerful enough to make a decisive difference, but they were in the right areas and with fighters joining in the attacks, they were as effective as they could be.

The situation was already critical; the Greek forces further forward in Macedonia were soon crushed and Yugoslav resistance was crumbling too. It soon became clear that the only possible defensive line would be much further south across the base of the southernmost peninsula, but without adequate air cover, retreating to this line was a risky manoeuvre. RAF Blenheim squadrons continued to do their best to slow down the German advance. Fighter escorts and some cloudy weather helped keep losses low; nearly 100 day sorties were flown in the first seven days with the loss of only one Blenheim. The 13th was a day of maximum effort. The morale of British forces fighting a rearguard action at Ptolemaida was boosted by the appearance of low-flying Blenheims, which strafed the German tanks the British artillery had just successfully repulsed.[25] It was not a co-ordinated, planned intervention, as the bombers were on their way to bomb more distant targets, but it was symptomatic of an RAF desire to support the ground force whenever possible. However, on this day of maximum effort, just thirty-five Blenheim sorties were flown. It was also the day of greatest loss, with an unescorted formation of six Blenheims wiped out by

Bf 109s.[26] On subsequent days the dwindling number of serviceable planes continued to apply what pressure they could.

As the weather improved the retreating Commonwealth forces experienced the full force of the Luftwaffe, adding to the strain of constant retreats punctuated by fierce rearguard actions. Dispatching pairs of Hurricanes to try and break up the Stukas was all the RAF could do. To add to the RAF's problems, the Luftwaffe was inflicting heavy losses on the ground. At Larissa, fourteen Hurricanes were destroyed by strafing fighters, and ten Blenheims were lost at Niamata. By 15 April, there were only twenty-one Blenheim bombers and forty-two fighters left, and fourteen of the latter were Blenheim 1F night fighters. On 17 April, Yugoslavia capitulated, freeing more German units for the push south. The dwindling RAF could do nothing to stop the Luftwaffe exploiting its total air supremacy. Any hopes of holding even the southern part of Greece were abandoned and plans made to evacuate the British forces.

The entire campaign became a continuous fighting retreat, culminating in evacuation under cover of darkness from beaches in the south of Greece. The rearguard actions were often skilfully conducted with well-directed artillery fire, but even the artillery support could be silenced by the mere appearance of unopposed German spotter planes seeking to pinpoint their location. As in France the previous spring, there were no fighters to drive them away. With the Luftwaffe attacking the retreating British, New Zealand and Australian forces almost at will, it was not surprising that the Allied troops once again believed that they had been abandoned by their air force comrades.

The RAF in Greece had actually done as well as could be expected. Fighters had been used flexibly, patrolling above the retreating Allied forces, escorting the bombers and joining in the attack of ground targets whenever possible. Bombers had been used in the right areas, and for the most part had avoided excessive losses. In all, eight bombers were lost during the course of 125 Blenheim and sixteen Wellington day sorties. With the quality and quantity of planes available, there was no question of even attempting to challenge German air superiority. It was, however, an excellent demonstration of how a small air force equipped with second-rate planes could use its limited resources to best effect in a situation of air inferiority – if that was how the RAF wanted to be judged.

The RAF, however, was not a minor air force – the UK-based force possessed over 150 squadrons. On 15 April, the day that single-seater fighter strength in Greece fell to just twenty-eight, there were in reserve in Britain ready and available for immediate issue over 400 Spitfires.

These were riches undreamt of by Middle East Command. As in Norway in 1940, British forces had been committed without anything like the necessary air support. As in Norway, Gladiators were still being used as frontline fighters. The Blenheim was still the best day bomber RAF squadrons had. Britain had been in possession of Martin Maryland and Douglas Boston light bombers for nearly a year, but neither had yet dropped a single bomb. If air support had to be limited in quantity, the pilots risking their lives should at least have been given the best available equipment.

Personnel combat losses were relatively light, but in a constant retreat with damaged planes having to be abandoned, and airfields at the mercy of Luftwaffe attack, material losses were heavy. Of the 129 Blenheims that had been sent to Greece, just thirty-eight returned to Egypt, and only nineteen of the 126 Hurricanes and Gladiators made it back.[27] There was next to nothing to replace these losses. Six complete squadrons from Fighter Command were now on their way to the Middle East, an unprecedented scale of reinforcement, but this rebalancing of resources had come too late and Allied ground forces paid the price.

By any measure the Greek campaign was a catastrophic debacle. Heads would roll, and Longmore's was a very obvious head. On 1 May, as the last of the troops rescued from the beaches in Greece were making their way to Crete, Churchill called Longmore back to London to discuss the 'changed situation' in the Middle East. Longmore suggested that given the critical situation that existed, perhaps he should delay his return. The immediate response that he should return as requested did not bode well. He apologized to his heir apparent, Tedder, about the difficult situation he was leaving him in and wished him luck.[28] Within days, Portal was assuring Tedder that he had his full confidence and that he should feel free to change any orders issued by Longmore. It would be another month before Tedder officially took over from Longmore, and even then the first indication that his position was now permanent came from Longmore.[29] There had indeed been much debate about Longmore's successor; Churchill had vigorously opposed Tedder's appointment. Tedder sensed the doubts, indeed doubted his own ability to carry out the role, and did not think it would be long before he too got his marching orders. So short did he expect his tenure to be, that he told his wife that it would not be worth her while moving out to join him. (It was January 1943 before Tedder's wife would fly out. Tedder watched helplessly as the plane crashed on landing, killing all on board.)

Longmore could not be blamed for the catastrophe in Greece. He had done his best with what the Air Ministry in London had deemed appropriate. Longmore had committed as many air units as he dare from what he had, but in the final analysis, for a battle that Churchill considered so crucial to British interests, the RAF could only deploy around 150 planes, about a third of those available in the Middle East, but a small fraction of the 2,500 planes available to the RAF. In contrast, the Luftwaffe deployed what it considered necessary, about 1,000 planes out of its total strength of over 4,000. With internal lines of communication, it was much easier for the Axis forces to switch resources to the Mediterranean. Yet the Allies had scarcely been taken by surprise. The Middle East was a theatre Churchill wanted to make the centre of gravity of the war, a theatre where he hoped Britain could take the initiative. This might have been a misjudgement, but having made the decision, Churchill never appreciated the need for a proportionate tactical air force to go with the ground forces he was so willing to commit, and Portal was too committed to the RAF's strategic mission to want to enlighten the Prime Minister. Portal's last-minute change of heart came far too late to save Greece, but it was the beginning of a significant change in attitude towards the Middle East's air requirements.

There was still much to fight for. The surviving Allied forces had retreated to the relative safety of Crete, the possession of which was one of the reasons Churchill had wanted to get involved in Greece. The British had been on the island since November and there had been plenty of time to prepare the defences. Two radar stations had been set up and work had started on a number of airfields to supplement the main air bases at Maleme and Heraklion. This was the type of situation in which the RAF felt most comfortable – defending an island from which fighters could be directed by radar to the approaching bombers, with no frontline or advancing enemy to worry about. Malta had set a precedent for holding island fortresses. Crete was a similar distance from enemy airfields and was in a far less isolated position. Another mini-Battle of Britain was in prospect – if the fighters could be found to fight it.

However, there were very few fighters. Only one squadron was in permanent residence to defend the island, No. 805 Squadron Fleet Air Arm, which operated a mixture of Fulmars, Sea Gladiators and Brewster Buffalos. To these were added the squadrons that had retreated from Greece — No. 30 with Blenheim IFs and Nos 33, 80 and 112, mostly flying Hurricanes Is with a few Gladiators. It was felt the Blenheim IFs of No. 30 Squadron would be unable to contribute much and they were pulled back to Egypt. The four remaining RAF and Fleet Air Arm squadrons formed a basis for a defence, but could muster just thirty-six fighters, half of which were unserviceable and the remaining half rather the worse for wear.[30] The Greeks were still determined to carry on the struggle, but could offer no assistance in the air. Around 800 Greek Air Force personnel had retreated to the island, of which 157 were pilots, but all they had to fly were half a dozen Avro trainers.[31] The Wildcat fighters the Americans had promised had got as far as Suez.

The Luftwaffe was soon building temporary airfields in the south of Greece and islands in the Mediterranean, from where even short-range fighters could operate over Crete. Britain had been working on airfields on Crete throughout the winter of 1940/41 and should have been well placed to meet the threat, but only Retimo was anywhere near ready to join Heraklion and Maleme. There was, Longmore insisted, plenty of suitable locations on the island for dispersed airstrips and many more could have been made ready if, as he put it, 'we had been content with strips instead of trying to make "Croydons"'[32] (Croydon was London's main civil airport at that time). The over-sophistication of these aerodromes, however, was not a misjudgement. The Air Staff wanted substantial airfields that heavy, long-range bombers could operate from, not simple airstrips that fighters or short-range tactical aircraft might be able to use.

The situation on Crete might be no more desperate than the situation on Malta, but Crete was an island the Germans planned to occupy. Enigma intercepts revealed that General Kurt Student's Airborne Army was being deployed in the Balkans, and an air and seaborne invasion of the island was planned. If Britain intended to retain control of the island, action needed to be taken quickly. There was no shortage of troops on the island, but units evacuated from Greece were battle-weary and had left much of their heavy equipment behind. However, the German airborne and seaborne forces would also lack heavy firepower. A defence of the island was still a practicable proposition, but the defenders would need all the air support they could get.

At the time, the limited air resources in the Middle East could not have been more stretched. In the west, Malta was still top priority. In the south, operations in East Africa were ongoing and still encountering some stiff Italian resistance. To the east, the Iraqi government, egged on by Germany, was taking exception to British forces based in their country. Iraqi forces had surrounded the RAF training base at Habbaniya and Churchill was urging Wavell to take firm action. To the north, German forces were massing for an invasion of Crete.

These commitments were more than enough to stretch resources in the Middle East to breaking point, but Wavell and Churchill were anxious to take the offensive against Rommel's Afrika Korps in the Western Desert. It scarcely seemed the time for such ambition, but Enigma intercepts convinced Churchill that Rommel was very low on supplies; the prime minister was keen for Wavell to strike as quickly as possible. Reinforcements for Rommel were arriving fast, so fast that Churchill had taken a gamble on rushing the Tiger convoy – with some 300 tanks – through the Mediterranean. These arrived on 12 May and Churchill was expecting Wavell to make prompt use of them. Meanwhile on Crete, General Bernard Freyberg, the British-born New Zealander commanding the Allied forces there, was appealing for as much military equipment as possible, but all he got was a handful of light and medium tanks.

Wavell was planning to strike Rommel, even before the Tiger reinforcements could reach him. His own intelligence also suggested that the Germans were only holding the front with light forces. Indeed, there was evidence Rommel was already planning to pull back to stronger positions west of Tobruk until reinforcements arrived.[33] It seemed like too good an opportunity to miss. Tedder was as enthusiastic as Churchill and Wavell. For Tedder, it was an opportunity to capture airfields from which more distant targets could be bombed.[34] Freeman in London, Portal's deputy, had similar ideas. On the same day that Tedder was enthusiastically describing his plans to bomb Benghazi from the airfields he hoped would be captured, Freemen sent him advice on how to do it. Freeman was very worried that Tedder might not be aware of the latest developments in air warfare and hurriedly penned a memo, describing how in Europe incendiary bombing was proving devastatingly effective. Tedder should try to make maximum use of this new technique, Freeman suggested. In the hot, dry Middle East, cities like Benghazi and Tripoli might 'burn like torches'.[35] Planning the destruction of distant cities scarcely seemed the priority, but for Tedder it appears to have had a higher priority than defending Crete.

Wavell's Operation Brevity had as its aim the recapture of the key defensive positions at the Halfaya Pass and Sollum, and, if possible, Allied the forces would then push on to relieve Tobruk. The sketchy forces available to Wavell included only around fifty tanks, supported in the air by just two Hurricane and two Blenheim squadrons, but Wavell hoped he would be pushing at an open door. The attack was to be launched as the defenders of Crete awaited the airborne invasion which Enigma intercepts warned was imminent.

The damage that events in Greece had done to RAF/Army harmony was apparent in the wrangles over how the tiny air force available should be used. The commander of the Commonwealth ground forces, General William Gott, wanted the RAF bombers to target German tanks, but Air Commodore Collishaw pointed out that aircraft invariably had little effect on armoured fighting vehicles and it was the soft-skinned supply vehicles that were the Achilles heel of the German panzers. This was entirely reasonable, but to a suspicious Army it looked like another example of the RAF wanting to operate too far from where the fighting was actually taking place.

With the experience of Commonwealth troops in Greece still fresh in their minds, Gott and Wavell also insisted on permanent fighter patrols over their advancing forces. It was by no means the first time the Army had requested such cover, and the RAF had previously obliged, but it was indicative of the cracks now opening up in army/air relations that this became a major bone of contention. Both Tedder and Collishaw wanted to use the few fighters available more offensively, but again to the Army this smacked of an air force wanting to distance itself from the fighting on the ground. Under pressure, Tedder agreed to use the fighters as the Army wanted. Indeed, for Brevity the RAF was used pretty much as it had been under Longmore's stewardship.

The challenge for the Hurricanes would now be much greater than before. On 19 April, Bf 109Es had been encountered for the first time, claiming four Hurricanes for the loss of one Messerschmitt.[36] It was just one Luftwaffe fighter group with three squadrons but it transformed the balance of power in the air, just as the arrival of a handful of Hurricanes had done for the Commonwealth forces six months before. Now it was the Hurricanes that were struggling.

On 15 May, British forces began their advance. Rommel was indeed taken by surprise and his forces were soon falling back. The Blenheims bombed German motor transport and retreating columns, while Hurricanes dutifully patrolled above the advancing troops and communications to the rear. However, air opposition was slight, with just a brief clash with Bf 109s on the first day, and the Hurricanes were able to turn their attention to the retreating German forces.[37] Rommel, however, was quickly organizing counter-attacks, and after making some initial gains, including the key Halfaya Pass, the Commonwealth forces were halted and then flung back. On the second day of the battle, the fighters were back in action strafing enemy columns, this time to cover the retreating Allied forces. Tank losses were heavy and all the gains, apart from the Halfaya Pass,

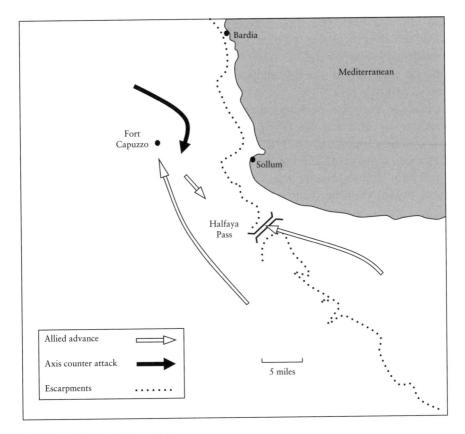

Operation Brevity May 1941

were lost. In just two days it was all over: Operation Brevity had indeed been brief.

Taking the initiative in the Western Desert was a gamble that had backfired. The need to support this attack inevitably deprived Crete of the air and ground reinforcements it desperately needed. Far from securing the western flank, Commonwealth forces on the ground had suffered heavily and German forces were threatening further advances. The captured Halfaya Pass was a useful springboard for future offensives and Wavell was determined not to lose this as well, but hanging on to it pinned down more forces.

Meanwhile, attempts to counter German raids on Crete were soon whittling down the meagre fighter resources. Freyberg made it abundantly clear to Wavell, and indeed his government in New Zealand, that resistance was impossible without effective air support. RAF losses during Brevity had been light, but with Rommel looking to recapture

135

the Halfaya Pass, the RAF was needed more in the Western Desert after the Brevity offensive than before. Tedder was in an impossible position. He simply did not have the resources to cover so many fronts, and he was well aware that dispersing what little he had would make the situation worse.[38]

Fighter resources on Crete were always far too limited to defeat the German air offensive. For the pilots flying the few available planes it was a torrid time. A handful of Hurricanes were flown in as reinforcements, but these were insufficient even to make good losses. This was a 'Battle of Britain' the Luftwaffe was going to win. However, this should not have meant that the RAF would have no role to play in the invasion. Grand ideas of establishing air superiority were not realistic, but the RAF was still capable of offering useful support to the defending forces.

Would RAF commanders rise to the challenge of supporting the troops in a situation of air inferiority? The omens were not good. The fighter Blenheims of No. 80 Squadron had already been pulled back to Egypt because they could play no part in the pre-invasion aerial battle. This was true, but if they were held back until the invasion, they might be able to shoot down Ju 52 transports and would certainly be capable of causing mayhem amongst the helpless paratroopers as they landed. This would be far easier from Crete than airfields in Egypt. In the Western Desert, Tedder had been quite happy for his fighters to strafe the enemy if there was no aerial opposition or if an emergency suddenly developed, to cover retreating forces. Planning to use your fighters in this way even before the battle begins was not something that came naturally to RAF commanders.

While the defenders awaited the invasion, Tedder's natural inclination was to use his air force to strike deep in the enemy rear. The only way he saw the Blenheims helping in the defence of Crete was low-flying attacks on enemy airfields. He brought in Wellingtons from Iraq and replaced them with Blenheims to increase his long-range capability and intensify attacks on the ports the Germans were using.[39] This was not what was required. As was the case in Greece, the further afield you go, the less immediate impact bombing can have. With the Luftwaffe swarming over Crete, bombing the airfields they were operating from seemed logical targets, but these raids did not usually achieve much. Shooting down a Ju 52 packed full of paratroopers was more useful than destroying an empty parked Ju 52 on a distant airfield. For Tedder and most RAF officers, bombing distant targets was what air forces were supposed to do; they were not supposed to attack targets a mile or two from troops fighting on the ground. That was the job of ground forces.

Far from flying in air reinforcements, Group Captain George Beamish, the commander of air units on the island, ordered a withdrawal to Egypt. Initially a couple of flights of Hurricanes stayed, but on 19 May, even these were withdrawn. Tedder fully supported the decision.[40] The air battle had been lost, so it was time to save the few surviving aircraft for the next battle. It was the mindset of commanders fighting their own independent air war. For the Army and Royal Navy, the battle was about to begin. As it turned out, the 19th was the day before the German invasion – unfortunate timing which did nothing for the RAF's reputation. Exactly one year before, a similar decision had been made to withdraw RAF units from France on the eve of the Arras counter-attack. History was repeating itself. Freyberg rather lamely accepted the decision as Gort had done a year ago in France. Although Churchill was still insisting that Crete had to be held at all costs, he too backed the decision. The prime minister was still not aware of how interlinked air and ground warfare was.

The only air support the island would get would have to come from Egypt, which for those like Churchill and many RAF commanders impressed with the long-range reach of air power was not seen as a problem. Indeed, the ability to operate from distant bases was the great advantage of air power. For the Germans, capturing the airfields was crucial if they were to take the island. Operating aircraft from them should have been just as crucial for the forces defending the island. However, the failure to appreciate how useful even limited close air-support might be meant there were no plans to make any use of them.

On 20 May, the invasion began with German airborne troops landing close to the airfield at Maleme early in the morning and later in the day at Heraklion and Retimo. A makeshift invasion fleet set sail for Crete to consolidate the ground captured by the paratroopers, but it was savaged by the Royal Navy, albeit at huge cost as German bombers sank two cruisers, four destroyers and damaged many more vessels. Nevertheless, the Navy had done its job. There would be no reinforcements arriving by sea. The German airborne troops would be on their own.

The early fighting on Crete suggested that the naval heroics might not be in vain. The air-drops did not go well; many of the troops landed in the wrong places, they were widely scattered and were often under fire long before they even reached the ground. The slow, low-flying Ju 52 transports were even more vulnerable than the seaborne transports the Royal Navy had destroyed. A few Marylands from No. 39 Squadron, flying from Egypt and using the bomber as a long-range fighter, claimed a couple of the Ju 52s, but much more could have been done from the airfields on the island. Initially the defences of the airfields held and the follow-up waves of Ju 52s found themselves having to land wherever they could. The island was soon strewn with wrecked planes. On the ground, German airborne forces suffered further heavy losses; even a handful of ground-attack planes operating from the besieged air bases could have only added to their problems.

Cretan civilians fearlessly took up any weapon that came to hand to take on the invader. No doubt had the Greek pilots on the island had any aircraft to fly, they would have been equally fearless. As it was, it was the German fighters and dive-bombers, operating from distant bases, that dominated the battlefield, strafing and dive-bombing the defenders. Nevertheless, at the end of the first day all the airfields were still in Allied hands. An unfortunate miscommunication between the forces holding Maleme led to an unnecessary withdrawal during the night, allowing the Germans to occupy the airfield the next day, but the other airfields remained in Allied hands throughout the campaign.

Counter-attacks to regain Maleme airfield faltered in the face of determined resistance on the ground and attack from the air. The capture of the airfield was the turning point. Ju 52s immediately started flying in reinforcements, even though the airfield was still under fire. On 23 May, a handful of Bf 109 fighters began operating from Maleme, enabling a more permanent fighter presence to be maintained. Unlike the RAF, the Luftwaffe was willing to use airfields that were only a few minutes' flying time away from the fighting.

It was only at this point that the RAF intervened in any strength. As the paratroopers descended on Crete, the focus of attention in Egypt was preventing Rommel from making any further progress. For the first three days the RAF attacked airfields and ports in Greece, but attacking such distant targets could not possibly influence the battle on Crete. It was 23 May before any substantial effort was made to directly support the defenders on Crete. Blenheims bombed and Hurricanes, using long-range tanks designed for ferrying rather than combat, strafed Maleme airfield, but by this time Crete's fate had been decided.[41]

Ironically, on the same day that the Luftwaffe moved it first fighters into the captured Maleme airfield, the RAF made a belated attempt to use the Heraklion base it had abandoned a few days before. The first attempt ended in failure as the six Hurricanes were scattered by friendly anti-aircraft fire, the gunners apparently not expecting any Allied planes in the area. One found the airfield but the other five headed back to Egypt. A second attempt saw six more Hurricanes land at the airfield. The aircraft were supposed to attack enemy forces at Maleme, but the local army commander insisted they be used to help his forces defend the airfield, much to the annoyance of the Air Ministry. In the official enquiry into the Allied defeat which followed, the Air Ministry, while conceding that in this particular situation it had made no difference, warned that such interference, without reference to any RAF commander, 'might jeopardise the outcome of an entire campaign'.[42]

One can understand the annoyance at having one's orders ignored, but it demonstrated that army commanders on the spot knew what they needed the aircraft to do. RAF indignation lost some of it potency as the failure to have any aircraft operating from the airfields on the island probably had jeopardized the outcome of this particular campaign. After a few sorties, the surviving Hurricanes flew back to Egypt.[43] It was the sort of improvised air intervention one might have expected from an attempt to occupy the island, rather than from those trying to defend it. On 25 May, the defenders of the Heraklion airfield were still reporting that it was serviceable and fuel stocks were available, but no more aircraft tried to use the airstrip.[44]

Instead of operating from Crete, aircraft tried to provide cover from Egypt. However, finding targets in Crete was much easier from airfields on the island than it was after a long sea crossing from bases in Egypt. Blenheims. Marylands, Beaufighters and long-range Hurricane did their best, but no more than thirty sorties a day were flown and in three days twenty planes were lost, a very high proportion of the available strength. It was for Tedder merely a question of flying the flag; Beamish had conceded defeat on the 19th when he decided to pull out. 'It will be said Crete was lost through lack of air support but it was lost through lack of secure bases,' he protested to Portal.[45] In fact the RAF had abandoned the bases before the invasion even began, and the failure to provide the ground forces with air support from those bases was one of the reasons the battle for Crete was lost. Cause and effect were getting confused.

The Fleet Air Arm did its best to assist. The aircraft carrier HMS *Formidable* set sail on 25 May from Alexandria with twelve Fulmars and fifteen Swordfish and Albacores on board to attack the Scarpanto airfield in the Dodecanese. Like all Royal Navy aircraft carriers, the planes it carried were not capable of competing with any land-based planes they might meet. Fortunately, a dawn attack on 26 May achieved complete surprise. Four Albacores bombed and four escorting Fulmars strafed the Ju 87 and Fiat CR.42s lined up on the airfield, destroying one and damaging nine aircraft, without loss. *Formidable* was able to make its escape, but when it seemed to have reached safety it had the misfortune to cross the path of a Ju 87 operating from North Africa. The Stuka attacked and inflicted severe damage. The carrier limped back to Alexandria and out of the war for six months. The entire venture seemed far riskier than operating a few aircraft from besieged airstrips on Crete.

As late as 27 May, Churchill was insisting that the battle was a turning point in the war and Wavell was ordered to throw everything into it, but the game was already up. The defensive lines were beginning to collapse. Wavell told Churchill that 'the continuous and unopposed air attack' would force even the stoutest troops to give ground. Crete was no longer tenable and the surviving forces were ordered to battle their way to the south coast, where the Royal Navy would once more be called upon to rescue as many as possible.[46] The invading German forces had suffered enormous losses and had come perilously close to being routed. It was here in Crete that there had been the opportunity for the stunning victory Churchill wanted, not against Rommel in the Western Desert. Defeating the German invasion of Crete would have done much to undo the damage the Greek defeat had inflicted, just as the Battle of Britain had helped bury the memory of Dunkirk.

Instead, it was yet another ignominious defeat. More worryingly, it was a reminder of what might still happen to the defenders of another much larger island off mainland Europe if they too had to battle an invasion without any close air-support. The enquiry that followed the defeat gave the War Office the opportunity to vent its frustration:

> 'Until the power of the air arm as a weapon of close support on the battlefield is fully appreciated and exploited, the army will continue to labour under a severe handicap and will be prevented from developing its full force either in attack or defence. German methods must be seriously studied and applied.'[47]

Up to this point, it had been a UK problem. The War Office was broadly correct in believing the attitude to air support in Greece and Crete was more influenced by Air Ministry thinking than was the case elsewhere in the region. The scale of the German intervention in Greece may have been impressive, but in method it involved nothing that Middle East Command had not tried on a much smaller scale. In the Western Desert and in East Africa, beyond the reach of the theorists in the Air Ministry, effective close air-support had begun to emerge. In the Middle East, it was not the method that was at fault, it was the material that was available to apply the method. Engaged only by less well-equipped and led Italian forces, the inadequacy of the available air resources had not been so obvious. In deciding how these limited resources should be used, common sense had prevailed over dogma and the available aircraft had been used in the most practicable and useful fashion. In Africa, army and air force had been working closely together, without any need to refer to German methods.

The progress made, however, was undone by events in Greece and Crete. The fault lines had perhaps always been there, but Longmore was enough of an inter-service man to make it work. He had always been sympathetic to Army requirements, and with good will on both sides differences of outlook had been overcome. The far more well-equipped Luftwaffe had exposed the chronic shortage of aircraft and lack of quality. The façade of Commonwealth air strength and with it army/air force unity had disintegrated. The breakdown in air/army relations was even more acrimonious than the collapse in confidence that followed Dunkirk. This time there was no Fighter Command close at hand to distract attention from the controversy with a glorious victory. Indeed, this time the fact that the plentiful but underused resources of Fighter Command were over 1,000 miles away simply added to the controversy.

Nor was there any Longmore to try to restore a degree of unity. Longmore had established a reputation for his less than diplomatic approach when dealing with his masters in Whitehall, but had provided Wavell with the air support he needed. Tedder was not a natural advocate of battlefield air support; while working in the Air Ministry, he had vigorously argued against the specialist close-support bombers the War Office wanted.[48] Nor was he likely to question Air Ministry policy. Tedder believed it was his duty to defend the Air Ministry and would show complete loyalty to his superiors in London, even if that meant a few harsh exchanges with his counterparts from the Army and Royal Navy.

In Egypt the mood was ugly. At every level from the lowest rank to high command, the ill-feeling between Army and RAF personnel was very apparent. The RAF was the object of bitter ridicule. As 'Rare As Fairies' was one re-interpretation of RAF; the 'Royal Absent Force' was another, although the earthier alternative for the 'A' perhaps gave a truer idea of the depth of resentment. Soldiers freely vented their bitterness, resentment and hostility on anyone in air force blue, verbally and on occasions physically. Feelings were every bit as intense at higher levels of command.

A tired, worn-down Wavell reported to London that the defeat in Greece and Crete was due to a lack of air support. He did not do this with bitterness or rancour; it was just a straightforward statement of fact. The obvious lack of air support might have concealed more fundamental weaknesses in Army strategy, tactics and training, but to claim air support in Greece and Crete had been lacking was scarcely controversial. Tedder, however, was furious when he discovered what Wavell had told London. Tedder, like Portal and the Air Staff, was still in denial about how the war was being fought and how far off-beam Air Staff thinking was. They all felt it was the Army that was getting it wrong. Tedder believed there was a 'grave danger that incorrect conclusions may be drawn from these operations and one of the fundamental principles of air operations be obscured or forgotten', and he promised Portal that he would continue to try to 'educate' Wavell and the Army about what these principles were.[49] It was not an approach that was likely to heal wounds.

In private, Tedder fully understood why there was so much bitterness within the Army and Royal Navy on the air-support issue, and was largely right that little more could have been done with the resources available.[50] The evacuation of the RAF the day before the invasion of Crete was very unfortunate, but in Greece the limited resources that were available could not have been employed any more effectively. If Tedder had simply said the RAF lacked the strength to do any more, he and his force would perhaps have won more sympathy. Instead, he blamed the Army for the problems. It was the fault of ground forces not protecting RAF bases. The RAF could not possibly be expected to operate without airfields, he insisted. The RAF had failed in Greece not because it only had 150 largely second-rate aircraft and lacked the means to support the Army or prevent the Luftwaffe from supporting German ground forces; it failed because Allied soldiers had failed to hold the airfields in the Larissa plain.

Possession of airfields was the aim. As far as Tedder was concerned, the Army's role was to ensure the RAF had the bases from which it could determine the outcome of battles and ultimately the war. In the struggle for Crete, the Germans and Italians had dominated the battle area because they had possessed aerodromes in the Dodecanese and Greece. 'This campaign is primarily a battle for aerodromes,' Tedder proclaimed.[51] He warned Wavell that the troops encircled in Tobruk would be similarly dealt with by the Luftwaffe unless the Army won airfields for the RAF in eastern Cyrenaica. It was an air-orientated strategy from an RAF used to thinking independently. As far as Tedder was concerned, the aim was not to relieve Tobruk; the aim was to gain airfields within range of Tobruk. Emerging from the shadows was Trenchard's RAF, where everything revolved around the needs of the air force. The RAF was not there to serve the Army; the Army was there to serve the RAF. Each Army advance would win the RAF the bases it needed to further its aims. It was an air force-centric view of how the war would be won.

Admiral Cunningham, naval commander in the Mediterranean, was more forthright than Wavell in his dealings with Tedder. The lack of protection the Navy had received was unacceptable, he said. The only solution, the naval chief insisted, was for the Navy to have its own 'Coastal Command'. Tedder had absolutely no sympathy with the Navy. As far as he was concerned, they had brought their problems on their own heads, for denying air power made sea power irrelevant. The Admiralty had indeed underestimated the importance of air power, and this had disastrous consequences in the Norwegian campaign. The Royal Navy would continue to be vulnerable as long as the best aircraft aboard its carriers were Albacores and Fulmars. However, the defence of Crete had hardly suggested the naval surface vessels had been made obsolete by the aircraft. It was Royal Navy warships that had turned back the seaborne invasion of Crete, not the RAF. All the Navy wanted was for the RAF to keep the Luftwaffe off their backs while they did their job. 'They should worry more about their shortage of light craft and submarines before they worry about long-range fighters,' was Tedder's advice.[52]

Vice-Chief of Air Staff Freeman commiserated with Tedder on his problems with Cunningham. It was the same on the home front, he complained. Air force operations in support of the Royal Navy seemed to bring precious little reward. Long-range fighter patrols had flown 1,200 hours for just one enemy aircraft shot down, he lamented. RAF commanders again found it difficult to see beyond the narrow air war. Freeman was measuring Coastal Command success by how many enemy planes were shot down, when it was how many ships that were saved that counted. Freeman had Air Marshal Philip Joubert de la Ferté, who was just taking over command of Coastal Command, investigating 'all the operations of his command, to discover which, if any are profitable'.[53] It was not surprising that the Admiralty wanted more control. Cunningham would eventually get his 'Coastal Command', although the Air Ministry would not agree to such a title. No. 201 General Reconnaissance Group would become No. 201 Naval Co-operation Group in October 1941, which put naval tactical air support on an equal footing with army tactical air support (No. 204 Group) and long-range bombing (No. 205 Group).

Louis Mountbatten, who had been aboard one of the destroyers that had been sunk by air attack, also laid into Tedder on army/air as well as naval/air co-operation. If the RAF carried on like this, he insisted, the Army and Royal Navy would both need to have their own air arms.[54] In Mountbatten's view, the RAF in its present form was simply not up to the task. The Germans had demonstrated how it should be done. They had moved their air units forward swiftly to bases close to the front, and from there they provided their army with close support on the battlefield on request. Tedder countered by pointing out that Britain did not have a large fleet of transport planes, it did not have the communications systems to enable the Army to call in close support and it did not have the air superiority such operations required. The obvious question was why Britain was fighting a war without transport planes, close air-support communication systems and the means to establish air superiority. Perhaps more pertinently, what had the Air Ministry done to rectify these faults in the first two years of war?

It was an issue being taken up at an even higher level. It was not just Freyberg who was letting Commonwealth governments know about how disgruntled he and his troops were about the lack of air support. General Thomas Blamey, who had commanded Australian forces in Greece, was keeping his government informed and advocating an army-controlled Air Corps to make sure the troops got the air support they needed. He wanted his government to get assurances that in future Commonwealth forces would match the 'unity of action' the German air and ground forces possessed.[55] The Australian government did indeed make known these concerns, and to make matters worse for Churchill, they had been leaked to the Australian press.[56] The New Zealand ambassador was complaining about the lack of air support in Greece and Crete, and South Africa's Smuts was joining in the chorus of discontent, with his talk of aircraft being unnecessarily hoarded in the UK.[57] It was becoming a political as well as a military issue.

Portal kept Tedder informed about the numerous reports emanating from the Middle East that painted an unfavourable picture of the RAF. The British ambassador in Cairo was expressing his serious concern at the lack of air support Commonwealth forces had received in Greece and Crete, and, by chance, the New Zealand Prime Minister was in Cairo at the time to hear these concerns.[58] The American Ambassador was apparently sending reports back to the United States of the rampant discontent among Australian and New Zealand forces and low morale among RAF personnel because of the poor equipment they had to fly in combat. Tedder had to scurry around Cairo trying to put right these misunderstandings.[59] There was a lot of 'educating' to do.

Tedder did his best to play down German superiority. He noted that the Stukas actually caused relatively little physical damage and were extremely vulnerable. Hurricanes, Tomahawks and Martlets were perfectly capable of dealing with Ju 87s and their escorts, Tedder confidently informed Portal.[60] This might have been true for the Stukas, but not quite so true for the escorts. Tedder was quite right that the Ju 87 was vulnerable. The problem was that the Air Ministry had been pointing this out ever since the stunning success these bombers had achieved in Poland in September 1939, but, if it was so obviously vulnerable, why was it still succeeding? The RAF might well be right that they did not inflict much physical damage – its bark was probably not as fearsome as its bite, as Slessor put it – but this seemed to be missing the point. It worked: terrorize your enemy and you are well on the way to winning the battle.

Perhaps the Stuka had no right to be successful, but unless the Allies deployed sufficient fighters to prevent the Luftwaffe using it, the Stuka would carry on terrorising frontline troops and the German Army would continue to take advantage. The Germans were merely demonstrating that low-performance aircraft could be extremely effective in short-range tactical air support if the enemy allowed them to be. Tedder should have been arguing that the RAF needed a lot more fighters to make sure the Germans could not use the Ju 87. Instead, he told London that all the troops he had spoken to were not in the least bit bothered by the Stuka' its efforts to terrorise just provided them with 'harmless amusement'.[61] Tedder was telling the Air Ministry what it wanted to hear. It was not what everyone else in the Middle East was hearing.

Tedder's assessment that low-level strafing attacks by fighters had been far more effective than dive-bombing was correct. By the spring of 1941, the War Office was thinking along similar lines.[62] As a tactical weapon, the fighter had the enormous advantage that it could look after itself – a very useful capability if an air force did not have enough fighters to provide protection. For the same reason, fighters were also taking on the tactical reconnaissance role. The problem was that the fewer fighters there were to establish air superiority, the more they were needed to fill other roles. It was a vicious circle which only a dramatic increase in fighter deliveries could resolve.

The lack of fighter cover was the biggest cause of bitterness. Troops found attack from the air a greater strain than ground fire. The individual soldier always felt the dive-bomber or strafing fighter was targeting him personally in a way conventional ground-based fire did not. Clearly more fighters would have helped, but the RAF was right in insisting that they were not the only means of beating off dive-bombers. Unfortunately, the barriers and arbitrary divisions that separated the British armed services tended to encourage all three to see problems as the fault of a sister service. The soldier's sense of helplessness was heightened by the feeling that air defence was not his responsibility.

It was a way of thinking that the Air Ministry had unintentionally encouraged by insisting all matters related to the air were its concern. If troops were fired on by machine guns or artillery, it was an Army problem, but if troops were bombed or strafed, it was the Air Force's fault and something the Air Force should deal with. The RAF had managed to burden itself with responsibility for problems that it could and should not have been held entirely responsible for. Fighters could help defend armies, but the final line of defence always had to be anti-aircraft fire and, if the enemy was flying low enough, any automatic weapons to hand, as so many low-flying RAF crews had found to their cost. The Army had to take more responsibility for its own defence and play its part in defeating the Stuka.

Similarly, the Air Force had to take some responsibility for the defence of airfields, not just with the aircraft it flew but with ground personnel. Tedder had made airfield defence a huge issue, and with the advent of airborne troops, however far behind the frontline airfields were, there was always a chance they could come under attack. In Crete, the evacuation of the remaining RAF planes had left a large number of ground personnel with no aircraft to service. When the German paratroopers arrived, the ground crews were hurriedly formed into units to help defend the airfields. It was not a task they were prepared for and, pitted against battle-hardened elite German paratroopers, what followed was often a very one-sided battle.

Servicing aircraft had always been considered a non-combat role; ground crews were not trained to fight.[63] Again the artificial barriers that separated Air Force and Army roles were at the root of the problem; as far as the RAF was concerned, defence of airfields was an Army problem. When Wavell signalled Tedder about the 'deplorable' lack of air support, Tedder retaliated by signalling back that his comments were frankly unhelpful, especially as he and Collishaw were not complaining about the 'deplorable shortage of the defence of our airfields'.[64] Churchill was not sympathetic. He was appalled when he discovered how many able-bodied men were tied up in Air Force support services and had no intention of letting airfields 'become the abode of uniformed civilians in the prime of life protected by detachments of soldiers'.[65] In future all ground crew were to be regularly drilled and become proficient in the use of arms. If the scenes in Crete were repeated in Britain, ground crews would be expected to defend their airfield, to the death if necessary, Churchill insisted with characteristic melodrama.

The defeats in Greece and Crete shook the system in a way the defeat in France did not. After that defeat, things had rapidly returned to normal for the Air Staff. Britain once again had no ground commitment on the continent and the absence of any other way of winning the war increased the need for the Air Staff's independent bombing strategy. Any fighting in the Middle East with Italian forces could be quietly forgotten about, especially when the Army appeared to be getting by with the minimum of air support. This all changed with the arrival of German forces. Commonwealth troops now had to contend with the Wehrmacht, and once again they were being trounced. The air support that German forces received was perhaps not the most important reason for German success, but it was the most striking feature. Army/air co-operation was back in the public spotlight once more. The knives were out for the RAF and Churchill was beginning to take a closer interest in the whole army air-support issue.

Chapter 8

The War Office Strikes Back

Churchill had never seen the development of tactical air support as an issue that required any special attention. His ideas on air warfare never got much beyond believing the bomber had almost unlimited powers of destruction. When Greece needed help, Churchill sent Wellingtons – there was an almost mystical belief in the ability of the heavy bomber to exert an influence over an entire region. For Churchill, bombers were bombers, an oversimplification the Air Staff was quite happy to encourage and indeed, to a large extent, subscribed to itself. The Army had the least important role to play in this war, and Churchill was not even aware that the type of bomber the Army required was an issue.

This began to change after the Greek fiasco. The ease with which the Germans had flung the Allies out of Greece stunned Churchill and the War Office. The panzer and Stuka were no longer a surprise, and the Greek terrain should have made it reasonably easy ground to defend. Such a comprehensive and rapid collapse had not been expected. Far from tying up German forces on a Balkan front, the threat to the German southern flank had been dismissed with contemptuous ease, leaving Hitler free to strike wherever he wanted. An invasion of the United Kingdom might only be weeks away.

Brooke had spent the winter well. He still only had three armoured divisions, and not the six he wanted to feel confident about defeating an invasion, but the regular Army and Home Guard were now much better trained. On the ground, progress had been made. In the air, however, it seemed to Brooke that nothing had improved. Indeed, things seemed to be going backwards. Goddard, the Director of Military Co-operation, was supposed to be liaising with War Office chiefs over their air requirements, but he seemed to be taking a particularly hard line. He refused to believe that there could be circumstances where bombers might support troops on the battlefield. He was prepared to do some preliminary development of the communication systems that close air-support might require, but he believed that there was no point in involving actual squadrons in exercises as the crews would probably soon be lost on normal missions.[1]

In private, Goddard was even less sympathetic. He moaned about the War Office obsession with the dive-bomber or any 'small bomber', the two invariably being lumped together. Their supposed advantage was that they were more manoeuvrable at low level, but flak defences made such an approach impossible, Goddard insisted; so, with low-level ruled out, 'It follows that the fast heavy bomber will be as good or even better than light bombers for any form of support.'[2] Large heavy bombers were all that was needed for any role, he believed, and that now meant Stirlings, Halifaxes and Lancasters.

Portal spoke confidently of how his bomber fleet was much better prepared to strike ports where any invasion fleet might be gathering, and Peirse claimed he was prepared to use his bombers by day, but Bomber Command was by this time a specialist night bomber force. Losses in combat meant there were now few crews with the necessary experience in formation flying required by daylight operations. Only No. 2 Group was trained to operate by day, and this group still had nothing better than the Blenheim and was in serious decline as a force. By the summer of 1941 it was down from a peak of thirteen squadrons the previous summer to just half a dozen.

Army co-operation squadrons were even less well prepared for an invasion. There were not enough for all corps and armoured divisions to have one, and those that existed had just eight planes each. Apart from three squadrons of Tomahawks, Army Co-operation Command was still relying on the Lysander and these were still expected to provide close air-support as well as reconnaissance. Most Lysander squadrons had half their machines capable of mounting 20mm cannon, but there was growing doubt about the value of this weapon. The armour-piercing shells that were becoming available were unreliable and ball ammunition restricted penetration to 30mm, which was not enough to pierce the heavier Panzer III and IV. It took five-and-a-half hours to fit the cannon and, it was argued, with the British Army now far better equipped with anti-tank guns than it had been in the summer of 1940, it was an emergency measure that was no longer required. It was an argument which rather summed up the Air Ministry attitude to any such support. The better equipped the Army was, the less air support it would need. If the Lysanders were needed for army support, they could still carry bombs.[3] Whatever armament the Lysander carried, as the spearhead of Britain's close-support bomber force, it hardly inspired confidence.

Rommel's advance in North Africa began to change things. The way German tanks were once more ripping through Allied armies in the Western Desert alarmed Portal. He believed the ground forces were not mobile enough to deal with tanks, it was too easy for them to go round defensive positions – especially in the desert of Libya – and he took on the responsibility for doing something about it: 'The need is obvious and extremely urgent. If the Army cannot stop the German armoured fighting vehicles, then we must.'[4] It was a strident call for action that demonstrated that Portal was well aware of how much the air force could contribute tactically. Nevertheless, there was still an element of the RAF stepping in to save the day once the Army had failed, rather than an attempt to see how the two services could work together to deal with the panzer threat.

Initially it was the panzer threat in the Middle East that was worrying Portal, but Beaverbrook was soon persuading him he should be more worried about the home front. Beaverbrook did not want any more 20mm cannon-armed planes to go to the Middle East; dealing with a possible invasion of the UK had to come first, and Portal agreed. With a large number of cannon-armed Hurricane IIs and Beaufighters in service, the availability of armour-piercing shells would provide an immediate and potentially powerful anti-tank force, especially against the light and medium tanks that would probably be the first to land.[5] An improved shell was about to enter production, but even without these, Portal was quite right in believing the Hispano Suiza cannon was a very useful ground-strafing weapon.

Not everyone was so enthusiastic about using cannon-armed planes for ground attack. Sholto Douglas at Fighter Command was far from pleased about the prospect of losing his night-fighter force, even during a temporary crisis an invasion would create.[6] The worst of the Blitz was over. Britain had come through the experience battered but unbowed. The German bombing had not even come close to defeating the nation. Yet for many the bomber was still thought a greater danger than an invasion. 'We shall be exposing ourselves to a knock-out blow which the enemy will not hesitate to deliver the moment he feels he has got us weak enough,' Douglas warned.[7]

As German panzers raced through Greece, Portal became even more anxious to develop a weapon that could stop them. The 20mm cannon could not penetrate heavy armour and Portal felt only a 40mm weapon would do. By good fortune, Vickers and Rolls-Royce had been developing such a weapon for the next generation of bomber interceptors, and Beaverbrook suggested they could be used as anti-tank weapons. Portal agreed and thought the Beaufighter might be a suitable carrier. Portal initially saw the weapon as being particularly useful in the open plains of the Libyan desert, but Beaverbrook again reminded him of the danger of invasion. With Allied forces in Greece in headlong retreat, Portal agreed that the weapon might be needed to prevent similar scenes occurring on British soil. 'Days or even hours may count,' he warned.[8]

Trials with a Beaufighter armed with a Rolls-Royce 40mm cannon were not a great success. The Beaufighter was not manoeuvrable enough and the weapon was not very penetrative. A single-seater fighter seemed better and the Hurricane seemed ideal. The project was given top priority, but the Vickers cannon would not be available until the autumn.[9] It was all rather strange. The War Office had caved in to Air Ministry pressure to give the strategic bomber priority, but it was the Air Ministry that was leading the way in the development of a tactical anti-tank aircraft.[10]

On 1 May 1941, Beaverbrook took on the greater responsibilities of the Ministry of Supply and his place was taken at the Ministry of Aircraft Production by John Moore-Brabazon. Beaverbrook had championed the Army cause in 1940, but after ordering hundreds of dive-bombers, had not done much more to help the War Office. The Air Ministry viewed his successor, Moore-Brabazon, as a more dangerous foe. In the winter of 1939/40, he had proposed building large numbers of cheap, expendable army-support planes and had even come up with a design of his own.[11] His appointment as Minister of Aircraft Production now caused unease in Air Ministry circles. Freeman hoped he had now been 'cured of his thousands of hedge-hopping army co-operation planes'.[12]

Portal was soon making sure any possible problems were nipped in the bud by sending the new minister a reminder of Air Ministry priorities. Portal explained how the Air Staff was generally against any specialist types, although there were exceptions for the all-important strategic air war. A specialist high-altitude long-range bomber and high-altitude interceptor, both with pressurized cabins, were needed, and both these were being developed. There was also a need for a specialist night fighter, a specification for which the Air Ministry hoped to get to the MAP in the next few weeks. There was, however, no need to develop any specialist bombers to support the

Army; Army support was a normal mission for the bombers already being delivered to Bomber Command. If something more specialist were ever required, there would always be the American Bermuda and Vengeance dive-bombers.[13]

Tizard, now working for the Ministry of Aircraft production, thought Portal was focusing too much on strategic air warfare at the expense of tactical ways of using airpower. It did not seem unreasonable to assume that one day the Allies would have the air superiority the Germans now had, and would thus be able to use low-performance ground attack planes just as the Germans were using the Stuka. It would take two years to develop such a plane, but by this time the war might look very different. Land operations might be playing a far more important part in the conflict, and Portal's and the government's strategic bombing strategy might no longer be the best way of winning the war.[14] The status quo was being challenged.

These ideas were very much in tune with Moore-Brabazon's, and the new minister was soon making his presence felt. He was none too impressed with War Office efforts in developing close air-support. He wrote a note to the Secretary of State for War, David Margesson, in which he was highly critical of the Air Ministry for focusing entirely on long-range bombers and short-range interceptors, but also chided the War Office for not doing anything about it. Nor had the War Office done anything to push the development of dive-bombers or mounting of 40mm anti-tank cannon on aircraft. All the initiatives seemed to be coming from the Ministry of Aircraft Production. Moore-Brabazon enclosed a copy of a letter from Tizard, describing how aircraft carrying 40mm anti-tank guns might effectively make the tank obsolete, and that instead of trying to build bigger and better tanks, Britain would do better to focus on making best use of this new weapon. Tizard also mentioned the Bell Airacobra, one of the fighters ordered from the United States and due to arrive soon, which had a built-in 37mm cannon firing through the airscrew hub that could fire armour-piercing shells. There were plenty of possibilities. The MAP had the power to order any appropriate development, Moore-Brabazon insisted. He was just waiting for the War Office to request some action.[15]

On 3 May, an emboldened Brooke went on to the offensive, launching a stinging denouncement of Air Staff policy and attitude. The needs of Bomber, Fighter and Coastal Command had prevented him from speaking out earlier, Brooke explained rather apologetically, but he could not hold back any longer. He expressed his great frustration at the slow development of army air support. The Wann-Woodall trials

The fearsome-looking but rather bulky Hawker Tornado (above) and Hawker Typhoon (below). Both were designed to intercept unescorted bombers, so there was no need for pilots to worry about their rear. Only later did the Typhoon get a bubble canopy. (*Crown*)

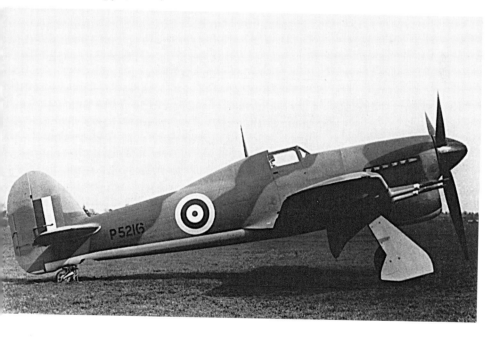

The Spitfire III with clipped wings. With its Merlin XX engine, it was by far the best fighter available for production in 1940. (*Crown*)

The Hurricane II. The less-advanced Hurricane airframe was in more need of the extra power the Merlin XX provided. The four-cannon armament was excessive for air combat and reduced performance, but made the fighter ideal for the ground attack role. (*Crown*)

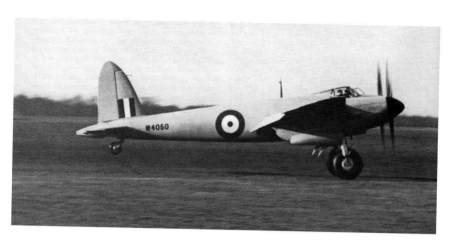

Three more aircraft that needed the power of the Merlin XX: (top) the de Havilland Mosquito prototype, (middle) the Bristol Beaufighter II and (bottom) the Boulton Paul Defiant II. (*Crown*)

High altitude bombing was thought to be the next big danger. Britain's contender for the role, the Vickers Wellington VI (above), had a pressurized cabin for the crew. (*Crown*)

The Westland Welkin, with its high-aspect ratio wings, was designed to deal with high-altitude bombers. (*Crown*)

Development of the jet-powered fighter was accelerated to deal with the German high-altitude bomber menace. The E.8/39 Gloster Whittle 1 demonstrator (above) and the Gloster Meteor (below), the fully developed fighter. (*Crown*)

The Bisley/Blenheim V was originally a specialist armoured low-level attack bomber with solid nose (above), but eventually emerged as a medium bomber (below). (*Crown*)

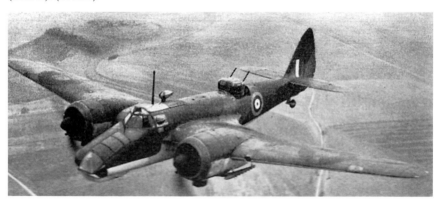

The Bristol Buckingham was the next generation of close-support bomber. With dorsal turret and ventral gun position, it was a large plane for low-level attack. (*Crown*)

The War Office wanted smaller, more manoeuvrable planes, so the Vultee Vengeance (above) and Brewster Bermuda (below) were ordered from the United States. (*Crown*)

The mighty Short Stirling was expected to lead the bomber offensive. (*Crown*)

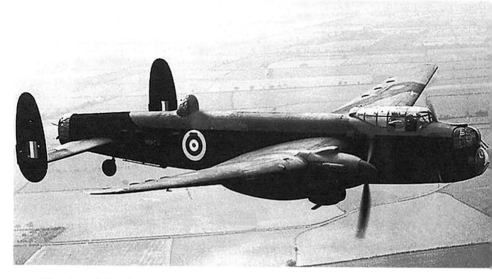

The Avro Manchester – forerunner of the Lancaster – was the second of the heavies to join the bomber offensive. (*Crown*)

The Handley Page Halifax was the third of the new heavies to enter service. It was another plane that was powered by the Merlin XX. (*Crown*)

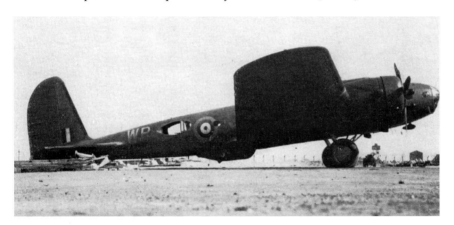

The Flying Fortress was tried as a high-altitude bomber. Its open gun positions made life very difficult for the crew. (*Crown*)

The Consolidated B-24 Liberator. Most, like this one, were used by Coastal Command for anti-submarine patrols in the mid-Atlantic. (*Crown*)

The Gloster Gladiator remained a frontline fighter in the Middle East well into 1941. (*Crown*)

The Curtiss Mohawk should have provided a far more modern immediate replacement, but only a handful ever reached the front. (*Crown*)

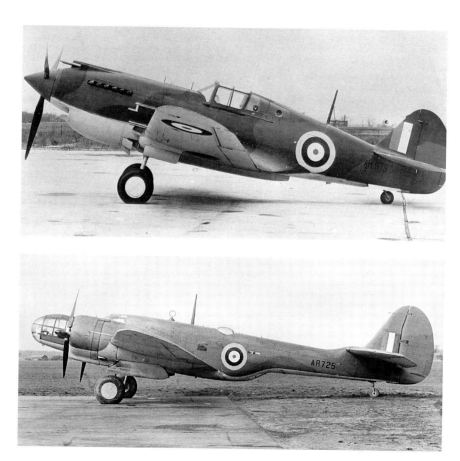

Other American planes that were slow to reach the front included the Curtiss Tomahawk (top), Martin Maryland (middle) and Douglas Boston (bottom).

Greek pilots had to soldier on with obsolete fighters like the Polish PZL P.24 (above). The Grumman F4F Wildcat (below) was ordered from the United States but ended up in the Fleet Air Arm. (*Crown*)

Hawker Hart trainers were used in action in the defence of Habbaniya air base in Iraq. The Air Ministry also thought they would make ideal dive-bombers if Britain was invaded. (*Crown*)

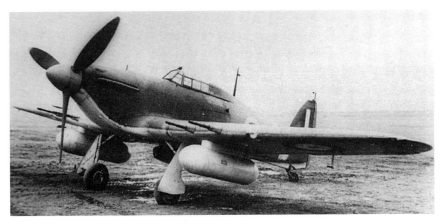

A Hurricane II with 40-gallon ferry tanks. These were used on missions to extend the range of the fighter. (*Crown*)

Either with bombs (above) or rockets (below), the Hurricane II made a versatile ground attack fighter. (*Crown via T. Buttler*)

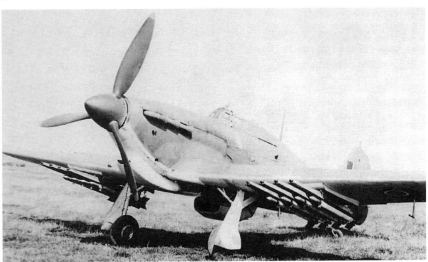

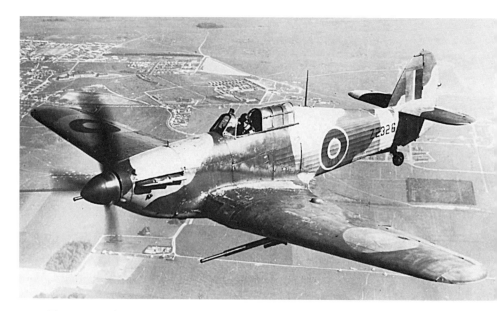

The anti-tank Hurricane II with 40mm cannons. (*Crown*)

The Vickers 40mm cannon. (*Crown*)

RAF airmen having their first look at the American Bell Airacobra, which had the engine behind the cockpit. It was an excellent ground attack fighter, but after equipping one squadron, Britain sent its allocation to the Soviet Union. (*Crown*)

A Hurricane II of No. 151 Wing operating from Murmansk. (*Crown*)

Fleet Air Arm Swordfish (above) and Albacores (below) were used for nocturnal tactical bombing in the Western Desert. (*Crown*)

The naval Fairey Fulmar, developed from the Fairey P.4/34 bomber, was not a success. (*Crown*)

in Northern Ireland had been given the go ahead the previous August and the Cabinet had declared close support was an RAF role. The Air Ministry had also agreed that close support would be required to defeat an invasion, but no suitable plane had been developed. The only support could come from No 2 Group and this now only had five squadrons, he claimed. Instead of 500 training sorties in the close-support technique planned for the group, only forty had taken place, and now the entire training programme had been suspended. It had been agreed that three army-co-operation squadrons should get the Tomahawk and the rest the Blenheim as interim equipment, but there were no plans for anything to replace the Blenheim with something more suitable, and even the interim Blenheim part of the deal seemed to have fallen through. Army air co-operation had gone backwards, Brooke insisted.[16]

Brooke wanted the Lysanders replaced by Tomahawks and Blenheims as soon as possible. Looking further ahead, he wanted sixty reconnaissance and close-support squadrons for the planned fifteen armoured divisions, and a suitable close-support bomber, preferably one with a dive-bombing capability.[17] Brooke was also fast coming round to the view that the only way the Army would get the Air Force it required would be to create its own Army Air Force, however inefficient that might be in terms of duplicating resources. The War Office, stung by the criticisms of inaction, joined the offensive. Brooke had only mentioned armoured divisions, but once the air support for twenty non-mechanized units had been added, the figure required rose to some eighty squadrons. With twelve aircraft each, this was nearly 1,000 planes. At a time when Bomber Command was supposed to be aiming for 4,000 planes in 260 squadrons, but had a mere forty-two squadrons, the War Office was well aware of the enormity of its demand. The War Office made it clear that it understood there was no question of these demands being met immediately, but there had to be plans in place for a future time when the planes and pilots existed for such a force.[18]

The Air Ministry had a collective fit at the sort of air resources the War Office was expecting. It disputed the claim that the Air Ministry had ever committed the RAF to a close air-support role in an invasion scenario. Barratt was given the task of checking back through all the minutes of the relevant meetings. When this clearly showed these commitments had indeed been made, a desperate Goddard attempted to reinterpret the relevant minutes. A reference Eden had made, for example, to the RAF's commitment to provide close air-support had been referring to 'when the Army takes the field', which, Goddard insisted, obviously meant when the Army fought overseas, not on British soil. If the training No. 2 Group had undertaken in early 1941 had been used to prepare crews for counter-invasion operations, that was only because Barratt had taken it upon himself to ignore instructions to prepare the squadrons for close support overseas. Goddard's crowning argument was that all the top positions in the Air Ministry had changed since any commitments made in the summer of 1940, and views on close air-support were different now. The present incumbents could not be held responsible for commitments made by their predecessors. An infuriated Barratt accused Goddard of attempting to rewrite history.[19]

As far as Goddard was concerned, the problem was Barratt. He blamed the Army Co-operation commander for allowing Brooke to come to the conclusion that the Air Ministry had shown bad faith in its efforts to meet Army requirements. He told Freeman he had 'had enough' of the man. Barratt, he claimed, appeared to resent Goddard's own co-ordinating position, the responsibility for operational matters that came with Freeman's position and the right of the Air Ministry Plans department to develop policy. Barratt had been perfectly placed to present to Brooke all the Air Ministry arguments for focusing on the strategic air offensive, but had failed to make any effort to do so. Goddard bluntly told Barratt that it was his attitude that was causing problems.[20] Freeman coldly informed Barratt that his role had only ever been intended for training purposes, and if invasion came he would immediately cease to be the commander of the Army Co-operation Command as 'there would be no need to deal with Air Staff policy', which was clearly seen as Barratt's weak point.[21]

Slessor, who had just returned from the United States and was about to take over No. 5 Group from Air Vice-Marshal Norman Bottomley, had his typically forthright say. He could not believe such ill-conceived ideas had emerged once more in his absence, and unleashed his frustration and fury in a remarkable outburst. Moore-Brabazon's ideas with his 'flying infantryman' concept (a reference to his 1939 proposal for a close support plane powered by a pusher engine behind the cockpit) were 'nothing short of fantastic'.[22] Once again Slessor insisted the aircraft was not a battlefield weapon. The Luftwaffe had only had success with close air-support because it had always possessed overwhelming air superiority, it had bombers in enormous numbers and opposing anti-aircraft fire had been minimal. If, in the winter of 1939/40, Slessor went on, so much time had not been wasted on the Army air support issue, and Moore-Brabazon's 'flying infantryman' in particular, the General Staff might have been less surprised by the invasion of Norway and the collapse of France. It was the Army's responsibility to destroy tanks, not the Air Force's. In the event of an invasion, the infantryman with his 'Molotov Cocktail or whatever the latest anti-tank bomb is called' was perfectly capable of dealing with the tank. It would be a complete waste of time having aircraft scouring the Kent countryside for enemy armour, Slessor insisted, perhaps not realizing that this was pretty much what his RAF chief was proposing with his anti-tank 40mm cannon-armed planes. If the Army could not stop individual tanks, then let them go on, Slessor continued. They might do a bit of damage while their fuel and ammunition lasted, but without petrol they were so much junk. Once the crew got out, as they would have to eventually to refuel, eat or sleep, then conveniently placed infantrymen could eliminate the crews with their rifles, Slessor explained.[23] So much for Moore-Brabazon's 'fantastic' ideas.

As far as the Middle East was concerned, Slessor recommended hitting the supply ports of Tripoli and Benghazi rather than shooting up tanks at the front. Slessor was on much more secure ground with this assessment. However, he grossly overstated the case by claiming that attacks on ports alone could be decisive. If the RAF had been employed correctly, he argued, the tanks the Army now wanted destroyed would never have got to the front in the first place. Close air-support could only be justified in an emergency, but the emergency would never arise if air power was used properly, he concluded triumphantly.[24]

It was pure 1920s Trenchardism. Air power used properly would do more than ensure victory on the battlefield, it would make it impossible for armies to fight battles. If this argument were to be true anywhere, it was in the Middle East, where Axis lines of communications were especially vulnerable, with Malta straddling Axis shipping routes to North Africa. However, despite Slessor's claims, even here air power could not win the battle alone. It could not stop every tank getting to the frontline. A land battle would ultimately have to be fought, and without adequate air power at the front it would be lost, however much damage bombers had caused in the rear.

It was a point made by a suddenly more forthright CIGS Dill in a stinging criticism of Churchill's war strategy. He accused the prime minister of putting at risk the security of the United Kingdom with the priority he was assigning to Egypt, the latest manifestation of this being the dispatch of 300 tanks to the Middle East in the Tiger convoy. Dill insisted that Britain could afford to lose Egypt and still continue the war, whereas a successful German invasion of Britain would end the war. Churchill's policy of reinforcing the Middle East meant the UK only had half the number of tank divisions required to defeat an invasion. Churchill was incredulous that Dill appeared to believe Egypt was expendable, an idea the Empire-orientated Churchill considered so absurd it scarcely needed rebutting.[25]

In the furore this caused, Dill's comments on air power might perhaps have been overlooked, but these seemed equally heretical. Dill did not believe the RAF could be decisive on its own, in a strategic or tactical context. He had no great faith in Bomber Command's ability to sink an invasion fleet in port before it even departed. Nor would it succeed against an invasion force en route across the Channel or be able to destroy it as it landed. Bomber Command was unlikely to have the resources to bomb all the ports of embarkation the Germans would be using, and was no more likely to disrupt the disembarkation than the Luftwaffe had been able to interfere with the Dunkirk evacuation. Dill described how the war had been dominated by the 'paramountcy of armoured forces supported by a powerful Air Force' which had recently proven itself yet again in terrains as different as the mountains of the Balkans and the deserts of Libya. To counter an invasion, Britain needed 'large reserves of counter attacking tanks, anti-tank weapons and aircraft', but Britain had 'no air forces designed and trained for close bombing co-operation with the Army'.[26]

Dill's views on the exaggerated importance of Egypt might have dumbfounded Churchill, but some of the criticisms of army/air co-operation were striking a chord. The German bombing of British cities in the Blitz had caused immense suffering, but had never come close to defeating the country. Not even the all-powerful Luftwaffe could deliver the much-predicted and feared 'knockout blow'. Churchill was beginning to appreciate that the bomber was not the all-conquering, fearsome weapon he had always imagined it to be. Perhaps Dill was right; perhaps it was a mistake to place too much reliance on bombing as a defensive weapon – or indeed a war-winning weapon.

Brooke now had more support for the cause, with General Henry Pownall replacing Haining as his Vice-Chief of the Imperial General Staff. Haining had never impressed Brooke, and Pownall before the war had always been bullish in his attempts to extract more effective close air-support from the Air Ministry.[27] Dill had made his views clear. Moore-Brabazon, unlike his predecessor Beaverbrook, was not a member of the War Cabinet, but the Secretary of State for War read to the Cabinet the letter Moore-Brabazon had sent him, along with Tizard's letter on aircraft-mounted anti-tanks guns. A debate followed and there was sufficient disagreement for a meeting to be arranged for

13 May at 10 Downing Street, with all relevant parties present, where the issue could be thrashed out.[28]

It would prove to be an acrimonious affair, where Brooke, in his own words, 'became a bit heated' as he laid into Portal 'and his awful satellite Goddard' for their attitude to army co-operation.[29] Army squadrons were beginning to get American fighters, but only a few of the 500 in the country had reached the squadrons. Brooke accused the Air Ministry of reneging on their repeated promises to develop an effective bomber support capability. Dill and Brooke insisted Bomber Command was only equipped and trained for an independent air war role and could not therefore provide the close support the Army wanted. Portal countered with the standard line that in defence bombers were best used for attacking targets well to the rear, and the whole of Bomber Command would be available for this. Brooke, quite unnecessarily, accepted that it might be difficult to organize close air-support in a defensive situation. However, the defence of the United Kingdom rested on the ability of British armoured forces to counter-attack and eliminate enemy bridgeheads. This was offensive action, which even the Air Ministry did not deny needed air support. Brooke insisted that bomber support would be needed to help eliminate 'centres of resistance' in the path of these counter-attacks.[30] Churchill, Portal's erstwhile ally, swung his support behind Brooke, insisting the armoured counter-attacks on which the defeat of an invasion so relied must have full air support.

Bomber Command could not provide the close support the Army required, and with their current equipment nor could the army co-operation squadrons. Tomahawks were fine for tactical reconnaissance but they could not carry bombs. Blenheims had to be found to give army co-operation squadrons some strike capability.[31] Portal was more than happy to agree that army co-operation squadrons should have bombing as one of their roles, and that was why he was planning to equip them with American Vengeance and Bermuda dive-bombers, which, he claimed, were expected to arrive in July. Churchill wanted to know why three army co-operation squadrons could not be equipped with Blenheims straight away. Goddard had to admit that the transfer of army co-operation crews to Bomber Command agreed in February had so reduced strength that what was left was scarcely capable of filling the Army's reconnaissance requirements. If close support was required, Bomber Command would have to supply it, but this was not good enough for Brooke. Squadrons supporting the Army had to be under Army, not Bomber Command, control.[32]

With Churchill siding with Brooke, Portal found himself on the defensive. Churchill demanded that as many Tomahawks be got into service as quickly as possible, even if they were still not fully operational. Goddard complained that it was scarcely worth it since American dive-bombers would be available so soon, but Churchill insisted. The fourteen army co-operation squadrons were to be equipped with Tomahawks and Blenheims as quickly as possible.[33] Blenheims would be used as an interim bomber-reconnaissance plane, but by the following year, Churchill insisted, a plane 'perfectly adapted' for army support must be developed.[34]

With the chorus of complaints about the absence of effective air support from military and naval commanders in the Middle East, not to mention the leaders of the Dominion countries involved in the fighting, Churchill – perhaps for the first time – was beginning to understand the problem and what needed to change. In future, the drive for effective tactical air support for the Army would have the prime minister's personal backing. For Portal and the Air Staff, the winds of change were blowing.

Churchill's insistence that the army co-operation squadrons could not await the arrival of the American dive-bombers was far more justified than he could have known. There was no question of either of these reaching the squadrons in the summer of 1941. All the Tomahawks in the United Kingdom would now go to equip these squadrons instead of to the Middle East and Fighter Command. As it turned out, the RAF was so short of Blenheims that only three squadrons were to get the bomber, leaving eleven to be equipped with the Tomahawk.[35]

Brooke was absolutely delighted with the way the meeting went. Indeed, it signalled the beginning of a change of attitude towards the Army and its role in the war. In the Middle East, Wavell had demonstrated that it could do much more than just defend the Nile Delta. His offensives had conquered most of East Africa and had come close to wiping out the Italian Army and clearing North Africa of Axis forces. Even with German forces in North Africa, Churchill was already contemplating a scenario in which more victories in this theatre might lead to an invasion of Italy. It was still difficult to imagine the Army bringing about the downfall of Germany, but it might knock Italy out of the war. However, if this were to be achieved the Commonwealth armies would have to start getting something like the air support the German Army was getting.

Portal and Goddard scurried back to the Air Ministry to try to work out what line the Air Ministry should take in these new circumstances.

From the inner sanctum of the Air Ministry, the situation did not seem as threatening as it had in 10 Downing Street. It was thought unfortunate that outside Ministry walls some half-baked ideas were emerging, and it was hoped that the foolishness of these ideas would soon be exposed by some rational analysis. There was 'considerable difficulty' in envisaging exactly what Brooke had in mind.[36] He appeared to be contemplating 'the attack of "centres of resistance" immediately in front of the forward troops', a requirement which, it was rather dismissively suggested, was apparently based on a study of German methods.[37] Considerable doubt was expressed as to whether such attacks were possible so close to friendly troops. They would certainly be extremely costly, and could not possibly be forthcoming in time at the speed land operations were likely to be developing. However, to keep the War Office happy, some token effort would have to be made. The War Office wanted the RAF to provide bombers to take part in exercises. Peirse thought that three would be enough, Harris – the Deputy Chief of Air Staff – thought one would do, and everyone agreed Army Co-operation Command should supply it.

The consensus within the Air Ministry was that the best 'direct support' Bomber Command could give would be bombers flying roving patrols in prescribed areas as part of a pre-arranged attack. This Bomber Command could do without any extra training. Army co-operation aircraft would have to perform the closer support Brooke appeared to want, and Army Co-operation Command would have to try to find out exactly what the War Office meant by 'centres of resistance'. Clearly this would require the specialist Wann-Woodall communication systems that were being developed, but no system was likely to be capable of coping with the sort of close support Brooke appeared to be wanting, it was argued, even though this was what the trials in Northern Ireland were supposed to be all about. The Air Ministry felt it was its duty to warn the War Office that should it insist on going down this path it could expect heavy losses for little return, but it was up to the War Office what it did with its army co-operation squadrons.[38] Brooke was indeed sent a note asking him to clarify what he meant exactly by 'centres of resistance'. The Army commander replied instantly, referring the Air Ministry to a joint Air Ministry/War Office memorandum issued the previous December which listed them, barely concealing his frustration behind an expression of surprise that the Air Ministry could be in any doubt about what these targets might be.[39]

For tactical reconnaissance, Goddard was soon extolling the virtues of the Lysander and insisted there was no need to rush to the single-seater fighter as an alternative. It was perfectly capable of operating in situations of air superiority, and even in France, where the enemy had air superiority, he claimed that only three had been lost during the course of seventy-five sorties.[40] It is not clear where Goddard got his figures from: around twenty Lysanders were lost in action in the first twelve days of the German offensive.[41] Nevertheless, Goddard was correct that low-performance planes could operate successfully in situations of air superiority, as the Ju 87 was constantly demonstrating. Indeed, they could operate reasonably successfully even without air superiority, provided they were not expected to operate too far beyond the frontline. However, the single-seater fighter was clearly proving itself to be a far better way of collecting tactical information, and with no shortage of American fighters, there was no excuse for not replacing the Lysanders.

The Air Ministry was in retreat on all fronts. Portal could only play for time and hope the storm would pass. The War Office was anxious to take advantage of the momentum gained and resolve the differences between the Army and RAF as rapidly as possible, but Portal insisted there was no need to rush. He pointed out that this was a long-term project and could not be brought into effect in time for the current 1941 'invasion season'. This, of course, was the second 'invasion season'. Portal was hoping to have something in place in time for the third, 1942 'invasion season'.

It was agreed that No. 2 Group should restart the close-support training programme. By 1 September, each squadron would have been withdrawn for a week of training and exercises. Portal felt it would be better to wait until No. 2 Group had completed this training and Woodall's tentacle system had been tried out in the autumn Bumper exercises before discussing the issue again.[42] This conveniently put any possible expansion of army support units to one side for the time being and gave Portal time to draw up his own plans for a massive expansion of Bomber Command.

Meanwhile, Trenchard was trying to stiffen the pro-strategic bombing lobby in any way he could. Slessor, commanding No. 5 Group, passed on to Freeman notes provided by Trenchard on the Army Co-operation Command issue, a command 'created in a hurry to satisfy the Army's inferiority complex', Trenchard ventured. 'No-one denies they need some support', Trenchard conceded, indeed even 'faster and more manoeuvrable bombers than heavy bombers', but low-level close support was too costly and only worked against Poles, Norwegians, Yugoslavs and Greeks. There could never possibly be enough to go round, so the Army should accept such units could only have the lowest priority. There was no question of there being any need for specialized support. 'We must remember the psychological factor of the Army feeling they have a share of control,' he patronizingly suggested. 'Should an Expeditionary Force materialise', and 'if and when the land battle becomes decisive', heavy bombers would be just as good for supplying close support. There was no reason why it could not provide an army in France with this support from bases in the UK, just like the Germans had done in Crete.[43] It was the old Trenchardian idea of large heavy bombers dominating entire theatres from distant bases. Trenchard seemed to think that the Luftwaffe had been conducting operations against Crete from bases in Greece by choice. He overlooked the fact that airfields on Crete had been the German top priority, and that as soon as they captured them, the Luftwaffe moved in.

Trenchard circulated more widely a memorandum that he proposed to publish, in which he demanded the bomber offensive be intensified, with no diversion of effort to support the Army or Royal Navy. He claimed the German people were far more susceptible to bombing than the British, and all bombers should concentrate on targets in Germany so that the 99 per cent of bombs that missed the target would kill Germans. Such a policy would bring a far swifter end to the war than any attempt to win on the ground. He hoped his contribution would 'squash the notion which many constantly press that a large number of machines must be built for use in purely Army operations at home', a force which could not contribute anything to the critical bombing offensive.[44]

Churchill thought Trenchard was 'flogging a good horse to death' and persuaded him not to publish.[45] Portal essentially agreed with Trenchard, even with the notion that Germans were more susceptible to bombing than the British, although he was anxious that British 'superiority in temperament' should be backed up by ways of alleviating the effects of bombing.[46] However, he realized that at this point in time any interventions like Trenchard's were likely to do more harm than good for the strategic bombing cause. Indeed, the likes of Portal and Slessor may have been impressed with the clarity of Trenchard's reasoning, but for Churchill the more extreme the presentation, the clearer the flaws in the argument became.

Meanwhile, the War Office was putting together a more ambitious air programme. Longmore, summoned home in disgrace by Churchill, was on hand to provide a first-hand account of how tactical air power could influence a battle. On many points he agreed with the standard Air Ministry line. The Ju 87 dive-bombers had proven to be extremely vulnerable to fighters and anti-aircraft fire, and the damage they inflicted was often minimal. Even a dive-bomber lacked the accuracy to hit small battlefield targets. There was no doubting the psychological impact the plane could have on troops, but with effective fighter and anti-aircraft cover, even this problem could be minimized. Fighters, he felt, were far more effective at striking battlefield targets. However, he disagreed with the Air Ministry view that only army co-operation squadrons should be attached directly to the Army. The Army needed bombers and fighters under its control, and Longmore suggested that an army co-operation wing, with two fighter and two bomber squadrons, in addition to a reconnaissance squadron, should be attached to each armoured division or infantry corps.[47]

For the Air Ministry this was mutiny within the ranks. To counter Longmore's opinions, Tedder's views were sought on the sort of air support that should be attached to the Army. Tedder tried to steer a middle ground, suggesting that perhaps one bomber and one fighter squadron would be an appropriate number of squadrons to attach to each corps.[48] Portal trumped them both. He did not think it should be two or four squadrons; the entire RAF should be at the disposal of the Army, he boldly and enthusiastically proclaimed, but only 'after the other necessary tasks such as general fighter protection' had been taken care of.[49] Portal was only talking about air support in the Middle East. Outside this theatre, the other 'necessary tasks' also included the strategic bomber offensive, and with a bomber force of 4,000 required it was doubtful that this would ever be taken care of.

Longmore's suggestion that bomber and fighter squadrons should be attached to the Army removed any lingering Air Ministry doubts about his suitability for command. He had not been ordered home because he was one of the few RAF commanders with experience of handling a tactical air force. He had been hauled home by Churchill to explain himself. Heretical talk like this was not going to win him back any friends. It merely sealed his fate. His premonition that he would not be returning to the Middle East had proven correct, although there was more than just a degree of self-fulfilling prophecy about it. Longmore joined other commanders who had failed to tow the Air Staff line, on inspection duties.

This did not stop Longmore from arguing the case for more army air support. To keep the War Office happy, Longmore and Barratt were instructed to write a report on how air support should be organized. Portal made it very clear that this was air support for an armoured force operating outside the United Kingdom. The report included many suggestions for improving the mobility of squadrons and ensuring their defence in fluid situations. In a covering letter, Longmore could not resist the temptation to propose that some of the suggestions might also be applicable during an invasion.[50] Portal, however, was determined to maintain the distinction between battles fought in north-west Europe and those fought elsewhere in the world.

Meanwhile, the War Office was busy recalculating its needs on the basis of Longmore's proposed army support wings. Each corps and armoured division would need a tactical reconnaissance squadron in addition to the four fighter and bomber squadrons. In the United Kingdom, just one bomber and fighter squadron would suffice as Bomber and Fighter Command could be relied on for more support. The ten corps and eight armoured divisions to be created in the UK would therefore require fifty-four squadrons. Another fifty-five squadrons would be needed by units in the Middle East, Iraq and Malaya. This brought the total number of squadrons required worldwide to 109, half of which would be single-seaters and half multi-seaters.[51] In addition, the War Office also wanted three observation AOP (Air Observation Post) squadrons and a communication squadron in each theatre. It also wanted sufficient transport planes to move a brigade of troops.

The transport demand was the opening Portal needed. The Air Ministry calculated that the Army was effectively asking for a frontline strength of 1,744 combat planes and a fleet of 1,000 transport planes. If this was not frightening enough, a recalculation took the number of transport planes required to 2,000, and the overall figure to 3,888 aircraft. The Air Ministry laid down the grim consequences if such a force were to be developed. The RAF would be left with no light bomber squadrons in the Far East or Middle East, no medium bomber squadrons anywhere, and the number of heavy bomber squadrons would be cut from 260 to 130. The number of night-fighter squadrons would be reduced to twelve, putting British cities in grave danger. In total, the War Office demand was the equivalent of taking 215 squadrons away from independent air force operations.[52]

It was a message that was designed to scare politicians into falling into line. War Office plans would deny their own troops on the ground vital bomber support and expose British civilians to a renewed German blitz, all just to enable ten divisions to land on the continent and be crushed by an overwhelmingly stronger German Army. Even in this extreme piece of scaremongering, Portal's Bomber Command was only being cut back to some 2,000 planes, which some might argue ought to be ample.

The problem for the Air Ministry was that nearly two years into the war, despite the apparent success of the bombing campaign, there was no tangible sign that the policy was taking Britain any closer to victory. In the meantime, the British Army, without adequate air support, was suffering defeat after defeat every time it took on the Wehrmacht. It was becoming increasingly difficult to justify giving the strategic bombing offensive priority over the development of tactical air support. The Air Ministry claimed it was all beyond its control. The 'lack of adequate air support in land operations hitherto has been due to circumstances beyond the control of both the Air Force and the Army', the Plans department insisted, but did not venture to suggest any ways in which the RAF and Army might set about acquiring control of these circumstances.[53] All the Air Ministry could suggest was that the Army should make do with strategic bombers for air support. The Air Ministry gamely stuck to its guns. The war would be won first by destroying German industry and only then, if it was still necessary, tackling the German Army.

With Churchill siding with the War Office, Portal felt he had to come up with some sort of alternative plan to the War Office demand for fifty-four squadrons in the UK, preferably without giving away too much. He suggested expanding the existing army co-operation squadrons to twenty, although this was only a return to the planned target before the freeze agreed in February. Ten of these would be fighter/reconnaissance and ten bomber/reconnaissance. No. 2 Group would be restored to nine squadrons, possibly equipped with the American Martin B-26 Marauder. This was still fewer than it had in the summer of 1940, and the Marauder was very much at the heavy end of the medium-bomber spectrum, and even less capable of close support than the Blenheim. Since Douglas had declared his fifteen Hurricane II squadrons could only be used for roles like 'ground strafing in the event of an invasion', these could also be added to the total.[54]

This brought the number of potential air support squadrons to forty-four, just ten short of the War Office demand. However, only the army co-operation squadrons would be under direct Army control. The medium bomber and fighter squadrons would remain under the control of Bomber and Fighter Command respectively and would continue to play a full part in the operations of these commands. The fifteen Fighter Command squadrons would get special training in ground strafing, but only after the summer of 1941 and the threat of a renewed German air offensive had passed.[55] This was of course also after the threat of a 1941 invasion had passed.

It had the appearance of a reasonable compromise, but it did not give the Army what it most needed – control. Having the squadrons spread across three different commands, two of which it had no control over, was not what was required. Nevertheless, Portal was being forced to give ground. The proposal effectively ended any hopes of No. 2 Group following No 1 Group into the heavy bomber fold. Portal probably realised that it was not enough to satisfy the War Office, but it might satisfy Churchill.

The prime minister had no intention of letting the issue slip. He instructed General Hastings Ismay, his military adviser, to keep a close eye on developments.[56] Ismay was able to report back that the No. 2 Group close-support training programme was underway and confirm eleven of the fourteen army co-operation squadrons were in the process of converting to the Tomahawk, with seven expected to be operational by 1 September. Portal was doing just enough to keep the critics at bay. With any further meaningful discussions put off until after the autumn Bumper exercises, Portal had negotiated another tricky invasion season without giving too much away.

With the close air-support issue temporarily shelved, Portal turned his attention to ensuring the strategic air offensive got the priority it needed. Portal knew it was essentially a struggle for production capacity. If aircraft had to be diverted to Army needs, they had to come from the United States and not reduce British bomber output. Churchill might want a close-support plane 'perfectly adapted' for Army support, but Portal insisted that the American Bermuda and Vengeance covered this requirement. The two American dive-bombers were becoming very useful assets for the Air Ministry. Every time the Army demanded specialist close-support planes, the Air Ministry could point out that the Bermuda and Vengeance were on their way.

The War Office wanted two types of aircraft: a fighter-reconnaissance and a bomber-reconnaissance. For the former it wanted a 350–400mph fighter with the manoeuvrability of a Tomahawk. It would also have to carry four cannon for ground attack. The bomber-reconnaissance plane was also to be fast and manoeuvrable at low level, carry 1,000lb of bombs and have rear defence. It also had to be capable of operating by night and in poor weather. It seemed that a Bermuda/Vengeance type plane was still expected.[57] The War Office emphasized that steep dive-bombing was not necessary if it reduced performance; shallow dive-bombing would do. Although the War Office still wanted a two-seater bomber, the cannon-armed single-seater demonstrated that it also recognized the ground attack potential of the single-seater fighter.

In the fighter-reconnaissance role, a replacement for the Tomahawk would soon be required as all future deliveries were going straight to the Middle East. The next fighter on the American taxi rank was the North American Mustang. This fighter was the result of a 1940 decision made by the British Purchasing Commission to humour a rather outlandish proposal by the North American aircraft company. The British wanted the company to build Tomahawks under licence, but rather boldly, given that it had very little experience in designing fighters, it suggested it could build something much better. The company was given a contract to build 320, provided it could come up with a satisfactory prototype within 120 days.[58] It seemed rather optimistic to believe the firm could do better than an experienced producer of fighters like Curtiss, and do it in a fraction of the time. If the Air Ministry team had spent more time considering the idea, it would probably have been rejected out of hand, but it was May 1940 and in desperation the British were willing to buy just about anything that flew, even anything that had not flown or indeed, in the Mustang's case, a plane which had not even been designed. It did not attract any interest from the USAAC, which rather fortunately meant there were no home contracts to compete with. Deliveries were due to begin in late 1941, and it seemed a natural successor to the Tomahawk.[59]

Off-loading responsibility for tactical aircraft on the American aircraft industry was not going to solve all Portal's problems. He knew that even if the British aircraft industry did not build any tactical planes, it still did not have the capacity to deliver the bomber fleet he needed. The American aircraft industry would have to make up the difference. General Arnold was hopefully already turning American production over to heavy bombers, but any tactical planes Britain ordered would inevitably cut into the number that might be available. Even with American help, it was difficult to see how a 4,000-strong bomber fleet could be created. Nevertheless, Portal remained upbeat. At the Chiefs of Staff meeting at the end of May, he launched a belligerent defence of the strategic bombing strategy. Hard choices had to be made. Either everything went into the existing air programme and the Army made do, or vice versa, but there could be no compromise. If it was decided to land a major force on the continent, there would have to be a rethink about the type of air force required.

This was an interesting change of tack from Portal. The standard Air Staff line had always been that no special aircraft or training were required to support the Army. He warned that such a landing would require the creation of a 2,000-strong specialist long-range fighter force to gain air superiority until the beachhead could be expanded to accommodate standard short-range fighters.[60] This, on the face of it, seemed like recognition that air superiority fighters were key, but Portal was really just trying to demonstrate how absurd it would be to create such a large specialist force that would only be needed for a short period of time. It was Portal at his scaremongering best. Whether an entirely new fighter had to be developed just to have the range to operate on the other side of the Channel was debateable.

Portal maintained that no major landing on the continent would ever be required. The strategic bombing alone could bring Germany to the point where it would be forced to sign an armistice. In 1918, continuous defeats on land had forced Germany to hand over substantial quantities of military equipment in exchange for a ceasefire. Portal sketched out a similar scenario in which German morale would be so undermined by the bombing offensive that they would agree to hand over all their aircraft and armoured fighting vehicles just to put an end to the bombing. Portal was convinced there was no need for Britain to build tanks or assault craft to batter their way into the continent. Instead, the country should focus on building bombers.[61] Britain would be pinning all its hopes on Bomber Command winning the war single-handedly. Dill was not impressed. The Army chief was willing to agree that an intense and sustained bombing offensive might bring Germany close to defeat, and might even bring chaos and revolution. However, the German armed forces would remain in existence and, however successful the bomber offensive was, there would be a battle somewhere in northern France before victory could be achieved, and this would require large numbers of tanks supported by a powerful tactical air force.[62]

Portal's scenario was breathtaking enough, even by the standards of the pre-war spectre of the apocalyptic death and destruction bombing would bring. It was even more extraordinary given the problems the bomber offensive was already facing. Just about everything was going wrong. The long-awaited 1936 generation of heavy bombers on which such high hopes had been placed were not proving a great success. The four-engined Stirling struggled to fly above 14,000ft, a deficiency that was to make it easy prey for interceptors and ground fire for its entire operational career. The Manchester's Vulture engines were proving even more dangerous to Bomber Command crews than the ever-more-efficient German defences. Only the Halifax could reasonably claim its teething problems were manageable.

Hopes that the cheap plywood and steel Albemarle would help bulk out the bomber fleet were fast disappearing. One thousand were on order, but in February 1941 the prototype crashed. The following month, cancelling the project completely was considered but plans to mass-produce the plane were too far advanced to abandon production entirely.[63] The second prototype flew in April, but could only get into the air if flown 3,000lb below the intended maximum weight, which effectively meant without three-quarters of the planned bomb load. Boscombe Down eventually got it to take off fully loaded, but only with a huge take-off run.[64] Trials in August revealed the plane's defensive armament was not very effective, and it had difficulty flying on a single engine. By this time, half of the 1,000 on order would have to be built just to use up the various components that had accumulated.[65] There was no way of using production capacity to build another bomber. The whole point of the Albemarle was that it was a plane whose components could be built by companies outside the aircraft industry. It was decided to go ahead with a batch of 200, with just the first twenty getting engines for trials, while the rest were mothballed for some future emergency.[66]

Only the Manchester, Stirling and Halifax were just about useable, and production of these was hopelessly behind schedule. Even worse, evidence was growing that the bombers were not delivering their bomb loads with the accuracy that crews were claiming. It was already recognized that there was a problem finding the targets, and the Telecommunications Research Establishment was already working on new navigational aids like GEE to help crews. However, it was generally assumed that if crews found the target, they could hit it. Photo-reconnaissance should have been able to verify these claims, but as is always the case, successful intelligence-gathering relies on asking the right questions. The early photo-reconnaissance planes were sent out to find out how much damage the bombers were causing. When no damage could be seen in the low-quality images, it was assumed the cameras were not good enough to detect the damage. There were issues with the quality of cameras available, but if the intelligence experts had been asking whether the bombers were causing any damage, there might at least have been more pause for thought. When photo-reconnaissance did not support the claims of pilots, it was the latter who tended to be believed.

For those who wanted to look, there was plenty of circumstantial evidence that crews were not hitting their intended targets. Successive bombers attacking the same objective would each claim to have caused the first fires in the target area. Crews flying on dead reckoning above thick cloud would miraculously spot their intended target in a sudden break in the cloud. Crews claiming to have bombed a target deep inside

Germany, would then be unable to find their own airfield. By the end of 1940, there was already enough evidence to suggest that precision bombing by night was only possible if conditions were favourable. When they were not, crews could only be reasonably asked to aim their bombs at a city centre. With the Blitz raging, there seemed ample justification for such an indiscriminate approach. In December 1940, the centre of Mannheim was targeted as a deliberate act of retaliation. One hundred and two bombers claimed to have hit the target.

By this time, Bomber Command had its own photo-reconnaissance unit and a high-quality German Zeiss Ikon photo-lens salvaged from a crashed Luftwaffe Ju 88. In future, images of bomb damage would be a lot clearer. A few days after the Mannheim raid, a reconnaissance Spitfire recorded only scattered, light damage. Even worse news was to follow a few days later when oil refineries which Bomber Command believed had been heavily damaged were photographed fully intact.[67] Still the penny did not drop. It was suggested that the Germans were hurriedly patching up damaged installations and factories to make them look as if no damage had been inflicted. Confidence remained high. The Luftwaffe was using advanced navigational systems to aid its night bombers, but no-one in the Air Ministry could understand why. 'We use no beams ourselves but we bomb just as successfully as the Germans bomb, deep into Germany,' Arthur Harris, the Deputy Chief of the Air Staff, smugly commented in February 1941.[68] Not all shared this optimism; most accepted there were problems, but no-one appreciated the scale of the problem. Bomber Command and the Air Ministry still had no idea how little their bombers were achieving.

Chapter 9

Disunited

While there were some doubts about the scale of the damage Bomber Command was inflicting on German industry, there was no doubt that in the Mediterranean the British and Commonwealth armies were suffering defeat after defeat. The progress made in army/air co-operation against Italian forces had been undone by defeats at the hands of the far better-equipped and led German forces. More than ever, the Middle East needed the air reinforcements Longmore had been demanding.

His successor, Tedder, could not have been more different to the straight-talking Australian. Tedder was very much Portal's man, and Portal was determined to keep it that way. Portal kept up a personal correspondence with Tedder, which both valued highly. Tedder was far from confident he would hold down his new position and was grateful for the constant support he received from London. From Portal's perspective, the close personal contact made it more difficult for Tedder to be more demanding or awkward. The correspondence also helped remind Tedder about Air Ministry policy. The influence London had on air policy in Greece would now extend to the Western Desert.

Tedder was determined not to cause problems for the Air Ministry. Whereas Longmore had joined forces with Cunningham and Wavell to try to get the air resources that all three agreed were needed, Tedder had no intention of embarrassing his masters in London by making similar demands. Wavell and Cunningham insisted air power in the region was disproportionately weaker than naval and army strength, and wanted a joint approach by all three commanders to demand that air support be increased.[1] Tedder knew all too well how this had gone down in London during Longmore's time in command, and would only agree to a joint request for reinforcement of all three services. As

170

welcome as more tanks and warships might be, these were not Wavell and Cunningham's first priority; it was air support and protection for what they already had that they wanted above all else.

This imbalance was reflected in the contents of the emergency Tiger convoy, rushed through the Mediterranean at great risk to enable Wavell to take the offensive. The convoy carried some 300 tanks, including 100 of the latest cruiser type, much to Dill's annoyance as he felt they were desperately needed to deal with a possible invasion. Alongside these precious tank reinforcements were fifty-three obsolete Hurricane Is, and these were only last-minute additions as Portal belatedly came to realize he had to get more fighters out to the Middle East. Fighter protection was hopelessly out of kilter with the size of the Mediterranean army. The RAF fighter force was far too few in numbers and, now that the Luftwaffe was the opposition, hopelessly inferior in quality.

The issue of quantity was being addressed. Churchill too was beginning to appreciate there was a problem. Having lambasted Longmore for not doing anything with the large numbers of planes in the Middle East and having the audacity to spread the rumour that Beaverbrook was hoarding aircraft in the UK, Churchill was now beginning to ask questions about the 'splendid accumulation of Hurricanes and Spitfires' in RAF stores in Britain.[2] On 10 May, he left Portal in little doubt about the new priority: 'The result of the Battle for Egypt now depends more upon the air reinforcements than the tanks.' Churchill wanted fighters sent to the Middle East, 'from every quarter and by every route'.[3] The Chief of Air Staff had come to the same conclusion before his prime minister, but only just. Still in awe of the power of the heavy bomber, Churchill also envisaged the dispatch of another six Wellington squadrons.[4]

Meanwhile, Tedder, far from educating his Army and Navy colleagues, found himself fending off criticism and trying not to give away too much ground. It was perhaps ironic that the pressure for Tedder to be more accommodating to army requirements came from the Air Ministry in London. Portal was soon letting Tedder know about the intense pressure he was under to do something about the army air support problem. Portal warned Tedder that the performance of the RAF would be under scrutiny during the forthcoming offensives. Critics 'in political circles' were complaining about the failure of the RAF to hit targets in and around the battlefield. The RAF was spending too much time bombing distant lines of communication rather than the artillery and tanks engaging the troops. All this, the critics were pointing out, was in stark contrast to the German use of air power, where an army commander could apparently radio for air support every time he got into difficulty. Portal encouraged Tedder to continue his efforts to 'educate' the army about how air power could best be used, but if persuasion failed, he was to concede to army wishes and put on record his objections for future reference.[5]

The 'political circles' included Winston Churchill, who was chaffing at the bit, anxious that the tanks and aircraft he had rushed through the Mediterranean at such huge risk should be used to send Rommel's forces packing. Most of the convoy arrived, but one ship was lost with fifty-seven tanks and ten Hurricanes. It could have been a lot worse. Portal assured Churchill that ten squadrons would be immediately available to give direct support to the offensive, with three-and-a-half squadrons of heavy bombers providing indirect support. It was enough, he believed, to give the RAF air superiority. He saw no reason why some elements of the seven squadrons converting to new aircraft should not be added to increase this advantage.[6] But a suspicious Churchill insisted on knowing precise details of how this air strength was going to be used to support the ground forces. News from Wavell that he had only been promised eight squadrons did nothing to ease Churchill's suspicions that the Air Force was not willing to engage fully.

While Churchill was growing increasingly suspicious about the RAF's willingness to support the army in the Western Desert, a training school at the opposite end of the Middle East Command was concluding a textbook demonstration of how close air-support should work. The training school was at Habbaniya in Iraq, where increasing anti-British feeling had culminated in a coup on 1 April 1941, which saw the establishment of a new government under Rashid Ali. Encouraged by German success in Greece and promises of German support, Rashid Ali set out to challenge Britain's right, by virtue of a 1930 treaty, to maintain and move military forces around the country as it pleased. Using pro-Vichy Syria as a staging post, German advisers and even Luftwaffe units were being fed into Iraq. British control of Iraqi oil fields was under threat.

Much to Churchill's annoyance, it was a threat Wavell felt he did not have the resources to deal with and he urged a political settlement that would relieve him of yet another military burden. Churchill would have none of it, and General Claude Auchinleck, the British commander in India, stepped into the breach by dispatching Indian troops to Basra in southern Iraq. In response, Iraqi forces occupied the plateau overlooking the RAF Habbaniya training base, 40 miles west of Baghdad. There was no real plan to occupy the base; Rashid Ali just wanted to apply a little extra pressure. The Iraqis announced that any attempt to fly from the base would draw Iraqi fire. They set up their artillery and waited to see how the stand-off would develop. It was just a small-scale local conflict, but in many ways what followed proved to be a microcosm of the much larger conflict being fought out over two continents.

After two days, advice reached Air Vice-Marshal Harry Smart, the commander of the air base, suggesting that he should attack the forces surrounding him, even though there was no sign of them doing any more than maintain an intimidating presence on the plateau above the base. Escalating the crisis was a huge risk – the 2,000 defending troops were scarcely capable of defeating a determined effort to take the base, and there was the additional complication that many British citizens who had fled from Baghdad were sheltering in the base.[7]

The ground forces defending the airfield were far too weak to attack; the only offensive option was the aircraft on the base. Smart organized the trainers into three bomber and one fighter squadron, flown by instructors and the more advanced trainees. The Banquet scheme, the plan drawn up in the summer of 1940 to help repel an invasion of the UK, was about to be given a trial run in Iraq. Twenty-five Hawker Harts and seven Fairey Gordons bombers were available. Thirty Audax army co-operation planes designed to carry four 20lb bombs were hastily adapted to carry two 250lb bombs, and twenty-seven Oxford trainers, which normally carried no ordnance at all, were fitted with bomb racks for four 20lb bombs. In total, the base mustered eighty-nine planes capable of carrying bombs and nine Gladiator fighters. However, there were only thirty-nine pilots capable of flying them, and many of the instructors had no operational experience.[8] Longmore provided some long-range support by flying eighteen Wellingtons from Nos 70 and 37 Squadrons to Basra.[9]

Smart issued his own ultimatum to the Iraqi forces – withdraw or face attack. This brought no response, so as dawn broke on 2 May 1941, Smart's planes, supported by the Wellingtons from Basra, attacked the Iraqi troops surrounding the base. Throughout the day they maintained the pressure as best they could, fearing that any relaxation might encourage the Iraqis to storm the base. During the course of the day, forty-six planes flew an impressive 193 sorties. The planes were operating in extremely difficult circumstances. As soon as the Iraqi forces came under attack, they opened fire on the base and the Iraqi Air Force delivered some punishing attacks with Northrop 8As, Breda 65s, Savoia-Marchetti SM.79s and, ironically, Audax bombers bought from Britain. However, no attempt was made to storm the airfield. Iraqi anti-aircraft fire was heavy but RAF losses were relatively light. Two planes were lost to ground fire and another three, including one of the Wellingtons from Basra forced to land at Habbaniya, were destroyed by shell fire on the airfield. However, many had been damaged and the sortie rate was soon dropping. The next day, thirty-three planes managed 119 sorties, but by 4 May the number was down to just fifty-three sorties.[10]

More reinforcements began to arrive from Egypt. A detachment of four Blenheim IVs of No. 203 Squadron arrived on 3 May, and these and the Wellingtons were used to attack Iraqi airfields, while the trainers continued to concentrate on the guns firing at the air base. Gladiators and Blenheim IVs flew standing patrols over the airfield to counter Iraqi raids, but could not prevent a sharp low-level raid on 6 May destroying four RAF planes. On the same day, the trainers prepared for a day of maximum effort as fears grew that the Iraqi forces were about to attack the base, but instead reconnaissance revealed the plateau had been abandoned. Instead of fending off an attack, the thirty-nine available trainers flew 139 sorties, strafing and bombing Iraqi forces caught on open roads retreating towards Fallujah.[11] For the purists it was a demonstration of how air power could win battles on its own, although it was never really a battle. In many ways the Iraqis on the plateau were more exposed than the troops defending the air base, and with no intention of attacking and bombs raining down on them, there was little point in staying there.

A few days later in Crete, Allied troops would find themselves defending airfields from which no aircraft were operating. The largely symbolic Iraqi forces that threatened the airbase at Habbaniya could hardly be compared to the battle-hardened paratroopers that were surrounding the RAF's bases in Crete, but even so, events in Iraq gave some idea of what might have been possible in Crete. Ironically, some of the pilots at Habbaniya were Greek.[12] They might have preferred to fly their trainers in defence of Cretan airfields against the German invader rather than help Britain out in a colonial dispute.

By this time Wavell had been persuaded to dispatch a relief force, led by Major-General John Clark, from Palestine, and Longmore had sent more Hurricanes and Blenheims. By the time the ground reinforcements from Palestine arrived on 18 May, the Iraqis had established defensive positions in Fallujah, protecting the bridge across the Euphrates and blocking the path to Baghdad. With a Luftwaffe He 111 and Bf 110 squadron, flying in Iraqi Air Force colours, to provide air support and far less exposed than they had been in the desert outside Habbaniya, the Iraqi forces posed a considerable barrier.

174

On 19 May, the Allied forces prepared to capture Fallujah. Colonel Ouvry Roberts, who had taken over from Smart after the latter was injured in a car accident, was anxious to avoid house-to-house fighting in the town, and following their success in defending the Habbaniya airfield, there seemed no reason why the RAF could not complete the defeat of the Iraqis single-handed. Ground forces took up positions around Fallujah, including a force landed in the rear on the Fallujah-Baghdad road by six Valentia and Bombay transports. It was hoped that an aerial bombardment of the town would be sufficient to underline the hopelessness of their position and the Iraqis forces would surrender.[13] Air power would allow land forces to occupy the town unopposed. It was, on a very small scale, the British strategy for defeating Germany.

On the eve of the attack, Air Vice Marshal D'Albiac took over the command of air units and Clark took over the ground forces. Clark and D'Albiac doubted the intimidatory impact of air power alone could achieve victory. Clark would have preferred the land forces to take advantage of the air assault by moving forward simultaneously. D'Albiac had no objections to a ground assault taking advantage of a brief air assault, but the primary role of the air force was to attack airfields in the rear, not targets the army could engage. However, it was too late for changes and the air attack went ahead as planned.[14]

The next day, forty-seven trainers and ten Blenheims attacked 'those points in Fallujah which it was known (from air reconnaissance and from ground reports) were held by enemy troops, the chief object of this aerial attack being demoralization'.[15] It was not so clear how such targets had been so accurately identified in a built-up area. It seemed more like a thinly disguised return to the indiscriminate policies of colonial 'Air Control' that Iraqis were already very familiar with. With Allied troops positioned around the town and the Iraqi Army occupying the town, it was a legitimate tactical target, but with no initial attempt to make any use of this assault to cover an attack on the town, the bombardment from the air was purely intimidatory. Following the air attack, leaflets were scattered on the town calling for Iraqi forces to surrender, but they showed no inclination to do so and continued light air attacks did not look like changing their minds. Finally, in mid-afternoon, the ground troops were ordered forward. The frontline Iraqi trenches were 'dive bombed and pattern bombed' by the trainers, and following a thirty-five-minute artillery barrage, the advance began and the town was rapidly captured. What had started as an attempt to win a battle by air power alone had ended as a classic example of air and ground forces working together to achieve victory.[16]

There was more evidence of the value of close air-support three days later, this time in a defensive situation. The Iraqis counter-attacked with the aim of recapturing the bridge over the Euphrates, and initially made good progress, but dive-bombing trainers helped stiffen the defences. Determined to retain the initiative, despite the relative weakness of his forces, Clark pushed on to Baghdad, and again the improvised RAF trainers played their part, engaging Iraqi strongpoints holding up the advance. With British forces approaching the capital and no more support coming from Germany, Rashid Ali fled the country and a more pro-British government was installed.[17]

The Habbaniya training unit found itself getting practical first-hand experience of a topic not on the normal syllabus – using an air force to provide close air-support in defensive and offensive situations. The campaign turned into a tutorial in army air support. Just about every application was covered. In Iraq it was the British who were boldly using close air-support and even landing airborne troops in the enemy rear. Aircraft had helped break up a threatening concentration of enemy forces surrounding the base, supported ground forces attempting to break through fortified positions, continued to support the troops on the ground as they advanced and helped break up counter-attacks. It was close support; targets were less than 1,000 yards from the Allied forward positions. Ironically, this support was being provided at the very time the Air Staff in London was puzzling over how the War Office expected 'centres of resistance immediately in front of forward troops' to be successfully attacked by the RAF. In practice, in real situations, finding targets was not the problem it seemed to be from the confines of the Air Ministry.

Just like the squadrons in the Western Desert and East Africa, the training units found themselves performing this role not through any application of a thoroughly thought through air doctrine, but simply because in the circumstances it seemed the best way to employ the available aircraft. As was so often the case in the Middle East, tactical air power was relatively easy to apply because the forces engaged were small and the fronts narrow, often just a single road. It was also more straightforward because there were no obvious strategic targets to muddy the waters and, more importantly, no air doctrine to cloud the mind. It was only when air commanders tried to apply Air Staff-inspired fundamental principles of air strategy that the RAF lost its way.

Once again obsolete planes had been used for ground attack, and once again it seemed that as long as the targets they were attacking were close to the frontline, hit-and-run attacks could be successful even with ancient biplanes. The Iraqi forces might not be as well equipped as the first wave of a German invasion, but there was some evidence that the RAF's Banquet scheme might have been able to achieve useful results.

It was always the Air Ministry way to say that no lessons could be learned from wars with so-called uncivilized opponents. It was not a proper enemy or a proper war. Lessons learned in a colonial context were only applicable in a major war when they happened to coincide with Air Staff thinking. The Air Staff was quite happy to apply the colonial tactic of using bombers to intimidate in the war with Germany, but tactical applications of air power were not so readily applied. What the RAF did in Iraq was no more than what Longmore's air force had managed against the Italians and what the Luftwaffe inflicted on Commonwealth forces in Greece and Crete. The scale and sophistication were different, but the principles were the same.

More experience was gained in Syria. The Vichy-controlled French colony had provided a staging post for the German forces that had flown to the assistance of the Iraqis, and the German presence on French airfields had already attracted Allied attacks. During one of these, on 14 May 1941, No. 250 Squadron, still forming on Tomahawks, flew the first mission by the American fighter, some seven months after the first the first batch arrived.

The possibility of German forces continuing to operate from Syria could not be ignored, and Commonwealth forces moved into the territory on 8 June. Initially there was little resistance, but it gradually increased as the French moved reinforcements in and there was some fierce fighting. The Allied forces were supported by an army co-operation squadron with Hurricanes, two Blenheim squadrons and two fighter units – a Hurricane squadron and No. 3 RAAF Squadron, with the Tomahawk. Many of the RAF Tomahawks were in fact French-ordered planes taken over by the British when France surrendered. It was unfortunate that their first victims should be French. There was also a flight of Gladiators. The bombers included a flight of four Blenheims specifically for close air-support duties. A Fleet Air Arm Fulmar squadron provided cover for Royal Navy ships that were to provide fire support for the advance along the coast.

The French initially had less than 100 aircraft, but reinforcements would bring this up to nearly 300. French fighters included the Dewoitine D.520, which was superior to the Hurricane I and had an even greater advantage over the two-seater naval Fulmars. The Fulmars were soon struggling and fleet protection duties had to be taken over by the RAF, stretching the available fighter resources even more thinly. Bombers attacked targets in the rear and on the battlefield. The fighters provided escorts, protected the troops and, whenever the opportunity arose, strafed enemy forces. The majority of bomber sorties were flown against targets beyond the battle zone, but any hold-up in the advance brought in the Blenheims to attack gun positions and strongpoints.[18]

The French response in the air was fierce. Fighters and reconnaissance planes joined the bombers in the assault on the advancing Allied columns. Even ancient Potez 25 biplanes bombed by night. The French attacks on occasion inflicted heavy losses and imposed severe delays. An Allied drive from Iraq was stopped dead in its tracks by French bombers. The French deployed their air resources resolutely and flexibly against their former allies, in a way they had not managed against the German invader in the Battle of France. Allied bombing sorties were fairly equally divided between ports, communication centres in the rear, aerodromes and battlefield targets.[19] As in Greece, overall, bombing was considered to have had less effect than ground strafing. In one case, nearly 50,000lb of bombs and incendiaries reportedly dropped on one airfield resulted in the destruction of just five planes, whereas strafing attacks on French airfields had inflicted some heavy losses, particularly in the second half of the campaign.[20] It was 12 July before the French finally agreed to an armistice.[21]

Tedder kept the Air Ministry up to date with the lessons learned in the Syrian campaign. He was never afraid to criticize what he saw as ponderous Army frontal assaults, and complained about the way every time a gun fired the Army wanted to know why the RAF had not destroyed it – it was the sort of talk that was always likely to go down well in the Air Ministry.[22] Real progress was made with close air-support; Tedder reported that air strikes requested by forward troops were delivered in forty-five minutes, and it was hoped to get this down to twenty-five minutes.[23] It was the sort of response time that Portal had been so certain was impossible.

While the fighting was raging in Syria, Wavell, under intense pressure from Churchill, was preparing to take on the Wehrmacht in the Western Desert. Whether this was wise while his forces were so heavily engaged further east had to be questionable. Rommel had already demonstrated what a formidable foe his Afrika Korps could be. The Luftwaffe was also arriving, and although numbers were small, planes of the quality of the Bf 109 were capable of having a huge impact. Wavell needed to be able to focus all his resources in the Western Desert if he was to have any chance of defeating Rommel.

Portal was at least now doing something about the Allied numerical weakness in the air. The increased flow of aircraft he set in motion was too late for Greece, but in April, around 200 planes arrived in the Middle East, compared to just seventy-eight in March. Another 200 arrived in May and nearly 400 in June. However, quality was still an issue. Tedder would have the first squadron of Tomahawks, No. 250, and No. 2 SAAF Squadron was also using Tomahawks alongside its Hurricanes. Although an enormous improvement on the Hurricane I, the Tomahawk was still inferior to the Bf 109E. The Hurricane IIs assigned to the Middle East were still only going to Malta, and, in any case, despite the altitude performance of the Merlin XX, it was no match for the Bf 109E. Tedder did, however, have the first squadron of Maryland bombers, a SAAF squadron transferred from East Africa making use of the allocation of Marylands sent to South Africa. A year after the first Marylands had been delivered to Britain, it was left to the South African Air Force to make first Allied use of the plane as a bomber since French Air Force missions in the May-June 1940 campaign.

On 15 June, even before the tank reinforcements Churchill had dispatched in the latest Tiger convoy could be fully incorporated into frontline strength, Wavell launched Operation Battleaxe. The rather grand objective was no less than the complete destruction of all Axis forces in North Africa. On the ground, Commonwealth forces had a two-to-one advantage in tanks, although many of the British tanks were either too slow or too lightly armed to challenge the panzers. In the air, Churchill saw no reason why the resources being devoted to the Middle East should not guarantee the Allies air superiority. Dill signalled a concerned Wavell that 'your greatly superior air strength is surely your greatest asset'.[24] Tedder wondered where London was getting its figures from. Churchill instructed Tedder to comb his rear units for every operational plane and crew. Aircrews and equipment from units still converting to or waiting for new equipment were used to reinforce frontline squadrons, but Tedder could still only muster around 240 planes, compared to the 360 the Germans and Italians could put into the air.[25]

The army and RAF entered the battle divided about how best to use the Air Force. Collishaw, the Air Force commander, wanted to use them aggressively against enemy airfields and support vehicles. Wavell, with the mayhem the Luftwaffe had caused in Greece very much in mind, again wanted them to cover the advancing Allied forces.[26] Both were right and both were needed, but with so few fighters available choices had to be made. With Portal's warning that in the current circumstances

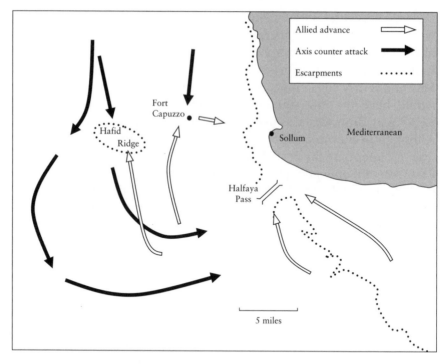

Operation Battleaxe June 1941

the army should be given what it wanted, Tedder let Wavell have his way.

The Allied plan was for a coastal drive through the Halfaya Pass with outflanking thrusts towards Hafid Ridge and Fort Capuzzo. At the Halfaya Pass, German 88mm anti-tank guns decimated the British tanks and the advance made no headway. The thrust towards Fort Capuzzo, however, made good progress and the strongpoint was captured. The Allied force then struck east for the coastal town of Sollum in an attempt to cut the line of retreat of the German forces holding the Halfaya Pass, but on 17 June the Germans were still stubbornly holding the coastal road.

In London, Dill, Churchill and Portal were following the progress of the battle from the War Room. Dill told Wavell to get Tedder to throw in the available bomber squadron against the forces holding the Halfaya Pass, 'as our troops were bombed in Crete', he suggested somewhat vengefully.[27] Portal reinforced the message with an instruction to Tedder to dispatch escorted Blenheims to deliver an intensive bombardment of German positions in the pass. Just a month before, Portal and the

180

Air Staff had claimed to be totally puzzled by what the Army meant by the 'centres of resistance' the RAF squadrons were supposed to attack. Portal now had no difficulty recognizing a 'centre of resistance' from 2,000 miles away and was urging the local commanders to throw everything at it.

Wavell could only reply that the situation was far too confused for such action. In fact, communications had completely broken down. Tedder had his Blenheims and Marylands on standby to strike, but no targets could be identified. Meanwhile, German forces were counter-attacking on the flanks. Fort Capuzzo was recaptured and German forces were dangerously poised to the south-west of the Allied troops attacking the Halfaya Pass. These movements were picked up by RAF reconnaissance, and two strikes were ordered against the threatening German columns. The Allied offensive was now in trouble and fighters were switched from air protection to ground attack in an attempt to slow down the advancing Germans. The ground forces pulled back as best they could, but large quantities of materiel had to be abandoned.

In the air it should have been no surprise that the Hurricane would struggle against the Bf 109E. Hurricane losses in combat with the German fighter rose rapidly, seven (and two more Tac/R Hurricanes) failing to return on 15 June, followed by three more the next day. The 17th was especially expensive, with eight lost in air combat and another two shot down by flak while ground-strafing. About a fifth of the available Hurricane force had been lost in a single day. The Tomahawk did not fare much better. No. 250 Squadron emerged from its first combat with Bf 109s on 16 June unscathed, but the next day four Bf 109s took seven Tomahawks by surprise, shooting down three without loss. On this evidence the Tomahawk was not the answer.[28]

The superiority of the Bf 109 was not mentioned in Tedder's report on the operation. This would seem too much like the carping his predecessor had been accused of. Instead of blaming the quality of the available equipment, Tedder preferred to point the finger at the inexperience of so many of his pilots and the overconfidence of those arriving from East Africa, where the opposition had been less effective. Collishaw was blamed for the rash way he had used his fighters, and was sacked. There was also the army to blame by insisting that fighters be used to provide permanent cover. It meant there were none available for other duties, including bomber escort, and this therefore placed a limit on the air support that could be provided. Nor were there enough to provide permanent cover. Fighters had to be dispatched in small formations and were therefore always outnumbered.[29] This might have explained some of the heavy losses, but even when the Allied fighters outnumbered the enemy, they still often came off worse. The Commonwealth air forces needed to outnumber the enemy just to offset the superiority of the Bf 109E, not to mention the superior tactics used by German fighter pilots. The bottom line was that the Allied forces did not have enough fighters for all the tasks they were expected to perform, and this had been the case in every land battle the Army had been engaged in since the outbreak of war.

Tedder would claim that the RAF had successfully performed its task, as on only two occasions were ground troops bombed in the first two days. Wavell felt he had been 'let down' on these two occasions. It was a question of glasses half empty and half full, although on this occasion the RAF seemed more in the right. There was a tendency by the army commanders of all nations to complain if their troops were bombed. Wavell was by no means blaming the failure of Battleaxe on the lack of air support, but the failure to gain air superiority was cited as one of the reasons. The Air Force, he claimed, had been unable to prevent enemy movement in the rear, but this accusation also seemed rather harsh. Portal felt obliged to ask Dill to make sure Wavell appreciated that with control of the air in the balance, to prevent all enemy movements was an unrealistic expectation. Even in Greece, with the total control of the air the Luftwaffe had possessed, the Germans had been unable to prevent Allied movements in the rear.

As far as Tedder was concerned there was no point in Wavell complaining about the lack of air support, if the army failed to make any use of what there was. On only one occasion during the offensive was a direct request for close support made by the army. This was for the destruction of a battery in the Halfaya Pass, which the RAF claimed to have carried out successfully, albeit at the cost of the single plane involved. Tedder claimed his bombers could have been involved in the fighting around Halfaya within ninety minutes if targets had been forthcoming. Wavell conceded that in this respect the British had a lot to learn from the Germans.

They did indeed. The air and ground elements of the Wehrmacht were much more focused. The British Army and RAF were very separate organizations which could work well together when everything was going well, but, quite literally, tended to spring apart when the going got tough. During Wavell's successful offensive against the Italians, the air and ground commanders had worked side by side. For Battleaxe, the air and army headquarters were some eighty miles apart. It was difficult enough to gather and act on intelligence at the best of times, but self-inflicted physical separation made successful co-operation even more difficult. Air/ground co-operation seemed to be going backwards. At least from this low point things could only get better. Portal may have ridiculed those who claimed German commanders could call up their 'pet' close-support plane every time they encountered a difficulty. However, in Syria, Allied squadrons were beginning to do this, and Tedder for one wanted to know how to do it better. He asked for personnel involved in the Northern Ireland close air-support trials to be sent to the Middle East.[30]

Events in the Mediterranean did not auger well for a successful defence of the United Kingdom should Hitler decide to invade. Tedder may have believed that all the expertise in ground air co-operation resided in the UK, but there was precious little sign of it at squadron level. A full year had passed since the British armies in Norway and France had experienced the effectiveness of German air support, but the Army and Air Force seemed no nearer to achieving the co-ordination and co-operation that might match it. Britain could not necessarily rely for ever on Hitler deciding that he had more important things to do than invade Britain.

The events on Crete seemed particularly alarming, with island defences overwhelmed by a largely airborne invasion. The British were not to know that the fierce resistance put up by the defenders and the huge material and personnel losses inflicted on the German airborne troops would ensure that this was the last major German airborne operation of the war. In Britain, two years into the war, the Air Force and Army were still locked in battle over how much air support the Amy could expect, the form it should take, who should control it and the means by which it would be delivered. Indeed, there was still a debate about whether the Army should get any bomber support on the battlefield. The RAF was even less capable of providing effective air support in the event of an invasion than it had the year before. Bomber Command had become an even more night bombing-orientated strategic force. To cap it all, there were doubts about the quality of the latest British fighters.

The only good news was that it seemed German forces were massing on the frontier with the Soviet Union, not the coast of the English Channel.

Chapter 10

A New Ally – New Approach

O n 22 June 1941, German forces, along with their newly acquired eastern European allies, launched a massive offensive along 1,000 miles of frontier with the Soviet Union. Britain had a new ally, not a minor player like Greece that could only field twenty divisions, but a major power with an army that dwarfed that of the British. Taking on the mighty Soviet Union dramatically shifted the balance of power. At a stroke, the German armed forces were now outnumbered by the enemies they faced.

This development did not immediately make Britain feel any more secure. No-one believed the Soviet Union would be any more successful than any of Germany's previous opponents at halting the Wehrmacht. Most gave the Red Army just a couple of months, and Germany would then be able to turn its full attention to Britain once more. It would be a rerun of 1940. Britain had gained another brief breathing space, no more; there might still be plenty of time for an autumn invasion. As the Soviet Army initially suffered crushing defeat after defeat, it seemed nothing could stop this prediction becoming a reality.

It was clearly in Britain's interests to assist the Soviets as much as possible, even if only to keep its new ally in the war a little longer and buy more time for Britain. Helping allies was something Britain was not very good at. It had also been in Britain's interests to keep Poland, Norway, Holland, Belgium, France and Greece in the war as long as possible, but had managed to lose all of them, often with much ill-feeling about how little support Britain had been able to provide.

On the face of it, the Soviet Union was the last country Churchill would want as an ally, but he immediately put aside his vehement hatred of all things communist and promised Stalin Britain's full support. Promising allies full support had never been a problem; delivering it had always

184

been the issue. The Soviet Union first and foremost wanted Britain to open a second front in Western Europe to take the pressure off the hard-pressed Soviet Armies. The pleas were incessant, and so logical that they generated considerable public support, with the arch-capitalist Beaverbrook one of the more notable and unlikely advocates.

It was a possibility the three Chiefs of Staff had not even begun to think about, let alone prepare for, and there was no immediate desire to start contemplating such a possibility. Dill may have argued that a land battle in northern France would eventually have to be fought, but he had no intention of fighting one in 1941. He was quite happy to go along with the Chiefs of Staff assessment that German forces were so powerful that even if the Soviet Union held on in the east, it would be impossible to defeat them in the west. It was a pretty damming assessment of Britain's fighting capabilities, and rather begs the question of how the British Army was supposed to defeat an invasion when there were no distractions in the east. For an invasion of Europe to succeed, the naval blockade, RAF bombing and resistance fighters on the continent would have to pave the way. Only when local uprisings had undermined German authority would the British Army step ashore. The consensus view was that the Soviet entry into the war did not improve Britain's chances of going onto the offensive. Interestingly, an American intervention was felt to be a very different matter. This would not only make victory certain, but might also make it very swift.[1]

For Churchill, an invasion of France was so inconceivable it did not even warrant the briefest of investigations. Britain's refusal to even consider this possibility, however, increased the pressure to meet Soviet demands for help in other ways. Stalin appealed for massive quantities of raw materials and equipment, including 6,000 modern bombers and fighters.[2] The sheer scale of the Soviet demands made them that much easier to reject, so beyond Britain's means were they. However, Sinclair, the Air Minister, suggested that a small number of Britain's American allocation might be diverted to the Soviet Union. It was decided that 140 Tomahawks in the UK and sixty straight from the United States could be spared.[3] Given the fuss that surrounded the transfer of sixty Tomahawks to the Greek Air Force just a few months before, this alone represented a major shift in attitude. The Lend-Lease Act had been passed and Britain was not actually paying for any of these aircraft, so it cost nothing, but it still represented a sizeable number of planes. No questions were asked about the quality of Soviet pilots or the ability of Soviet engineers and ground staff to handle modern equipment.

Nor was it suggested that spare parts might be a problem. Convoy PQ0 therefore set sail late in August with the first Tomahawks.

Beaverbrook was pushing very hard for far more substantial aid, and Churchill was soon asking the MAP and Air Ministry to do more – including the dispatch of British-built planes. Churchill had in mind a further 200 British fighters. Again, by comparison with previous efforts to aid allies the scale was staggering. No doubt Churchill reasoned that the 'splendid accumulation' of fighters he had become aware of in British stores could contribute far more to the war effort by being used on the Eastern Front. The Air Ministry was taken aback by the request, but as long as it did not involve parting with any of Britain's precious long-range bombers, it could live with the commitments Churchill and Beaverbrook were willing to make. The Air Ministry sought from Beaverbrook, and got, cast-iron guarantees that under no circumstances would the Soviets get any long-range bombers.[4] These were of course the last combat planes Stalin needed to halt the German advance. He only wanted fighters and tactical bombers.

The Air Ministry dutifully set about investigating what fighters could be sent. A dispassionate look at production and loss rates for the Hurricane and Spitfire led to a rather surprising conclusion. The underused Spitfire squadrons in the United Kingdom were losing fewer aircraft than were being built, while the hard-pressed Hurricane squadrons abroad were losing aircraft faster than they could be built. It therefore seemed more logical to supply the Russians with Spitfires. The uproar this would have provoked in the Middle East prevented this entirely logical but nevertheless bizarre option getting any further.[5] It would have indeed been strange if the first fighter pilots to fly the Spitfire from bases outside the UK had been Russian. Vice-Chief of the Air Staff Freeman drew up a plan which involved freeing 200 Hurricanes by re-equipping some Hurricane squadrons with Spitfires, presumably Mark Is which were still coming off the production lines, and by dipping into the quite substantial reserves.

Portal objected, not to the number of fighters involved but to their destination. He had to concede that with the fighter resources that existed in the United Kingdom, there could be no objection to such a large transfer of fighters overseas. Portal, however, claimed that the Eastern Front was not the place where the 'maximum dividend' would be obtained. Very few would reach the frontline, so the effect on the military situation would be minimal, he claimed. Portal seemed to be assuming the Russians would be just as slow getting these planes into service as the RAF had been with American imports. Portal suggested a far bigger 'dividend' would be gained by sending these planes to the Middle East, the Far East or, rather remarkably, Turkey.[6] The suggestion that the Middle East should get them was a measure of Portal's conversion to the need to reinforce that theatre, which must have left Longmore and the Greeks wishing Portal, or perhaps more pertinently Churchill, had taken a look at the reserves building up in the UK a little sooner. However, the Middle East was still in competition with other overseas theatres. With hindsight, the Far East seems like a reasonable destination for reinforcements, but scarcely a priority at the time when forces in the Middle East were in action and those in the Far East were not. The Turkey option was bizarre. Portal clearly still had hopes of setting up a base from which strategic bombing operations could be launched, but Turkey was not even a fully committed ally. Equipping the Turkish Air Force with Hurricanes that RAF squadrons in the Middle East needed was scarcely likely to be popular.

Even Churchill seemed to be losing interest in any further Balkan adventures. On 29 August, he promised Stalin the delivery of an additional 200 'eight and twelve gun Hurricanes that we have found very deadly in action'.[7] One hundred would be delivered in September, followed by another fifty in each of October and November. They would all be Hurricane IIs. This was an unprecedented level of support for an Allied air force. Just months before, the Air Ministry had offered the Greeks Gladiators and, when pushed, upgraded to Defiants. It refused to send Hurricane Is, and Hurricane IIs were never on the agenda. Now the Soviets were to get Hurricane IIs while most RAF squadrons in the Middle East were still struggling with the Hurricane I.

Stalin was extremely grateful for the sale of these planes and totally dumbfounded when he discovered there was no sale involved – the planes were a gift. This did not stop him asking for more. After a brief stabilization of the front in late summer, an alarmed Stalin warned Churchill that German forces were once again surging forward and only drastic measures could save the Soviet Union from defeat. His demands included the supply of 400 aircraft and 500 tanks a month.[8] If a second front in Europe was impossible, he also suggested that twenty-five to thirty British divisions should be transferred to the Eastern Front.[9] The request for British divisions was greeted with incredulity by Churchill. Britain could best support the Soviet Union in its desperate struggle by engaging the Luftwaffe with fighter sweeps over northern France and by bombing German industry by night, Churchill explained, which was no doubt greeted with equal incredulity by Stalin.

However, Churchill was now anxious to go even further with military aid. The Americans were also promising help, and a conference was organized in Moscow at the end of September to finalize details. Even before this meeting, Churchill promised Stalin that Britain would meet half of Soviet demands from British production, which put Britain's commitment at 200 planes a month. These would be delivered by convoys that would have to run the gauntlet of German warships, submarines and aircraft operating from Norway. This was one ally Churchill was determined not to lose.

The sudden demand for fighters alarmed Air Marshal Courtney's Supply and Organization section. Preparation of the first batch of 100 Hurricanes had, they claimed, cleared out the reserve; the second batch could only be sent at the expense of the Middle East.[10] An analysis of the RAF's future fighter needs revealed a rather disturbing picture. The Hurricane was due to be phased out by April 1942, but Spitfire output was only going to increase slightly. Combined Spitfire/Hurricane output would drop from 456 planes in September 1941 to just 280 in April 1942. The Typhoon was supposed to replace the Hurricane and eventually the Spitfire, but this was in all sorts of trouble. The American Mustang, Airacobra and Lightning fighters might fill the gap, but all were unproven designs.[11] The MAP suggested it was in the interests of the Air Ministry to play up the doubts about these planes to underline the difficulty of maintaining the promised delivery of fighter to the Soviet Union. There was little need to pretend. American designs never inspired much confidence, and there was little need to exaggerate the doubts about the Typhoon.[12]

The Tomahawk and its successor, the Kittyhawk, were supposed to re-equip Hurricane squadrons in the Middle East. In the UK, continuing Hurricane production ought to just about cover the declining number of squadrons equipped with the plane, but it was difficult to see how there would be any available to deliver to the Soviet Union. Indeed, with question marks about the Typhoon, it was difficult to see how Fighter Command strength could be maintained. Existing plans called for seventy-five day and twenty-five night fighter squadrons, but planned Spitfire production would only allow only sixty day squadrons with no reserve, or more realistically, fifty squadrons with a small reserve, and this was assuming none were delivered to the Soviet Union.[13]

The conclusion was that Britain could not possibly supply the Soviet Union with British planes, unless the Airacobra, Lightning or Mustang proved to be as good as the Spitfire, in which case Spitfires could be sent. There was a second conclusion that might have been drawn from these figures. Even for Britain's own needs, never mind Soviet ones, Britain was simply not building enough Spitfires, or indeed fighters of any description. As far as the Soviet commitment was concerned, the only alternative to British fighters was to use American Lend-Lease fighters, which would mean Britain was just borrowing planes off the United States to give to the Russians. Indeed, the aircraft would go straight from American factories to the Soviet Union, which might seem a rather odd way of supporting the Soviets.[14]

Beaverbrook set off for the Moscow conference determined to give the Soviets everything they needed. The Soviets were not expected to, nor did they intend to, justify their huge list of requirements. Nor, in the view of the Anglo-American team, did they show much appreciation. As far as the Soviets were concerned, Britain and the United States were just paying with military equipment for the sacrifice Soviet soldiers were making. The frosty, demanding, unconciliatory Soviet attitude did not discourage Beaverbrook from trying to offer even more. He contacted London to ask if he could offer 100 Spitfires, instead of Hurricanes, in the first batch of 200.[15] Just months before, he had been pleading with Churchill not to send a handful of Hurricanes to the Greeks.

Portal finally put his foot down. He told Churchill that Beaverbrook (and he might have added the prime minister, but perhaps thought better of it) was almost casually handing away hundreds of fighters. The planned commitments constituted about one-third of single-seater fighter output and two-thirds of total Hurricane production. There was going to be a desperate shortage of fighters the following spring – instead of the planned eighty-seven squadrons with reserves, Fighter Command might end up with just sixty-seven squadrons supported by no reserves. Demand from the Middle East for Hurricanes was rising, and there might not be enough to equip any Hurricane squadrons in the UK. The new Tornado and Typhoon were still unknown quantities and could not be relied on. If Fighter Command had to depend on the Spitfire, production at best could support fifty, possibly sixty squadrons. Portal pleaded to at least delay the start of any fighter deliveries to the Soviet Union.[16]

The Soviet request for Spitfires was even more worrying. An initial batch of 100 would be the thin end of the wedge, Portal protested. Even if the Soviets did not insist Spitfire deliveries continued every month, fifty to sixty would be required a month just to make good wastage. More likely, the Soviets would soon be demanding 200 cannon-armed Spitfires Vs a month.[17] With Beaverbrook's cavalier approach to Russian aid, Portal had every reason to fear the Soviets would get them.

To Portal's, and indeed Churchill's, relief Stalin's interest in Spitfires evaporated rather quickly. Perhaps one lesson Churchill drew from this was that Hurricanes and Spitfires were not as interchangeable as he thought; Spitfires were rather more valuable than Hurricanes. The British commitment was still huge. The massive aid programme to the Soviet Union agreed on 1 October required Britain to deliver 200 Hurricane IIs a month, plus 100 American fighters and 100 American light bombers from its Lend-Lease allocation.[18]

The Soviets were in desperate need of this aid. The German advance had forced them to uproot entire factories and transfer them further east. As the battle reached a crucial stage, Russian production was in freefall. The Russians may have complained about the machine-gun armed British and American fighters, and it was true that neither the Tomahawk nor the Hurricane II were as good as the Soviet Yak-1, but the Soviets had few of these. Most squadrons were still making do with obsolete biplane Polikarpov I-15 and only slightly more modern monoplane I-16s. The Russians needed every plane they could lay their hands on, and in the winter of 1941–42 the Tomahawks and Hurricane IIs were priceless acquisitions.

During the autumn and winter of 1941–42, the PQ convoys carried their precious cargoes through the arctic waters to Murmansk and Archangel, braving U-boat and Luftwaffe attack. On 7 September, Nos 81 and 134 Squadrons, equipped with Hurricane IIs, flew off the aircraft carrier *Argus* to Murmansk to help introduce the Hurricane to Soviet pilots. They would also provide air defence for the port and support Soviet forces defending the town. In fact they were mainly used to escort Soviet bombers over the frontline, which was not far west of Murmansk. The Soviets were quick to make use of the Hurricanes and Tomahawks. The first Tomahawks arrived at the beginning of September 1941. The planes were assembled, pilots trained to fly them and six weeks later the Tomahawks were flying operations over the front.[19] It was all very different to British efforts to get American fighters into action.

Once the floodgates had been opened, there seemed to be no stopping Churchill. He suggested that the seventy-five day and twenty-five night fighter squadrons Douglas at Fighter Command considered the very minimum to secure Britain against air attack was a rather generous allocation now that Germany was engaged against the Soviet Union and was also heavily involved in the Middle East. He now wanted twenty more fighter squadrons transferred overseas. It seemed that finally something was going to be done about the imbalance between the air resources doing little in the UK and the overstretched resources elsewhere. However, Churchill's idea was not more support for Stalin or to provide Wavell with overwhelming air superiority.

Churchill had become very familiar with the Air Staff belief that fighters should wherever possible be used for radar-controlled interception. As a document of the time casually reminded everyone, 'As is well known, the aeroplane is an extremely inefficient defensive weapon, except when used as part of a highly organised static defence system.'[20] This had always been used as a reason for not sending fighters abroad. Defending Allied armies in France in 1940 was a poor use of fighters because they could shoot down more aircraft if they were directed by radar over the UK, even if the British Army was being bombed and the UK was not. For the Air Ministry, the primary aim was always a high victory/loss ratio, rather than providing protection. The prime minister seemed to have taken this lesson to heart. His idea was that a chunk of Fighter Command – complete with radar, communications and sector stations – should be moved lock, stock and barrel to the Iran/Iraq/Syria area. For reasons which Churchill did not elaborate on, he believed that the existence of this force would compel the enemy to attack it, and the RAF could recreate the circumstances which had been so successful in the Battle of Britain, with fighters closely controlled by radar being used in a pure air battle. This, Churchill believed, would be 'a more paying business' than the fighter sweeps across northern France.[21]

It was a proposal that underlined the way radar tended to dominate and shape British air policy. For all radar's enormous benefits, air warfare could not always be fought like the Battle of Britain. In 1940, during the Battle of France, Dowding had encouraged the opening of the strategic air offensive in the hope that it would persuade the Luftwaffe to stop bombing Allied armies and start bombing the UK. Now Churchill was extending the idea by hoping to persuade the Luftwaffe to attack Fighter Command by moving it around the world. Commanders in the Middle East might argue that if the resources could be found to maintain a twenty-squadron fighter force in the barren deserts of Iraq, then surely something similar could be organized over the frontline in the Western Desert. Commonwealth troops needed fighters in the tactical zone, not an air defence system hundreds of miles in the rear.

Portal could see the logic of Churchill's argument but felt it might be difficult to recreate the sophisticated communication network in the deserts of the Near East. An Air Ministry study of the proposal pointed out that there were also only seventeen Hurricane squadrons left, so sending twenty would require the transfer of Spitfire squadrons, which was not considered a good idea.[22] Even sending all the Hurricane squadrons would cause problems, as Hurricane output would not cover combat losses, especially as the delivery of the first batch of 200 Hurricanes to the Soviet Union had 'cleared the Hurricane shelf'.

Nevertheless, Portal was still keen to do something along the lines of what Churchill was suggesting. Portal still feared a surprise German invasion of the UK in the spring of 1942, but keeping the Germans occupied in the Middle East was one way of making it less likely. As he explained:

> 'Air inferiority can be accepted with less risk where armies are not actually or potentially in contact than in areas where the enemy's air superiority may enable land forces to achieve a decision.'[23]

Allied commanders in the Mediterranean might have wished he had come to this conclusion a little sooner.

Portal reassessed Middle East fighter requirements and decided an extra seventeen squadrons would provide scope for a reasonable central reserve that could be used to defend Iraq or Turkey if the Germans occupied the Caucasus. This was eight more than the Tedder was asking for; the drive to send more fighters overseas was coming from London, not the Middle East. Again, however, Portal was trying to have it both ways by putting the onus on the Middle East to find the material for these squadrons. Four would have to come from resources in the Middle East, including half-formed South African squadrons and the remnants of the Greek Air Force. This left thirteen to find from Fighter Command.

However this number was soon to be whittled down. It seemed Hurricane output would not be able to cover the losses from so many Hurricane squadrons. Britain seemed to be in a position where it had fighter squadrons it did not dare use, because of the losses they would suffer. Douglas was adamant that his Fighter Command had to be kept up to strength, so the number of squadrons to be transferred was reduced to just six. Douglas only accepted this because a German air offensive was unlikely during the winter months, but he wanted replacement squadrons in place by the following spring. Douglas saw the seventy-five day fighter squadrons as a bare minimum, not a reserve for deployment overseas, just as Dowding had viewed Fighter Command during the Battle of France. He reminded Portal that invasion was still a real possibility in 1942, and of course there was always the fear of a purely aerial knockout blow.[24]

Like all commanders, it was of course Douglas's duty to get the best possible deal for his Fighter Command. Indeed, the air defence of the

United Kingdom deserved every fighter it could get. The risk of an aerial knockout should have been discounted by this time, but an invasion was still a real possibility and Douglas put up a strong argument for ensuring Fighter Command was kept up to strength. Douglas had always been more interested than most in tactical bombing, and he was becoming particularly interested in the ground-attack potential of the fighter. Ground-strafing Hurricanes had been very successful in recent operations over France, and he believed they would be particularly effective against naval vessels and the light tanks the German would probably have to use in the early stages of an invasion. With the 40mm cannon then being trialled, all enemy tanks would be vulnerable. He hailed the Hurricane II as Britain's answer to the dreaded Stuka. So enthusiastic was he about the ground-attack potential of his squadrons that he wanted them all trained in the role. Douglas clearly saw ground attack as a primary role for his force, not just for emergencies or if his fighters had nothing more useful to do. He warned Portal that if Fighter Command dropped below seventy-five squadrons, and there was an invasion, he would not have enough fighters to use any for ground attack.

Given that commanders rarely get everything they want, Douglas was doing much better than most. However, he was also highlighting the underlying problem more clearly than most:

'We have only to look back at the past history of the war – Norway, the Battle of France, the Middle East, Crete, the Russian campaign. The one cry all the way through was "More Fighters".'[25]

In this he was absolutely right. Britain had to start building more fighters. It was not a lack of industrial capacity that was preventing this. The Air Staff had a choice: Britain could build one Stirling heavy bomber or five Spitfires. The Air Staff preferred the Stirling. From a limited supply of fighters, Douglas was perhaps doing better than he should have been, but the real issue was that too few fighters were being built.

By emphasizing the versatility of Fighter Command as an air combat and ground-attack force, Douglas was putting the case for more fighters far more forcefully and effectively than Tedder. The Middle East was actually in far greater immediate need of fighters for both these roles, but Tedder was not demanding more fighters so he could use them for ground attack. He was not criticizing the quality, as Douglas was. He was not even demanding more for the air combat role.

Fighter Command was serving one useful purpose. It would be some time before the Middle East could go on to the offensive again, and all Churchill had to offer Stalin was the bomber offensive and Fighter Command sweeps over France. The RAF had been flying these sweeps over northern France since the beginning of 1941 as part of the more offensive spirit Douglas was determined to instil in his force. It was a straightforward struggle for air superiority that Fighter Command was only slowly adjusting to. Douglas's fighters were not designed for fighter-versus-fighter combat, and required various modifications. The way the carburettor-fed Merlin engine temporarily cut out when the pilot put the nose down to dive had not been a problem for a bomber interceptor, but German fighters, with their fuel injection system, did not have this problem. In dogfights, the Spitfires and Hurricanes were at a major disadvantage. Beatrice 'Tilly' Shilling at the Royal Aircraft Establishment came up with a simple modification which helped reduce the disadvantage, and this was fitted to fighters during the first half of 1941.

Poor manoeuvrability at high speed was another issue that was not a problem for a bomber interceptor, but it was a handicap for a dogfighter. Replacing the fabric covering on the ailerons with metal helped, and this improvement was introduced in the summer of 1941. The Air Ministry would always claim that British fighters were better armed than their German opponents, but in reality their armament was another disadvantage. Four cannon were not needed, their weight only making the Hurricane II even less suitable for fighter-versus-fighter combat. Fortunately, it was not possible to fit the Spitfire with four cannon; the two it carried were more than ample. The Bf 109F was very successful with just one cannon.

The tactics fighter pilots were using were also only slowly evolving. Squadrons gradually moved from the tight formations required for mass attacks on unescorted bombers to looser, more flexible pairs of fighters, which were far more suitable for fighter-versus-fighter combat. It was only in April 1941 that this became official policy, a delay the official narrative rather defensively sought to justify by claiming the new tactics were so obvious, they did not need to be dictated from above.[26] This was just another way of saying the pilots were expected to work it out for themselves. Even those who flew in pairs could not be expected to acquire instantly the expertise German pilots had gained over the years.

In the first five months of 1941, Fighter Command had lost heavily in its operations over France. A pause at the end of May caused by poor weather might have become permanent if intelligence reports had not spotted the movement of Luftwaffe units to the east. Portal asked his commanders to consider ways that this movement might be stopped, 'particularly in event of operations developing against Russia'.[27] Douglas suggested that it might be a good idea to pretend to be making preparations for an invasion of France. It gives some idea of how fanciful such an operation was viewed that it was dismissed out of hand. The Germans would never for one moment believe that Britain would be foolish enough to try. The RAF would have to distract German attention as best it could on its own. Douglas's fighter offensive would have to continue, with possibly heavier bombers like the Stirling joining the Blenheim on escorted missions to give the Luftwaffe more reason to respond.

From mid-June, there was a dramatic increase in Fighter Command sorties over France. Losses, however, rose proportionally. Once the Germans launched their attack on the Soviet Union, Fighter Command had to maintain the offensive. The German fighter pilots continued to react only if the fighters were escorting bombers, and only then if the tactical situation favoured the defenders, and this would remain the case as long as it was occupied France that was being bombed. There was no need to withdraw air units from the east. If the RAF was to provoke a stronger reaction, the bombers would have to fly deeper into enemy airspace by day and hit targets inside Germany. For Bomber Command it was an opportunity to kick-start its daylight bombing offensive. However successful night bombing might be (and there were already serious doubts), clearly it was easier to find and hit a target by day. If Bomber Command was going to dominate the skies above Europe, it was not going to be done scurrying around under the cover of darkness.

Peirse at Bomber Command was enthusiastic about giving daylight operations another go. With the German fighter force focusing on the Eastern Front, there might be more opportunities. The new generation of heavy/medium bombers (the Stirling, Halifax and Manchester) were better armed. No longer did anyone imagine that these would be capable of blasting their way through powerful fighter defences, as Peirse himself had once believed, but there did seem to be a chance that with fewer fighters in the west, the German defence might be caught out by the odd daylight raid inside Germany.[28]

Churchill wanted to go much further than this. Early in June, with evidence of the movement of Luftwaffe units eastwards mounting, he was encouraging Portal to reopen the day offensive and reconsider his ideas on the practicality of long-range fighters to escort them. This would not only enable Germany to be bombed on a 'severe scale' by day, but targets in the eastern Mediterranean like Crete and the Dodecanese would be within range. If the range of fighters was not extended, 'you will be helpless in the West and beaten in the East', he warned Portal.[29] It was one of Churchill's more perceptive observations. The way to air superiority was through the fighter, not the bomber, but short-range interceptors could not win this battle. For air superiority and escort, more range would be essential.

The Air Staff had never believed a long-range escort fighter was possible, partly because a fighter weighed down by the extra fuel would not be able to compete with a short-range interceptor carrying less fuel. Portal saw no reason why this would ever change. Single-seater escorts seemed especially unsuitable as they would always be vulnerable to attacks from the rear when the time came to head for home, but providing rear defence would make the fighter even less capable of dealing with shorter-range single-seaters. Portal pointed to the failure of the German Bf 110 as evidence that fighter escorts did not work.[30] The best efforts of the British aircraft industry to develop a long-range escort fighter seemed determined to prove Portal right.

The latest attempt was a specially modified long-range version of the Spitfire II. This project can be traced back to Douglas' decision in March 1940 to order 100 medium-range Spitfire fighters, making use of the rear fuselage tank first used in the photo-reconnaissance (PR) Spitfire. Supermarine pointed out that the installation of the tank would require the repositioning of certain equipment, much of which had not been required in the PR Spitfire, and in any case all the PR Spitfires had been individually modified. If a long-range version was to be mass-produced then it would be far simpler if a 29-gallon slipper tank was fitted to the starboard wing, an arrangement which had been successfully used on one of the PR versions of the Spitfire. Supermarine assured the Air Ministry that the reduction in top speed would be a mere 3mph. At the beginning of June 1940, with the crucial Battle of Britain looming, Dowding was taken aback by a request to nominate three squadrons to re-equip with this long-range version of the Spitfire I. Dowding could not believe that fighter operations over the continent were being contemplated at this delicate stage of the war. It seems some were delivered to No. 602 Squadron in Scotland, but Dowding made sure no more squadrons get the modified Spitfire.[31]

In the spring of 1941, the project was revived. It was not just the need to escort Bomber Command that was focusing minds. The new Merlin XX and 45 engines had higher fuel consumption, which meant even lower endurance if no extra fuel could be carried. In April 1941,

Supermarine was told to resurrect the long-range Spitfire project, this time using the Spitfire II, and rather than a 29-gallon tank, a 40-gallon tank was to be fitted to the port wing. This was no longer the neatly faired slipper tank of the previous proposal; it was nothing short of a carbuncle, totally at odds with the ultra-sleek lines of the rest of the fighter.

Surprisingly, tests carried out in May reported no loss of performance, and in July Nos 66, 152 and 234 Squadrons converted to the fighter. Pilots were far from happy with their new plane and soon discovered that, despite what the experts claimed, maximum speed, manoeuvrability and climb were all seriously affected by the wing-tank. The operational debut on 10 July 1941, a raid on Cherbourg, revealed the plane was not only a failure, it was also a dangerous failure. One pilot was seen bailing out after his plane suddenly went into an uncontrollable spin, and another only regained control of his plane after falling several thousand feet.[32]

Boscombe Down was immediately instructed to carry out a more thorough examination of the plane. Far from having a top speed of 354mph, Boscombe Down now conceded it was capable of a mere 325mph. Another way had to be found of extending the Spitfire's range. Either more fuel had to be carried internally or drop tanks had to be used.[33] As events would show, there was no reason why both approaches could not be adopted, but at this stage they were seen as alternatives.

It was still not so obvious that a jettisonable tank held any real advantages over internal tanks. Once the petrol in an internal tank was used up, the weight of the tank was not a huge handicap. The externally mounted tank, on the other hand, increased drag until its fuel was used up, thereby reducing the extra range gained. There was also a reluctance to throw away valuable metal and indeed supply the enemy with useful scrap metal. The easiest way for the Spitfire to carry extra fuel was the spaces in the inboard wing leading edge, where the abandoned evaporative cooling system used to be. There was only space for 10 or possibly 15 gallons in each wing, but this was deemed sufficient and would become standard in future versions of the Spitfire. Until these became available, drop tanks would be used. The Air Ministry initially wanted 100 Spitfire Vs modified on the production line to carry 30-gallon jettisonable tanks and sufficient tanks for thirty sorties. In August, Douglas doubled the number of Spitfires that were to be capable of carrying a drop tank, but it was still a timid approach in terms of extra fuel carried and the number of fighters that would use the tanks.[34]

Even the drop tanks would not be available until the end of the year, and in the meantime pilots were told they would have to make do with the existing long-range Spitfire II with its permanent wing tank.[35] An attack on German warships based in French Atlantic ports would provide an opportunity to see whether an escort combined with the new bombers reaching Bomber Command would make a return to daylight operations a practicable proposition.

Despite the dramatic sinking of the *Bismarck* in February 1941, the Battle of the Atlantic was not going well for Britain. In March 1941, an alarmed Churchill instructed Portal to switch Bomber Command's effort to naval targets. Chief amongst these were the pocket battleships *Scharnhorst* and *Gneisenau*, which had been in Brest since the sinking of the *Bismarck*. Both were well placed to strike the Atlantic convoys. The ships were very small target for bombers to hit. Photographic evidence of the fall of bombs during a night raid by fifty-four Wellingtons on the Bremen Focke-Wulf factory on the night of 12 March 1941 demonstrated just how difficult such raids were. The raid was carried out in ideal conditions, but just twelve of the 200 bombs carried by the attacking bombers hit the target. Superimposing the outline of the *Scharnhorst* on the centre of the factory revealed that had the pocket battleship been the target, none of the bombs would have hit the ship. To have any chance of success, bombers would have to attack the warships by day. Brest was far further than Circus missions had been able to reach, so it would be an opportunity to find out if Bomber Command could operate by day beyond the range of the standard fighters available to Fighter Command.

It was a raid that would see Bomber Command try out most of the available options for deep penetration daylight bombing. The newly arrived American Boeing B-17 Flying Fortresses would be used at high altitude, the new Manchesters and Halifaxes would be tried out by day and the long-range Spitfires would provide escort. The Fortresses would open the attack and try to draw enemy fighters into the air prematurely. Three squadrons of long-range Spitfire IIs would provide close escort for a second wave of Hampdens. Then the main strike would be made by Wellingtons, Manchesters and Halifaxes, with the two remaining long-range Spitfire squadrons providing a looser, indirect escort. It was hoped that by this time the German interceptors would be returning to base. At the last minute the Manchesters, with their notoriously unreliable engines, were grounded. Further complications arose when, just before the raid was due to be launched, the *Scharnhorst* moved to La Pallice, beyond the range of the Spitfire escort. The Halifaxes would take on this target without an escort.

On 24 July, three Fortresses followed by the eighteen Hampdens and, a little later, seventy-nine Wellingtons bombed Brest, while fifteen Halifaxes tackled the *Scharnhorst* at La Pallice. German defences proved stronger than expected, with pilots from operational training units joining regular Luftwaffe squadrons. The initial attack failed to draw the sting of the German defences. The three Fortresses avoided interception, but ten Wellingtons and two Hampdens, 12 per cent of the force, were lost. Losses among the closely escorted Hampdens were not significantly lower than among the less well-protected Wellingtons. The fifteen unescorted Halifaxes suffered more heavily, with five shot down and all the rest damaged. The overall loss rate was an unacceptable 15 per cent. Tactically the raid was a partial success, with *Scharnhorst* suffering damage that kept it out of action for several months. However, the high loss rate did not bode well for any attempt to attack targets in Germany by day.[36] Long-range Spitfires had not provided enough protection, and the new more heavily armed Halifax bombers had been unable to defend themselves. Even stiffer resistance could be expected against targets in Germany.

A huge amount of effort had gone into this operation. Formation flying was a rapidly disappearing skill within Bomber Command, and the Hampdens had been practising for a month. The standard of formation flying was far from perfect, but this was not felt to be a significant factor. Arguably, one mission was not enough to assess the value of the fighter escort, but the idiosyncratic handling characteristics of the lopsided Spitfires scarcely encouraged too much experimentation.

Work continued on adapting the Spitfire V to carry a 30-gallon jettisonable tank, but none would be available until 1942.[37] Even with the drop tank, the Spitfire could still not reach German air space. An extra 30 gallons was a useful increase, but it did not offer the single-seater fighter any real strategic value. Going any further did not seem possible as 'the Spitfire does not lend itself to [drop] tanks bigger than 30 gallons', it was rather dogmatically decided.[38] While getting fighters to carry more fuel seemed to pose all sorts of problems in the UK, in the Middle East, Tedder was rather guiltily admitting that his technicians, in 'an interesting and highly illegal sideline', had been fitting Hurricanes with internal wing tanks, without needing to remove any guns or ammunition, turning the plane into a 'useful long-range fighter'.[39] Like many other innovations, what seemed to require endless debate and controversy in the UK just evolved naturally in the Middle East. Portal was forced to concede that Hurricanes in the Middle East had a range of 900 miles, nearly twice that of the standard model, but continued to insist they could only operate where there were no enemy fighters.[40] It was almost as if the Air Staff was hoping escorts were not the answer. A huge fleet of escort fighters could only make the strategic air offensive even more unaffordable. The 2,000 long-range fighters the Air Ministry had claimed an invasion of Europe would require had been used to demonstrate how unrealistic War Office ideas for landings in France were. There was no reason to suppose it was any more realistic to create such a fleet to protect the 4,000-strong bomber force Portal was hoping to build.

The high-level bombing experiment with the American Fortresses did not look like the solution either. The bomber could only carry a relatively small bomb load, and the RAF was soon discovering all the disadvantages of operating at such extreme altitudes. Guns froze and other equipment failed as aircrews struggled to cope in appalling conditions on the edge of the stratosphere. Time and again the appearance of condensation trails forced missions to be aborted. Of the fifty-one sorties flown by the RAF Fortresses, half had to be abandoned for one reason or another. Initially it seemed that the effort at least meant German defences could be evaded, as German fighters were sometimes spotted far below, struggling to reach the bombers. However, interceptions started becoming more frequent, culminating in a disastrous raid on Oslo by four Fortresses on 8 September, when one was shot down by fighters, another was badly damaged and a third failed to return for reasons unknown. The experiment was ended and No. 90 Squadron disbanded.[41]

Development of the Wellington VI continued, and its pressurized cabin ought to ease some of the problems, but hitting targets from such high altitudes was not as easy as the makers of the much-vaunted Sperry bombsight were making out. The Americans observers came to similar conclusions. The Fortress had never been designed for high-altitude bombing, and the British experience reinforced their view that future models of the bomber should attempt to beat off fighter attack at medium altitude.

There was always the high-speed option, and with the Mosquito the RAF had an outstanding 'speed bomber'. The plane had a rather odd early history. An early incarnation of the twin-engined wooden bomber had suffered the indignity, with hindsight, of being rejected in favour of the ill-starred Albemarle. Before a much-revised prototype flew, fifty had been ordered in the spring of 1940, but this apparent display of confidence did not reflect Air Staff opinion of the plane's potential. There was little faith in the plane as a bomber, or indeed in

200

any role other than reconnaissance. The Air Staff thought the idea of an unarmed high-speed bomber was a myth, and the plane was not manoeuvrable enough to be a fighter. Beyond reconnaissance, its only role would be filling a Fleet Air Arm requirement for a target tug. When the Reaper twin-engined fighter was abandoned to allow Gloster to focus on its Meteor jet fighter, the Mosquito was accepted as a second-best substitute and thirty of the fifty on order were to be built as night fighters. Even after the prototype flew in November 1940, the value of the plane was still not appreciated. In December, it was proposed that another 150 be ordered to meet the Admiralty requirement for a target tug, with possibly a few more for the RAF for similar duties.[42]

Then, early in 1941, everyone suddenly realized what the RAF had and everyone wanted it. Coastal Command wanted the plane as a long-range fighter, and Peirse at Bomber Command was pestering the Air Ministry for a bomber version and was none too pleased when told the night-fighter version was getting priority.[43] Even now, the MAP still seemed in the dark about the value of the plane. It complained that de Havilland could not possibly deal with all these new requirements, being too busy making the plane suitable for target towing. In June 1941, the Admiralty was still expecting its Mosquito target tug. Nobody seems to have got round to telling the Admiralty there was no chance of arguably Britain's best and most versatile warplane being using to haul practice targets around.[44] However, despite Peirse's interest and the plane's remarkable performance, the Air Ministry was right to believe it could not be relied on to deliver the strategic bombing offensive. It could only carry a relatively small bomb load, and at any time a new faster German fighter might make the unarmed bomber obsolete overnight. It would be very useful for hit and run nuisance raids, but no more.

On 29 July 1941, Peirse conceded that he had been too optimistic. Germany's preoccupation with the Eastern Front was not going to enable his bombers to operate by day.[45] This, however, would not put him off attempting a fortnight later a daring low-level strike on the Ruhr with the day-bombers of No. 2 Group. A raid on the Ruhr power stations had been one of Bomber Command's favoured projects in the late Thirties. It would finally get an opportunity to see if the low-level, unescorted approach would work. It would not be on the scale envisaged in the Thirties; only the Blenheims of No. 2 Group would take part, and only two power stations would be targeted. Every effort was made to distract the German defences: Fighter Command flew patrols over northern France, twelve escorted Hampdens bombed St Omer airfield and Gosnay power station, and four unescorted Fortresses, flying at over 35,000ft, bombed Cologne and De Koy airfields and Emden. Nothing this elaborate had been planned to support the pre-war plans. Whirlwinds escorted the Blenheims as far as they could, but when the bombers crossed the Dutch coast they were on their own. Of the fifty-four Blenheims taking part, ten were lost to flak and fighters. Even with the Luftwaffe concentrating on the Eastern Front, there was plenty left to defend the Reich. Not even the occasional surprise attack was going to embarrass the Germans.

Escorted raids over northern France were not going to force the Germans to switch fighters from the Eastern Front, and to make matters worse, these were proving ever more expensive. The Luftwaffe lost just eighteen fighters in August compared to the 108 lost by Fighter Command. In three months, 277 RAF fighters were lost over France, which meant losing the same number of pilots. Even inflated claims by British pilots could not hide the fact that Fighter Command was continuing to come off worse.

The losses came at a time when Britain was desperately short of fighters. More were being sent to the Middle East and hundreds promised to the Soviet Union. The Hurricane was being phased out, the Typhoon was not ready to replace it and Spitfire production was not increasing to compensate. The Air Ministry knew there was going to be a severe shortage over the winter months. Fighter Command could not afford to throw away fighters on missions over France that were achieving little. In September, Fighter Command was told to scale back operations; the priority was to conserve strength.[46]

This decision was taken just in time, for the struggle was becoming even more one-sided. In September, British pilots began encountering a fast and manoeuvrable radial-engined fighter. These were initially identified as Bloch 152 or Curtiss H75 (Mohawk) fighters captured from the French, tantalizing evidence for those who wished to believe that Bomber Command was having a real impact on German war output. The new fighter the RAF was now encountering had many of the fine qualities of the American Curtiss H75, but the American fighter never flew this fast. Intelligence soon confirmed that pilots were not dealing with captured French fighters; the long-awaited Focke-Wulf FW 190 had arrived.

The appearance of this outstanding new German fighter looked like another blow for Douglas. The expectation was still that Germany would defeat the Soviet Union, although there was huge relief that Russian resistance had at least delayed a renewal of the offensive against Britain until 1942. Douglas had already judged the Fighter Command of 1941 to be inferior to the force that had existed in 1940. However, if anything the prospects for the spring of 1942 appeared even worse. At altitude, the Bf 109F was clearly superior to the Spitfire V. Now at low and medium altitudes the Spitfire was outclassed by the FW 190. British fighter design was slipping ever further behind.

Yet, despite the alarming reports from the pilots, it was still not the dogfighting capabilities of British fighters that was causing the Air Ministry or Douglas concern. There was a lot of talk about needing to improve performance, but no rethink about what needed improving, apart from the need to fly ever higher. British intelligence was expecting the Luftwaffe to have in service by 1942 bombers and fighters which could operate between 35,000 and 40,000ft, outflanking the United Kingdom's air defences. This was the challenge British fighter designers were expected to meet. Douglas wanted a general purpose fighter with a service ceiling of at least 36,000ft, preferably 40,000ft, with a top speed in excess of 400mph, and a specialized high-altitude interceptor with a service ceiling of at least 41,000ft, but eventually 45,000ft.[47] Douglas did not have these fighters in 1941 and knew he was unlikely to get them before the spring of 1942. It was this, not the extraordinary manoeuvrability of the FW 190 at medium and low altitudes, that worried him.

Douglas accepted that by the spring of 1942, the Hurricane II would be obsolete as a fighter. If the Typhoon's technical problems could be sorted out, it might be able to deal with medium-altitude bombers, but the plane lacked the ceiling to deal with future high-altitude fighters or even the existing Bf 109F. The Tornado might offer slightly superior altitude performance, but was slower than the Typhoon. The high-altitude versions of the Spitfire V and the Merlin 61-powered Spitfire might eventually give Douglas fighters that could reach bombers above 35,000ft, but there was nothing planned that could climb above 40,000ft. Development of specialized high-altitude interceptors continued apace. The Vickers 432 joined the Westland Welkin in the development programme, but neither was anywhere near a first flight.

American imports offered no immediate solutions to the high-altitude problem. The Allison engine which powered most American fighters did not perform well at high altitude. The Mustang had already been relegated to army co-operation duties. By January 1942, it was planned to equip seven squadrons with the Bell Airacobra, also powered by the Allison. Although not capable of the promised 400mph, the Airacobra was another extremely useful low/medium-altitude fighter which was up to 30mph faster than the Spitfire V at altitudes up to 18,000ft. With its excellent range, it was considered a useful asset and indeed, like previous American fighters, it was ideal for low/medium-altitude tactical air fighting.[48] However, it seemed that the poor altitude performance of the Allison engine would condemn any American fighter powered by it.[49]

The Lockheed Lightning looked like it might buck the trend. The twin-engined fighter also used the Allison, but the engines were boosted by a revolutionary but rather complicated turbo-supercharger system, a feature which dictated its clumsy twin-boom layout. The Air Ministry expected this to be able to match German fighters at any altitude, although clearly it was again only thinking about speed and service ceiling, not manoeuvrability. The twin-engined, twin-boom layout did not lend itself to agility and dogfighting. Unfortunately, the first 177 were going to be delivered to Britain without the turbo-supercharger, which would mean they would have all the disadvantages of a twin-boom layout without the compensations of the supercharger. Three Fighter Command squadrons were supposed to have the fighter by January 1942.[50]

The jet engine seemed to be a ray of hope. Tizard, at the Ministry of Aircraft Production, did not believe that piston engines more powerful than the Sabre or Vulture were possible, and was convinced that Britain had to start thinking seriously about moving to jet power. Portal was hoping for speeds of 475mph from the next generation of fighters, and Tizard thought this would only be possible with jet engines.[51] The Gloster/Whittle jet fighter was still only a design on the drawing board, but Tizard was convinced the revolutionary power plants could hasten victory and that there was no reason why jet fighters could not be in production by 1942. Turning to jet power so soon might be a gamble, but he felt it was a gamble worth taking.

The Treasury was persuaded, and early in 1941, twelve prototype jet fighters were ordered and Gloster was told to start preparing for the delivery of eighty per month from the beginning of 1942.[52] If such a timetable was to be achieved, the Spitfire/Merlin 61 high-altitude fighter might become obsolete before it even flew. In May 1941, the Gloster G.40 experimental research plane took to the air, the first flight by a plane using Whittle's revolutionary jet engine. In September, Gloster's Thunderbolt twin-engined fighter, the future Meteor, was considered so promising it was included in production schedules, with the first delivery expected in February 1942. The Gloster G.40 had demonstrated the practicality of the jet engine, but attempts to increase the output of the engine were proving more difficult than anticipated. Even so, Churchill was so worried by what unopposed bombers flying at high altitude might do that in the summer of 1941 he was suggesting a chance be taken and work start on a production run of 1,000 Thunderbolt fighters before the prototype had even taken to the air.[53] Huge risks were being considered to deal with high-altitude bombing, while virtually no thought was being given to developing a fighter that could dominate the skies over the battlefield at lower altitudes.

The Spitfire in any form was still Douglas's first choice fighter. He was decidedly nervous about any of the alternatives living up to expectations, and argued that Spitfire production should be increased to guard against disappointment. Douglas had good reason to be suspicious. The Tornado was already on the brink of being abandoned. Its Rolls-Royce Vulture engines were not only unreliable, they were competing with the Merlin for production space, and with all the available machine tools being siphoned off into the massive effort to build up Napier production capacity, there was little left over for Rolls-Royce.[54] Indeed, planned Sabre production exceeded demand, so there would be no problem increasing Typhoon output. Abandoning the Tornado and its ill-starred Vulture would free Rolls-Royce to produce more Merlins. This in turn would allow more Hurricanes to be built to help meet the Soviet commitment.[55] In October, Rolls-Royce was instructed to terminate production of the Vulture.[56] Enough were to be produced to complete those Manchesters still being built, but no fighters were to be powered by the engine. Six weeks after the first Tornado airframe left the assembly lines, production of the fighter was cancelled. The Sabre-powered Typhoon was scarcely any nearer to overcoming its problems, but at least Camm, Hawker's chief designer, would now only have one fighter to worry about.

Only the Spitfire seemed to offer the prospect of reliability and reasonable performance in 1942, but it was only reasonable performance. The Spitfire V fitted with the Merlin 46, tweaked to improve output at altitude, gave the fighter a service ceiling of 40,000ft and would just about satisfy the general-purpose fighter requirement. The Spitfire VI, a makeshift high-altitude version with the Merlin 47, which offered a degree of pressurization for the pilots, was about the best bet for the high-altitude role. Neither was ideal. Only about 100 of the specialized Spitfire VI were to be built, and there were doubts as to whether the marginal performance advantage at altitude warranted the disruption to production this small production run would entail. The best bet seemed the Merlin 61-powered Spitfire VII. Development of the Merlin 60 series engine was going well; it was now hoped to have the Merlin 60 bomber version of the engine in production in 1941, with the Merlin 61 fighter version following early in 1942, but Spitfires with the engine (the Spitfire VII) were not expected before April 1942. These were still seen as specialist high-altitude fighters that would only have mediocre performance at lower altitudes

By January 1942, Douglas hoped to have sixty Spitfire V, fifteen Hurricane II, four Typhoon, seven Airacobra and three Lightning squadrons. In the spring of 1942, the Spitfire V would still be numerically by far the most important fighter available to Douglas. It would also be his best, yet it was inferior to the Bf 109F and FW 190, and there was nothing in the pipeline that promised to be better. The future was not looking good. Come the spring of 1942, Douglas feared that his command would be even less well prepared to take on the Luftwaffe than it had been the previous spring.[57] Fighter Command was losing more ground.

Out of the blue, however, a ray of hope appeared. It seemed that the Merlin 61 might offer far more than even Rolls-Royce had anticipated. In the early summer of 1941, the Air Ministry was still assuming that the Merlin 61 powered-Spitfire would offer excellent performance at high altitude but would be inferior to the Merlin 45 Spitfire V below 27,000ft. In June 1941, however, Rolls-Royce surprised the Air Ministry by announcing that the Merlin 61 was going to be a far more versatile engine than anticipated. Trials had revealed the engine was going to combine the high-altitude performance that the Merlin 60 series was designed to produce without losing the low-altitude performance of the Merlin 45.[58] The Spitfire III airframe was given to Rolls-Royce to try out the engine. This flew in September 1941, and it soon became clear that the Merlin 61 could do even better than that. The Merlin 61 Spitfire not only had a service ceiling of 42,000ft and an astonishing 75mph speed advantage over the Spitfire V at 30,000ft, it was also some 30mph faster at low and medium altitudes. This was an unexpected bonus. The Merlin 61 Spitfire met fighter Command requirements at all altitudes.[59]

As well as the Mark VII with a pressurized cockpit, a Mark VIII without pressurization would also be built. Both would have a new wing which would incorporate the 14-gallon leading edge tanks, although this was not going to offer much additional range. Much of this extra fuel would be needed to compensate for the increased fuel consumption of the Merlin 61. The MAP believed that both versions of the Spitfire could be in service in reasonable numbers by the summer of 1942.[60] Douglas would not be getting the 45,000ft ceiling he felt he needed, but he was getting a manoeuvrable, single-engined fighter that was vastly superior to the Spitfire V at all altitudes.

Even more was expected from Griffon-powered Spitfires. In its early single-stage form (Griffon IIb), the engine only offered high power at low altitude. In November 1941, the first Spitfire IV, with the single-stage two-speed Griffon, took to the air. Above 24,000ft, the Merlin 61 Spitfire was far superior, but below that altitude the Spitfire IV was quicker. At very low altitudes it was as much as 30–40mph faster. However, Rolls-Royce planned to incorporate the same two-stage supercharging that had made the Merlin 61 so successful. If the Griffon 61 produced the same performance advance as the Merlin 61, the Griffon-powered Spitfire would be superior at all altitudes to both the Merlin 61 Spitfire and Typhoon.[61] As 1941 drew to a close, the medium/long-term prospects for the fighter force were beginning to look much brighter.

In the short term, the Ministry of Aircraft Production was still confident that the Typhoon could be turned into a successful fighter. The first squadrons began converting to the Typhoon in September 1941, but the engine was giving so much trouble that at the end of the year the plane was still not ready to fly operations. With every passing month, the case for abandoning the Typhoon was growing stronger. The Spitfire was a proven airframe, it was lighter than the Typhoon, more manoeuvrable and had a higher rate of climb. It was an easier plane to fly and was powered by an infinitely more reliable engine. The Merlin 61 and eventually the Griffon 61-powered Spitfires were the best way of closing the gap that was opening up between British and German fighters. Two-stage supercharging was something Napier engineers could only dream about as they struggled to tame their single-stage Sabre.

Camm was under no illusions about the Typhoon's shortcomings. Hawker was already working on the design of the far more refined Typhoon II (the future Tempest), with completely new, thinner elliptical wings. Two prototypes were ordered in late 1941. Whether it was needed was debateable. The Spitfire already provided the RAF with an excellent thin-wing fighter. It was difficult to make any sort of a case for sticking with the Typhoon – except that so much effort had gone into preparations to mass-produce its Sabre engine. The Air Ministry and MAP had been ruthless with the Tornado, but that decision had been relatively easy because scrapping the Vulture engine had freed Rolls-Royce capacity to produce more Merlins. There was no way of using the surplus Sabre capacity so easily. Too much had been invested in the Typhoon/Sabre combination to scrap it now. It had to be made to work.

As with the Hurricane II at the beginning of the year, the RAF found itself having to rely far too heavily on a fighter that was inherently flawed.

Chapter 11

Butt Bombshell

Despite the problems, the Air Staff was still convinced the bomber offensive would prove to be a war-winning weapon. Peirse was more aware than most of the problems. Only when conditions were good could he expect a reasonable number of his crews to find their targets, and losses were rising. Bomber Command had already demanded the development of warning devices, and better defensive armament was back on the agenda again. In the winter of 1940–41 operations were cut back as there was no point risking highly trained aircrews unnecessarily when a new generation of heavy bombers was about to enter service. However, even with the latest bombers, losses continued to rise. The loss rate reached 4 per cent again in March, fell back to 3 per cent in April but then steadily climbed as Bomber Command turned more of its attention to targets inside Germany. In the first eighteen days of August 1941, the loss of 107 bombers caused sufficient concern for the problem to be discussed by the Cabinet. Overall, losses in August broke the 5 per cent barrier for the first time.

It was not difficult to explain why losses were increasing. Reports from agents, Enigma intercepts and monitoring German radar emissions had enabled British intelligence to build up a fairly clear picture of how German radar was being used. Long-range early warning was provided by the Freya system, which was operating on a 2.5m wavelength, far lower than the British Chain Home system. The 53cm wavelength Wurzburg system was not as advanced as British centimetric radar, but it was accurate enough to guide searchlights, anti-aircraft guns and fighters. It was more difficult to work out the radar systems that German night fighters were using, but there was every reason to suppose the Luftwaffe had developed techniques similar to those used by Fighter Command.[1]

The Air Ministry had always preferred to blame anti-aircraft fire rather than fighters for bomber losses. Admitting fighters were causing the problem called into question the fundamental Air Staff belief that bombers could fight their way through to any target. Nothing could be done about anti-aircraft fire; that was just bad luck. The evidence that flak was the main problem was rather suspect. The damage on planes that made it back was invariably caused by flak, so it was assumed, incorrectly, that most aircraft that did not return were also victims of anti-aircraft fire. In fact, the evidence merely demonstrated that bombers were more likely to survive anti-aircraft fire. Bombers caught in the gun sights of a fighter were not so likely to make it back.

As the RAF knew all too well, it was extremely difficult for a fighter to find the attacking bomber, even with the help of radar. However, if the interceptor succeeded in making contact with the bomber the tables were turned, and it was the lone bomber that was at a severe disadvantage. The approaching fighter was difficult to spot and the German fighters were equipped with cannon, while the bombers only had rifle-calibre machine guns. As radar interception techniques improved, there was a danger the bombers might end up even more vulnerable than when they were flying in formation by day.

By the summer of 1941, Slessor at No. 5 Group was demanding some action. He believed it was only a matter of time before night fighters using airborne radar would be able to shoot down bombers without even seeing them, and he wanted his crews to have their own radar to tell them where the enemy fighters were.[2] The previous November, Bomber Command had asked for ways of using radar to be investigated; the Interception Committee was supposed to be looking into it.

In June 1941, Peirse passed on to the Air Ministry Slessor's requests for some sort of warning devices for his bomber crews, with the reminder that they had made a similar request the previous November. However, it seemed that the Interception Committee had never discussed the matter and the Air Ministry was forced to concede that his request had apparently 'got lost' and nothing had happened.[3] Peirse made sure the issue would not be forgotten again, and the Telecommunications Research Establishment (TRE) set to work. Their research would eventually lead to Boozer, a passive warning device that would tell the crew if any German radar was tracking them, and Monica, an active device that would use centimetric radar to locate any enemy fighter approaching a bomber from the rear. Even as these were being developed, the Air Ministry was very aware that any active system like Monica that transmitted signals was telling the enemy where the bomber was. There was a grave danger enemy fighters would use the signal to home in on the bomber. The TRE also set about creating ways of neutralizing German equipment, or at least reducing its effectiveness. The long-range early warning Freya stations seemed most vulnerable, and Mandrel jamming was hurriedly devised to drown out their signals, but the shorter-wavelength Wurzburg stations would prove more of a challenge.[4] It was a cat and mouse game in which it was far from clear who might emerge the victor.

Improving the bomber's defensive armament was back on the agenda; once more the Air Staff was demanding all-round protection. Ideally, power-operated nose, tail, dorsal and ventral turrets were needed, but this required major modifications to existing designs and even if possible meant unacceptable reductions in bomb load and range. Ventral defence might have to rely on simpler periscopically aimed guns, but these had to be developed and would not become available until the end of 1941.[5] In the meantime, crews might have to make do with a gun poking through the side or floor of the plane.[6] In January 1941, the possibility of replacing the rifle-calibre machine guns with cannon was discussed, but nothing had changed to make it any more possible. Even the idea of using heavier 0.5in machine guns had to be abandoned.[7] By May 1941, Bomber Command at least wanted the twin-gun dorsal turrets replaced by four-gun turrets, but even this was only possible on the Halifax.[8]

There was no new generation of bombers in the pipeline capable of carrying heavier defensive armament. The Air Ministry was quick to blame Beaverbrook for this. The cancelled B.1/39 cannon-armed bomber had been revived after the disastrous December 1939 Wilhelmshaven raid, only for Beaverbrook to cancel it again in the panic rationalizations of 1940. However, there was no reason to believe that any future generation of bomber could carry all-round cannon defensive armament. Indeed, there was no clear idea about where bomber design should or could go next. There was not even an attempt to draw up what might be required of successors to the 1936 generation.

All that existed were efforts to revamp existing models. There was a proposal from Short for a scaled-up version of the Stirling (the Short B.8/41) with four of the 2,000hp Centaurus engines then being developed.[9] The design was considered extremely promising and late in 1941, before the prototype had even flown, had found its way into production schedules. Even this massive bomber, weighing in at over 100,000lb, only had a mixture of 0.5in and 0.303in guns in its four turrets, and the spiralling weight of the plane was already forcing the MAP to suggest the number of heavy machine guns should be reduced.[10] The Air

Ministry found itself going down the same path it had been forced to follow in the late Thirties, and the arguments and conclusions were the same – bombers could not match in every direction the firepower an intercepting fighter only had to have in one direction.

In the summer of 1941, the future for Bomber Command was not looking very bright. With doubts growing about the effectiveness of the bombing campaign, the War Office putting in its plans for a large tactical air force to support the Army and Churchill wavering in his support for the bomber offensive, Portal felt the need to reassert the primacy of Bomber Command's role in the war. The Air Ministry sketched out precisely how Bomber Command was going to win the war. The 4,000 figure Portal was bandying about had been plucked out of the air and was by no means officially approved. Slessor demonstrated it was possible to build the airfields to house such a force.[11] American help to build the bombers had been solicited via Arnold of the USAAC. Now a study of the German blitz on Britain was used to demonstrate why such a force would do the job. It was estimated six Coventry-scale attacks ought to be enough to put a city 'beyond all hope of recovery', and the destruction of forty-three key German cities would effectively win the war.[12] No-one was talking about precision attacks on key industries. The aim was to destroy cities. It was conservatively estimated that on any given night, only 25 per cent of the bombers dispatched would find their targets, so a frontline strength of at least 4,000 heavy bombers would be required. With such a force, Portal assured the prime minister victory would come within six months.

The proposal did not quite have the intended result. His figures caused considerable consternation among government planners and members of the Cabinet. Maintaining such a huge bomber force would involve Bomber Command taking over British war production. Sinclair reported unease in political circles at the prospect of relying so heavily on just one means of winning the war. Although intended as a bold reassertion of the key role Bomber Command had in British war strategy, it began to look like an admission of defeat. With doubts about the accuracy of the bombing, concerns about the loss rate and fears that the country could not afford to build the huge number of bombers required, the prospects for the strategic bombing offensive did not look good in the summer of 1941 – but they were about to get a lot worse. Fears had been growing for some time that far too many aircrews were not even finding their targets. However, nobody was prepared for the bombshell that was about to hit Bomber Command, the Air Ministry and the government.

It was not just Peirse and the Air Ministry that was growing concerned about bombing accuracy. Ominously for Portal, Churchill was also worried. Reports Churchill was getting from the United States suggested observers on the spot were not seeing the damage Bomber Command was claiming. Churchill asked Lindemann to find out exactly how well or badly Bomber Command was actually doing. David Bensusan-Butt, a member of Lindemann's staff, was given the task of carrying out the first systematic survey of the accuracy of British bombing. In July 1941, with the situation in the Atlantic not as critical as it had been, Bomber Command had been able to return its full attention to German industry. By this time a reasonable number of bombers carried cameras which recorded where bombs had been dropped, and Butt compared the photographic evidence with the pilots' reports. Even the most pessimistic within Bomber Command found it hard to believe the conclusions he came to.

In June and July, two-thirds of crews claimed to have hit their target; Butt set out to find how many of these had actually done so. He adopted the generous definition of finding the target as dropping bombs within 5 miles of it. The evidence available to Butt suggested that on average only one-third of crews claiming success were in fact managing this. French coastal targets were relatively easy to find, with two-thirds of bombers actually bombing within 5 miles, but targets inside Germany were far more elusive. Against targets within the Ruhr, the proportion dropped to one-in-ten. This was one-in-ten of crews who claimed to have bombed the target. If those who admitted to not finding the target were included, only 6 per cent of bombers dispatched were getting anywhere near the most important industrial targets in Germany.

By Butt's criteria, success was measured as the ability to drop bombs within an 80 square mile area around the target. Clearly most of the bombs Butt was counting as successfully dropped were not only missing their intended targets, but were quite likely to be missing any worthwhile target at all. Many were probably falling on open countryside.[13] Post-war analysis would confirm that these findings were essentially correct. Up to this point in the war, bombing had made virtually no impact on German industrial output. This was the offensive that was supposed to be leading the country to victory. It was not that the results were disappointing. The shocking truth was that a year of bombing had achieved almost nothing. Rarely in the history of warfare can so much have been invested in the development of a strategy that produced so little military gain.

It was a shattering result. Many had been expecting the worst, but no-one had expected this. Peirse for some time had been voicing his doubts about the accuracy of pilots' claims, but he simply refused to believe that it could be this bad. He rather desperately scribbled on his copy of the report, 'I don't think at this rate we could have hoped to produce the damage which is known to have been caused.' Even Peirse was in denial. All sorts of attempts were made to explain away the results: perhaps cameras had only been issued to inexperienced crews; could the photographic evidence be believed?

The bomber strategy was in far more serious trouble than anyone previously imagined. Bombers could not find their targets by night, and all the alternatives had been tried and failed. Long-range Spitfire escorts over even relatively short ranges had not worked, and attempts to use the new better-armed heavy bombers unescorted by day had been no more successful. High-flying Fortresses had also failed. Bombing by night was the only option, and it was not working.

It was now a lot clearer why German night bombers had been using radio beams to guide them to their targets. The idea that British aircrews did not need such support was now recognized as a major error. Much was expected of GEE, and operational trials were already taking place. As soon as Butt's report was issued, GEE was ordered into production. There were other promising lines of research that would now get top priority. In June 1941, the TRE had put forward its Oboe blind bombing system which would use radar to ensure a bomber flew a fixed distance from the transmitter in the UK, with a separate signal to indicate when the plane was about to fly over the target. It was rather optimistically hoped that this would enable a plane to drop its bombs in a 130 by 200 yard area on targets as distant as Berlin.[14]

The government and Air Staff had already accepted that sometimes indiscriminate bombing might be the only option. In April 1941, it was already conceded that without good moonlight, only 'Blitz type' attacks on 'working class and industrial areas in towns' were possible.[15] After the Butt report, it was no longer a fall-back option when bombing conditions were not ideal; it became Bomber Command's only method and with it came an even more ruthless attitude to bombing. In September, Peirse agreed with a suggestion from Slessor, at No. 5 Group, that to reduce losses and 'spread the morale effect', small agricultural towns where local fairs were taking place should be bombed.[16]

This sort of indiscriminate attack did not actually need manned planes to be used at all. The pilotless cruise missile approach had been abandoned in the early Thirties because of its inherent inaccuracy.[17]

Albert 'Jimmy' Rowe, the TRE Director, reminded Tizard of the experiments with the Larynx pilotless bomb in the late Twenties and argued that the navigational devices the TRE was developing for manned bombers would work equally well in a pilotless plane. An accuracy of a quarter of a mile might be attainable, and even 1 mile would not be totally useless.[18] Given the findings of the Butt report, this would be a considerable improvement on what Bomber Command was currently achieving. Rowe suggested that a cheap expendable missile might be built around the jet engine, 'which can more or less be made out of bashed out tin and very cheaply', he speculated rather optimistically.[19] At least with the pilotless planes, Slessor's ruthless approach would not be necessary. With no aircrew losses to worry about, there would be no need to choose poorly defended towns.

The option was investigated by Tizard, but with Britain geared up for the mass production of manned bombers, switching horses mid-stream seemed a rather drastic step to take. The Americans were known to be working on pilotless planes and associated guidance systems, including guidance by a television camera, and it was decided to leave any such research in their capable hands.[20] It was one of many areas of research that the British were leaving to the Americans. It would not be long before Germany also began taking the pilotless approach more seriously with the V-1 and V-2 as a way of retaliating for RAF attacks.

The Butt report was not the only bad news for the bomber offensive. Portal's 4,000 target frontline strength required the production of around 12,000 bombers a year. Britain at best could manage half of this. The Americans had proposed to deliver most of their heavy bomber output to Britain, and this went some way to making up the balance. In August 1941, Churchill and Roosevelt, along with their military commanders and advisers, met in Placentia Bay, Newfoundland. Arnold was there, and Freeman represented the Air Ministry. Freeman went hoping he could persuade the Americans to increase their contribution. To his horror, he discovered they planned to cut it.[21]

The bomber strategy did not hold the same dominant position in overall American planning as it did in Britain. Arnold was as keen as ever, but his USAAC was part of the US Army, which had its own massive expansion plans. General George Marshall and Admiral Harold Stark, the American Army and Navy chiefs, made it clear that the United States was not going to be relying on long-range bombing to win wars. They did not agree with Arnold's emphasis on long-range bombers and warned that attempting to build them would mean Dill and Dudley Pound not getting the tanks and ships they needed.[22] Even a sympathetic Arnold was dumbfounded by the number of bombers Freeman was expecting. Arnold suggested it might be possible to switch a couple of new factories from B-26 Marauders to heavy bombers, but that was about it.[23]

Instead of the 6,000 bombers the British were hoping for, and the 4,000 bombers the United States had promised by July 1943, they could now only expect little more than 1,000. Freeman was stunned. Before leaving, he left a note for Harry Hopkins, Roosevelt's top adviser, in the hope that he might persuade Roosevelt to overrule Marshall and Stark. He described how depressed he was after hearing the strident US Army and Navy opposition to heavy bomber production: 'Has anyone in the world yet produced any other theory other than bombing, for winning the war? The answer is - No!'[24] However, the Americans did have other ways. Churchill stood by the bomber policy, but he was mulling over what he was hearing and was also beginning to see other options.

On his return to the United Kingdom, another apparently minor incident also set Churchill thinking. It all started as a relatively minor inter-service spat. In the wake of the Battleaxe fiasco, Wavell was replaced by Claude Auchinleck and dispatched to the backwaters of India. There he wrote up his account of his time in charge. Portal was not impressed by Wavell's complaints about the lack of air superiority and inadequate air reconnaissance. However, it was one particular incident during Rommel's earlier advance in April that aroused Portal's ire. Wavell described how the disintegration of the armoured division during the retreat had been caused by incorrect information provided by RAF reconnaissance. On 13 April, two separate reconnaissance sorties had reported enemy columns heading for Musa, which, Wavell claimed, were in fact friendly forces. As a result of this information, the fuel dumps had been destroyed and the armoured division left short of fuel.[25]

Portal objected to this apparent attempt to lay the blame for the defeat at the door of the RAF, and he launched a full-scale investigation. The commanders were asked to comment and the pilots involved in the fateful reconnaissance missions were tracked down for their views. The whole issue was clouded by uncertainty; the RAF pilots had reported Italian trucks carrying large numbers of troops, which in itself was not conclusive as the British were using a large number of captured Italian vehicles. The column had then been strafed and bombed by the RAF, and aircrews reported seeing swastika flags and were greeted with heavy anti-aircraft fire. Portal concluded that it probably was an enemy column. The upshot was that Auchinleck withdrew the claim

215

on Wavell's behalf. It looked like a victory for the Air Ministry and that seemed to be the end of the matter.[26]

However, Churchill had been following the case and was drawing far more general conclusions. Whatever had happened, Churchill insisted, the pilots could not be blamed; it was the system that was wrong – and it was not just tactical reconnaissance that Churchill was referring to. 'The lack of effective and intimate contact between the air and ground forces calls for drastic reform,' he concluded, adding:

'The needs of the Army should be met in a helpful spirit by the Air Ministry. It is the responsibility of the Air Force to satisfy the Army now that the resources are growing. We need not go into the past but if the Army is not well treated in the future, the Air Ministry will have failed in an essential part of its duties.'[27]

These were indeed strong words.

Portal was deeply offended. 'I very much hope that your minute … is not intended to be read to imply that the Air Ministry have been unhelpful in meeting the needs of the Army in the past,' he protested Lest there be any misunderstanding, Churchill wrote back, explaining that was exactly what he meant:

'I have certainly sustained the impression that the Air Ministry in the past has been most hard and unhelpful both to the Army and to the Navy in meeting their special requirements. The Navy succeeded in breaking away before the war, but the Army lies under a sense of having been denied its proper Air assistance. To some extent this can be excused by the plea that the need of increasing the RAF was paramount. Now that that need is no longer overwhelming, I trust the Army's grievances and complaints will be met.'[28]

It was a reply that sent shock waves ringing round the Air Ministry. The comment 'Now that that need is no longer overwhelming' seemed especially ominous. The RAF's special status as the central pillar in Britain's war-winning strategy was in serious jeopardy. Just to make it clear that this was not just about tactical reconnaissance, Churchill added:

'There is a widespread belief that we have not developed dive-bombers because of the fear of the Air Ministry that a weapon of this kind specially associated with the Army might lead to a formation of a separate Army wing.'

216

Churchill softened the personal criticism by claiming, 'All these things happened before your time, but their consequences are with us today.'[29] But Portal knew that not all of them happened before his time; he had been very much a part of this policy, and indeed it was his total belief in the strategic air offensive that had won him Churchill's favour in the first place.

On his return from his meeting with Roosevelt, Churchill also found the Butt report waiting for him. The prime minister reminded Portal how 'serious' Butt's findings were, and wanted to know what he was going to do about it.[30] Portal's promise that once he had his 4,000 bombers Germany would be broken in six months now looked distinctly hollow. Indeed, without American help, it seemed unlikely that Portal would ever get the 4,000 bombers to find out if this would be enough. Portal could not complain about the prime minister's determination to get the bombers Portal wanted. Churchill harangued Beaverbrook, Moore-Brabazon and anyone else with any power to do anything about it, demanding that another 3,500 bombers be squeezed out of British factories. To achieve this, drastic decisions might have to be made, cutbacks in Admiralty and War Office programmes might be necessary, workers moved from building new factories to building bombers and old bomber types kept in production longer.[31] However, even these draconian measures would not produce anything like the number of bombers Portal needed.

The Air Ministry was willing to take drastic steps. The Warwick could carry twice the bomb load of the Wellington, but Freeman suggested that dropping it would mean more Wellingtons could be built.[32] This might help achieve the production targets, but it was only going to increase short-term output at the expense of long-term lifting capability. In the Thirties, smaller bombers had been produced to hoodwink the enemy; now the MAP and Air Ministry just seemed to be trying to fool themselves. The performance of the cheap Albemarle was so poor that the MAP had decided to mothball the engineless airframes for some future emergency. This now seemed to be that emergency. Albemarle production would be counted against the new target, even if the plane was quite unusable.[33] Even with these measures there would still be a short fall of 2,000 bombers, and that assumed the Americans would reverse their decision to cut deliveries. The harder Churchill, the MAP and Air Ministry tried, the more obvious it should have seemed to everyone that it simply could not be done.

While the Air Ministry and MAP struggled even to come up with a plan that might enable the bomber offensive to succeed eventually,

Stalin was still expecting more immediate help in the form of a second front. Stalin was not alone; there were also growing demands in the British press for a more active response in the west. It did not seem unreasonable. More than a year had passed since the defeat at Dunkirk, and most of the German Army was now tied up in Russia. Surely the time had come for Britain to take advantage of the situation and go on to the offensive?[34] It seemed a reasonable suggestion. If Britain had spent that year developing the ground/air forces required to defeat an invasion of the UK, then the country would have been well on the way to creating the sort of force that might be capable of mounting an invasion of the continent. If newspaper editors had had any inkling about how unprepared Britain's armed forces were even to deal with a German invasion, they would perhaps not have been so enthusiastic about attempting to cross the Channel.

Churchill still considered such an operation inconceivable in the short term, but his doubts about winning the war by bombing were growing. He had spent the Thirties warning the government and nation about the horrendous consequences of aerial bombardment, but he was beginning to realize that he had been seriously misled by the inter-war bomber zealots. There was an air of resentment as Churchill complained to Portal how exaggerated the talk of the all-conquering power of the bomber had been. The bombing of Britain in the winter of 1940–41 had not had the catastrophic consequences so many had feared. Indeed, far from breaking the morale of the British people, it had strengthened their resolve. There was also the possibility that air defence would ultimately triumph over the night bomber, just as it had the day bomber. Churchill now believed it was 'very disputable' whether bombing would be a decisive factor in the present war: 'The most we can say is that it will be a heavy and I trust a seriously increasing annoyance.'[35] It was a conclusion that sent more shock waves through the Air Ministry.

Portal reminded the prime minister that the strategic air offensive had been the cornerstone of Britain's strategy since the fall of France. British production plans were built around the premise that the bomber would win the war. If Churchill had changed his mind about this and had decided that the Army should become the principal means of defeating Germany, 'we should require an air force composed quite differently from that which we are now creating'. If this was the case, Churchill should release new instructions to the Chiefs of Staff without a moment's delay.[36]

It was a fine display of brinkmanship. If Churchill was changing his mind, all existing plans would have to be torn up and a fresh start made. However, the reasons Portal put forward for persevering with the aerial offensive were scarcely convincing. He pointed out that the scale of attack the Air Staff was proposing was far in excess of anything the Germans had tried, and he doubted any country could withstand indefinitely such an assault. Furthermore, the 'consensus of informed opinion is that German morale is much more vulnerable to bombing than our own'.[37] This combination of speculation and belief in the superiority of the British race were not compelling reasons for Britain to commit itself so totally to a single means of achieving victory. Even in the best-case scenario, Portal was not expecting the bomber force to become the decisive weapon he was predicting until 1943. A lot could happen before then.

Churchill's reply again made much of the previous exaggerated claims made for long-range bombing. He blamed these for the decision to abandon Czechoslovakia in 1938. He reminded Portal that during the Blitz, 750,000 beds were ready to deal with the expected flood of civilian casualties, but only 6,000 had been needed. By 1943, German industry might be so dispersed throughout Europe that it would no longer offer a viable target. Churchill insisted that he had done everything he could to create the bomber force the Air Staff wanted, but he cautioned: 'It is an unwise man who thinks there is any certain method of winning this war.'[38] Churchill admitted that aerial bombardment was the most potent method of undermining enemy morale available at that time, but he was already thinking ahead to a time when the United States was in the war and multiple landings of Allied forces along the coastline of German-held Europe would provoke uprising in the occupied lands and the defeat of Nazism. The winds of change were indeed blowing.

There was also the Soviet factor. Many had predicted a rapid defeat for the Red Army, but as the conflict entered its third month, despite heavy defeats, the Soviet Army was still fiercely resisting. In a memo to the Chiefs of Staff in September, Churchill instructed his commanders to consider the possibility that the Soviet Union might still be holding on in the following spring. In such circumstances, the premise that the Allies would be unable to land on the continent of Europe for some considerable time had to be reconsidered. Britain had to do something with a largely unemployed Army stagnating in the United Kingdom, and with most of Germany's armed forces tied up in the east there might be an excellent opportunity to strike a surprise blow in northern France, Churchill suggested, but only if planning started immediately. Taking on board Portal's comments, he suggested there would indeed be a need for long-range fighters, and, rather ominously from Bomber

Command's point of view, a need to switch bombers from Germany to support the landings.[39]

The tide seemed to be turning against the strategic bombing strategy. With the Soviet Union showing no signs of succumbing, the prospect of taking on what the Germans could afford to deploy in the west was beginning to look a little more attractive to the War Office. In October, an emboldened Dill again insisted that the RAF bomber offensive could not win the war – this could only be done by defeating the German Army – and proclaimed that this was what the War Office was preparing for. But air support was crucial. The British Army could only defeat the Wehrmacht with air force squadrons under its control, not with squadrons carrying on their normal duties with Bomber and Fighter Command. Dill rejected the accusation that the War Office just wanted to rigidly tie squadrons to army units; the Army just needed a pool of resources that army commanders could call on.[40] Portal believed that the RAF was that pool of resources and that the Luftwaffe the War Office seemed so anxious to copy was centralized just like the RAF. However, as the War Office pointed out, the difference was that the Luftwaffe was geared up for tactical air-support, whereas the RAF was trained and equipped for strategic operations. The German Army did not need the control the British Army was seeking.[41]

The American Army Chiefs of Staff added to the pressure on the Air Ministry. The United States may not be in the war yet, but its supplies were vital to the Allied war effort, and under Lend-Lease these were now being offered free of charge. In the Atlantic, the US Navy was already fighting alongside the Royal Navy. The United States believed it had earned the right to have some say in the way the war was being fought. The War Cabinet Joint Planning Committee was well aware of American criticisms that not enough importance was being attached to the role of the Army. The British planners hoped it was a misunderstanding rather than a disagreement, but this was scarcely the case. The British believed that the Americans were simply underestimating the need to reduce the fighting capabilities of Germany by air bombardment before any attempt was made to land on the continent. Even so, it seemed best to at least start considering some sort of landing, if only to deflect American criticism.[42] Thus began planning for Operation Roundup, a full-scale invasion of France if it suddenly appeared Germany was about to collapse.

Churchill was already suggesting large-scale raids anywhere from Brest to Norway. These would require all three services to work together. This was not the direction the Air Ministry wanted to go in. Air Commodore William Dickson, the Director of Plans and a future

Chief of the Air Staff, made it clear that these schemes were only worth considering if resources existed beyond those required by the existing bomber strategy. Since this involved building a 4,000-strong bomber fleet, it was likely to be a very long time before the Air Ministry felt it needed to consider them.

General Brooke, in charge of forces in the UK, was set the task of coming up with plans for these landings, a task he approached with almost as little enthusiasm as the Air Ministry. He was far from sure he had the forces to defeat an invasion, never mind launch one of his own, but doubts about the air support that was likely to be available provided a very real justification for his pessimism.[43] With land-based forces, the War Office could at least attempt to tackle the deficiencies, but air support was beyond its control. To overcome the inter-service barriers the services themselves had done so much to create, Churchill brought in the confident young Mountbatten to take over a beefed-up Combined Operations Command, which would oversee and co-ordinate the plans of all three services. Mountbatten had been about to take over command of the aircraft carrier *Illustrious* and was not in the least bit enthusiastic about Churchill's offer, until the prime minister made it clear that the commando raids the Combined Operations Command was currently organizing were just a stepping stone towards the landing of a British army on the continent.[44]

In December 1941, the beaches of Normandy were mentioned for the first time as a possible landing site. The War Office and Army Co-operation Command were working on Operation Striker, a large-scale raid which would capture the Cherbourg peninsula. The limited endurance of RAF fighters came to the fore. With current equipment, it would only be possible to patrol the bridgehead for thirty minutes. However, an even bigger barrier to progress was the mindset the Air Staff's air-only strategy engendered in RAF commanders. Douglas was one commander who had shown an interest in using his squadrons for army support, but even he was making it clear that he had an absolute right to withdraw fighter support at any time during the operation if he considered the defence of the United Kingdom required it.[45] Fighter Command had been set up to defend the UK, and putting the defence of the Army over the defence of the country did not come naturally to its commander. It was an attitude that demonstrated why the Army needed to have more control of the aircraft that were supposed to be supporting it.

The landings would require the sort of mobility that Barratt and Longmore had outlined in their report, with aircraft using advance landing grounds within the bridgehead. It was not the sort of mobility that the rather static RAF commands in the UK were used to providing. Even mobility within the UK was a problem. Ideally, bombers should be operating from airfields as close as possible to the landings to reduce response time and increase sortie rates. Peirse, however, insisted that his bomber squadrons would not be capable of operating from airfields in the south of the country; they would have to use their home bases, which meant flying to targets on the other side of the Channel from as far afield as Lincolnshire. It was all part of the general lack of flexibility that pervaded the RAF, which was very real but at the same time very convenient for a force that did not want to get too closely involved in tactical operations.

Meanwhile, the Joint Planning Staff was working on Operation Roundup. This envisaged an initial landing by five infantry and five tank brigades between Dieppe and Deauville, either side of Le Havre. This would rise to six infantry divisions supported by six tank brigades and six armoured divisions. In addition to the full support of the Metropolitan, UK-based RAF, twenty-four fighter, ten reconnaissance and twelve army support squadrons would need to operate from the continent, with six fighter squadrons based within the beachhead by the second day.[46]

The problems were many, but at least they were now being tackled. Fighter Command was told it would have to increase the number of airfields in southern England to enable more fighters to operate over the continent. The long-range Spitfire with a 30-gallon jettisonable tank, the first of which came off the Supermarine production lines in December 1941, became even more important. The lack of fighters again came to the fore. It would be difficult to provide all bombers with escorts, which once again saw Fighter Command claiming that establishing general air superiority would enable bombers to operate without escorts. This was a laudable aim, but this too required a large number of fighters.

The Army thought it unlikely such widespread air superiority would be possible with the number of fighters available. Army support bombers would have to react immediately, and the only sure way of protecting them was to have them accompanied by fighters. The War Office feared that over-aggressive, ambitious attempts to win overall superiority would take the fighters too far from where they were needed. With fighter endurance so limited, fighters could not afford to stray far from the bombers. They were all very familiar arguments, some of them dating back to the First World War.

The shortage of fighters also meant there would not be enough to provide high and low cover over the landings. To be of maximum use to the Army, the planners decided that fighter effort would have to be concentrated at 5,000–8,000ft. Having no fighters at altitude was not ideal, but it was recognition that in a tactical setting, low-level fighter cover was vital. Ground attack fighters would also be very useful for attacking reinforcements moving towards the landings. For closer support, brigades and battalions within the bridgehead would have radio links to call in air support if required, including direct links with bombers already heading for targets so that new targets could be assigned.[47] These were all aspects of air support that had been lacking during the 1940 campaign in France, and about which so little had been done in the eighteen months since. By the end of 1941, these should have been well-established procedures to help deal with a possible invasion. Instead, the RAF still did not have the right planes and the aircrews had received only the sketchiest of training.

Officially, strategic bombing still remained the main offensive weapon, but the gauntlet was being thrown down. Alternative military options were now on the agenda. The Air Staff's strategic air offensive had competition just as Bomber Command's problems seemed to be multiplying. GEE seemed to offer an excellent way of helping bomber crews find their way around a blacked-out continent, but before it was even ordered into production, a Wellington trialling the system was shot down over Germany. The self-destruct mechanism probably worked, but nobody knew. Even if it worked, the fact that one was used would certainly start the Germans thinking about what needed destroying. Further trials were banned and the aircraft taking part in the trials had all traces of the equipment removed. It would be six months before sufficient had been built to use on a large scale. If the Germans had the device, it was estimated it would take them three months to put in place jamming systems. German scientists might already be working on counter-measures.

In November, Portal was able to tell Churchill about another possible breakthrough in navigational aids. Previous efforts to develop a downward-looking radar that gave crews an idea of what they were flying over had not brought much success. However, the TRE was working on a centimetric system (H2S) that provided an image of the terrain below which could distinguish land from sea and built-up areas from countryside. There were, however, problems. Centimetric radar was a priceless secret that Britain's night defences relied on. Portal feared that Britain might well lose more than it gained by taking the risk of using it over enemy territory.[48] The early claims for the Oboe guidance system were proving a little exaggerated. It transpired that it could only be effective over targets as distant as Berlin if a second plane halfway to the target was used to retransmit the signal. Without this complication, 250 miles was a more realistic range.[49] All these navigational aids (GEE, H2S and Oboe) had great potential, but it was far from clear they could solve Bomber Command's problems.

Little progress was made with improving defensive armament. Trials in the autumn of 1941 with additional dorsal turrets revealed they imposed a far greater loss of performance than expected.[50] Slessor at No. 5 Group demanded the question of cannon armament be reconsidered, but the manufacturers insisted that cannon turrets were simply not practicable. Even formation flying by night was being considered, so bombers could rely on some mutual protection.[51] The rather grim conclusion was that operating by night, radar-guided fighters had all the advantages.[52]

The night of 7/8 November 1941 was the worst so far for Bomber Command. In atrocious weather, nearly 400 bombers set course for targets in France, Belgium and Germany. Aircraft attacking targets in France and Belgium escaped without loss, but 12 per cent of those sent to Berlin and 13 per cent of those targeting Mannheim did not return. Thirty-seven bombers had been lost in a single night, a loss rate of nearly 10 per cent. To Churchill it seemed pointless to suffer such losses when, it was now clear, very little damage was being inflicted on the enemy. Churchill instructed the Air Staff to reduce the scale of attack. Bomber Command was to be conserved in the hope that new navigational aids and defensive electronic countermeasures might allow a return to full-scale operations the following spring.[53]

Chapter 12

Air Strategy at the Crossroads

The equipment and methods of Bomber Command were not proving up to the task. Strategic bombing was failing, but was tactical air support any closer to becoming effective? Despite Churchill's demands that something be done about improving the forces available for co-operation with the Army, the Air Ministry was going to be very reluctant to comply when it did not believe in the policy and knew it could only suck resources away from the strategic air offensive it did believe in. In the Middle East, ongoing operations provided an incentive to develop army air support, but in Britain the threat of invasion was never enough to overcome the Air Ministry's ingrained opposition to using air power tactically. With a dominant Bomber Command and a powerless Army Co-operation Command, the system was set up to ensure tactical air support would not flourish.

Progress was agonizingly slow in all areas. In May 1941, it had been agreed that eleven of the fourteen army co-operation squadrons would be equipped with the Tomahawk. The War Office made it clear that using fighters for tactical reconnaissance was not a temporary interim solution; it wanted at least half of all future army support squadrons to be equipped with single-seaters. With the Mustang expected to be another American failure and already lined up as a replacement for the Tomahawk, the War Office seemed to be getting its way.[1]

However, the re-equipment programme encountered obstacles at every level. To be useful, the Tomahawks needed cameras. Two types were needed: vertical mounted cameras for high-level reconnaissance and sideways looking cameras for low-level missions. There was nothing especially novel about fitting cameras to single-seater fighters; 8in and 14in cameras had been mounted in the rear fuselage and under the wings of the Spitfire for vertical and oblique photography. Early in 1941, similar arrangements had been improvised on the Hurricane in the Middle East. The Air Ministry and MAP, however seemed to be determined to find problems organizing something similar for the Tomahawk.

In April 1941, Brooke was told the Tomahawk could not carry vertical cameras as they were too difficult to aim and too complicated to install. They would also overload the airframe and result in an unacceptable reduction in performance.[2] These were issues that had not stood in the way of modifying Hurricanes and Spitfires. Brooke accepted that, initially, priority would be given to fitting oblique cameras, but insisted the long-term aim was to fit vertical cameras as well.[3] In the meantime, for vertical photography, tactical reconnaissance squadrons would have to continue using two-seaters, which meant initially Lysanders and eventually the Bermuda or Vengeance.

There was little urgency about overcoming the problems mounting vertical cameras in the Tomahawk. Indeed, the problems were used as a reason for giving the task a low priority, which scarcely seemed the most productive approach.[4] The programme meandered along without much purpose until late summer, when Barratt injected some urgency into the work. He made it clear that he did not accept the previously cited problems and late in August issued instructions for a mock-up with vertical cameras to be ready for inspection within a week. The mock-ups presented were just drawings, but they were good enough for Barratt and he demanded the decision not to mount vertical cameras be reversed.[5] Tests went ahead and the previously cited unacceptable reduction in performance with the 8in camera turned out to be just 5mph.

Nevertheless, the objections to the vertical camera mounting continued. It was claimed that only a 5in or possibly an 8in camera could be fitted, which would force planes to fly far too low and cover too little ground.[6] Barratt persevered, insisting that three Tomahawks fitted with vertical cameras should be attached to each army co-operation squadron.[7] This was agreed, provided Army Co-operation Command did the work itself and the modifications enabled the vertical cameras to be rapidly replaced by oblique cameras. This proved to be impossible to do, but by the end of the year it was finally conceded that twenty Tomahawks would be modified to carry the vertical cameras. It had taken an entire year to get this relatively simple modification approved. By this time, first deliveries of the necessary parts had been pushed back well into 1942.

It seems that the problems of equipping single-seater fighters with cameras were exaggerated partly to justify using the Bermuda and

Vengeance to equip army co-operation squadrons. Bomber Command did not want them in No. 2 Group, and their supposed tactical reconnaissance capabilites was another good reason for assigning them to 'army co-operation squadrons', as the Air Ministry still liked to call them. Multi-purpose dive-bomber/reconnaissance squadrons ought to fill all War Office requirements and relieve pressure on Bomber Command to provide the Army with support. The War Office and Barratt, however, were trying to separate the strike and reconnaissance roles. Indeed, Barratt was insisting that photo-reconnaissance planes should not be used for ground attack as their specialist pilots were far too valuable.[8]

Single-seaters could not perform all photo-reconnaissance missions; longer-range aircraft that could carry bulkier equipment and operate in all weathers were also needed. However, the solution was not two-seaters like the Vengeance or Bermuda, which managed just 280mph and struggled to reach 23,000ft. The de Havilland Mosquito could fly 100mph quicker and nearly 10,000ft higher, and was a much better alternative. It could also have been available much sooner. The Mosquito was flying long before the Vengeance (first flight March 1941) or the Bermuda (first flight June 1941), but the plane never managed to break the stranglehold the heavy bomber had on British production priorities. Desperately few were ordered for the wide range of roles the aircraft was capable of, and army support roles always had the lowest priority. Photo-reconnaissance versions of the Mosquito were among the first to be delivered, flying their first strategic reconnaissance mission for the No.1 PRU in September 1941, but it would be late 1943 before any could be spared for army reconnaissance squadrons.

Developing or acquiring specialist ground attack planes was making even slower progress. At the beginning of 1941, the only British plane on offer was the Bisley, and the Air Ministry still hoped it could get out of that commitment. Freeman wanted the Blenheim phased out and the Bisley to 'die a natural death' with it.[9] This would have been fine if the Air Ministry had a more suitable alternative in mind, but the aim was simply to clear the decks for more heavy bombers. There was no sign of the American Vengeance or Bermuda arriving. Only the standard Blenheim was available, but not even the Air Ministry thought this could be used for low-level ground attack. In any case, there were so few being built that the Air Ministry was reluctant to part with any for army co-operation squadrons.

Outside the army co-operation squadrons, the only source of bomber support for the Army was Bomber Command's No. 2 Group, and this was far from being a specialist army support force. No. 2 Group had just about continued to exist as a day bomber force, partly because it demonstrated the RAF had some tactical day bombers, but it was also a convenient home for any experiments in long-range daylight bombing. The Flying Fortresses of No. 90 squadron were attached to this group. No. 105 Squadron with Blenheims was supposed to be trying out the Mosquito as a high-speed bomber, although it would be November 1941 before the squadron could lay its hands on any examples for training.

The need to tie down as much of the Luftwaffe as possible in the west in order to help the Soviets gave No. 2 Group a new lease of life. The bombers were supposed to provide the Germans with some incentive to engage the fighters escorting them. The escorts were lavish. No. 2 Group bombers could rely on large numbers of fighters sweeping ahead of the bomber formation, others providing close escort and still more operating at altitude providing top cover. Such comprehensive escorts had been unthinkable when, the previous year, No. 2 Group had been engaged against targets in the same part of France in desperate attempts to slow down the German advance. For bombing missions laid on to help prevent the destruction of the British Army, any sort of escort was only provided with great reluctance, but when Fighter Command required the bombers for their own battle with the Luftwaffe, the escorts were lavish and organized in fine detail, and all for bombing raids that were attacking trivial targets. At least it kept No. 2 Group, and its tactical day bombing capability, in business.

It was still planned to re-equip No. 2 Group with Douglas Bostons, but the needs of the night fighter squadrons prevented the delivery of the first Boston bomber until August 1941, and then it was decided to send them to the Middle East. The first Boston bomber sortie from the UK was not flown until February 1942. The Bisley/Blenheim V was beginning to replace the Blenheim IV on the production lines, but a lack of vital items of equipment would prevent it reaching squadrons until well into 1942 – remarkably late for a plane that had started life in late 1939 as a hasty, temporary interim solution. It was, however, now just a conventional light bomber rather than the heavily armoured low-level assault aircraft originally envisaged; instead of 600lb of armour, the production version had just 120lb.[10] The Blenheim V was faster at lower altitudes than the Blenheim IV, but as a low/medium-altitude attack bomber it was inferior to the American Boston or Maryland. Throughout the summer of 1941, the Blenheim IV remained the only day bomber in the UK suitable for any sort of tactical operations.

Various planes were being considered as future equipment for No. 2 Group. The American Martin B-26 Marauder medium bomber was one contender, the Bristol Buckingham another. Like the Bisley/ Blenheim V, this was mutating into a conventional medium bomber. By 1942, expected range had been increased to 1,600 miles.[11] The Air Ministry also began thinking in 1941 about a Mosquito replacement. Specification B.11/41 required a 400mph unarmed bomber with a range of 1,500 miles, but the Air Staff still found it difficult to do without a power-operated turret. Designers were asked to make provision for a retractable four-gun dorsal turret in case it was required. Hawker's B.11/41 proposal created much interest. Norbet Rowe, the MAP Director of Technical Development, believed it was good enough to be ordered off the drawing board and thought it might eventually make use of the Whittle jet engine.[12] But like the Bristol Buckingham, the 'Camm Bomber' was another medium bomber.

All these bombers were at the top end of the tactical bomber spectrum, useful for attacking targets behind the battlefield but not on it. Nor were there plans to build many. Production schedules called for just twenty-five Buckinghams a month. As Portal freely admitted, it was just enough to keep the British aircraft industry in the medium bomber business. Freeman provisionally ordered 200 'Camm Bombers' in October 1941, but it proved to be very provisional.[13] By June of the following year, Freeman had decided he could do without them and the plane was cancelled.[14] For future equipment, the Air Staff was quite happy to rely on anything the Americans might be willing to offer. Relying so entirely on the United States for light/medium day bombers seemed risky, but in truth, if the supply dried up and No. 2 Group had to re-equip with heavy bombers, from the Air Staff point of view that was no bad thing.

None of the officially sponsored efforts to develop a genuine close air support capability were making much progress, but, quite by chance, what was needed was emerging. Ironically, for the weapons close air support required, it was the much-feared long-range bomber threat that provided the stimulus. Top of the list was the Hispano Suiza HS.404 20mm cannon. This was introduced to deal with large bombers, and to make sure no bomber would be safe, the Air Ministry had insisted that fighters carry at least four of these formidable weapons. This was far more than was necessary to deal with the largest bombers the Luftwaffe possessed, but it gave fighters like the Whirlwind and Hurricane II a fearsome built-in ground attack capability.

The decision to use Fighter Command Hurricanes and Whirlwinds in the ground attack role was not inspired by experience gained in the Middle East, nor did it come from Army Co-operation Command. The original idea was not even to provide the Army with air support. Douglas wanted to use ground-strafing fighters as another way of prodding German fighters into action over France. With both the Whirlwind and Hurricane II lacking the qualities required for air combat, ground attack was a good way of using these planes. Pilots flying sweeps over northern France had always been encouraged to attack any targets on the ground they came across if there was no opposition in the air. However, in the second half of the year, fighters started to get specific targets to attack.[15] In the autumn of 1941, fifteen Hurricane II and Whirlwind squadrons were formally assigned the ground attack role, but by the end of the year Douglas wanted all his fighter squadrons to be capable of what he was now referring to as army support missions.[16]

Portal had already proposed increasing the Hurricane's firepower by arming it with 40mm cannon. This was another weapon that had been originally designed as an anti-bomber air-to-air weapon. By July it had been decided to go ahead with a version of the Hurricane armed with two Vickers 40mm cannon and the prototype flew in September 1941. By October 1941, trials had proven the weapon worked, and Moore-Brabazon wanted 500 ordered.[17] Again, the original motivation was not to improve army/air co-operation. It was very much the Air Ministry's weapon. Portal hoped to surprise an invading German army. Training would take place in secret and the plane would only be unleashed once an invasion was underway. There does not seem to have been much desire to share this secret with the War Office.[18]

Another method of attacking bombers investigated in the Thirties was dropping 250lb bombs on formations. The idea was revived in 1940, and a couple of Hurricanes had been ordered with strengthened wings for trials.[19] The idea went no further, but in April 1941 the squadron leader of No. 87 Squadron suggested using these Hurricanes to dive-bomb the German pocket battleships sheltering in Brest. Trials were ordered, but before they could get started it was decided that 250lb bombs were unlikely to cause a battleship much damage and the plan was abandoned.[20]

Nevertheless, it was decided to go ahead with the trials anyway, to see what such a plane might be able to do. Ships or tanks were seen as possible targets, or it could be used as an intruder against enemy airfields. Trials demonstrated that the Hurricane could not be used as a dive-bomber, but low-level attack was possible. It was found that the Hurricane II required few modifications to take a couple of 250lb bombs.[21] Douglas was enthusiastic about having another way of attacking targets in northern France, and two of his squadrons were equipped with 'Hurribombers'. These flew their first missions in October 1941.

Douglas thought they might be very useful for attacking tanks, as his thoughts turned more to the army support role his squadrons might soon have.[22]

Interestingly, these fighter-bombers immediately aroused the interest of Bomber Command. Peirse argued that any bomb-carrying planes obviously belonged to his Command, not Fighter Command. The Blenheims of No. 2 Group were suffering heavy losses in anti-shipping strikes and the 'Hurribomber' seemed like a good alternative. Fighter Command was keen to hold on to its latest acquisition, and argued that the planes did not have the radio equipment to operate outside the Fighter Command system.[23] It was an example of the trivial disputes and unnecessary friction the compartmentalized, role-based RAF commands tended to encourage. While Bomber and Fighter Command argued over who should have the plane, Army Co-operation Command did not even seem to be aware it existed.

Another weapon designed to bring down bombers was the ground-to-air unrotated projectile (UP). Alwyn Crowe, the Army's rocket expert, had been working on these unguided missiles since the mid-Thirties as a cheap alternative to the anti-aircraft gun. The Air Ministry also had hopes of adapting this rocket as an air-to-air anti-bomber weapon. In the summer of 1940, serious consideration had been given to fitting these to Beaufighters for use against day bomber formations or even radar-directed by night.[24] It was suggested the Beaufighter might carry twenty of the 55lb missiles. The idea of using radar to aim the missiles was aired at various times during the months that followed and dismissed as impractical, but following one such discussion in September 1941, Tizard suggested that instead of using the rocket against bombers, it could be used against ground targets, such as 'submarines, E-boats and tanks'.[25] It was decided that the Beaufighter would lack the manoeuvrability, but the Hurricane might be ideal and it was agreed that trials should be organized.

The Hurricane was reinventing itself as a ground attack fighter that could carry 20mm or 40mm cannon, bombs or rockets. It was an ironic turn of events. The Hurricane II's Merlin XX was the best high-altitude engine available, but the fighter was becoming primarily a low-level ground attack plane. Keeping the Hurricane in production for too long as a fighter suddenly seemed like a stroke of good fortune. The Hurricane II, together with a rethink about some anti-bomber weapons, provided Britain with a ready-made ground attack force. Indeed, far from just using up unwanted Hurricanes, Moore-Brabazon felt another 1,000 should be ordered. In October 1941, Leigh-Mallory at No. 11 Group wondered if the Typhoon might be adapted to carry a couple of 500lb bombs. With the problems the prototype was having, Douglas thought it might be a bit too soon to worry Hawker with this suggestion, but the possibility was on the agenda.[26] The War Office was getting the single-engined ground attack planes it wanted without the two to three-year design and development phase the Air Ministry was constantly insisting it would take.

With its new role and the large numbers of Hurricanes promised to the Soviet Union, it seemed that rather than being phased out, the Hurricane was growing in importance. Indeed, with the Hurricane II becoming the standard fighter in the Middle East, the Air Ministry was beginning to regret ever promising the Russian so many. Monthly deliveries to the Soviet Union (200) and the Middle East (150) exceeded production (300).[27] The only solution was to palm off more of the unwanted American fighters on their Soviet allies as a substitute. There were fears that there might be political complications if the Soviets objected to getting second-rate American fighters instead of Hurricanes, but Russia was scarcely in any position to argue. Plans to equip Fighter Command squadrons with Airacobras were abandoned, and these joined the Tomahawks Britain was already sending to the Soviet Union as a partial substitute for the Hurricane.[28] Moore-Brabazon thought they could have the Mustang as well, rather than part with any more Hurricane IIs.[29]

As it turned out, when the Airacobras started arriving, the Russians were delighted. The high-altitude performance of the Hurricane II had never been especially useful in the low/medium-altitude tactical air war the Red Air Force found itself fighting. The American Airacobra, on the other hand, was very fast and manoeuvrable at low and medium altitudes. The 20mm cannon the RAF version was armed with was a disappointment – the Soviets much preferred the 37mm weapon the American Airacobras came with – but the plane could carry a 500lb bomb and was ideal as a low-level attack fighter. It was preferred to the Hurricane the Air Ministry had opted for.

In Britain, plans were laid to extend Hurricane production. The problems with the Typhoon, the Hurricane's intended successor on the production lines, were still far from sorted out. The Sabre engine could still only be made reasonably reliable by building them individually, and output was a mere trickle. Airframe production was outpacing engine production, and Typhoons were having to be stored engineless. In these circumstances there was absolutely no point in increasing Typhoon production at the expense of Hurricanes. With the Hurricane taking on the ground attack role, continuing Hurricane production at a high level was an easy decision to make. There was, however, no attempt to increase Spitfire production for the pure fighter role to compensate. In effect, the ground attack fighter was being built at the expense of standard fighters.

For the December 1941 programme, it was agreed to build an extra 1,000 Hurricanes in the first six months of 1942 and, instead of phasing it out in July 1942, build another 1,300 after that. Production would now continue on a large scale throughout 1942 and would not peter out until the end of 1943. This was a remarkable turnaround for a fighter that just a few months before the Air Ministry had been demanding should be removed from the production programme as soon as possible. As a ground attack fighter it was rugged and manoeuvrable, and for hitting small battlefield targets was far more suitable than the Blenheim or Bisley.

The ingredients for an effective close air-support force were all there, but in the UK it was taking a long time for the pieces to fall into place. The Bumper exercises in October 1941 was the first full-scale Army exercise involving close air support. The value of the tentacle techniques pioneered in the Northern Ireland Wann-Woodall trials was clear. Even using airfields 50 miles away, the exercises demonstrated that aircraft could be over the target within fifty to sixty minutes of the request. War Office reports spoke enthusiastically about the time saved by briefing aircraft in the air on new targets. The possibility of having aircraft patrolling near the front, on call and ready to strike at targets as they emerged was another interesting option, although protecting the planes waiting to go into action would require more fighters than were likely to be available.[30] Brooke was already suggesting the forward controllers operate from armoured cars rather than unprotected trucks. More training was required to ensure army staffs appreciated the potential and limitations of the bomber, but Brooke was in no doubt the trials had proven the case for close air support. It was just a question of gaining operational experience and acquiring the right sort of aircraft.[31]

These were all exciting developments, but they were no more than the methods that had evolved quite naturally in the fighting in Africa. They had also been used during various inter-war colonial conflicts and had been standard RAF practice on the Western Front in 1918. The RAF in the UK was still trying to make up lost ground. This was especially true for the planes being used. The Bumper exercises had used Blenheims, which, the War Office pointed out, experience in the Middle East had already demonstrated were unsuitable. The single-engined Fairey Battle was closer to what the War Office wanted, and the Army regretted that the two Battle squadrons (Nos 88 and 226) that had been involved in the Northern Ireland trials were not available for the exercises. With these they believed it would have been possible to hit targets much closer to friendly troops.[32] Both squadrons were actually unavailable because they too were converting to twin-engined planes (the Douglas Boston). Bomber Command did not want any single-engined bombers.

Nor did it occur to anyone to use Fighter Command Hurricanes in the exercises. By the end of 1941, it had become very clear from experience in the Middle East that the single-seater fighter was the best option for ground attack.[33] The Hurricane I had done well but lacked cannon and the ability to carry a reasonable bomb load. In Britain, the Hurricane II was proving it had all the required qualities. Douglas was even enthusiastically describing how his Hurricanes could be used for army support, but he was also insisting they would only be available if he did not need them to establish air superiority. The ground attack fighters the Army needed existed, but they were under the wrong command and might be needed for something else.

When Barratt enquired about the possibility of the fifteen squadrons nominated for ground-attack duties taking part in Army exercises, the Air Ministry was rather concerned that he might believe such support would actually be available in the event of an invasion, when in reality all fighters would be required for the battle to control the skies. Fighters could perhaps be released to simulate the sort of air support the British Army might be on the receiving end of, to help familiarize British troops with ground strafing and dive-bombing, but there was no desire to ensure British troops would get similar support.

Meanwhile, the Air Ministry was still ploughing ahead with the twin-engined close-support Blenheim V bomber. Douglas might be convinced the ground-attack fighter was best and the Air Ministry might even agree, but fighter-bomber Hurricanes could contribute nothing to the strategic bomber offensive. As Britain entered the third year of the war, the need to build up a long-range bomber fleet was still dominating all decisions. As Douglas had emphasized, it was fighters that were in demand, as interceptors, air superiority fighters, fighter-bombers and reconnaissance planes. You could not have too many fighters, but Portal was constantly trying to peg back fighter production so that more bombers could be built.

Nothing much had changed since the summer of 1940. The Air Ministry was no closer to accepting the value of air support on the battlefield. Portal talked about the force of fifteen squadrons, along with cannon-armed night fighters, as an anti-invasion force, but in Portal's mind, opposing an invasion and supporting the Army were still not quite the same thing.[34] Portal still tended to see it as the RAF stepping in to make up for the deficiencies of the Army, rather than a joint enterprise that improved the country's defences. The Air Ministry continued to insist that genuine co-operation would only be needed when the time came to cross the Channel. As long as the War Office viewed this as an impossible undertaking, the Air Ministry would have time to get its strategic bomber offensive back on track. However, the task of defeating the German Army was beginning to look a little less daunting. The first cracks were beginning to appear in the apparent invincibility of the all-conquering Wehrmacht.

Following the failure of Battleaxe, heads rolled. Wavell had been replaced by Auchinleck, who had impressed Churchill with his handling of the Iraq crisis. Collishaw had been replaced by Air Vice-Marshal Arthur 'Mary' Coningham. Coningham was a New Zealander ('Mary' was a corruption of 'Maori') who had been commanding No. 4 Group in Bomber Command since March 1939. The commander of a heavy bomber group that was spearheading the strategic air offensive might not seem the most promising material to lead a tactical air force, but Coningham was not a hard-core bomber disciple and the problems he had achieving worthwhile results with his Whitleys did nothing to persuade him he should be. Towards the end of the First World War, he had commanded an S.E.5a fighter squadron and had extensive experience of fighter-bomber operations over the Western Front, which helped influence his outlook.[35] He believed the Air Force was there to support the Army and the two services had to work together. This did not necessarily mean he was wholeheartedly in favour of close air support on the battlefield, but he was willing to work with the Army, and this was a start.

Coningham took over at a time when trust between the two services had fallen to an all-time low. Once again there were demands from the Army and War Office for an independent 'Army Air Force' along the lines of the Fleet Air Arm. The Air Ministry might claim that any division of air resources could only be inefficient, but so little effort or thought and so few resources were going into army support that the War Office could scarcely be blamed for welcoming such inefficiency. A small force it had control over was far more useful than a larger force it had no control over.

As soon as he had replaced Wavell with Auchinleck, the ever-impatient Churchill was urging his new Middle East commander to get on with the task of defeating Rommel. The next offensive (Operation Crusader) would be another attempt to relieve Tobruk, and Churchill was already envisaging a follow-up offensive completing the liberation of North Africa (Operation Acrobat) and even the occupation of Sicily (Operation Whipcord). As it turned out, Churchill found Auchinleck even less obliging than Wavell. While Wavell had insisted it would be three months before he could attack again, Auchinleck wanted more like five months. It would be at least early November before his forces would be adequately equipped and trained, he insisted. This was a welcome respite for the RAF that would give the Commonwealth Air Forces time to incorporate the greater number of combat planes that were now arriving in the Middle East.

Once again, Churchill would make sure as much equipment as possible was sent to strengthen the army in North Africa, including the very latest Crusader cruiser tanks. This did not involve the same level of risk as previous reinforcements for the Middle East. With German forces still heavily engaged in Russia, it seemed safe to assume no invasion of the United Kingdom could be attempted before winter. It was also politically essential that Britain should be seen to be pulling her weight. Tackling the German army in North Africa was the only military way of assisting the Soviets. North Africa provided a second front of sorts, and action there might help deflect calls for a second front on mainland Europe.

The pause in the fighting in the Western Desert allowed the last remaining threats in the rear to be dealt with. Iran was occupied by Commonwealth and Soviet forces in August 1941, and in November the last Italian strongholds in East Africa surrendered. The Allies could now deploy all their Mediterranean-based air strength in the Western Desert. The quality of the fighters available slowly improved as more squadrons re-equipped with the American Tomahawk and Hurricane II. The Tomahawk was a reasonable match for the Bf 109E at low and medium altitude, although significantly inferior at high altitude. On paper the Hurricane II, with its two-speed Merlin XX engine, should have been at less of a disadvantage, but the Tomahawk was a much better fighter and despite its problems at altitude, it was the American fighter that was viewed by the Germans as the greater threat and tended to take on the air superiority role for Coningham's squadrons. The Hurricane tended to be used for the less-demanding escort and interception roles. Both types were in short supply. Russian commitments limited the number of Hurricane IIs available, and Curtiss were about to switch production from the Tomahawk to the improved Kittyhawk. The last batch of Tomahawks arrived in Takoradi in September, and there would be a two month gap before the Kittyhawks started coming through. The Curtiss Kittyhawk only offered a slight improvement over the Tomahawk, but did possess one major advantage. Unlike the Tomahawk, this version was designed to carry light bombs. It was not a modification requested by the British. The Air Ministry loftily proclaimed that it was still Air Staff policy that single-seater fighters should not be expected to carry bombs. However, to avoid unnecessary delays, the Air Ministry decided not to ask the Americans to remove this capability.

The Spitfire was still the only Allied fighter that could take on the German Messerschmitt on reasonably equal terms. The war was entering its third year, yet still no Spitfire fighters had been based outside the UK. It was a policy that placed the RAF and the British Army at a huge disadvantage. Reasons for not sending it abroad included the supposed fragility of the design and its narrow track outward retracting undercarriage, both of which made it less suitable for the more basic airfields usually found near the front. The rugged Hurricane, with its more stable wide track undercarriage, was better in this respect, but the Bf 109 also had a narrow track undercarriage and was even more delicate than the Spitfire, and German pilots still managed to get by operating it from less than perfect tactical airstrips. The use of the Spitfire later in the war in all corners of the globe scarcely supported the theory that it was too fragile to use abroad.

The real problem was that the bomber was still dominating all Air Force thinking. Defending the country against the knockout blow and a possible invasion meant Britain's air defences had to have the best fighters available. Even so, five years after the prototype flew and three years after it entered service, there was no reason why all the RAF's fighter squadrons throughout the world, even those in far-flung Malaya, should not have had the Spitfire by the end of 1941, but the bomber strategy prevented this. Britain never devoted sufficient resources to fighter, and in particular Spitfire, production. Everything had to be sacrificed to help build the massive bomber fleet the Air Staff wanted. Fighter squadrons overseas were having to make do with second best. This was not simply because home defence had too high a priority. It would have been equally wrong, and perhaps more dangerous, to equip overseas squadrons with Spitfires and leave home defence in the hands of Gladiators and Hurricane Is. The fundamental problem was that the bomber strategy was absorbing a dangerously high proportion of the country's resources.

There were so few Spitfires that Britain was rather reluctant to use any for fear of losing too many. The Middle East did not even get the Spitfire

I, lest it prove to be a tap that could not be turned off. In the summer of 1941, there was the first hint that the policy might change. In June, trials with a tropicalized Spitfire got underway and 200 sets of the necessary equipment were ordered, but it was only a precaution, in case Spitfires had to be sent overseas. There were still no firm plans to send Spitfire fighters abroad, although the possibility of supplying the Red Air Force with Spitfires did perhaps expose the absurdity of denying British forces the benefit of the protection the Allies' best fighter might provide.

It did not help that there was still no pressure from the Middle East for Spitfires. Tedder does not appear to have been too alarmed by the quality of the equipment available to him, or if he was, he was determined not to show it. He had not forgotten the fate that had befallen his predecessor. Longmore had irritated Portal and Churchill with his demands for the very latest combat types. Lest his successor have any similar ideas, Freeman was soon explaining to Tedder that such were the technical problems with many of the latest planes that they would cause more problems than they solved, which in the case of planes like the Stirling and Typhoon was undoubtedly true.[36]

Tedder, however, had no intention of being as awkward as his predecessor. After visiting London in June, Tedder did admit to being 'nervous' that the idea that obsolescent aircraft would do for the Middle East seemed to be gaining ground but he was happy to concede that the Home Front should have priority with the latest types.[37] He admitted that the Hurricane I was verging on the obsolescent, but at this stage he seemed perfectly happy with the Hurricane II or Tomahawk as a replacement. It was range and lifting power that he most wanted to improve; the Wellington II and Beaufighter were the planes he was after, not better single-seater fighters.

As 1941 wore on, however, the Air Ministry in London was becoming a lot less relaxed about the fighter inferiority Tedder seemed so willing to accept. Portal worried that 60 per cent of frontline Hurricane strength would still consist of the old Mark I version for the Crusader offensive. The long-term plan was still for American production to meet the majority of Middle East requirements, but there was a major question mark about the quality of American designs, especially their performance at altitude. It was hoped that the turbo-supercharged Republic P-47 Thunderbolt would address this problem, and Freeman did his best to hurry along deliveries, but none could arrive before March 1942 at the earliest.[38]

Until these arrived, as an interim measure Portal decided to break with the past and allow the first Spitfire fighter squadrons to operate outside the United Kingdom. In September 1941, he informed Tedder he would be getting a squadron of Spitfire Vs. Interestingly, Portal wanted the Spitfires used to deal with high-altitude bombers, not to challenge the high-flying Axis fighters over the front.[39] Portal was more worried about rear defence than air superiority over the battlefield. Tedder was warned to be very careful with them: he would only be getting an allocation of ten replacements a month. It was a start, but one squadron was not going to make much difference. Nor could Tedder expect them to arrive before the end of 1941, so they would not be in time for Auchinleck's Crusader offensive.[40] There were, however, soon some very good reasons for bringing forward the deployment of Spitfires.

The appearance of the Tomahawk and Hurricane II in the Western Desert was noticed by German pilots, who immediately demanded the latest Bf 109F to replace the Bf 109E to restore their advantage. The first of these were encountered by Allied pilots in October, and it was assumed that all German fighter squadrons would quickly re-equip with the improved Messerschmitt.[41] It was an interesting assumption, given that the conversion of the RAF fighter force from one model to another took so long.

To make matter worse, Italian units were beginning to get the Macchi C.202 Folgore. This was basically a Machhi C.200 re-engined with the same Daimler-Benz engine that powered the Bf 109E. With the benefit of the extra power, the outstanding flying qualities the basic design had always possessed were now backed up by a high top speed. The new fighter was faster and flew higher than the similarly powered Bf 109E. Also, unlike the Messerschmitt – and indeed the Hurricane and Spitfire – the Italian fighter retained its superb handling and manoeuvrability at high speed. With a fighter of this quality, the Italian Air Force became a significant factor.

The appearance of the Bf 109F in the Middle East prompted Churchill to request a comparison of the fighters available to both sides in the theatre. The RAF had by this time come into possession of a Bf 109F, and this confirmed that the fighter was far superior in climb and ceiling, although it was claimed, somewhat generously, that the Spitfire V was faster in level flight.[42] Not even Air Ministry wishful thinking could deny that the German fighter was far superior to the Tomahawk and Hurricane II. Having seen the performance figures, Churchill agreed that the discrepancy in the performance was serious and felt that there should at least be 'some of the best' in the Middle East, and he fully approved Portal's decision to send the Spitfires.[43]

Still there was no specific demand from the Middle East for better fighters, just the odd reference to what was becoming a serious problem. In October, with the forthcoming Crusader offensive just weeks away, Tedder startled Portal with a rather casual reference in a report to being up against enemy fighters that had better performance, allowing their pilots to choose their own time and place to intervene. This he regarded as a 'not unfamiliar situation'.[44] It was only mentioned in passing. Tedder was accepting this state of affairs without complaint; he was far more worried about how long it was taking for the latest fighter tactics to filter through to the Middle East from the UK, and wondered if someone could be sent out to pass on these ideas.

Portal should hardly have been surprised that Allied fighter pilots were so hard-pushed. Douglas had been telling him that even the latest version of the Spitfire was inferior to the Bf 109F. What the Middle East was having to use was vastly inferior. Indeed, Portal seemed more worried than Tedder about the Bf 109F danger, and was coming up with suggestions for dealing with it. He told Tedder to take risks, using Wellingtons by day, without escort if necessary, to knock out these dangerous fighters on their airfields.[45]

Tedder's estimate of the relative air strengths did not go down well in London either. Tedder's intelligence was predicting that in the forthcoming offensive the enemy would have 650 planes to the Commonwealth's 500.[46] Tedder was not in the least bit alarmed by this numerical inferiority, remaining confident that his squadrons would be able to carry out their duties. He certainly never imagined the effect his words would have in London.

Churchill was still facing severe criticism for the performance of Allied air forces in North Africa from Commonwealth leaders. The Australian government was far from happy at the way its troops were having to fight without the sort of close air-support German forces were getting. The New Zealand government upped the stakes by demanding assurances that its troops would only be committed if Allied forces had air superiority.[47] Churchill was therefore considerably embarrassed by Tedder's claim that he did not expect his air force to be numerically superior in the forthcoming battle. Portal told Tedder his assessment of relative air strength had caused him 'considerable disappointment' and suggested he was getting his figures wrong. He told Tedder the figures he should be using, and that to 'help you still further' seventy-five more fighter pilots were on the way, which Portal suggested would get his strength up to 600. These would be followed by another 100 pilots by the end of November.[48]

It was only the issue of numerical superiority that was causing the furore in London. No account was being taken of the quality of the planes involved. Fighter Command and the Air Ministry were worried enough by the growing technical inferiority of the fighters like the Spitfire V being held back to defend the United Kingdom. The fighters they were expecting the Middle East to use were far inferior and this should have been a factor in assessing the relative strengths of the opposing forces. The tactical skills of Allied fighter pilots, which was so worrying Tedder, was another factor which should have been taken into account. Nor was it just fighter tactics that was worrying Tedder; the heavy losses in Greece and Crete had caused a shortage of experienced wing and section leaders to lead the 'raw material' that had been rushed though operational training units to replace losses, and which he rated at a 'village cricket' level of performance.[49] In truth, the Allies needed numerical superiority just to compensate for their inferior quality.

Tedder's efforts not to cause trouble by keeping his demands to a minimum were not having the desired effect. Churchill was losing confidence in the compliant, dutiful Tedder as fast as he had lost confidence in the ever-complaining Longmore. Freeman was sent out to investigate, and Churchill, always liable to blame the sender of the message rather than believe the message, made it clear to Auchinleck that if he felt Freeman – a leader he believed to be of 'altogether larger calibre' than Tedder – would make a better air commander than Tedder, then he would stay in the Mediterranean. Freeman, horrified when he discovered he had been given the 'Judas' role, would have nothing to do with it. Portal did not believe it made any sort of sense to change commanders on the eve of a battle, and was willing to resign over the issue, although this would not stop him making it clear to Auchinleck that if he wanted, Tedder could be replaced as soon as the battle was over.[50] It was scant loyalty from someone who had disapproved so strongly of Longmore conniving with army commanders. In fact Auchinleck and Tedder got on very well, and Auchinleck was not the least bit interested in having Tedder replaced.

Freeman's main purpose for going to Egypt was to study the intelligence data and come up with some better figures. By combing through rear areas, and a contribution from Iraq, the Commonwealth force was squeezed up to 660, and a careful review of intelligence estimates arrived at a more precise figure of 642 Axis planes. It all seemed a rather pointless exercise, as the final difference was a 'guesstimate' of eighteen planes more instead of fifty less. Churchill begged to differ. 'The only difference was that the first version stated that we should be inferior and the revised version that we should be superior,' Churchill the politician barked back. 'It is only the kind of difference between plus and minus, or black and white,' he added, just in case anyone was still not clear.[51] This marginal advantage, coupled with the rather dubious claim that Commonwealth ground crews would keep more aircraft serviceable than their Axis counterparts, and Tedder's confidence in the superior fighting qualities of his pilots, was enough for Churchill. He was able to reassure Commonwealth governments with a clear conscience that their troops would be fighting with air superiority. If these governments had been aware of the clear technical superiority of German fighters they might not have been so easily persuaded. Nor would Tedder's confidence in the superior fighting qualities of his pilots have impressed them so much if they had known Tedder was in fact genuinely concerned about their inexperience and the tactics they were using.

Portal was still planning to send one, possibly two, Spitfire squadrons to the Middle East, but only after Crusader had been launched. With Churchill anxious to impress Stalin with a military victory in the Middle East and reassure Dominion governments about the quality of the fighter cover that would be provided, there were excellent political and military reasons for getting Spitfires out to the Middle East sooner. The Air Ministry, however, was soon coming up with some reasons not to: 'To use Spitfires would introduce a new type to the Middle East of which they have no experience and which no provision has ever been made.' This was a very good argument for never deploying any new aircraft in the Middle East.[52] When Douglas got wind of the decision, he was horrified. He foresaw all sorts of difficulties: the Spitfire was too fragile for operations in the desert and there were already too many different types operating in the Middle East. He saw no logical advantage in sending Spitfires to provide defence against high-altitude bombing raids. The Hurricane II may not be as fast as the Spitfire, but, he claimed, its rate of climb and service ceiling were the same as that of the Spitfire V. It was an upbeat assessment that was at odds with his own clearly stated desire to remove all Hurricanes from fighter duties as quickly as possible.

Just like Dowding before him, he saw the Spitfire as the country's insurance policy against invasion or the knockout blow. There were in his view already insufficient Spitfires in the UK and he could not afford to lose any. If even a few were sent to the Middle East, there would soon be demands for more. It was crucial that the Spitfire tap should not be turned on. 'If you add to this drain on our Spitfire resources, I sincerely believe that you will be laying this country open to a mortal blow next spring,' he warned in Dowding-esque tones.[53] Churchill may have come to appreciate the bomber threat had been exaggerated, but it was still haunting RAF commanders and dominating the conduct of the war. Portal reminded him of the need for a correct balance between UK and Middle East forces. The Spitfire was needed in the Middle East to boost morale as much as defend Alexandria against high-level bombing attacks, the Chief of Air Staff insisted, still failing to appreciate the vital importance of fighters over the battlefield. Portal was doing his best to move in the right direction, but even having the two Spitfire squadrons in the Middle East and forty-one Spitfire squadrons on the home front, where no fighting was taking place, was scarcely a satisfactory balance. Douglas insisted he could not afford to lose any Spitfire squadrons. He had to have a powerful Fighter Command to repulse any resumption of the German air offensive or possible attempt at invasion in 1942. With so many Hurricanes going to the Soviet Union and the Middle East, he would need every Spitfire he could get to keep his force up to strength.[54]

This seemed to finally break Portal's resistance. The approval for the dispatch of two Spitfire squadrons to the Middle East had just been confirmed when Portal suddenly changed his mind; the Spitfires would not go after all. Portal cited the need to retain a powerful home defence fighter force. Less convincingly, he explained that since the decision to send the two squadrons to the Middle East, it had been decided that another two would be needed for Operation Whipcord, the plan to occupy Sicily, and Portal did not want to be committed to both simultaneously. He therefore suggested delaying the two squadrons for the Middle East until after Whipcord.[55] It seemed a rather contrived reason. Whipcord would only happen if Crusader was successful and a follow-up offensive evicting Axis forces from the rest of North Africa (Acrobat) was also a success. Putting off the transfer until after Whipcord meant no Spitfires would serve in North Africa until after the continent had been cleared of Axis forces. Churchill seemed to agree rather easily with Portal's decision. Commonwealth troops would have to carry on waiting for the only Allied plane capable of challenging the best enemy fighters. There were not the howls of protest that Longmore might have greeted such a decision with. There was still no pressure from the Middle East to supply Spitfires. Tedder believed his Hurricanes and Tomahawks were capable of handling the Bf 109F satisfactorily, provided his pilots did not develop a complex about the capabilities of the German fighter. No doubt Tedder's willingness to play down the problems his pilots faced helped suppress any feelings of guilt within the Air Ministry.

Meanwhile efforts were being made to undo the damage the Greek fiasco had inflicted on RAF/Army relations. An inter-service committee was set up, the results of which were formalized at an air support conference in Cairo in September. On the 30th of that month, a directive was issued which attempted to clarify the responsibilities of the two services. On balance it was a compromise that leaned towards the Air Ministry view on tactical air support. The directive dropped the 'close support' label because it was deemed confusing. There would be indirect support, which would involve attacks on land and sea communication in the theatre, and direct support, which would have an immediate effect on the battle. Arguably 'direct support' was a very broad category, and removing the term 'close support' made it more difficult to discuss the balance between support on the fringes of the battle and more intimate support. Indeed, the directive insisted that more distant targets would usually be the more appropriate. These would generally be beyond observation from the ground and aerial reconnaissance would identify them. Targets reported by the tentacles with forward troops were not ruled out, but aircraft should only be used if the army had no artillery or other suitable weapons to call on. A rapid advance which had outstripped artillery support would be an example of such a situation. Targets as close as 500 yards to friendly forces were not ruled out. However, only fighter-bombers would be able to hit targets this close to friendly forces, and these would only become available when a 'considerable degree of air superiority' had been established. Normal practice would be for army commanders to indicate where they wanted support, and reconnaissance planes would operate in that area to seek out targets.[56]

For defence, army commanders could not expect permanent fighter cover, but it was agreed that some effort should be made to fly sweeps in the area where enemy attacks were more likely. Defence of individual ground units was first and foremost an army responsibility, and extra anti-aircraft units were to be dispatched to the Middle East to give troops the means to defend themselves. Fighters would be freed for more offensive duties.

The RAF was still not accepting that there might be situations where aircraft were a better way of dealing with a tactical target than the options normally open to ground forces. There was still an air of using the RAF to come to the rescue when the Army was in trouble. Bombing on the battlefield was still a last resort rather than normal practice. The need to wait for air superiority before there could be any closer support was Air Staff dogma flying in the face of reality. An army could not wait until the RAF had built up a 'considerable degree of superiority' before it could expect fighters to be employed in a close air-support role. In previous operations, fighters had been regularly switched from air superiority to ground attack, when the circumstances demanded it. From the army's point of view, this attitude made the flexibility of the fighter-bomber a major disadvantage. A fighter-bomber could be switched to the air superiority role, but a specialist dive-bomber or armoured close-support plane could not.

There was of course no reason why additional fighter squadrons could not be formed for the specialist fighter-bomber role, but this was not on the Air Ministry agenda. Fighter production was effectively capped by the need to build up the strategic bomber force. As far as the Air Ministry was concerned, fighter-bomber support was a bonus that the Army did not absolutely need and should learn to live without, rather than a key element of the fire-power available to the Army.[57]

The first Bomber Control Unit, as developed in the Northern Ireland trials, was now to be deployed in the Middle East. Further exercises and trials were conducted in the Middle East. Their role was expanded to cover reconnaissance and fighter support, and to reflect this wider role they were renamed Air Support Controls (ASC). Each army corps or armoured division was to have one ASC, each with seven tentacles deployed at the front.[58]

With air superiority the priority, only the medium/light Blenheims and Marylands would initially be available for army support. Supplies of Marylands, however, were drying up as the Martin plant switched to the Baltimore. This was the heavier four-seater update of the Maryland that the Air Ministry had specifically asked the Americans to build, but the required modifications made it even less suitable for the low-level attack role. To make up for the shortage of Marylands, as many Blenheims as possible were sent to the Middle East, but these too were in very short supply. In September, much to Bomber Command's dismay, Portal ordered that the Bostons which No. 2 Group was finally beginning to get should be diverted to the Middle East.[59]

Low-level ground attack missions with these twin-engined light bombers was particularly risky in the featureless desert terrain, with no natural features to help conceal the approach and achieve surprise. Even attacking from 1,000–3,000ft was considered risky unless anti-aircraft defences were known to be weak. Level bombing from as high as 8,000ft was the preferred option. This made hitting small battlefield targets difficult, which provided further justification for the Air Force preference for focusing on larger targets in the rear. There was one squadron capable of operating over the battlefield. The Hurricanes Is of No. 80 Squadron had been equipped with bomb racks for eight 40lb bombs, and these would be used to attack targets closer to the frontline.[60] There was a joint army/air force headquarters to try and ensure the two elements did not get separated in the heat of battle, either by circumstances or simply as a result of mutual antipathy. So much for the theory – it just remained to see how all this would work in the heat of battle.

Both sides were frustrated by the slow build-up of supplies. Holding the port of Tobruk meant all German supplies had to come along what were often very basic desert tracks. Rommel realized that he had to take the port before he could consider any further advance eastwards. Submarines, RAF Blenheims and Fleet Air Arm Swordfish operating from Malta were making sure he did not have the resources by playing havoc with Axis convoys. Ultra intercepts were providing precise information on the routes and times of Italian and German convoys. To ensure the enemy suspected nothing, reconnaissance planes were always sent to identify the position of the convoys, and then normal operating practices were allowed to run their course. Wellingtons from the Nile Delta kept up a continuous offensive against Benghazi, while Wellingtons operating from Malta struck Tripoli, but it was the attacks on the convoys that did the real damage. In August, 35 per cent of supplies crossing the Mediterranean were lost; in October this rose to 63 per cent. In five months, nearly 180,000 tons of Axis shipping had been sunk, over half as a result of air attack. The Italians gave up even trying to get supplies across to Tripoli. It was a very risky business for the Allied aircrews and aircraft losses were heavy, but the effects on Rommel's supplies were devastating.[61]

This was indirect support precisely as Slessor had always advocated. The offensive against Axis convoys was, by any standards, staggeringly successful, in large measure due to the priceless information provided by Ultra. However, not even this level of good fortune and success could eliminate the need for a land battle. Allied lines of communication were tortuously long, and arguably the success of the Malta-based squadrons merely compensated for the huge advantage of internal lines of communications the Axis forces possessed. Rommel would be handicapped and his plans disrupted, but a land battle would still have to be fought and won, and air support would still be required for this. Indeed, not providing the ground forces with the air support they needed to exploit German weakness would just be throwing away the advantage the courageous efforts of the RAF and Fleet Air Arm aircrews based on Malta had gained.

Some of the squadrons inflicting this horrendous damage on Axis convoys had been transferred, with enormous reluctance, from Bomber

Command. These included Blenheim squadrons from No. 2 Group and, more damagingly for the strategic air offensive, Wellington squadrons from No. 3 Group. From Bomber Command's point of view, this diversion of resources was a running sore that was preventing the bombers from getting on with the task of winning the war. However, even Portal had to concede it was difficult to deny the Middle East these bombers, at the expense of the stuttering Bomber Command offensive, when 'great results may flow from the destruction of the enemy's bases in North Africa'.[62] Just before the Crusader offensive, a fifth Wellington squadron joined the four already in the Middle East.

The contrasting contribution that squadrons in the two theatres could make was illustrated rather graphically by one particular No. 2 Group operation, which quickly attracted the wrath of Churchill. On 28 August, seventeen Blenheims, escorted by two long-range Spitfire squadrons, carried out a low-level strike on shipping in the port of Rotterdam. Two ships were hit, but seven Blenheims failed to return. Churchill publicly praised the devotion and gallantry of the crews. 'The charge of the Light Brigade at Balaclava is eclipsed in brightness by these almost daily deeds of fame,' he eulogised, but he privately expressed his disappointment to Portal that so many aircraft were being lost against targets of so little importance. Such losses might be acceptable attempting to sink a German battleship about to descend on an Allied convoy in the Atlantic or Tripoli-bound Axis convoys, but not to attack a couple of cargo ships in Rotterdam harbour.[63]

That the British naval and air forces were allowed to continue operating from Malta seemed almost too good to be true. It was only possible because the Italians seemed very reluctant to do anything about the Malta threat. The departure of the Luftwaffe in May to support the invasion of Crete released the pressure on the island, and the Italian Air Force showed little inclination to fill the breech; monthly Italian bombing sorties rarely rose above 100.[64] Indeed, it was the RAF units on Malta that were going on to the offensive. There was so little call on the Hurricanes as interceptors that they were being sent regularly over to Sicily to attack targets of opportunity with machine guns and 20lb bombs, even using the clumsy long-range ferry tanks that enabled them to get to Malta on operational missions to extend their range.[65]

With the Italians possessing no fighter capable of handling the Hurricane II, it was the Regia Aeronautica that was forced back on the defensive. In October, however, the Italians began to deploy their new Macchi C.202 fighters, and these soon began inflicting regular losses on RAF squadrons. It was still a very low intensity offensive;

just seventy-eight bombing sorties were flown against the island in October, rising, in an all out effort, to just 160 in November. However, the occasional appearance of the Macchi C.202 never caused the alarm that the Bf 109E had triggered earlier in the year. Indeed it was the RAF that was consolidating its position. In November it was planned to use *Ark Royal* to fly in three more squadrons (Nos 242, 258 and 605) of Hurricane IIs to the island in two batches. On 12 November, all of No. 242 Squadron and most of No. 605 Squadron were flown off, but the aircraft carrier was sunk at Gibraltar by a U-boat before it could deliver the remainder. It was a reminder of how difficult and expensive it was to keep the island supplied. The reinforcements that did make it, however, were ample to protect the strike force of two Blenheim, three Wellington, one Swordfish and one Albacore squadrons. The situation had become so comfortable on Malta that civilian BOAC flying boats, carrying personnel and supplies, were using the island for refuelling.

It was a state of affairs that was causing the German High Command enormous frustration. It could not understand why Italy had not simply occupied the island, and the Germans were forced to consider doing it themselves. First, though, they had to make sure Rommel had the supplies to launch his attack on Tobruk, planned for late November. So desperate had Rommel's supply situation become that transport planes had to be used to fly in supplies, and even some of these failed to evade marauding long-range Beaufighters and Marylands. Malta had to be neutralized. In October, Goring decided to switch an entire Fliegerkorps with sixteen bomber and fighter groups from the Moscow front to Sicily to back up the efforts of the Italian Air Force.

It was a move that simultaneously underlined how effective the operations from Malta were and how little effect Bomber and Fighter Commands were having on the course of the war. Bomber Command's air offensive against German industry and the efforts of No. 2 Group Blenheims and Fighter Command patrols over France had not caused a single Luftwaffe squadron to be withdrawn from the Eastern Front. However, a handful of Fleet Air Arm and No. 2 Group planes operating from Malta had led to the withdrawal of an entire Air Corps.

Meanwhile, Auchinleck was hoping to get his offensive to relieve Tobruk underway by mid-November. General Alan Cunningham would command the Commonwealth forces. He had 700 tanks, outnumbering the combined German/Italian force two-to-one. Despite the pessimistic intelligence estimates, in the air Coningham had a substantial advantage with 657 planes compared to the 171 German and 214 Italian machines at the front. However, the Italians had considerable resources close to hand, with another 227 planes in North Africa and many more not so far away in Italy.[66] There were nineteen Commonwealth fighter squadrons. Eleven had the Hurricane (including the Hurricane fighter-bomber squadron) and five had Tomahawks. A Royal Navy formation had two-and-a-half squadrons with Hurricanes and Martlets (the ex-Greek Wildcats). There was also a flight of Beaufighters. These were opposed by five German Bf 109 squadrons, of which four now had the Bf 109F, and three Bf 110 squadrons. The Italians had nine fighter squadrons with Macchi C.200s and Fiat G.50s. This gave the Axis forces around 170 fighters compared to some 240 of the Commonwealth air forces. Another nine Italian squadrons with the superior Macchi C.202 were in Italy and available, and would soon be flown in.

In response to Tedder's plea for some tactical guidance, Group Captain Basil Embry, a commander of a night fighter wing, and Flight Lieutenant Johnny Louden, a squadron commander, had accompanied Freeman on his trip to the Middle East. Embry encouraged the adoption of looser, more flexible formations with all pilots weaving rather than just a couple of weavers guarding the rear of the formation. There was some vague talk of fighters operating in pairs, but the 'pair' was not a team in the German sense, with one member of the team watching out for the enemy while the other concentrated on the enemy plane under attack. Embry did not specifically recommend the 'pair' formation should be adopted, and the advice was not the radical overhaul that was required.[67] German pilots did not notice any change in Allied tactics, and continued to be puzzled and surprised by the Allied persistence with fighting formations that gave Luftwaffe pilots so many advantages.[68]

For bomber support there were nine squadrons, six still equipped with Blenheim IVs, with just two with the Maryland and one with the Boston. There were five Wellington squadrons and a Fleet Air Arm Albacore squadron was available for tactical bombing by night. There were also two general reconnaissance squadrons with Marylands and two photo-reconnaissance squadrons with Hurricanes, Beaufighters and Marylands.

For the tactical bomber squadrons, Operation Crusader would prove to be the most difficult of battles. Even by the standards of the highly mobile warfare the open spaces of the desert made possible, the fighting would prove to be exceptionally fluid, with very little in the way of clearly defined frontlines. During the battle, both sides gambled on armoured penetrations deep in the rear of their opponents that relied on fragile lines of communication. In a battle of such confusion it was perhaps appropriate that the ground forces were commanded

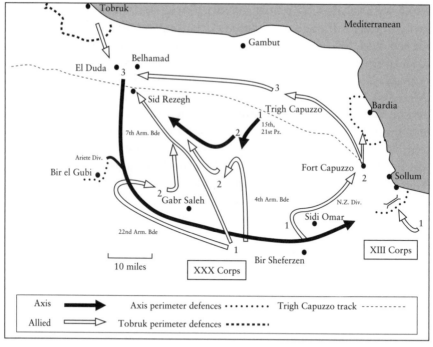

Operation Crusader November 1941

by General Cunningham, the air force by Air Vice-Marshal Coningham and the fleet by Admiral Cunningham.

The battle opened on 18 November with XXX Corps bypassing the Axis frontier defences and heading for the besieged port of Tobruk, leaving XIII Corps to tackle the German defences around Halfaya. The initial advance was concealed by atrocious weather. Enemy airfields in the area were waterlogged and many Axis air units remained grounded for several days. Allied airfields were not so seriously affected, and for once advancing Allied ground forces had the luxury of total air superiority. On the first day of the battle, despite the poor weather, Allied fighters flew over 100 sorties. Axis airfields in the rear were attacked by fighters and medium bombers. In one incident, Beaufighters of No. 272 Squadron caught five Ju 52s taking off and claimed all of them. Attacks on tactical targets were almost exclusively based on aerial reconnaissance. On the afternoon of the 18th, the first direct support mission was flown against enemy armour and vehicles, spotted earlier in the day by Allied planes stuck in waterlogged ground near Bir el Gubi.[69] On 19 and 20 November, around 400 fighter sorties were flown, and with little reaction from the Axis air forces, many pilots turned their attention to any targets on the ground they came across.[70]

On the 18th, the Allied ground forces met little resistance. The next day 7 Armoured Brigade pushed on to Sidi Rezegh, just 10 miles from the Tobruk perimeter defences. However, on the left, 22 Armoured Brigade was halted by the Italian Ariete Division, and on the right, 4 Armoured Brigade, to the east of Gabr Saleh, was severely mauled by Stukas and the 21st Panzer Division, leaving 7 Armoured exposed on both flanks. Neither 4 nor 22 armoured brigades requested air support. Thirty-one Blenheims and Marylands bombed concentrations of enemy armoured vehicles and transports identified by aerial reconnaissance in the Gambut-Bardia-Capuzzo region, well to the east of the main fighting, with Fleet Air Arm Albacores continuing the attacks under cover of darkness.[71]

The 4 Armoured Brigade fell back on Gabr Saleh and 22 Armoured Brigade was switched from Bir el Gubi to support it. On 20 November, two German panzer divisions struck towards Gabr Saleh. The 22 Armoured Brigade arrived too late to help, and 4 Armoured Brigade suffered more heavy losses. This time air support was requested, but when the bombers arrived there was no sign of the expected identification signals, and the attack was not delivered. Bombers were active elsewhere. Forty-five Marylands and Blenheims attacked enemy transports around Tobruk. The Blenheims got some protection from fighters patrolling the general area, but the Marylands had to do without any protection and paid the price. No. 21 Squadron SAAF ran into Bf 109s and lost four out of nine aircraft.[72]

On the 21st, the German panzers swung north of Gabr Saleh to attack 7 Armoured Brigade in the rear, but were themselves then pursued by 4 and 22 armoured brigades. On the same day, the Allied forces in Tobruk attempted to break out towards El Duda. For the next three days there was bitter and confused fighting in the Sidi Rezegh area. XXX Corps made more effort to call in direct air support than XIII Corps fighting around the Halfaya Pass, but the failure to display correct identification signals, poor weather and the hopelessly confused situation on the ground all made it difficult to put close air-support theory into practice.

It was by any standard an extraordinarily confused struggle. There were occasions when commanders overlooking the scene of battle had little idea which forces were friendly and which were hostile. The bombers had little choice but to confine their efforts to enemy columns on the fringes of the battle. The fighter-bomber Hurricanes of No. 80 Squadron were also involved in these attacks. Aiming the bombs proved difficult, and initially the strafing caused far more damage than the bombs, but as the battle progressed the pilots became steadily more proficient.[73]

On 22 November, the Luftwaffe made a determined effort to assert itself. In fierce clashes, ten Tomahawks were lost at the cost of six Messerschmitts.[74] Bomber losses on the 22nd forced a review of fighter escort policy. The Marylands had already suffered heavily, and on the 22nd four out of six Blenheims from No. 45 Squadron were shot down by Bf 109s. No longer could bombers rely on the indirect escort that offensive fighter sweeps provided; in future, fighters were instructed to stay close to the bombers they were escorting.[75] For its part, the Luftwaffe decided its small fighter force could not continue to sustain such heavy losses. In future it would avoid combat with any large Allied formations and confine itself to hit-and-run tactics, if the odds were favourable. In effect, Allied bombers would be safe provided they had an escort.

On the ground, the battles in the Sidi Rezegh region were not going well for the Commonwealth tank units: 4 Armoured Brigade had been virtually wiped out and the 22nd had less than fifty tanks left. The forces in Tobruk had advanced about 3 miles but had failed to break out. Further east, however, the New Zealand Division was having more success. This unit had encircled the German forces in the Halfaya and Bardia areas, and were pushing on along the Trigh Capuzzo track towards Sidi Rezegh. The excellent views provided by the escarpment allowed the tentacles attached to ground units to provide accurate information on targets for air strikes. For once, effective use was made of the tentacle system.[76]

Despite the Allied advance, Rommel was convinced he could eliminate the entire Allied force with an audacious drive towards the Egyptian frontier, simultaneously cutting off the remaining Allied forces in the Sidi Rezegh area and relieving the encircled Axis forces still holding on in the Halfaya Pass and Bardia. He instructed the 15th and 21st panzer divisions to disengage and swing south through Gabr Saleh to Sid Omar. The move caused total confusion within the Allied ranks, and units in the path of the Germans were swept aside. It caused considerable consternation in London that on such a vital day, Allied bombers flew only forty-eight sorties. With 100 bombers available, some 200 should have been flown, an enraged Churchill protested. The problem was that army commanders were in no position to provide accurate information on the whereabouts of the enemy. The bomber units stood by idle, waiting for instructions that never came.[77]

Once the direction of the panzers had become clear, the Allied air forces were able to intervene. The German panzers struck north and south of the encircled Axis forces around Halfaya, elements getting as far as Bardia, but elsewhere, as soon as the overstretched German forces made contact with substantial Allied units, their progress was halted. Where there were no substantial Allied units, the Allied air forces were able to intervene. No longer restricted by the possible presence of friendly forces, Allied bombers and fighters inflicted heavy losses on the German columns. On 25 November, over 100 bomber sorties were flown in the Sidi Omar and Bir Sheferzen regions, with fighters joining in these attacks whenever possible.[78]

The next day, the bombers switched their support to the New Zealanders threatening the German forces encircling Tobruk. Both Belhamed and Sidi Rezegh were captured, and the New Zealanders had linked up with the Tobruk garrison at El Duda. The following day (the 27th), direct support was divided between the Tobruk and Halfaya fronts, but the number of sorties fell to just sixty-six. Twenty-three of these were flown by the Hurribombers of No. 80 Squadron, which was managing to keep a higher proportion of its equipment serviceable. In the three days 25–27 November, the squadron flew forty-six fighter-bomber and twenty-three escort sorties without suffering serious losses.[79]

The battle was on a knife edge; both sides were over-extended and short of supplies. General Cunningham wanted to go on to the defensive, but Auchinleck was determined to persevere and replaced Cunningham with his like-minded deputy, General Neil Ritchie. Rommel was the first to show signs of cracking. On 28 November, the German commander felt compelled to abandon his advance on Halfaya and wheel his armoured divisions round to re-establish the German position around Tobruk. On 1 December, the Germans again sealed off Tobruk. There followed several days of fierce but inconclusive fighting to control the Sidi Rezegh region. From 28 November to 2 December, the medium bomber squadrons managed around 135 sorties against enemy units in the area.[80]

On 2 December, Rommel again ordered units to disengage and strike in a south-easterly direction to link up with the Halfaya defences. Again the attempt was foiled by a combination of counter-attack on the ground and air bombardment. Bombers were also in action against Axis forces in the Tobruk area, when they could be identified. By night, Wellingtons based in the Delta joined the Albacores in night attacks on motor transport and troop concentrations in the battle zone, often flying low enough to strafe the enemy.[81] This use of heavy bombers under cover of darkness was to become a regular feature of future RAF tactical air operations.

Meanwhile, Axis forces were being reinforced by the arrival of fresh units from the mainland, including Italian Machhi C.202 and German Bf 109 squadrons. The shortage of fuel limited the number of sorties, but the fighters that did get into the air took their toll. The Tomahawks suffered heavily, although when they broke through to the Ju 87 they were able to wreak their revenge. Hurricane losses were even heavier. On 6 December, five were shot down attempting to break through the fighters escorting Stukas. On the next day, another six Hurricanes were lost in similar circumstances. In these engagements, several enemy escorts were claimed, but only one bomber. The escorts had done their job. On 9 December, another seven Hurricanes were lost, along with four Tomahawks.

At this point Rommel decided his supply situation no longer enabled him to maintain the ring around Tobruk. The Axis forces were instructed to pull back to the Gazala Line. The retreat and the disruption it brought to Axis fighter squadrons brought some relief to the hard-pressed Allied fighter forces. The Germans and Italians were forced to abandon large numbers of unserviceable planes. Coningham was equally concerned by the losses his fighter force had suffered. It was now patently clear to Coningham that neither the Tomahawk nor the Hurricane II were a match for the Bf 109F. Nor were they a match for the Macchi C.202, which tended not to get the recognition it perhaps deserved. Commonwealth pilots preferred to believe they had been engaging the better-thought-of German Messerschmitt pilots.

The first Kittyhawks were arriving, but the improvement in performance was small and even before they were used in combat, Coningham realized that it was not the answer to the Bf 109. He made it very clear to Tedder that the Air Ministry had to stop believing second-best would do for the Middle East.[82] Faster and more powerfully armed fighters were required, and he suggested the Spitfire or American Airacobra. Tedder did not perhaps pass these warnings on with sufficient force, but he provoked an apology from Freeman that the Hurricane, Tomahawk 'and possibly even the Kittyhawk' were not up to the standard of the Bf 109F, and he promised Tedder that the tropicalization of Spitfires would be speeded up.[83]

A few days later, on 18 December, it was decided that Spitfires would now be sent to the Middle East – but they would not be going to the Western Desert. Coningham's doubts about the Kittyhawk appear to have made little impression on Embry. He reported back to London enthusiastically about the qualities of the latest American fighter, which helped settle nerves and perhaps ease guilt. The first two Spitfire squadrons would go to Malta.[84] Embry fully backed the decision; Malta's need was definitely greater, he insisted, which was perhaps true, but the Allied forces in the Western Desert came a very close second.[85]

Initially, the German retreat from Tobruk was allowed to proceed largely unhindered by air attack. The loss of five out of six unescorted Bostons on 10 December was a timely reminder of the need for close escorts, but the Axis forces were by this time beyond fighter range. By the 11th, Allied fighter units had moved to the Tobruk region, enabling escorted attacks on Axis forces to continue. Rommel briefly made a stand at Gazala. On 15 December, this position was attacked frontally by infantry, while 4 Armoured Brigade was used to swing around the flank of the Axis coastal defences to cut Rommel's line of retreat. However, the brigade arrived short of fuel and disorganized, and was able to contribute little to the battle. The German forces had, however, been squeezed into a relatively small area. It was the perfect opportunity for the RAF to intervene, but once again the problems of identifying friend from foe when forces were closely engaged proved impossible to overcome and the direct support squadrons played virtually no part in the fighting.[86] On the night of 16/17 December, Rommel pulled his forces out of the Gazala Line and fell back on Agedabia.

Commonwealth forces desperately tried to cut off Rommel's escape from Cyrenaica and inflict a defeat of the proportions that Wavell had achieved over the Italians twelve months before. Msus, just 40 miles from the German forces at Agedabia, became the advanced base from which fighters and Blenheim bombers could support Allied efforts to block the Axis retreat. Fighters operated in force over the area, attacking targets of opportunity, but there were few requests from the army for close support, even though Allied ground forces in the area were getting badly mauled by German panzers. The first unit to suffer was the Coldstream Guards on 23 December. On the 27th, 22 Armoured Brigade attempted to outflank the German defences but was hurled back with heavy losses. For most of this period, the Blenheims at Msus stood idly by. Five sorties were flown on 26 December in support of the Guards. No more direct sorties were flown until the 29th, when XIII Corps requested air support for the hard-pressed 22 Brigade, and twenty-four sorties were flown. The next day, aerial reconnaissance spotted thirty tanks and 200 vehicles bearing down on 22 Brigade, but only eleven successful sorties were flown. In the period 26 December to 7 January, only eighty-eight bomber sorties were flown in direct support of XIII Corps.[87]

Meanwhile, the deteriorating Axis position in North Africa and the need to neutralize Malta to restore lines of communication caused the movement of Fliegerkorps II from the Eastern Front to Sicily to be accelerated. The first units arrived towards the end of November and operations began in mid-December. Initially, the Germans sent over relatively small bomber formation with large escorts of Bf 109Fs and Macchi 202s, with the port and airfields the main targets. The impact was immediate. From September to the opening of the German offensive, ten Hurricanes pilots had been lost in action; from 19–29 December, this number had been doubled and many more aircraft were destroyed on the ground.[88]

These were alarming losses for such a small force. Not only were fighter losses heavy, but the Hurricane was having problems just catching up with the Ju 88 bombers. Only two Bf 109Fs were claimed by the defenders. Lloyd, the commander of the RAF units on Malta, was soon demanding more modern fighters to help restore the situation.[89] It was not surprising that he got his Spitfires before the far more acquiescent Tedder. Axis convoys were soon taking advantage: at the beginning of January, a substantial Axis convoy arrived in Tripoli unscathed.

On 7 January, Rommel, now under very little pressure from the exhausted Commonwealth forces, began pulling back to the more easily defended El Agheila position. To make life even more difficult for the advancing Allies, the Axis convoy had brought with it priceless aviation fuel, and once again Axis aircraft were much more active. Fiat CR.42 fighter-bombers were now being encountered in some numbers, whereas direct air support for Allied air forces was virtually non-existent. Four Commonwealth bomber squadrons had been withdrawn to refit and others were supporting the assault on the Halfaya Pass, where German forces were still holding on. From 7–11 January, only around twenty bomber sorties were flown in support of the forces in western Cyrenaica, although fighter support was still fairly comprehensive with around 100 sorties a day.

The retreating Axis mobile forces had left behind them their immobile forces encircled at Bardia, Sollum and the Halfaya Pass. In an effort to keep infantry casualties to a minimum, maximum use was made of air and naval fire power. A Royal Navy cruiser and gunboat and the four Blenheim squadrons of No. 270 Wing and Wellingtons from the Delta supported the artillery. Embry took the credit for organizing the air assault on Bardia. Four days of intensive artillery, naval and air bombardment preceded the advance on land. From 27–30 December, 259 Blenheim sorties were flown. The assault went in on 31 December, with Blenheims continuing their attacks on the port as well as responding to requests for more direct support from the advancing Commonwealth troops. On 2 January 1942, the fortress surrendered.[90]

The army hailed the capture of the port a great success. A potentially awkward objective had fallen in three days with only light casualties. The Air Ministry in London was not so impressed. Portal was horrified that bomber effort should be wasted against targets that were now 250 miles behind the frontline. The use of the Blenheims at Bardia certainly appeared to contravene the principles laid down in the Cairo conference, which had made it clear that aircraft should not be used for close support when substantial ground-based artillery was available.[91] It is interesting that there was no equivalent understanding that naval firepower should not be used when army artillery was available. The naval support passed off without controversy or even comment. Supporting the Army was part of the Royal Navy tradition, but it was not part of the Air Staff's idea of RAF tradition. The barrage provided by the navy and air force was hugely effective, as much for the psychological lift it provided for the advancing infantry as the damage inflicted, but, as far as Portal was concerned, there was still no place for air support in a set-piece assault.

Tedder appeared to agree with Portal and disowned all responsibility for the Bardia operation, dismissing the air support as 'misdirected enthusiasm' which he had 'checked immediately'.[92] However, his subsequent use of the air force suggested that he did not disapprove so heartily, or at least he did not feel he could disappoint army expectation. Bombers were used in the same way in the assault on the Axis forces holding the Halfaya Pass, with 281 Blenheim sorties flown between 4–16 January.

Tedder defended the decision to employ bombers so far in the rear by claiming that supply difficulties at the westernmost points of advance made it difficult to operate large numbers of planes from frontline airstrips there. He also pointed out that communications between the front and rear were too poor to enable these aircraft to be used to support the forces further west, and there was a lack of appropriate targets. This last claim was unfortunate, as it was while the Bardia assault was taking place that the Guards and 22 Armoured Brigade were suffering so heavily, but the communication and supply problems were very real.

In fact, both the surrounded Axis forces in the east and the fleeing Axis forces further west were suitable targets, if sufficient aircraft had been available to strike both. Portal was right that it was further west where air support was most needed: a successful encirclement of Rommel's retreating forces would have transformed the overall situation in the Mediterranean. However, Tedder was right that the logistic problems made it impracticable. Knowing where air strikes can cause most damage was one thing, but it had to be possible to deliver the support. The Army had not even been able to make use of the limited resources that were available to it in the Agedabia battles.

Crusader was an important psychological turning point – for the first time Commonwealth forces had forced a German army to retreat. It had, however, been achieved at a heavy cost in tanks and planes. Both sides had lost around 300 tanks. The best British tanks had proven inferior to the best German tanks. In the air, too, Commonwealth fighters had been inferior. The tank crews could at least console themselves with the knowledge that they had been given the best that Britain had. This was not the case for the fighter pilots.

In the end, the army got the sort of fighter cover it wanted. Having been given the freedom to allow his fighter force to roam far and wide, Coningham had come to the conclusion his pilots were most likely to meet the enemy if they operated over the army. He was at pains to point out that this was not a return to the standing patrol or 'air umbrella' policy, and indeed there were not enough fighters to provide permanent cover. However, it seemed sometimes that the army's desire for an 'aerial umbrella' and the RAF preference for 'fighter sweeps' was merely semantics. Permanent cover was impossible, but there was nothing intrinsically correct about providing patchy air cover; it was just an unfortunate consequence of the shortage of fighters.

Coningham's attitude rather betrayed the air force tendency to see air warfare as an independent activity. Coningham rather ruthlessly saw the army struggling below as bait for his fighters:

'If the effect on our forces is one of protection, then all concerned, except perhaps the enemy, are happy but I do not want our own tactical thinkers to be led astray into considering the operation as any more than an ordinary O.P. [offensive patrol].'[93]

For Coningham it seems the protection his fighters were offering was a by-product rather than the aim of the process. The air force was still more interested in how many planes it shot down rather than how much protection it was providing. RAF commanders still seemed to want to fight their own private air war with the Luftwaffe.

It was rather reminiscent of the First World War, when 'offensive-defensive' and 'close-offensive' patrols had been inaugurated, which essentially fulfilled the Air Force need to be offensive while operating where the Army wanted it to operate and where enemy aircraft were most likely to be found – in the vicinity of the frontline.[94] Army and Air Force positions were not always as far apart as both parties would sometimes make out. Dogma seemed to drive the RAF to take extreme positions, but having apparently won the argument, it found itself drifting back to what the army had wanted all along. In years to come, as more fighters became available, the cover would become less patchy and there would be no shortage of 'aerial umbrellas'.

In such a complex battle, providing close air-support was always going to be difficult, and much went wrong. Only patchy close support had been possible, and there were far too many instances where air force units were unable to identify their targets. The fluid nature of the fighting had made it especially difficult to distinguish friend from foe. The lack of natural features in the desert made target identification especially difficult, and to complicate matters, both sides were using large quantities of captured motor transport. In the heat of battle, displaying recognition panels was often too much to expect of harassed troops in the firing line. There were also some unfortunate instances where friendly troops had been hit. By the end of the campaign, the bomber crews were reluctant to bomb anything closer than 50 miles to Allied forces for fear of attacking their own side. Much to the Army's dismay, it was decided to abandon any attempts to call in close support to hit targets just a few hundred yards in front of the frontline. It was, the Army hoped, only a temporary restriction.[95] One partial solution was to mark friendly vehicles, but with Axis air power still much in evidence, there was a reluctance to provide the enemy with such obvious guidance. From January, though, the Army did agree to mark its own vehicles, but only on condition that the RAF maintained air superiority.[96]

When support requested by ground forces was provided, there tended to be a two-and-a-half to three hour delay rather than the thirty minutes sometimes achieved in the less demanding atmosphere of exercises. The fact that the medium bombers had to operate from the larger airfields well behind the frontline and then pick up their fighter escorts on the way to the target added to the time required. During the closing stages of the offensive, some bombers being used for direct support were still operating from airfields that were by this time 200 miles from the fighting, not because the squadrons lacked mobility but simply because it was impossible to maintain more squadrons further forward. Larger twin-engined planes in particular made greater demands on the supply network. The Hurricane fighter-bombers of No. 80 Squadron, operating from airstrips much closer to the fighting, and providing their own escorts, had been able to provide much prompter support, rarely taking more than half an hour to arrive where they were required. Strafing had proved generally more effective than bombing. Something more powerful than 40lb bombs were needed to knock out tanks, but it was more evidence that the fighter-bomber was the way forward.[97] The huge distances the battle was fought over also emphasized the need for longer-range twin-engined reconnaissance planes. A handful of Mosquitoes would have been a priceless asset.

Close air-support was very much a work in progress. The air force had enjoyed most success against columns, spotted by RAF reconnaissance, heading deep into the Allied rear and not being directly engaged by ground forces. These strikes had played a vital part in the battle, but closer support was also needed to swing tight battles the Allied way. Tedder was frustrated at the Army's failure to make better use of the available bomber resources, but it was very much a problem that both Army and Air Force had to work on. Some of the ground lost by the Greek debacle had been recovered, but there was still not the degree of respect and understanding between the service leaders and they were not working together as closely as had happened in some of the earlier campaigns.

What was happening in the Middle East should have been helping to shape attitudes in London. Wavell's 1940 offensive had taken everyone by surprise. For Crusader, the political and military leaders were all keenly following the ebb and flow of battle. It was not so easy to divide the world up into theatres where conventional land battles were fought and those where the air weapon would decide the issue. The mighty Wehrmacht could be beaten, and there was no reason why this could not happen in north-west Europe.

The Commonwealth forces had achieved a degree of air superiority. There was a strong air presence throughout the battle and, when escorted, Allied bombers had been able to operate without interference. From 18 December to the end of January, only three escorted bombers were lost to enemy fighters.[98] But it was a fragile superiority, achieved with technically inferior planes. The superiority of the Bf 109 and Macchi C.202 meant the Allied fighter units had paid a high price for any dominance achieved. The need for higher quality as well as a higher number of fighters should have been clear, but Embry's enthusiasm for the Kittyhawk did nothing to speed up the delivery of the Spitfires that the Allied squadrons needed. With its manoeuvrability at low altitude and ability to carry a bomb, the Kittyhawk was an ideal replacement for the Hurricane in the low-level fighter-bomber role. However, the Allied air forces needed a quality medium/high-altitude fighter to challenge the Messerschmitts and protect the fighters operating below.

Crusader was not the complete success Wavell had achieved the year before; the Afrika Korps had been able to withdraw in reasonable order and was, as Rommel would demonstrate all too soon, far from beaten. However, for the first time the British had forced a German army to retreat. This was progress indeed, coming as it did little more than six months after the humiliating defeats in Greece and Crete. Nor was this the only Allied success. In the Soviet Union, far from being overwhelmed, the Red Army was also taking the offensive and pushing the German Army back from the gates of Moscow. While the strategic air offensive had stalled, the war on land appeared to be turning in favour of the Allies.

In the midst of these successes, on the other side of the world a Japanese fleet launched its fateful strike on Pearl Harbor. Simultaneously, Japanese troops began advancing against American, British and Dutch territories. Allied forces in the Far East faced dire times, but the United States was now in the war and its vast manpower resources would enable Allied armies in the west to match the strength of the Red Army in the east. Churchill warned the nation that this turn of events was not the end, nor even the beginning of the end. But was it the end of trying to win the war by bombing the German nation into submission and the beginning of an attempt to use air power to help win the war by defeating the German Army on the battlefield?

Conclusion

The second year of war had seen Britain suffer yet more defeats at the hands of the Wehrmacht. For a third time, the British Army had been ignominiously evicted from the continent of Europe. Once again, Allied troops cursed the lack of fighter cover and anything to match the fearsome Stuka. For two years the unwavering conviction that the long-range bomber was a war-winning weapon had ensured these failings had not got the attention they deserved. For the Air Staff, the bombing strategy had become an article of faith, and like all beliefs based on faith rather than evidence it was remarkably enduring. Air Staff certainty was not in the least shaken by the fact that in the first two years of war, Germany had defeated country after country, not by the merciless massacre of their civilians or the destruction of their industries, but by defeating their armies on the battlefield. In each victory, tactical air power had made a significant contribution. Yet the more the evidence mounted, the more passionate the defence of the bombing strategy became.

Pleas from the commanders of British and Allied armies for tactical air support were met with assurances that the methods the enemy were using so successfully were an incorrect use of air power. The Air Ministry was so focused on fighting the bomber war everyone had predicted that they could not see that the war raging around them was being decided by completely different methods. Air Staff thinking had become trapped in its own doctrinal straitjacket. They could not see any other way of defeating Germany apart from bombing.

The corollary of the Air Staff's faith in the bomber as a war-winning weapon was the fear that Britain could easily lose the war by an aerial knockout blow. During the Blitz, Britain had endured the worst the Luftwaffe could throw at the country without the government or people ever coming close to considering surrender. Yet there was still a belief that if the country dropped its guard, the Luftwaffe was capable of delivering a devastating blow. The emphasis on bomber production meant fighters were in short supply, but for those that were available, the priority had to be preventing a knockout blow. Defending cities, not armies, was the priority.

An invasion of the UK was an ever-present possibility, but even this battle the Air Staff believed the RAF could win on its own. Bombers would destroy an invasion fleet in port or as it crossed the Channel. Fighters would secure air superiority. However, there was no thought about how this could be exploited. Air superiority was seen as the aim, not the conditions which would make it easier for the Air Force to support the Army on the battlefield.

Building long-range heavy bombers was the Air Ministry's top priority, followed by developing bomber interceptors. The development of aircraft for tactical air support came a very poor third. Building specialist army support bombers was seen as a waste of resources. No thought was given to the sort of fighter that would be required to win a tactical air battle. Air forces, not armies, won wars and the primary role of the RAF was to bomb Germany and stop the Germans bombing Britain.

For the Air Staff, tactical air forces were more than just a misuse of airpower; they were a threat to their strategic aspirations and therefore a danger to Britain's chances of winning the war. Britain did not have the resources to build a large strategic bomber force and a tactical air force. Building one meant not having the other, so any plans to create the air force the British Army wanted had to be nipped in the bud. The failure to develop tactical air power was not an oversight or a misjudgement; it was a relentlessly pursued policy. The Air Staff hoped that by delaying its development it could buy enough time for the bombing offensive to work. The Air Staff was convinced that this was in the best interests of the country.

In reality it was placing the country in grave danger. Far from strengthening Britain's military position, the bomber policy had seriously weakened it. In the most favourable circumstances, the British Army would struggle to match the battle-hardened German Army. Trying to do it without air support might make a difficult task impossible. In 1940, Britain had won a breathing space, but the time was not used to develop the tactical air force the country needed. Instead, British air policy continued to plough down the wrong road. The next ignominious defeat suffered by the British Army might not be in Norway, France or distant Greece; it might be on home soil. Britain was only a Hitler whim away from discovering how ill-prepared the RAF was to help the Army deal with an invasion.

The sort of air force required to defeat an invasion was also what was required to support an advancing British Army. The failure to develop one meant no progress had been made towards creating the other. Without a powerful tactical air force, any attempt to land troops on the continent was a very daunting prospect. The War Office had always viewed an invasion of France as a near impossible undertaking. By not developing the air support the Army would need, the Air Ministry was justifying the generals' pessimism. It was a vicious circle that the War Office made only half-hearted attempts to break free from.

The only army support bombers the Air Ministry was willing to consider were planes that could also contribute to the strategic bomber offensive. The Air Ministry insisted that for tactical purposes, these were as good, if not better, than any specialist army support bombers. In reality, they were only suitable for indirect support beyond the battlefield. This conveniently meshed nicely with the independent ethos that permeated all Air Staff thinking. If the RAF had to support the Army, it would be by attacking enemy communications. This was something only the Air Force could do. It could do it on its own; it did not require any intimate co-operation with other services. Interdiction was as far as the Air Staff was willing to go with army support.

For the Air Staff, any closer co-operation smacked of subservience; it was feared that giving the RAF any role that was not in some way autonomous was tantamount to accepting an independent air force was not needed. If the Army had failed and was in retreat, then, as a desperate last resort, the air force might intervene on the battlefield to save the day, but again this gave the RAF a quasi-independent role. Close co-operation and co-ordination did not come naturally to a force that prided itself on its independence. Ironically, the more the Air Staff resisted close co-operation on the battlefield, the stronger the case became for an Army-controlled air arm.

As 1941 wore on, the Air Staff found its bombing strategy and its attitude to army support coming under increasing scrutiny. The Air Staff not only had to contend with the obvious evidence that tactical air support was working very well for the German Army, it also had to face the growing evidence that its bomber offensive was not working. Bomber Command was not achieving anything like the degree of destruction everyone had been assuming. In Britain's darkest hour, the bomber policy had given the country hope. Before the defeat of France, the Air Staff believed a powerful strategic air offensive was the best way of winning the war. After France was defeated, it seemed the only way Britain had of winning the war. The belief that the country had a route to victory did much to strengthen resolve in the summer of 1940, when a negotiated surrender might have seemed a tempting alternative.

However, as it became clear that Bomber Command was achieving far less than even the most pessimistic had imagined, it seemed time to rethink Britain's war strategy. Success in Africa had demonstrated that Allied armies were also capable of rapid advances. With the Soviet Union fighting alongside Britain, there was no longer any need to rely on the bomber. With Bomber Command achieving little and tactical air power helping to win battles in the Western Desert, it was very difficult to see a way forward for the bomber strategy. The dream of winning wars by the action of bombers alone looked like it would remain just a dream.

By good fortune, the tools needed for an effective close air-support capability already existed. A whole range of weapons that had been designed to shoot down bombers happened also to be suitable for attacking ground targets from the air. The Hurricane was of questionable value as a fighter, but it provided a fast and manoeuvrable way of carrying these weapons. In the war on the ground, new options were opening up. By the end of 1941, the Red Army had not just halted the German Army; in front of Moscow it was pushing the invader back. In the Western Desert, Rommel was also retreating. The United States was also now in the war. The Allies had the manpower and industrial resources to defeat Germany on the battlefield. Indeed, with the German Army struggling to hold on to its gains, outright victory might not be such a distant prospect.

Japanese advances in the Far East would ensure there were still many dark days ahead, but in Britain the fears of defeat were fast receding. Now it was a question of how to defeat Germany as quickly as possible. As 1942 dawned, British air strategy, and overall military strategy, was at a crossroads. The direction both should take and how air power could best contribute to victory hung in the balance.

Notes

Chapter 1

1 NA AIR2/2896, 26 July 1940
2 Baughen, G., *The RAF in the Battle of France and the Battle of Britain* (Fonthill: Stroud, 2016), p.161
3 Churchill, W.S., *Their Finest Hour* (Reprint Society: London, 1952), p.368
4 NA CAB66/11/50, 14 September 1940
5 Baughen, G., *The Rise of the Bomber* (Fonthill: Stroud, 2015), pp.194–95
6 Mason, F.K., *Battle Over Britain* (McWhirter Twins: London, 1969), pp.348, 411
7 NA CAB66/13/7, 27 October 1940
8 NA CAB66/13/7, 27 October 1940
9 Price, A., *The Spitfire Story* (Jane's: London, 1982), pp.117–18
10 NA AIR8/450, 28 January 1941
11 NA AIR62/2
12 NA AVIA15/3922, 8 August 1939
13 NA AVIA15/478, 21 May 1940
14 NA AIR8/450, 7 May 1941
15 NA AVIA10/233, 28 August 1940
16 NA AIR2/5170, 27 July 1940
17 Buttler, T., *British Secret Projects, Fighters and Bombers 1935–1950* (Midland: Hinckley, 2004), p.45
18 Baughen, G., *Blueprint for Victory* (Fonthill: Stroud, 2014), Chapter 7
19 Baughen, *Blueprint for Victory*, p.91
20 NA AVIA46/120
21 NA AVIA15/639, 16 September 1940; NA AVIA46/69, 2 October 1940
22 NA AIR6/33, 3 February 1938
23 NA AIR20/279, 25 April 1940
24 AIR8/421, 31 July 1940
25 NA AIR2/2622, 24 May 1940
26 NA AVIA10/233, 27 August 1940
27 NA AIR20/3461, 27 September 1940
28 NA AIR19/226, 27 August 1940; NA AIR16/688, 2 October 1940
29 NA AVIA46/69 2 October 1940; NA AVIA15/639, 29 December 1940

30 NA AIR16/688; Lloyd, I., and Pugh, P., *Hives and the Merlin* (Icon Books: Cambridge, 2004), p.116
31 NA AIR8/450, 30 January 1941
32 NA AIR8/450, 9 February 1941
33 NA AIR16/691, March 1941
34 Price, p.142
35 NA AIR16/688, 11 December 1940
36 NA AIR16/691, March 1941
37 NA AIR8/450, August 1941
38 NA AIR8/450, 25 January 1941
39 NA AIR16/326, February 1941
40 NA AIR8/450, 25 January 1941
41 NA AIR41/18, pp.79–80
42 NA AIR41/18, p.86
43 Hooton, E., *Eagle in Flames* (Arms and Armour Press: London, 1997), p.110
44 NA AIR41/18, p.90
45 Franks, N., *Fighter Command Losses* (Midland: Hersham, 2008), p.117
46 NA AIR8/450, 1 February 1941
47 NA AIR8/450, 1 February 1941
48 NA AIR8/450, 11 February 1941
49 NA AIR8/452, 27 April 1941
50 NA AVIA46/120, 10 May 1941
51 NA AIR8/410, 27 April 1941
52 NA AIR19/486, 10 November 1940
53 NA AIR19/486, 12 November 1940
54 NA AIR39/33, 20 February 1941
55 NA AVIA15/921, 5 December 1940
56 NA AVIA15/921, 15 March 1941
57 *Milwaukee Journal*, 12 February 1941
58 NA AVIA15/2613, 14 May 1941
59 Arnold, H., *Global Mission* (TAB: Blue Ridge Summit, 1989), p.233
60 NA AIR8/410, 11 April 1941
61 NA AIR8/410, 6 March 1941

Chapter 2

1 NA AIR8/412, 7 September 1940
2 Webster, C., and Frankland, N., *The Strategic Air Offensive Against Germany 1939–1945*, Vol. 1 (HMSO: London, 1961), pp.300–01
3 NA AIR8/982, June 1941
4 NA AIR14/2196, 14 November 1940
5 Slessor, *The Central Blue* (Cassell: London, 1956), pp.327–28
6 Churchill, *Their Finest Hour*, p.448
7 Webster, Frankland, Vol. 1, p.159, Vol. 4, pp.128–29

8   Webster, Frankland, Vol. 1, p.244
9   Churchill, *Their Finest Hour*, p.535; NA AIR41/40, p.121
10   Webster, Frankland, Vol. 1, p.156
11   NA AIR2/7310, December 1940–January 1941
12   Baughen, *The Rise of the Bomber*, p.208
13   NA AIR2/7922, 20 November 1941
14   NA AIR14/614, 3, 17 November 1940
15   Middlebrook, M., and Everitt, C., *The Bomber Command War Diaries* (Penguin: London, 1990), p.104
16   Webster, Frankland, Vol. 1, pp.398–99
17   Churchill, *Their Finest Hour*, pp.541–42
18   NA AIR14/614, 3 November 1940
19   NA AIR14/614, 3 November 1940
20   NA AIR2/7230; NA AIR20/3461, 27 September 1940
21   Bowyer, M., *Aircraft for the Many* (Patrick Stephens: Yeovil, 1995), p.81; NA AIR2/2899, February 1941
22   NA AVIA10/124, 30 October 1940
23   NA CAB65/11/14, 15 January 1940
24   Buttler, p.118
25   NA AIR20/3066, September 1940
26   Bowyer, M.J.F., *No. 2 Group RAF* (Faber and Faber: London, 1974), p.195
27   Bowyer, *No. 2 Group RAF*, Chapter 10
28   Webster, Frankland, Vol. 1, p.159
29   Furse, A., *Wilfred Freeman* (Spellmount: Staplehurst, 1999), pp.214–17; Arnold, p.222
30   Bowman, M., *USAF Handbook 1939–1945* (Sutton Publishing: Stroud, 1998), p.20

Chapter 3

1   Longmore, Sir A., *From Sea to Sky* (Geoffrey Bles: London, 1946), p.176
2   NA AIR41/27, p.5
3   Shores, C., *Fighters Over the Desert* (Neville Spearman: London, 1969), p.15
4   NA AIR41/44, p.52
5   NA AIR20/3461, 7 July 1940
6   NA AIR41/44, p.52
7   NA AIR41/44, p.49; NA CAB66/12/18, 26 September 1940
8   NA AIR20/3461, 13 September 1940
9   NA AIR8/544, 10 October 1940
10   NA AIR8/544, 28 October 1940
11   NA AIR8/316, 28 October 1940
12   NA AIR8/544, 24 October 1940
13   NA AIR41/44, p.67
14   NA CAB66/12/49, 14 October 1940
15   NA AIR8/507, 12 October 1940

16 Churchill, *The Fight at Odds*, p.249
17 NA AIR8/483, 8 March 1941
18 NA AIR8/316, 19 November 1940
19 NA AIR39/139, 20 December 1940
20 NA WO193/495, 1 January 1941
21 Air 41/27, pp.68–69
22 NA WO193/678, 1 January 1941
23 NA AIR8/982, August 1940
24 WO106/5152, 21 March 1940
25 NA AIR39/16, 16 May 1941; NA AVIA10/126, 24 August 1940
26 NA WO106/5151, 28, 30 July 1940
27 WO106/5151, 31 December 1939
28 WO106/5151, 14 July 1940
29 NA WO106/5151, 15 February 1940
30 NA AVIA15/227, January–March 1940, 11 June 1940
31 NA AVIA15/227, 15 June 1940
32 NA AVIA46/110, NA AIR20/3461, 7 July 1940
33 NA AIR20/3461, 3, 7 July 1940
34 NA AVIA46/110, NA AVIA15/227, July 1940
35 NA AVIA15/227, 12, 14 August 1940
36 NA WO106/5151, 21 March 1940
37 Baughen, *Blueprint for Victory*, p.183
38 NA AIR9/137, 2 August 1940
39 WO106/5151, 14 July 1940
40 NA AIR2/7280, 7 September 1940; NA AIR39/139, 6 September 1940
41 NA AIR2/7280, 27 August 1940
42 NA AIR39/16, 16 May 1941 summary
43 NA AIR25/518, July–December 1940
44 NA AIR39/139, 9 September 1940
45 WO106/5162, 18 November 1940
46 NA AIR2, 7280, 27, 28 November 1940
47 NA WO193/678, 10 October 1940
48 NA WO193/678, 10 October 1940
49 NA AIR39/139, 20 November 1940
50 NA AIR20/4301, 17 November 1940
51 NA AVIA46/125, section 1
52 NA AIR2/7280, 6, 14 December 1940
53 NA AIR2/7280, NA AVIA15/695
54 NA AVIA10/353, 10 February 1941
55 NA AVIA46/125, p.1; NA AVIA15/772, 27 May 1941
56 NA AIR8/452, November–December 1941
57 NA AIR19/498, 16 December 1940
58 NA AIR19/498, 14 December 1940
59 NA AIR19/498, 16 December 1940

60 NA AIR39/16, 16 May 1941 summary
61 NA AIR39/16, Enclosure 20A
62 NA WO233/60, p.145, 17 March 1941
63 NA WO233/60, p.113
64 NA AIR39/139, NA WO233/60, pp.12325
65 NA AIR39/139, NA WO233/60, p.125
66 Baughen, *Blueprint for Victory*, p.183
67 NA WO233/60, p.132
68 NA AIR39/142
69 NA AIR39/16, report May 1941
70 WO106/5162, 23 October 1940
71 WO106/5162, 23 October 1940

Chapter 4

1   Cruickshank, C., *Greece 19401941* (Davis-Poynter: London, 1976), pp.51–61
2   NA AIR8/316, 8 November 1940
3   NA AIR8/316, 12 November 1940
4   NA AIR41/44, pp.70, 72
5   NA AIR8/507, 2 November 1940
6   NA AIR8/544, 28 October 1940
7   *Hansard*, 28 November 1934
8   NA AIR8/544, 28 October 1940
9   NA AIR8/316, 1 November 1940
10 NA AIR8/316, 2 November 1940
11 AIR8/544, 28 October 1940
12 AIR8/544, 7 November 1940
13 NA AIR8/544, 6 November 1940
14 NA AIR8/544, 7 November 1940
15 NA AIR41/44, p.70
16 Cruickshank, pp.53–56
17 NA AIR8/316, 617 November 1940
18 Tedder, Lord, *With Prejudice* (Cassell: London, 1966), p.82
19 Shores, C., Cull, B., and Malizia, N., *Air War for Yugoslavia, Greece and Crete 1940–1941* (Grubb St: London, 1987), p.27
20 Shores, Cull, Malizia, *Air War for Yugoslavia, Greece and Crete*, pp.1121
21 NA AIR19/487, 24 November 1941
22 NA AIR8/544, November 1940
23 NA AIR8/544, 3 November 1940
24 NA AIR23/6375, 5 November 1940
25 NA AIR23/6375, 5 November 1940
26 NA WO193/678, 3 September 1941
27 NA AIR8/544, November 1940
28 Shores, Cull, Malizia, *Air War for Yugoslavia, Greece and Crete*, p.39

29 NA AIR8/544, 19 November 1940
30 NA CAB65/16/7, 19 November 1940
31 NA AIR23/6375, 7 November 1940; AIR2/7084, 15 August 1941
32 NA AIR41/28, p.16
33 NA AIR41/28, p.11
34 NA AIR41/28, p.15
35 NA AIR41/28, p.33
36 NA AIR23/1338, 1 January 1941
37 NA AIR19/487, 23 November 1940
38 NA AIR8/544, 4 December 1940
39 NA AIR19/487, 20 November 1940
40 NA AIR19/487, November 1940
41 NA AIR41/28, p.34
42 NA AIR19/487, 24 November 1940
43 NA AIR19/487, 27 November 1940
44 NA AIR19/487, 23 November 1940
45 NA AIR19/487, 23 November, 14 December 1940
46 NA AIR19/487, 12 December 1940
47 NA AIR19/487, 15 December 1940
48 NA AIR19/487, 17 December 1940
49 NA AIR19/487, 18 December 1940
50 NA AIR19/487, 22 December 1940
51 NA AIR19/487, 24 December 1940
52 NA AIR19/487, 25 December 1940
53 NA AIR41/32, p.31
54 NA AIR19/487, 15 February 1941
55 NA AIR19/487, 15 February 1941
56 NA AIR41/28, p.34
57 NA AIR19/487, February–March 1941
58 NA AIR19/487, 7–14 January 1940
59 NA AIR41/28, pp.21–22
60 NA AIR41/28, pp.109–11
61 NA AIR8/544, November 1940
62 NA AIR8/544, 17 November 1940
63 NA AIR8/544, November 1940
64 NA AIR8/507, 5 December 1940, 5 January 1941

Chapter 5

1 NA WO193/678, 1 January 1941
2 NA AIR8/507, 2 November 1941
3 NA AIR41/44, p.72
4 NA AIR41/44, p.72, Appendix XXII
5 NA AIR41/44, p.77

6 NA AIR8/507, 15 December 1940
7 NA AIR41/44, p.79; Santoro, G., *L'Aeronautica Italiana Nella Seconda Guerra Mondiale* Vol. 1 (Apollon: Rome, 1957) p.295
8 NA AIR23/1341, 31 January 1941. Shores, *Fighters Over the Desert*, p.24
9 NA AIR41/44, p.78; Santoro, Vol. 1, p.29
10 NA AIR23/1341, 31 January 1941
11 AIR41/44, pp.8082
12 NA AIR41/44, p.82
13 NA AIR8/507, 17 December 1940
14 NA AIR23/809, ACM Longmore dispatch
15 NA AIR22/211, 23 March 1941
16 NA AIR2/7210, 14 March 1941
17 NA AIR41/32, NA AIR8/483, 8 February, 8 March 1941
18 NA AIR2/7244, 16 January 1941
19 Churchill, *Their Finest Hour*, p.561
20 Churchill, *Grand Alliance* (1952), pp.23–24
21 NA AIR8/316, 6 January 1941
22 NA AIR8/507, 5 January 1941
23 NA AIR41/44, p.84
24 Churchill, *Grand Alliance*, p.42
25 Churchill, *Grand Alliance*, pp.42–43
26 Richards, D., *Portal of Hungerford* (Heinemann: London, 1977), p.231
27 NA AIR41/44, pp.87–88
28 NA AIR41/44, p.91
29 NA AIR41/27, pp.82–93, Appendix H
30 NA AIR41/27, pp.82–93, Appendix H
31 NA AIR41/27, pp.150–55
32 Shores, C., *Dust Clouds in the Middle East* (Grub St: London, 2016), pp.157, 16061

Chapter 6

1 NA AIR14/268, 5 December 1940
2 NA AIR14/268, 5 December 1940
3 NA AIR14/268, November 1940
4 NA AIR14/268, November 1940
5 NA AIR2/7210, 9 January 1941
6 NA AIR14/563, 16 December 1940
7 NA AIR14/268, November 1940
8 NA AIR14/268, November 1940
9 Alanbrooke, Lord, *Alanbrooke War Diaries 19391945* (Weidenfeld & Nicolson: London, 2001), p.138
10 NA AIR14/564, 15 January 1941
11 Baughen, *Blueprint for Victory*, pp.188–90

12 NA WO216/59, 19 February 1941
13 NA WO216/59, 19 February 1941; NA AIR8/982, 19 February 1941
14 NA WO233/60, p.143
15 Alanbrooke, p.139
16 NA WO216/59, 27 February 1941
17 NA AIR14/268, 29 March 1941
18 NA AIR39/16, 25 March 1941
19 NA AIR39/16, 25 March 1941
20 NA AIR14/268, 9 March 1941
21 NA AIR19/487, 21 February 1941
22 NA AIR19/487, 23, 25 February 1941
23 Shores, Cull, Malizia, *Air War for Yugoslavia, Greece and Crete*, p.48
24 NA AIR23/6375, 11 March 1941
25 NA AIR41/28, p.13
26 NA AIR2/7084, 15 August 1941
27 NA AIR41/28, pp.11–12
28 NA AIR41/28, pp.38–42
29 NA AIR2/7084, 15 August 1941
30 NA AIR2/7084, 15 August 1941
31 NA AIR2/7084, 15 August 1941
32 NA AIR41/28, pp.43–45, 112–13
33 NA CAB65/22/4, 6 March 1941
34 NA CAB65/22/5, 7 March 1941
35 NA CAB65/22/5, 7 March 1941
36 NA AIR41/28, Appendix J
37 NA AIR8/483, 11 March 1941
38 NA AIR19/48, 16 February 1941
39 NA AIR8/558, 23 February 1941
40 NA AIR8/558, March 1941
41 NA AIR8/483, 11 March 1941
42 NA AIR19/487, 4 March 1941
43 NA AIR8/519, 26 March 1941
44 NA AIR8/316, 22 February 1941
45 AIR8/519, 3 March 1941
46 NA AIR8/558, 12 March 1941
47 NA AIR8/519, 24 March 1941
48 NA AIR8/519, 19 March 1941
49 NA AIR2/7244
50 NA AIR8/316, 20 March 1941
51 NA AIR8/316, 21 March 1941
52 NA AIR8/316, 21 March 1941
53 NA AIR8/519, 24 March 1941
54 NA AIR8/558, 27 March 1941
55 NA AIR8/316, 17 February 1941

56   NA AIR8/316, 5 April 1941
57   NA AIR8/316, 6 January 1941

Chapter 7

1   Shores, C., Cull, B., and Malizia, N., *Malta: The Hurricane Years* (Grubb St: London, 1999), pp.xi, 6
2   Shores, Cull, Malizia, *Malta: The Hurricane Years*, p.399
3   Santoro, Vol. 1, p.43
4   Shores, Cull, Malizia, *Malta: The Hurricane Years*, p.122
5   Hooton, p.79
6   NA AIR8/504, 16 February 1941
7   NA AIR8/504, February 1941
8   NA AIR8/504, 8 March 1941
9   NA AIR41/28, p.55
10 NA AIR19/487, 26 March 1941; NA AIR8/504, 6 March 1941
11 NA AIR8/558, 25 March 1941
12 NA AIR8/558, 25 March 1941
13 NA AIR8/316, 26 March 1941
14 NA AIR19/487, 26 March 1941
15 NA AIR8/483, 25 March 1941
16 NA AIR8/483, 27 March 1941
17 NA AIR8/483, 27 March 1941
18 NA AIR8/558, 28 March 1941
19 NA AIR8/316, 4 April 1941
20 NA AIR41/28, Appendix J
21 NA AIR23/6486, 22 April 1941
22 NA AIR23/6486, 22 April 1941
23 NA AIR19/487
24 Shores, Cull, Malizia, *Air War for Yugoslavia, Greece and Crete*, p.230
25 Liddell Hart, B., *History of the Second World War*, Vol. 2/2 (Purnell: London, 1970), p.497
26 NA AIR41/28, p.114
27 NA AIR41/28, p.77
28 Tedder, p.82
29 Tedder, p.83
30 NA AIR41/29, p.8
31 NA AIR41/29, p.8
32 NA AIR41/29, p.83
33 NA AIR41/44, p.154
34 NA AIR19/482, 11 May 1941
35 NA AIR20/2791, 11 May 1941
36 Shores, *Fighters Over the Desert*, p.36
37 NA AIR41/44, p.155

38 NA AIR41/29, p.9
39 NA AIR23/139, 11 May 1941; NA AIR41/29, pp.1920
40 NA AIR41/29, pp.2122
41 Shores, *Fighters Over the Desert*, pp.39–40
42 NA WO201/99, p.39
43 NA AIR41/29, pp.46–47
44 NA AIR1/29, p.59
45 NA AIR41/29, pp.73–74
46 Churchill, *Grand Alliance*, p.236
47 NA WO201/99, p.42
48 AIR9/132 (undated late 1939); Baughen, *The RAF in the Battle of France and the Battle of Britain* (2016), p.35
49 NA AIR41/29, p.75; Tedder, pp.113–14
50 NA AIR41/28, p.75
51 NA AIR41/29, p.54
52 NA AIR41/29, p.75
53 NA AIR8/584, 16 June 1941
54 NA AIR23/1395, 31 May 1941
55 Parkin, R., *The Urgency Of War: The Development Of Close Air Support Doctrine In The Second World War*
56 NA AIR8/982, July 1941
57 NA AIR23/1395, 28 May 1941
58 NA AIR41/29, pp.70–71
59 Tedder, pp.15253
60 NA AIR23/1395, 20 June 1941
61 NA AIR20/2792, 15 May 1941
62 NA AIR39/16, 30 May 1941
63 NA WO233/60, p.119
64 Tedder, p.122
65 Churchill, *Grand Alliance*, p.605

Chapter 8

1 NA AIR39/16, 25 March 1941
2 NA AIR39/16, 19 February 1941
3 NA AIR39/22, 14 March 1941
4 NA AIR8/568, 14 April 1941
5 NA AIR8/715, 17 April 1941
6 NA AIR8/715, 26 April 1941
7 NA AIR8/410, 16 April 1941
8 NA AIR8/568, 14 April 1941
9 NA AIR8/715, July 1941
10 NA AIR8/715, 17, 19 April 1941; NA AIR2/7230, 29 April 1941; Baughen, *The RAF in the Battle of France and the Battle of Britain*, pp.161–62

11   Baughen, *The RAF in the Battle of France and the Battle of Britain*, p.57
12   NA AIR20/2791, 5 May 1941
13   NA AVIA10/231, 10 May 1941
14   NA AVIA10/232, 20 May 1941
15   NA AIR39/16, 9 May 1941
16   NA WO193/678, 3 May 1941
17   NA AIR39/16, 3 May 1941
18   NA WO193/678, 3 May 1941
19   NA AIR39/16, 19 May 1941
20   NA AIR20/2812, 16 May 1941
21   NA AIR20/2812, 4 June 1941
22   NA AIR39/16, 6 May 1941
23   NA AIR39/16, 6 May 1941
24   NA AIR39/16, 6 May 1941
25   Churchill, *Grand Alliance*, pp.336–38
26   Churchill, *Grand Alliance*, p.337
27   Baughen, *The RAF in the Battle of France and the Battle of Britain*, pp.1314; Alanbrooke, pp.140, 146
28   NA AIR39/16, 3 May 1941
29   Alanbrooke, p.157
30   NA AIR8/982, 13 May 1941
31   NA AIR8/631, 13 May 1941; NA AIR8/982, 13 May 1941
32   NA AIR8/982, 13 May 1941
33   NA WO193/678, 13 May 1941
34   NA AIR39/93, 31 May 1941
35   NA AIR2/7294 21 March 1941; NA AIR8/982, 13 May 1941; NA AIR39/93, 31 May 1941
36   NA AIR8/982, 16 May 1941
37   NA AIR39/16, 16 May 1941
38   NA AIR8/982, 16 May 1941
39   NA AIR39/16, 19 May 1941
40   NA AIR8/631, 14 May 1941
41   Binhgam, V., *Blitzed* (Air Research: New Malden, 1990), pp.201–12
42   NA WO233/60, p.153
43   NA AIR20/2812, 27 July 1941
44   Webster, Frankland, Vol. 4, pp.194–97; Boyle, A., *Trenchard* (Collins: London, 1962), p.724
45   Richards, p.224
46   Webster, Frankland, Vol. 4, p.200
47   NA AIR19/482, 11 May 1941
48   NA AIR19/482, 22 May 1941
49   NA AIR19/482, 22 May 1941
50   NA AIR39/17, 30 May 1941
51   NA AIR39/16, 30 May 1941

52 NA AIR8/986, 25 June 1941

53 NA AIR8/986, 25 June 1941

54 NA AIR8/452, 18 August 1941

55 NA AIR8/982, undated summer 1941

56 NA AIR8/986, 20 June 1941

57 NA AIR39/16, 30 May 1941

58 Hardy, M., *The North American Mustang* (David and Charles: London, 1979), pp.10–11

59 NA AIR39/93, 31 May 1941

60 NA CAB79/11/56, 31 May 1941

61 NA AIR8/982, June 1941

62 NA AIR8/982, June 1941

63 NA AVIA46/106

64 Bowyer, M.J.F., *Aircraft for the Many* (Patrick Stephens: Yeovil, 1995), p.112

65 NA AIR10/232, 29 May 1941

66 NA AVIA46/106

67 Brookes, A., *Photo-Reconnaissance* (Ian Allan: London, 1975), pp.103–05

68 Jones, R.V., *Most Secret War* (Coronet: London, 1981), p.227

Chapter 9

1 Tedder, p.115

2 NA AIR8/410, 22 April 1941

3 Churchill, *Grand Alliance*, p.594

4 Churchill, *Grand Alliance*, p.594

5 Tedder, p.123

6 Tedder, pp.122–23

7 NA AIR41/30, pp.1821

8 Lyman, R., *Iraq 1941* (Osprey: Wellingborough, 2006), p.22

9 NA AIR41/30, pp.12, 17

10 NA AIR41/30, pp.22–33, Appendix G

11 NA AIR41/30, pp.34–36, Appendix G

12 Lyman, *Iraq 1941*, p.41

13 NA AIR41/30, pp.54–56

14 NA AIR41/30, pp.56–57

15 NA AIR41/30, p.55

16 NA AIR41/30, pp.55–59

17 NA AIR41/30, pp.66–61

18 NA AIR41/31, p.23

19 NA AIR41/31, Appendix p.20

20 NA AIR41/31, p.44

21 Shores, *Dust Clouds in the Middle East*, Chapter 7

22 NA AIR41/31, Appendix H

23 NA AIR8/986, 24 September 1941

24 Tedder, p.118
25 Playfair, I., *The Mediterranean and Middle East* Vol. 2 (HMSO: London, 1956), p.166
26 NA AIR41/44, p.167
27 NA AIR8/582, 17 June 1941
28 Shores, *Fighters over the Desert*, pp.44–45
29 NA AIR8/582, 21 June 1941
30 NA AIR23/1395, 23 June 1941

Chapter 10

1 NA AIR8/877, 31 July 1941
2 NA AIR20/2958, 29 June 1940
3 NA AIR19/287, 25 July 1941
4 AIR8/591, 27 August 1941
5 NA AIR8/258, 27 August 1941
6 NA AIR20/3904, 27 August 1941
7 NA AIR19/287, 6 September 1941; Churchill, *Grand Alliance*, p.361
8 Churchill, *Grand Alliance*, p.363; NA AIR19/287, 4 September 1941
9 Churchill, *Grand Alliance*, p.367
10 NA AIR19/287, 16 September 1941
11 NA AIR19/302, 19 September 1941
12 NA AIR19/302, 18 October 1941
13 NA AIR19/302, 19 September 1941
14 NA AIR19/302, 19 September 1941
15 NA AIR19/287, 29 September 1941
16 NA AIR19/287, 30 September 1941
17 NA AIR19/287, 30 September 1941
18 Churchill, *Grand Alliance*, p.361
19 Hill, A., *The Great Patriotic War of the Soviet Union, 194145* (Routeledge: Oxon, 2009), p.174
20 NA AIR8/584, undated
21 Churchill, *Grand Alliance*, p.398
22 NA AIR2/7560, 2 September 1941
23 NA AIR2/7560, 1 September 1941
24 NA AIR8/410, 6 October 1941
25 NA AIR8/410, 7 October 1941
26 NA AIR41/18, p.31 para 10608
27 NA AIR41/18, pp.96–97
28 NA CAB65/11/14, 15 January 1940
29 Churchill, *Grand Alliance*, p.600; NA AIR20/2925, 3 June 1941
30 NA AIR20/2925, 3 June 1941
31 NA AIR2/3037, 6 June 1940; NA AIR16/327, 2 June 1940

32 NA AIR16/327, 13 July 1941
33 NA AIR16/327, 19 July 1941
34 NA AIR16/327, 11 July 1941; NA AIR16/3975, 13 August 1941
35 NA AIR16/3975, 2 August 1941
36 Webster, Frankland, Vol. 1, pp.240–41; Middlebrook, Everitt, pp.184–85
37 NA AIR16/327, 2 January 1942
38 NA AIR2/3037, 21 June 1941
39 NA AIR20/2792, 1 May 1941
40 NA AIR15/556, 27 May 1941
41 Bowyer, *No. 2 Group RAF*, pp.195–206
42 NA AIR8/452, November 1940; NA AIR20/2884, 4 December 1940
43 NA AIR8/452, NA AIR14/251, 13 February 1941
44 NA AIR20/284, 30 December 1940–April 1941
45 NA AIR41/18, pp.103–04
46 NA AIR41/18, pp.104–06
47 NA AIR8/452, 18 August 1941
48 NA AIR8/452, 30 June 1941
49 NA AIR8/452, 18 August 1941
50 NA AIR8/452, 18 August 1941
51 NA AVIA10/231, 20 May 1941
52 NA AVIA15/1252, 24, 31 January 1941
53 NA AIR8/452, 13 July 1941
54 NA AVIA10/232, 25 August 1941
55 NA AVIA10/232, 30 September 1941
56 NA AVIA10/216, 10 October 1941
57 NA AIR8/452, 18 August 1941
58 NA AVIA10/312, 24 June 1941
59 Price, pp.128, 142
60 NA AVIA10/312, 6 November 1941
61 NA AVIA10/232, 7 July 1941

Chapter 11

1 NA AIR14/614, 24 June 1941
2 NA AIR14/614, June 1941
3 NA AIR14/614, June–July 1941
4 NA AIR41/13, chapter 7; NA AIR20/1454, 4 November 1941, 9 December 1941
5 NA AIR2/3126, 28 November 1940
6 NA AIR2/3126, 14 December 1940
7 NA AIR2/3126, 11 January, 21 May 1941
8 NA AIR2/3126, 13 May 1941
9 Buttler, p.115
10 NA AIR2/3126, undated after September 1941

11 NA AIR14/1113, 11 April 1941
12 Webster, Frankland, Vol. 1, pp.181–82
13 Webster, Frankland, Vol. 4, Appendix 13
14 NA AVIA7/3558, 18 June 1941
15 Webster, Frankland, Vol. 1, p.173
16 NA AIR14/614, 17 August, 6 September 1941
17 Baughen, *The Rise of the Bomber*, pp.55–56, 92
18 NA AVIA7/1518, 22 July 1941
19 NA AVIA7/1518, 22 July 1941
20 NA AVIA7/1518, 6 August, 14 October 1941
21 Air 8/591, August 1941
22 Air 8/591, August 1941
23 Arnold, p.253
24 Air 8/591, 11 August 1941; Furse, pp.220–22
25 NA AIR8/585, July 1941
26 NA AIR8/585, July 1941
27 NA AIR8/585, 19 August 1941
28 NA AIR8/585, 27 August 1941
29 NA AIR8/258, 27 August 1941
30 Churchill, *The Hinge of Fate* (1952), p.236
31 Churchill, *Grand Alliance*, pp.398–99
32 NA AIR46/70, 11 September 1941
33 NA AVIA10/232, 8 September 1941
34 NA CAB79/14/14, 8 September 1941
35 NA AIR8/258, 27 September 1941
36 NA AIR8/258, 2 October 1941
37 NA AIR8/258, 2 October 1941
38 Webster, Frankland, Vol. 1, pp.184–85
39 NA AIR8/877, 9 September 1941
40 NA AIR39/16, 22 October 1941
41 AIR8/986, 24 September 1941
42 NA CAB84/36, 11 November 1941
43 Alanbrooke, p.189; NA CAB79/14/14, 8 September 1941
44 Churchill, *Grand Alliance*, p.424; Leasor, J., *War at the Top* (Michael Joseph: London, 1959), p.126
45 NA WO233/60, p.155
46 NA AIR9/159, 24 December 1941
47 NA AIR16/754, 15 January 1942; NA AIR39/31, 1718 January 1942
48 NA AIR2/7922, 20 November 1941
49 NA AIR19/482, 16 July 1941
50 NA AIR2/3126, 4 October 1941
51 NA AIR14/614, 27 October 1941
52 NA AIR2/3126, 5 November 1941
53 Middlebrook, pp.21718; Webster, Frankland, Vol. 1, pp.185–86

Chapter 12

1   NA AIR39/93, 27 May 1941
2   NA AIR39/22, 6 April 1941
3   NA AIR39/22, 6 April 1941
4   NA AIR39/131, 12 August 1941
5   NA AIR39/131, 12 August 1941; NA AIR39/22, 3 September 1941
6   NA AIR39/22, 3 October 1941
7   NA AIR39/22, 15 October 1941
8   NA AIR39/22, September 1941
9   NA AIR8/452, 16 January, 4 March 1941
10 NA AVIA46/110
11 NA AVIA46/110, NA AVIA46/125, section V
12 NA AIR2/7568, 29 September 1941
13 NA AIR2/7568, 3 October 1941
14 NA AVIA15/1583, June 1942
15 NA AIR41/18, pp.116–17
16 NA AIR16/776, 3 January 1942
17 NA AVIA10/232, 20 October 1941
18 NA AIR8/715, October 1941
19 NA AVIA15/695, 27 September 1940
20 NA AIR2/7494, April–May 1941
21 NA AIR2/7294, 2 May 1941
22 NA AIR41/18, p.110
23 NA AIR16/517, 22, 26 July 1941
24 NA AVIA65/1868, 14 August 1940
25 NA AIR2/5146, 3 September 1941
26 NA AIR16/517, 29 October 1941
27 NA AIR2/7560, 1 October 1941
28 NA AVIA10/232, 20 October 1941
29 NA AVIA10/232, 20 October 1941
30 WO32/10403, November 1941
31 WO32/10403, 16 October 1941
32 WO32/10403, August 1941
33 NA AIR39/129, 2 December 1941
34 NA AIR41/49, p.8
35 Orange, V., *Coningham* (Methuen: London, 1990), pp.28–32
36 NA AIR20/2791, 5 May 1941
37 NA AIR23/1395, 20 June 1941
38 NA AIR8/558, September–October 1941
39 NA AIR20/2791, 29 September 1941
40 NA AIR8/558, 7 October 1941
41 NA AIR8/558, October 1941
42 NA AIR20/279, 23 October 1941

43 NA AIR8/558, 7 October 1941
44 NA AIR23/1395, 14 October 1941
45 NA AIR23/1395, 19 October 1941
46 NA AIR23/1395, 14 October 1941
47 NA AIR23/1395, 28 May 1941
48 NA AIR23/1395, 14, 15 October 1941
49 Orange, *Coningham*, p.83
50 Richards, pp.235–36
51 Tedder, p.184
52 NA AIR2/7560, 2 September 1941
53 NA AIR8/410, 7 October 1941
54 NA AIR8/410, October 1941
55 NA AIR8/558, 22 October 1941
56 NA WO32/10403, September 1941; NA AIR41/25, pp.57–61
57 NA WO32/10403, September 1941
58 NA WO32/10403, September 1941
59 NA WO32/10403, September 1941; NA AIR8/412, 5 August 1941
60 NA WO32/10403, September 1941; NA AIR41/25, pp.57–61
61 Shores, Cull, Malizia, *Malta: The Hurricane Years*, p.318
62 NA AIR8/412, 5 August 1941
63 AIR14/1929, 31 August 1941; Churchill, *Grand Alliance*, p.635
64 Santoro, Vol. 2, p.43
65 Shores, Cull, Malizia, *Malta: The Hurricane Years*, pp.319–23
66 Santoro, Vol. 2, p.110
67 Embry, B., *Mission Accomplished* (Methuen: London, 1957), p.217
68 Embry, p.217; Shores, *Fighters Over the Desert*, p.219
69 NA AIR41/25, pp.131–32
70 NA AIR41/25, pp.135–36
71 AI 41/25, p.136
72 NA AIR41/25, pp.137–38
73 NA AIR41/25, p.138
74 Shores, *Fighters Over the Desert*, pp.65–66
75 NA AIR41/25, p.149
76 NA AIR41/25, p.214
77 NA AIR41/25, pp.154–55
78 NA AIR41/25, pp.165–66
79 NA AIR41/25, pp.162, 164–65
80 NA AIR41/25, p.172
81 NA AIR41/25, pp.183–84
82 Tedder, p.205
83 NA AIR20/2791, 14 December 1941
84 NA AIR8/558, 18 December 1941
85 NA AIR8/558, 31 January 1942
86 NA AIR41/25, pp.199–209

87   NA AIR41/25, pp.248–49
88   Shores, Cull, Malizia, *Malta: The Hurricane Years*, pp.349–60
89   NA AIR41/49
90   NA AIR41/25, pp.255–58
91   NA AIR41/25, p.258
92   NA AIR41/25, p.258
93   Tedder, pp.206–07
94   Baughen, *Blueprint for Victory*, pp.99,170
95   NA AIR23/910, p.20
96   NA AIR41/25, pp.295–96
97   NA AIR41/25, pp.211–14, 292–97, Appendix G(I) p.4
98   NA AIR51/25, p.293

Appendices

LIST OF APPENDICES

Appendix I

UK production and imports 1940

	Jan	Feb	Mar	April	May	June	July	Aug	Sept	Oct	Nov	Dec
Beaufighter	-	-	-	1	-	2	5	23	15	21	25	19
Beaufort	23	25	30	35	50	62	33	36	21	14	15	15
Blenheim	86	65	75	91	124	167	173	177	112	154	163	134
Buffalo	-	-	-	-	-	-	19	-	1	11	-	-
Defiant	5	5	12	19	22	30	56	38	41	48	53	37
Halifax	-	-	-	-	-	-	-	-	-	1	2	3
Hampden	36	31	35	44	63	81	56	41	40	38	40	37
Hurricane	108	83	123	178	233	313	288	275	253	251	236	244
Lysander	26	43	35	29	46	56	78	66	58	51	77	54
Manchester	-	-	-	-	-	-	-	-	2	3	11	6
Mohawk	-	-	-	-	-	-	5	49	10	48	29	43
Spitfire	37	51	40	60	77	103	160	163	156	149	139	117
Stirling	-	-	-	-	1	1	4	1	1	-	1	4
Tomahawk	-	-	-	-	-		-	-	1	-	26	43
Wellington	38	17	35	56	80	108	141	134	84	97	102	105
Whirlwind	-	-	-	-	-	2	3	1	3	1	8	5
Whitley	22	18	21	30	40	50	45	39	39	32	27	24
Total	381	338	406	543	736	975	1,066	1,043	837	919	954	890

Appendix II

UK production and imports 1941

	Jan	Feb	Mar	April	May	June	July	Aug	Sept	Oct	Nov	Dec
Airacobra	-	-	-	-	-	-	2	6	14	8	45	23
Albemarle	-	-	-	-	-	-	-	-	1	-	1	1
Beaufighter	10	32	37	42	58	61	90	93	91	88	97	101
Beaufort	12	13	17	13	20	12	9	1	9	8	23	23
Blenheim	117	196	163	163	147	136	130	99	83	66	44	37
Boston	-	-	-	-	-	30	24	52	53	4	34	92
Defiant	36	72	60	54	49	28	27	19	33	19	38	17
Fortress	-	-	-	-	8	2	5	2	-	2	-	-
Halifax	4	6	9	8	11	14	9	12	20	18	26	25
Hampden airframe	-	-	-	8	3	4	4	8	10	10	6	2
Hampden UK	40	45	50	50	45	40	40	30	30	30	30	24
Havoc								1	-	21	13	17
Hurricane	139	269	303	273	247	250	271	271	333	292	248	271
Hurricane (Canada)	3	26	20	37	35	16	-	-	-	2	32	31
Kittyhawk	-	-	-	-	-	-	-	-	-	-	2	1
Lancaster	-	-	-	-	-	-	-	-	-	2	3	13
Liberator	-	-	-	-	-	-	-	4	4	2	6	8
Manchester	10	9	16	15	17	14	16	25	18	17	7	1
Maryland	21	17	2	-	-	-	-	-	-	-	-	-
Mohawk	7	5	6	1	1	-	-	-	-	5	2	1
Mosquito bomber	-	-	-	-	-	-	-	-	2	4	4	2
Mosquito fighter	-	-	-	-	-	-	3	2	2	-	-	2
Mustang	-	-	-	-	-	-	-	-	-	-	2	6
Spitfire	125	153	199	154	212	205	171	250	276	261	267	245

	Jan	Feb	Mar	April	May	June	July	Aug	Sept	Oct	Nov	Dec
Stirling	3	6	12	4	10	11	13	13	22	20	23	16
Tomahawk	40	41	30	63	21	29	41	91	9	36	2	1
Typhoon	-	-	-	-	-	1	-	2	6	12	-	7
Wellington UK	89	133	139	130	149	145	147	157	172	191	191	173
Whirlwind	3	9	10	11	14	11	10	8	6	4	3	1
Whitley	21	42	42	32	38	46	45	50	50	54	36	48
Total	640	1,033	1,085	995	1,064	1,026	1,016	1,196	1,244	1,176	1,185	1,189

Appendix III

Aircraft arriving in Middle East by all routes 1941

	Jan	Feb	Mar	April	May	June	July	Aug	Sept	Oct	Nov	Dec
Baltimore											4	9
Beaufighter					16	5		4	3	8	1	32
Beaufort								7	2	3	4	1
Blenheim	12	38	35	37	39	55	115	66	38	36	16	60
Boston										7	23	32
Fortress										3	1	-
Gladiator						5	3	2				
Hurricane	44	30	13	96	85	206	82	34	186	81	60	93
Kittyhawk											62	135
Lysander			6	6		17						
Maryland	1	2	6	7	6	22	46	14	3	2	2	3
Tomahawk			2	25	41	71	29	87	23	16		
Wellington	2	2	16	27	15	11	31	14	13	15	17	19
Total	59	72	78	198	202	392	306	228	268	171	190	384

Appendix IV

Aircraft Performance

(Unless otherwise stated, mg refers to 0.303 calibre machine guns.)

Fighters	First flight	Engine	Speed (mph)/ altitude (ft)	Range (miles)	Climb (ft/ min-sec)	Ceiling (ft)	Empty Weight (lb)	Loaded Weight (lb)	Wing area (sq ft)	Armament
Bell Airacobra	06/04/1938	1,150hp Allison V-1710	358/15,000	1,100	10,000/ 3-54	35,000	5,360	7,380	213	6 mg, 1 x 20mm cannon
Boulton Paul Defiant	11/08/1937	1,030hp Merlin III	315/16,500	465	15,000/ 10-6	30,350	5,868	7,510	250	4 mg
Brewster Buffalo	12/1937	1,200hp Wright Cyclone 9	313/13,500	650		30,500	4,479	6,840	209	4 x 0.5 mg
Bristol Beaufighter	17/07/1939	2 x 1,590hp Hercules	323/15,000	1,500	20,000/ 14-6	28,900	14,069	20,800	503	6 mg, 4 x 20mm cannon
Bristol Blenheim IF	1938	2 x 840hp Mercury XV	260/12,000	1,460	15,000/ 15-0	24,600	9,200	13,800	469	6 mg
Curtiss Kittyhawk I	22/05/1942	1,150hp Allison V-1710-39	354/15,000	700	15,000/ 6-22	29,000	6,350	8,100	236	700lb bombs 4 or 6 x 0.5 mg
Curtiss Mohawk IV	1937	1,200hp Wright Cyclone 9	323/15,000	603	15,000/ 4-54	32,700	4,541	5,750	236	300lb 6 mg
Curtiss Tomahawk II	10/1938	1,150hp Allison V-1710-33	345/15,000	730	15,000/ 5-06	29,500	5,812	8,058	236	4 mg 2 x 0.5 mg

	First flight	Engine	Speed (mph)/ altitude (ft)	Range (miles)	Climb (ft/ min-sec)	Ceiling (ft)	Empty Weight (lb)	Loaded Weight (lb)	Wing area (sq ft)	Armament
Dewoitine D.520	02/10/1938	910hp Hispano-Suiza 12Y45	329/19,685	777	13,120/ 4-0	36,090	4,608	6,129	172	4 mg, 1 x 20mm cannon
Focke-Wulf 190A-2	01/06/1939	1,360hp BMW 801	389/18,000	500	16,400/ 4-50	37,400	5,530	7,716	197	2 mg, 2 x 20mm cannon
Gloster Gauntlet	01/1930	775hp Mercury VIS	223/15,000	425	10,000/ 4-12	33,200	2,823	3,937	315	2 mg
Gloster Gladiator II	09/1934	840hp Mercury IX	253/14,000	410	15,000/ 5-48	32,300	3,554	5,020	323	4 mg
Grumman Martlet II	02/09/1937	1,200hp Wright Cyclone 9	315	1,100		28,000	4,649	5,876	260	6 x 0.5 mg
Hawker Hurricane I	06/11/1935	1,030hp Merlin III	315/16,500	425	20,000/ 8-21	34,500	4,743	5,672	258	8 mg
Hawker Hurricane II	01/06/1940	1,460hp Merlin XX	342/22,000	460	20,000/ 8-24	36,500	5,500	7,000	258	12 mg or 4 x 20mm cannon
Hawker Tornado	06/10/1939	1,980hp Vulture V	398/23,000		10,000/ 4-45	34,900	8,377	10,688	283	12 mg or 4 x 20mm cannon
Hawker Typhoon	24/02/1940	2,180hp Sabre	405/18,000	610	15,000/ 6-12	34,000	8,800	11,400		12 mg or 4 x 20mm cannon
Macchi MC.202	10/09/1940	1,175hp Alfa Romeo R.A.1000	370/16,400	475	19,685/ 5-55	37,730	5,181	6,459	181	2 mg, 2 x 12.7mm mg
Messerschmitt Bf 109E	Summer 1938	1,100hp DB 601A	354/12,300	412	16,500/ 6-12	36,000	4,421	5,523	174	2 mg, 2 x 20mm cannon
Messerschmitt Bf 109F		1,300hp DB 601E	390/22,000	440	19,865/ 5-42	37,000	4,330	6,054	174	2 mg, 1 x 15mm cannon
Messerschmitt Bf 110C	12/05/1936	2 x 1,100hp DB 601A	349/22,965	565	18,000/ 8-30	32,000	11,466	14,884	413	5 mg, 2 x 20mm cannon

	First flight	Engine	Speed (mph)/altitude (ft)	Range (miles)	Climb (ft/min-sec)	Ceiling (ft)	Empty Weight (lb)	Loaded Weight (lb)	Wing area (sq ft)	Armament
Spitfire II	Summer 1939	1,175hp Merlin XII	357/17,000	500	15,000/5-00	37,200	4,900	5,900	242	8 mg
Spitfire III	04/1940	1,460hp Merlin XX	401/25,000		20,000/7-48			6,530		
Spitfire V	20/02/1941	1,470hp Merlin 45	371/20,000	470	15,000/4-36	37,000	5,033	6,525	242	4 mg, 2 x 20mm cannon
Supermarine Spitfire I	05/03/1936	1,030hp Merlin II	360/20,000	575	15,000/6-30	31,900	4,482	5,819	242	8 mg
Westland Whirlwind	11/10/1938	2 x 885hp Peregrine	360/15,000		15,000/5-48	30,000	7,840	10,270	250	4 x 20mm cannon

Bombers

	Prototype first flight	Engine	Speed (mph)/altitude (ft)	Range (miles)	Ceiling (ft)	Empty Weight (lb)	Loaded Weight (lb)	Wing area (sq ft)	Bomb load (lb) / Armament
Armstrong Whitworth Albemarle	20/03/1940	2 x 1,590hp Hercules XI	265/10,500	1,300	18,000		22,600	804	4,000 / 4 mg
Armstrong-Whitworth Whitley I	16/03/1936	2 x 795hp Tiger IX	192/7,000	1,250	19,200	14,275	21,600	1,138	3,365 / 2 mg
Avro Lancaster I	09/01/1941	4 x 1,460hp Merlin 22	281/11,000	2,250	20,000	36,900	68,000	1,297	14,000 / 8 mg
Avro Manchester	25/07/1939	2 x 1,760hp Vulture	265/17,000	1,630	19,200	29,432	50,000	1,130	10,350 / 8 mg
Bristol Blenheim I	25/06/1936	2 x 840hp Mercury VIII	279/15,000	1,000	31,400	8,483	11,776	469	1,000 / 3 mg
Bristol Blenheim IV	24/9/1937	2 x 920hp Mercury XV	266	1,460	22,000	8,700	13,400	469	1,000 / 4 mg
Bristol Blenheim V	24/02/1941	2 x 950hp Mercury XX	245/5,900		26,000	10,775	12,500	469	1,000 / 5 mg

	Prototype first flight	Engine	Speed (mph)/altitude (ft)	Range (miles)	Ceiling (ft)	Empty Weight (lb)	Loaded Weight (lb)	Wing area (sq ft)	Bomb load (lb) Armament
Bristol Bombay	23/06/1935	2 x 1,010hp Pegasus XXII	192/6,500	2,230	25,000	13,800	20,000	1,340	2,000 2 mg
de Havilland Mosquito	25/11/1940	2 x 1,250hp Merlin 21	380/17,000	1,795	33,000	13,400	21,462	454	2,000
Dornier Do 17 Z-2	1934	2 x 940hp BMW 323	255/13,120	720	22,965	11,484	18,931	592	2,205 6 mg
Douglas Boston III	26/10/1938	2 x 1,600hp Wright Twin Cyclone	304/13,000	1,020	24,250	12,200	25,000	465	2,000 8 mg
Flying Fortress	28/07/1935	4 x 1,200hp Wright Cyclone 9	320/20,000	2,100	33,300	30,670	45,470	1,420	2,500 1 mg, 6 x 0.5 mg
Handley Page Halifax I	25/10/1939	4 x 1,280hp Merlin X	265/17,500	2,400	18,000	34,500	59,000	1,250	13,000 6 mg
Handley Page Hampden	21/06/1936	2 x 950hp Pegasus XVIII	254/10,000	1,460	24,300	11,761	18,750	718	2,100 3 mg
Junkers Ju 88 A-1	21/12/1936	2 x 1,210hp Jumo 211B/1	280/18,050	1,055	26,250	16,975	22,840	565	3,960 3 mg (2 fixed)
Martin 167 (Maryland)	14/03/1939	2 x 1,050hp Pratt & Whitney R-1830	294/13,000	1,870	27,200	11,000	17,890	452	1,800 6 mg (four fixed)
Martin B-26 Marauder	25/11/1939	2 x 2,000hp Pratt & Whitney R-2800	305/15,000	1,200	28,000	17,000	37,000	664	4,000 8 x 0.5 mg
Savoia Marchetti SM.79	08/10/1934	3 x 860hp Alfa 128 R.C.18	286/12,430	1,615	24,600	16,975	25,132	664	2,645 2 mg, 2 x 12.7mm mg, 1 cannon
Short Stirling I	14/05/1939	4 x 1,590hp Hercules XI	260	2,330	16,500	44,000	59,400	1,460	14,000 8 mg
Vickers Wellington III	15/06/1936	2 x 1,500hp Hercules XI	255/12,500	2,200	18,500	19,000	29,500	840	4,500 8 mg

Army co-operation/Ground attack	Prototype First flight	Engine	Speed (mph)/ altitude (ft)	Range (miles)/ Endurance (hrs)	Ceiling (ft)	Empty Weight (lb)	Loaded Weight (lb)	Wing Area (sq ft)	Bomb Load (lb) Armament
Fairey Battle I	10/03/1936	1,030hp Merlin III	241/13,000	1,050 mi	23,500	6,647	10,792	422	1,000 2 mg
Hawker Audax	1931	580hp Kestrel IB	169/5,000	3.5 hrs	21,500	2,938	4,386	347	160 2 mg
Hawker Hart	06/1928	580hp Kestrel IB	166/5,000	500 mi	20,600	2,780	4,592	347	500 2 mg
Junkers Ju 87 B-2	Spring 1935	1,200hp Jumo D	237/13,120	370 mi	25,071	9,321	26,248	343	1,102 3 mg
Hawker Hartebeest	06/1928	600hp Rolls Royce Kestrel	176/6,000	3 hrs	22,000	3,150	4,787	348	Light bombs 2 mg
Taylorcraft D Plus	1939	55hp Lycoming	110	275 mi	15,000	700	1,200	155	None
Brewster Bermuda	17/06/1941	1,650hp Wright Twin Cyclone CR-2600	274	1,650 mi	23,000	9,920	12,240	379	1,000 6 mg
Vultee Vengeance	30/03/1941	1,650hp Wright Twin Cyclone CR-2600	275	1,500 mi	22,500	9,725	14,300	332	1,000 6 mg
Westland Lysander	16/06/1936	890hp Mercury XII	229/10,000	600 mi	26,000	4,065	5,920	260	500 3 mg
Fairey Swordfish	17/04/1934	690hp Pegasus IIIM	139/4,750	546 mi	10,700	5,200	9,250	607	1,500 2 mg
Fairey Albacore	12/12/1938	1,065hp Taurus II	161/4,000	930 mi	20,700	7,200	10.600	623	2,000 3 mg

Bibliography

Adesr, G., *History of the German Night Fighter Force 1917-945* (Janes: London, 1979)

Air of Authority, www.rafweb.org

Alanbrooke, Lord, *Alanbrooke War Diaries 1939–1945* (Weidenfeld & Nicolson: London, 2001)

Arnold, H., *Global Mission* (TAB:, Blue Ridge Summit, 1989)

Baughen, G., *Blueprint for Victory* (Fonthill: Stroud, 2014)

Baughen, G., *The Rise of the Bomber* (Fonthill: Stroud, 2015)

Baughen, G., *The RAF in the Battle of France and the Battle of Britain* (Fonthill: Stroud, 2016)

Binhgam, V., *Blitzed* (Air Research: New Malden, 1990)

Bowman, M., *USAF Handbook 19391945* (Sutton Publishing: Stroud, 1998)

Bowyer, M.J.F., *Aircraft for the Few* (Patrick Stephens: Yeovil, 1991)

Bowyer, M.J.F., *Aircraft for the Many* (Patrick Stephens, Yeovil, 1995)

Bowyer, M.J.F., *No. 2 Group RAF* (Faber and Faber: London, 1974)

Boyle, A, *Trenchard* (Collins: London, 1962)

Brookes, A., *Photo-Reconnaissance* (Ian Allan: London, 1975)

Buttler, T., *British Secret Projects, Fighters and Bombers 1935–1950* (Midland: Hinckley, 2004)

Churchill, W.S., *Grand Alliance* (Reprint Society: London, 1952)

Churchill, W.S., *Their Finest Hour* (Reprint Society: London, 1952)

Clarke, R., *British Aircraft Armament Vol. 2* (Patrick Stephens: Sparkford, 1994)

Cruickshank, C., *Greece 1940–1941* (Davis-Poynter: London, 1976)

Divine, D., *The Broken Wing* (Hutchinson: London, 1966)

Douglas, W., and Wright, R., *Sholto Douglas* (Collins: London, 1966)

Embry, B., *Mission Accomplished* (Methuen: London, 1957)

Farrar-Hockley, A., *The Army in the Air* (Alan Sutton Publishing: Stroud, 1994)

Franks, N., *Fighter Command Losses* (Midland: Hersham, 2008)

Furse, A., *Wilfred Freeman* (Spellmount: Staplehurst, 1999)

Goulding, J., *Interceptor* (Ian Allan: Shepperton, 1986)

Green, W., *Warplanes of the Second World War Fighters Vol. 4* (MacDonald: London, 1966)

Gunston, B., *Rolls-Royce Aero Engines* (PSL: Frome, 1989)

Hardy, M., *The North American Mustang* (David and Charles: London, 1979)

Hastings, M., *Bomber Command* (Pan Books: London, 1981)

Hill, A., *The Great Patriotic War of the Soviet Union, 1941–45* (Routeledge: Oxon, 2009)

Hooton, E.R., *Eagle in Flames* (Arms and Armour Press: London, 1997)

Hooton, E.R., *Phoenix Triumphant* (Arms and Armour Press: London, 1994)

Irving, D., *The Rise and Fall of the Luftwaffe* (Futura: London, 1976)

Jackson, B., and Bramall, D., *The Chiefs* (Brassey's: London, 1992)

Johnson, J. E., *Full Circle* (Pan: London 1969)

Jones, R.V., *Most Secret War* (Coronet: London, 1981)

Leasor, J., *War at the Top* (Michael Joseph: London, 1959)

Liddell Hart, B., *History of the Second World War*, Vol. 2/2 (London: Purnell, 1970)

Lloyd, I., and Pugh, P., *Hives and the Merlin* (Icon Books: Cambridge, 2004)

Longmore, Sir A., *From Sea to Sky* (Geoffrey Bles: London, 1946)

Lyman, R., *Iraq 1941* (Osprey: Wellingborough, 2006)

Mason, F.K., *Battle Over Britain* (McWhirter Twins: London, 1969)

Mead, P., *The Eye in the Sky* (HMSO: London, 1983)

Meekcoms, K.J., and Morgan, E.B., *The British Aircraft Specifications File* (Air Britain Publication: Tonbridge, 1994)

Middlebrook, M., and Everitt, C., *The Bomber Command War Diaries* (Penguin: London, 1990)

Orange, V., *Coningham* (Methuen: London, 1990)

Orange, V., *Slessor: Bomber Champion* (Grubb St: London, 2006)

Parham, H.J., and Belfield, E.M.G., *Unarmed into Battle* (Picton Publishing: Chippenham, 1986)

Parkin R., 'The Urgency Of War: The Development Of Close Air Support Doctrine In The Second World War', https://www.army.gov.au/sites/g/files/net1846/f/1995_from_past_to_future_aust_experience_of_land_air_operations_0.pdf

Playfair, I., *The Mediterranean and Middle East Vol. 2* (HMSO: London, 1956)

Price, A., *Instruments of Darkness* (Macdonald and Jane's: London, 1977)

Price, A., *The Spitfire Story* (Jane's: London 1982)

Price, A., *World War II Fighter Conflict* (MacDonald and Jane's: London, 1975)

Probert, H., *High Commanders of The Royal Air Force* (HMSO: London, 1991)

Richards, D., *Portal of Hungerford* (Heinemann: London, 1977)

Santoro, G., *L'Aeronautica Italiana Nella Seconda Guerra Mondiale* Vol. 1, (Apollon: Rome, 1957)

Sharp, M., and Bowyer, J.F., *Mosquito* (Faber and Faber: London, 1971)

Shores, C., *Dust Clouds in the Middle East* (Grub St: London, 2016)

Shores, C., *Fighters Over the Desert* (Neville Spearman: London, 1969)

Shores, C., *Ground Attack Aircraft of World War II* (Macdonald and Jane's: London, 1977)

Shores, C., Cull, B., and Malizia, N., *Air War for Yugoslavia, Greece and Crete 1940–1941* (Grubb St: London, 1987)

Shores, C., Cull, B., and Malizia, N., *Malta: The Hurricane Years* (Grubb St: London, 1999)

Slessor, J., *The Central Blue* (Cassell: London, 1956)

Tedder, Lord, *With Prejudice* (Cassell: London, 1966)

Terraine, J., *The Right of the Line* (Sceptre: Sevenoaks, 1988)

Webster, C., and Frankland, N., *The Strategic Air Offensive Against Germany 1939-1945*, Vols 1, 4 (HMSO: London, 1961)

Wilson, T., *Churchill and the Prof.* (Cassell: London, 1995)

Index

Admiralty, 143, 201, 217

Air Ministry (see also Air Staff), 3, 13, 15, 22, 26-28, 38, 41-42, 45, 67-74, 79-80, 89, 92-93, 109, 114, 117, 124-125, 139-141, 143-146, 169, 171, 177-178, 186-187, 191, 194, 197, 201-204, 209-212, 232, 238-239, 242; bomber strategy, 2, 4, 29, 38, 48, 71-72, 84, 107, 218, 264-265; high altitude bombing, 5, 7, 18, 22, 36-37, 151; interest in jet, 8-9; fighter armament, 9-10, 231; tactical air support, 23, 49-65, 100-108, 148-154, 156-165, 216-217, 220-221, 225-229, 234-235, 237, 244-246, 262-264; attitude to foreign pilots,78, 83, 185

Air Observation Post (AOP), 49, 88, 163, 204-205, 210, 214, 217, 229, 232-234, 237

Air Staff (see also Air Ministry), 23, 176-177, 200, 221, 223, 262-264; army support, 1, 47-48, 50, 55, 63, 65, 107, 150-152, 164, 166, 229, 234, 244, 257, 263; bomber policy, 1-2, 31-32, 37-38, 44, 60, 68, 93, 103, 132, 142, 147, 148, 151, 193, 201 208, 213, 219; fighter policy 2-3, 5-6, 9, 15, 19, 23, 30-31, 44, 61, 151, 191, 195-196, 200, 236; meaning of air superiority 3, 4, 11; invasion of UK, 48-49, 263; bomber defence, 60, 70, 209-210, 224, 229

Aircraft production plans, 4, 12-13, 16, 30-31, 60, 168, 188, 233

Airspeed Oxford, 173

Ali, R., 172, 176

American aircraft deliveries, 44, 45; failure to use, 23-25, 37, 99, 130, 190

Arado Ar 68, 126

Argus, HMS, 190

Ark Royal, HMS, 248

Armstrong Whitworth, Whitley, 12, 235; Albemarle, 31, 167, 168, 200, 217

Army Air Force (British), 51, 54, 153, 235

Army role, 1-3, 44, 89, 142, 158, 220, 263; Europe, 29, 158, Middle East, 3, 41

Auchinleck, Gen C., 172, 215, 235, 239, 241, 248, 253

Avro, Tutor, 125, 132; Manchester, 15-17, 22, 30, 31, 35, 113, 126, 167, 168, 195, 198, 205; Lancaster, 16, 17, 22, 149

Banquet Scheme, 102, 103, 107, 173, 177

Barratt, AM A., 55, 58, 59, 63, 106, 153, 154, 162, 221, 226, 227, 234

Battle of Britain 1, 4-7, 10, 19, 21, 23, 78, 83, 131, 136, 140, 191

Battle of the Atlantic, 38, 117, 198

Beamish, Capt. G., 137, 139

Beaverbrook, Lord, 4, 12-14, 16, 21, 23, 30, 51, 53, 56, 67, 81, 108, 109, 117,

Westland, Lysander, 46, 56, 57, 59, 62,
    85, 88, 89, 95,115, 149, 150, 153, 159-
    160, 226; Whirlwind, 6, 12, 19, 229,
    230; Welkin, 8, 10, 18, 203
Whittle, F., 8, 204, 229
Woodall, Col., J., 55, 58, 59, 65, 85

Yugoslavia, 66, 90, 93, 111,
    124-129
Yugoslavian Air Force, 125, 126